# WAR, POLITICS

## &

# REVOLUTION
# IN PROVINCIAL
# MASSACHUSETTS

# War, Politics, & Revolution in Provincial Massachusetts

## WILLIAM PENCAK

WITHDRAW

Northeastern University Press   Boston   1981

Editors, Heather Felsen and Robilee Smith
Designer, David Ford

Copyright © 1981 William Pencak
Northeastern University Press

LIBRARY OF CONGRESS
CATALOGING IN PUBLICATION DATA

Pencak, William, 1951–
    War, politics & revolution in provincial Massachusetts.

    Bibliography: p.
    Includes index.
    1. Massachusetts—Politics and government—Colonial
period, ca. 1600–1775. I. Title.
F67.P38        974.4'02        80-39487
ISBN 0-930350-10-3


86  85  84  83  82  81    8  7  6  5  4  3  2  1
Printed in the United States of America

IN
MEMORY
OF
JOHN LAX

# CONTENTS

Preface                                                         xi

Illustrations and Tables Listings                              ix

I     Introduction                                              1
      Notes                                              7

II    The End of Puritan Politics: 1676–1694                    9
      Preserving the Charter: 1676–1686              9
      Revolution and Collapse: 1686–1691            14
      Installing a Royal Government: 1691–1694      18
      Ousting a Royal Governor: 1692–1694           23
      Notes                                         28

III   Forging Provincial Unity: 1694–1713                      35
      Consolidation: 1694–1702                      36
      Counterattack: 1702–1713                      45
      Notes                                         53

IV    Paralysis: 1713–1730                                     61
      The Popular Party Emerges: 1714–1723          62
      Crisis and Compromise: 1723–1728              76
      Stalemate: 1728–1730                          80
      Notes                                         83

V       Procrastination: 1730–1741        91

Neutralizing the Caucus: 1730–1735    92
Placating the Assembly: 1730–1735    95
Elite Opposition to Belcher: 1730–1741    98
The Land Bank: 1739–1741    101
Notes    108

VI      Crusaders and Critics: 1741–1756      115

Unfinished Business: 1741–1745    116
Louisbourg and Beyond: 1745–1748    119
Samuel Adams and Revolutionary Ideology:
  1748–1749    125
A Specie Currency: 1748–1753    129
Excise and War: 1753–1756    133
Notes    137

VII     The Fragmentation of Massachusetts:
        1756–1765      149

Winding Down the War: 1756–1760    151
Bernard's Broad-Bottomed System:
  1760–1765    158
Enter the Merchants: 1758–1763    163
The Sphere of Politics Broadens:
  1761–1765    168
The Court's Last Stand: 1763–1765    172
Notes    175

VIII    The Crowd Enters Politics: 1765–1775    185

The Pre-Revolutionary Crowd    185
Revolutionary Violence    191
Who Made the Revolution?    196
Notes    206

IX      Loyalist and Patriot Leadership: The Two
        Cultures of Revolutionary Massachusetts    213
Notes    229

X       Postscript: Massachusetts and the Mid-Century
        Colonial Crisis    233
Notes    239

Tables    241

Bibliography    287

Index    303

# LIST OF ILLUSTRATIONS

*The Virtuous Patriot at the Hour of Death*, from the cover of Low's
*Astronomical Diary*, 1775     193

*Traitor [Thomas Hutchinson] at the Hour of Death*, from the cover
of Gleason's *Massachusetts' Calendar*, 1774     195

# LIST OF TABLES

1   Cumulative Voting Records of Massachusetts Towns on All Roll Calls, 1726–1765     243

2   Roll Calls in the Massachusetts House of Representatives, 1726–1765     250

3   Leaders of the House of Representatives, 1715–1768     251

4   Towns with More Than Three Percent of House Leaders     257

5   Committee Activity of Members of the House of Representatives     258

6   Justices of the Peace in Massachusetts     260

7   New Councillors Elected Each Year, 1692–1776     261

8   Surviving Returns for Council Elections     262

9   Towns Formed in Massachusetts, Excluding Maine, 1630–1776     266

10   Votes Received by and Factional Affiliation of Successful Candidates for Boston Representatives, 1692–1774.     267

11   Annual Rental Value of Real Estate Assessed Per Household in Boston for all Male Inhabitants, Members of Revolutionary Organizations, and Loyalists, 1771     273

12   Percentages of Loyalists and Sons of Liberty with Mercantile Wealth on the 1771 Boston Tax System     274

13   Profile of Tea Party Participants     275

14   Profile of the North End Caucus     277

15   Profile of Committee, 1775     278

16   Revolutionaries' Ages of Marriage     280

17   Migration into Boston by Household, 1745–1773     281

18   Profile of Loyalist Leaders     284

19   Profile of Revolutionary Leaders     285

# PREFACE

*W*AR IS THE STARTING point for understanding royal Massachusetts. Military conflict shaped the province between the Glorious and American Revolutions as distinctively as "Puritanism" did the seventeenth century. For over half of the period between 1689 and 1765, Massachusetts mustered and taxed its inhabitants to a degree unduplicated in any other British colony. One has to turn to Frederick the Great's Prussia for a comparable contemporaneous mobilization.

The effect of Massachusetts' "total wars" on its political system, and by extension on its leading role in the American Revolution, has yet to be investigated. Twentieth-century Americans know only too well that great wars increase executive power at the expense of the legislature. Great wars also intensify the impact of the central government on ordinary citizens and severely circumscribe a "loyal opposition's" ability to reconcile patriotism and criticism. Eighteenth-century Massachusetts exhibited the same trends. The General Court became more cooperative with royal policy in war.

To suggest an analogy, Republican conservatives cried "socialism" when Franklin D. Roosevelt regulated the economy to fight the depression, but they tolerated far greater controls without a murmur to fight the Nazis. Similarly, Massachusetts' representatives spent years in peacetime demanding the supervision of every cent in the treasury. During war, they voted the governor and his supporters enormous sums. And if like the Republican "Old Guard," they complained of incompetence and corruption, they could not obstruct the government without jeopardizing its survival.

We in the twentieth century know that total wars cannot bring total victory. Mobilization invariably unsettles economic life and produces dissatisfaction with unequal burdens during the conflict. Common postwar problems include recession and unemployment. Nations face the unpleasant options of inflation or heavy taxes to pay off debts. Victors must maintain a large defense establishment to retain their territorial acquisitions.

Massachusetts suffered from all these consequences. Animosity against British officers and mismanaged expeditions marked the province's four great wars. Even military success left a bitter taste; for instance, in 1748 at the Peace of Aix-la-Chapelle, Britain returned to France the fortress of Louisbourg, which Massachusetts had captured three years earlier. The conquest of Canada brought glory to Generals Amherst and Wolfe but harsher trade regulations, heavier taxes, and a postwar depression to their staunchest colonial allies. War unleashed inflation, social disorder, and political discontent in eighteenth-century Massachusetts. Instead of rewards, the province suffered economic decline and increased British attention to the "defects" of its political system.

As in so many societies that make tremendous exertions for minuscule gains, the people of Massachusetts made scapegoats of those who had guided the war. During the 1760's, hatred of the "court," or "prerogative," faction, the leading legislators who had urged maximum support for war measures, accompanied disenchantment with Britain. The aftermath of the peace treaties of Utrecht (1713) and Paris (1763) led to the "country" or "popular" faction's resurgence. The new leaders won their spurs not through the administrative drudgery required to wage war, but by branding their opponents as self-seeking, corrupt enemies of the people. Conversely, the court faction, which had advanced its fortunes while urging sacrifices for the common cause, failed to appreciate the suffering its policies had caused.

The magnitude of Massachusetts' mobilization leads to an interpretation of the American Revolution as the reasonable response to severe, undeserved burdens. British arguments, during and after the French and Indian War, that the colonies could neither defend themselves nor pay those who did, may have held true elsewhere. They rang hollow in the province that had expended the greatest energy even though it had not been directly attacked since the early days of the eighteenth century.

Massachusetts' war effort ensured that its revolution would be radical, not conservative. The province's war-tested political leaders did not head the resistance. With few exceptions, obscure men had to seize the reins of power because prominent families took the British side. Precisely because Massachusetts, through war, had developed such a strong native court party, the revolutionaries had to resort to exceptional tactics to overthrow it. They took politics into the streets and used apocalyptic rhetoric. For the first time, large numbers of people became actively involved in political organizations on a sustained basis. To be sure, the Massachusetts revolution was not radical in a Marxist sense. Tracing names shows that people of all classes combined against a group defined politically, not economically. A society united to oppose its government.

The Massachusetts revolution was a true people's revolt. It was the product neither of personal elite squabbling, paranoid fear of British tyranny, nor class conflict. First, there are almost always some disgruntled individuals—the question is when and why they obtain a popular following. Second, Massachusetts' sufferings were real, not imaginary. If anti-loyalist rhetoric was hysterical, the province's unrewarded exertions had been equally extreme. The other colonies, which in the last analysis rebelled against Britain's punishment of Massachusetts for resisting the Stamp, Townshend, and Tea acts, faced a grim precedent. Finally, if significant conflict existed in Massachusetts between upper and lower orders, how can the absence of crowd violence against wealthy revolutionaries and of class cooperation against Tories be explained?

Why did I write this sort of book? Massachusetts provincial politics consisted of the major issues debated by the General Court. These can be ascertained by reading the legislative journals and the correspondence of governors and other political notables. For the most part, Massachusetts' lawmakers argued over defense in wartime and constitutional and currency disputes in peacetime. Issues such as the management of Harvard College or the settlement of the frontier intruded at times, but did not command attention over a comparable duration. In short, I analyze those matters the legislature deemed most worthy of its attention. I treat other issues only when they impinged on provincial concerns.

Next, I examine how controversy started, stopped, and altered its nature over time. Chapter one advances the thesis that only the pressure of events and problems themselves can adequately account for political change in Massachusetts. Religious, ethnic, personal, or regional explanations for strife are inadequate save in specific or exceptional cases. Massachusetts' relatively homogeneous society, combined with variable behavior by towns and representatives, indicates that its politics require a developmental, rather than a structural, interpretation. Only by focusing on the issues themselves can we explain why the majority of the General Court changed from opposing royal policy to supporting it.

After laying this groundwork, I spend most of the book discussing the General Court's behavior. However, the chapters dealing with the American Revolution move beyond the legislature to the general public. A different approach is necessary here for two reasons. First, the actual disputes between Governors Bernard and Hutchinson and the General Court have been discussed in virtually every history of the Revolution or of colonial Massachusetts, and I have nothing new to add. Second, the legislature no longer shaped politics without much popular input. Crowds and other quasi-governmental institutions took up the slack when the General Court could not resist British policy to general satisfaction. I therefore discuss the membership, tactics, and ideology of the revolutionary movement that centered in Boston. I then show how revolutionary politics produced a social and intellectual cleavage between Whigs and Tories that had been absent previously.

Not all readers, I am sure, will be convinced that my interpretation of eighteenth-century Massachusetts politics is the most fruitful. But I offer the above comments to explain where I believe I shed new light on provincial history and the American Revolution.

I thank the Massachusetts Historical Society; Massachusetts Archives; Houghton Library, Harvard University; the Boston Public Library; the New England Historic Genealogical Society; the Suffolk County Court House, the Social Law Library, New Court House, Boston; the American Antiquarian Society; and Butler Library, Columbia University for allowing me to peruse and quote from documentary material. Aimée Bligh, Winifred Collins, Molly Collingwood, Malcolm Freiberg, and Gertrude Fisher at the MHS, Helen and Leo Flaherty at the Archives, David Dearborn at the Genealogical Society, William Joyce at the Antiquarian Society, and Robert Brink and Charles Hammond at the Social Law Library went out of their way to make research pleasurable as well as profitable.

Alden Vaughan's painstaking, prompt, and courteous reading of my drafts made him an ideal sponsor for the dissertation on which this book is based. Chilton Williamson has been a great friend and never-ending source of inspiration—and helpful criticism—since my undergraduate days. John Murrin read the manuscript twice. I have benefitted enormously from his friendly but penetrating advice. Peter Onuf provided an invaluable, detailed critique. Eric McKitrick and

## Preface

Gordon Wood also enabled me to produce a better book. I am pleased to thank Ralph J. Crandall, Jack P. Greene, and John Schutz for their interest in my work, encouragement, and valuable suggestions for improvement.

Fellowships at Columbia University's Graduate School and an Andrew Mellon Fellowship at Duke University financed completion of the work, although my main backers—both financial and spiritual—have been my parents. My mother deserves an award for typing repeated drafts of this book as well as just about everything I've ever written. The Stevens Institute, Columbia, Tufts, and Duke Universities provided congenial and interested colleagues and students. I especially thank the undergraduates at Tufts for their great enthusiasm and competence in doing original research in Massachusetts history. William Frohlich and Robilee Smith at Northeastern University Press have been extremely patient and courteous. I would also like to thank Heather Felsen for her fine suggestions for improving the manuscript.

This book was to have been dedicated to my parents. On the death of my friend John Lax—who collaborated with me on "The Knowles Riot and the Crisis of the 1740's in Massachusetts"—they insisted the book serve as a memorial to John. Not only did the article mark an important turning point in my thought on Massachusetts politics, but knowing John and his family has been one of my most rewarding personal experiences. I hope the dedication expresses the affection and esteem with which John is remembered by many.

# ABBREVIATIONS

*A&R*  *The Acts and Resolves, Public and Private, of the Province of Massachusetts Bay* (Boston, 1869–1922), eds. Abner C. Goodell and Ellis Ames

*Boston* Boston Records Commissioners' *Reports,* (Boston, 1880–1902), ed.
*Records* William H. Whitmore et. al.

*CSP*  *Calendar of State Papers, Colonial Series* (London, 1869–  ), ed. W. Noel Sainsbury et. al.

*CSMP* Colonial Society of Massachusetts *Publications*

*House*  *Journals of the House of Representatives of Massachusetts Bay*
*Journals* (Boston, 1919–  ), ed. Worthington C. Ford et. al.

MHS  Massachusetts Historical Society

*MHSC* *Collections* of the Massachusetts Historical Society

*MHSP* *Proceedings* of the Massachusetts Historical Society

NEHGS New England Historic Genealogical Society

# INTRODUCTION

$\mathcal{S}$INCE 1629, when the Puritans first erected their "city upon a hill" to serve as a model society for a corrupted world, Massachusetts politics have been unusual. Massachusetts led the movement, culminating in the Hartford Convention, to oppose the War of 1812. In the next half-century, the State refused to let its militia fight in the Mexican War and spearheaded the anti-slavery crusade. During the 1960s, the Commonwealth contributed disproportionately to the protests that ended the Viet Nam War. "Don't blame me, I'm from Massachusetts," read bumper stickers during Richard Nixon's second administration, calling attention to the only state to cast its electoral votes for George McGovern in 1972.

Yet what can compare with Massachusetts' preeminence in the struggle for American independence? Who can imagine an American Revolution without James Otis and his attack on the Writs of Assistance, the great Stamp Act riots of 1765, the Boston Massacre, the Boston Tea Party, Samuel and John Adams, Paul Revere's midnight ride, and the "shot heard round the world" at Concord? When Americans study the causes of their Revolution, they learn mostly about developments in and around Boston. Why? Something must have been happening in prerevolutionary Massachusetts that distinguished it from its fellow colonies.

Domestic and Anglo-American factionalism in most colonies other than Massachusetts can be traced to socioeconomic divisions. In the middle colonies, ethnic, religious, economic, and geographic loyalties created an animated political life. Conflicting interest groups in New York and Pennsylvania had to fight out or compromise their differences. Candidates for public office campaigned actively to win the approval of a diverse public. Large election districts with socially diverse constituencies ensured that the political behavior of the middle colonies anticipated party politics in many respects.[1]

The southern royal colonies overcame their class violence and subsistence crisis by the early eighteenth century. These relatively homogeneous Anglican colonies grew tobacco and rice for export. Fear of a growing black slave population further united the white landholders. In the absence of internal strife, a well-entrenched planter class devoted most of its political energy to a "quest for power" against royal administration. The assemblies fought to control finances, to initiate legislation, and to meet regularly. The quest was successful; by mid-century the royal southern colonies enjoyed stable regimes. Only after 1740, with the rapid settlement of the backcountry by German and Scotch-Irish subsistence farmers, did new problems arise. Virginia expiditiously extended legal protection and political power to the newcomers, but the Carolinas had to endure the near-revolutionary Regulator movements.[2]

Massachusetts' factional development cannot be so neatly linked with either its social circumstances or a deficiency of power in the lower house of the legislature. First, the population of the Bay Colony was overwhelmingly Congregational and English. Although immigration did not cease after 1640, most of the settlers were descended from the large families of the pioneers who arrived between 1630 and 1640. Religious conflict at the provincial level was preempted by the province's strong tradition of local government. Towns chose their own ministers and enforced church discipline within relatively wide limits. Appeals on matters of faith, as on other issues, only reached the General Court on exceptional occasions. The provincial legislature was thus largely freed from involvement in local or regional squabbles.[3]

Class tensions, similarly, were not major determinants of provincial politics. All available evidence suggests that social unrest was rare. Compared with other provinces, the poor were usually subsidized, well-treated, and not in dire straits; and minority groups (while not regarded as equal members of the community) fared better than elsewhere in the English-speaking world. Members of all social classes approved of and participated in crowds, which before the Revolution were unconnected with legislative factionalism. Prominent officials, regardless of factional allegiance, tried to redress grievances the crowds protested (see chapter eight).

Sectional conflict, too, is difficult to find. Before 1740, many of the assembly's leaders, regardless of faction, came from a number of wealthy, interrelated families from Boston and a few other towns, even though the majority of the body came from inland rural communities.[4] After 1740, recognized leaders of both the court and country factions continued to come from wealthy seaboard families even though committee work in the house became decentralized. More importantly, an analysis of all roll calls before 1765 yields no pattern that can be linked with definable sectional interests although towns in certain regions tended to vote the same way.[5] Why, for instance, did the smaller inland towns in Suffolk and Worcester oppose royal demands while those in Middlesex and Hampshire supported them? Why did the smaller coastal towns in Essex and Barnstable favor the court while those in Bristol supported the opposition? The western frontier, Hampshire and Berkshire, provided eighty-four votes for the court and only thirty-five for the country over four decades; the eastern frontier, York, reversed the proportion forty-nine to sixty-three. (See Tables 1 through 5.)

Another feature of Massachusetts politics that is overemphasized is rivalry between elite families. Such quarrels certainly occurred, but they fail to explain why the majority of the assembly supported or opposed a governor. A few men (the Mathers around 1700, Elisha Cooke and his connections in the late 1720s, and the Otis family in the 1760s) attacked their governor for personal reasons. But they were impotent unless an issue emerged that the house perceived as threatening colonial interests. To be sure, much of the resentment against Thomas Hutchinson in the 1760s stemmed from his efforts to obtain positions for his unqualified relatives. But in the past, the descendants of the prominent Cookes, Dudleys, and Winthrops failed to interest themselves in politics.

Similarly, patronage functioned differently in Massachusetts than in England. At home in England, a prime minister could obtain votes and create a parliamentary majority by distributing lucrative posts to the right people. In the Bay Colony, small towns elected a house of representatives far too large to be bought off, and few of the available government posts paid well enough for wealthy, influential politicians to desire them for that reason. Furthermore, after Governor Jonathan Belcher vastly expanded the number of justices of the peace, roll calls indicate that many representatives who opposed the governor held appointive posts. Unlike in Britain, there were few sinecures to which the governor could appoint anyone. Judicial and militia officers had to be respected in their communities to maintain law and order to muster and command troops. (See Tables 2, 5, and 6.) High office was an index of prestige, a reward for having performed lower level tasks diligently, not a primary source of income. Leaders of the popular party preferred to be ineligible for patronage or service on the council rather than give up their principles.[6]

Some aspects of Massachusetts' relations with England also mitigated political strife. After 1691, it was the one royal colony possessing a charter guaranteeing it a legislative assembly that met annually. It was also the only one in which the assembly and outgoing council elected the new upper house subject to the governor's approval; elsewhere the Privy Council directed the governor's appointments. Massachusetts was never subjected to the incompetent placemen who plagued its fellow colonies. Every executive was either a native of the province, handpicked by Massachusetts agents or lobbyists, or (to cover the two exceptions, Bellomont and Bernard) an experienced and well-regarded administrator. British commercial policy, too, harmed Massachusetts in the breach but not in the observance. Those aspects of the Navigation Acts that restricted the province's trade were poorly enforced, whereas it shared in the shipbuilding and trading monopolies for English commerce within the empire.

Massachusetts and British interests coincided on the most important issue of all: defense. North America's most populous colony until well into the eighteenth century, Massachusetts was strategically located to repel or launch attacks against the French. The province's survival and expansion could only be ensured through cooperation with British defense policy. No violent internal conflicts (New York) or pacifist tendencies (Pennsylvania) dampened Massachusetts' enthusiasm. Throughout the eighteenth century, the Bay Colony proved far more diligent in raising men and money than any other.

At this point, the reader is perhaps wondering how serious political controversy could have occurred. Most Massachusetts representatives did not belong to any organized political group, but simply voted their interests and consciences. No preexisting factional ties disposed the assembly's small-town majority to associate with either the group opposing the governor or with the men who supported him. As issues arose, members took stands based on their independent judgments. To be sure, the house leadership could argue one way or the other, but both court and country always presented rival spokesmen. Extremely variable records of towns and representatives establish the followers' independence. (See Table 1.) For instance, the house voted to suppress

4

the Land Bank in 1739 and to sustain it in 1740; the votes for silver currency in 1749, the approval of the Explanatory Charter in 1726, and the agreement of 1733 permitting the council to appropriate money in the recess of the assembly were reluctant reversals of long-standing policies. The deputies repudiated currency inflation in 1751 and a plan of colonial union in 1754, less than a month after both had been approved. (See Table 2). The issues themselves, and the ability of house leaders to persuade members of the justness of their cause, formed the basis of factional divisions.

Somewhat paradoxically, Massachusetts' special privileges and intimate cooperation with British defense policy provoked as well as preempted some forms of conflict. In peacetime, Britain tried hard to bring its most favored royal province into line. Massachusetts' governors were compelled to insist on a large, fixed salary, the right to dispose of money approved by the house, and the power to veto the assembly's speaker. Britain also tried to curtail the province's right to issue paper money at will. After 1760, Parliamentary legislation threatened Massachusetts' self-government and harmed its economic interests. During war, Massachusetts was required to build forts, provide seamen for the navy, and furnish men, money, and supplies for the common cause.

Political factionalism in Massachusetts, therefore, waxed and waned according to the obnoxiousness of Britain's demands. Coherent groups that shaped legislative behavior cannot be identified on the basis of families (such as the Livingstons or Delanceys in New York), religion (such as the Quakers or Presbyterians in Pennsylvania), or geography (such as East and West Jersey men). The Massachusetts legislature consisted of two shifting, unorganized coalitions. The court or prerogative faction favored cooperation with British policy. The country or popular group resisted imperial demands.[7]

The strength of the court and country factions depended on the extent to which provincial welfare and imperial policy coincided. When Massachusetts was not fighting a major war (before 1689, 1713–1741, and after 1764), the country faction dominated the house of representatives.[8] Constitutional disputes over the governor's and assembly's powers were endemic. They only ended when one side gave up the struggle. In peacetime the prerogative party's strength was minuscule. Governors only enjoyed untroubled administrations by disregarding their instructions and taking the province's part against Britain.

Serious or impending warfare (1689–1713, 1740–1764) reversed the dominant and subordinate factions. The prerogative faction usually obtained most, if seldom all, of the supplies, men, and money required to mount an effective war effort. The court's supremacy in wartime, however, never matched the country's in peacetime. Many key votes only passed the assembly by narrow margins.

An interpretation of Massachusetts politics stressing the strength of the court faction in war and the country faction in peace helps resolve one major historiographical controversy. Some historians view the province's history as marked by "perpetual discordance" with Britain. Others note that political stability was achieved roughly between 1740 and 1760.[9] Political stability clearly existed if it means that the court prevailed most of the time and that paralyzing constitutional disputes ceased. But even though the court had the upper hand, there was always discordance of some kind.

Unlike peacetime disputes, politics during war inspired men to question the relationship between government and society. Once it lost control of the assembly, the popular faction developed new methods of protest. It no longer restricted itself to defending the deputies' powers. Instead, it attacked the corruption of the people's representatives and the government's violation of their natural rights. Such arguments appeared in the 1740s to oppose Governor Shirley's military policies.

Furthermore, war measures affected the average citizen far more directly than peacetime attempts to curtail legislative autonomy. Crowds protested impressment, recruiting parties, and heavy taxation. After 1740, Massachusetts multiplied its peacetime budget several times. The province mustered annually as many as one-fifth of its adult males for military service. As late as 1764 it supplied men for garrison duty against Indians in the Ohio Valley.

The greatest effect of war on politics, however, was that the problems it provoked became the principal issues in peacetime. Massachusetts' currency troubles stemmed from its military expenditures. The cessation of hostilities made debates over the settlement of the frontier in Maine possible. Most significantly, British efforts to strengthen the governor's powers, enforce trade regulations, and (after the French and Indian War) impose taxation, all stemmed from dissatisfaction with colonial assistance. Massachusetts felt more aggrieved at these measures than any other colony. Its extraordinary exertions did not win it any exemptions from general policy.

Massachusetts' disillusionment became especially acute in the mid-1760s. A victorious war offered the province new burdens and few fruits. The prerogative faction proved to be a major casualty of this discontent. Having predominated since the early 1740s, it continued to urge peaceful remonstrance against injurious measures. But once the French no longer posed a military threat, Massachusetts had no further reason to cooperate with British demands.

Massachusetts' prominence in the American Revolution can be explained by the depth of this dissatisfaction and the strength of its prerogative faction. Both must be attributed to the province's military exertions. Massachusetts had developed a dominant faction committed on principle to ensuring cooperation between the province and England. Unlike the people of Massachusetts, the court leaders had benefited from war and had advanced their careers through service as soldiers and administrators. They even held their own in the early 1760s. But when they favored acquiesence in the Stamp Act, a popular party invigorated by lawyers, merchants, and clergymen (all of whom had special reasons for discontent) eliminated the court faction within a few years.[10]

# *Notes to Chapter I*

1. Patricia U. Bonomi, "The Middle Colonies: Embryo of the New Political Order," in *Perspectives on Early American History: Essays in Honor of Richard B. Morris,* eds., Alden T. Vaughan and George A. Billias (New York, 1973), pp. 63–92.

2. Jack P. Greene, *The Quest for Power: The Lower Houses of Assembly in the Southern Royal Colonies* (Chapel Hill, 1963).

3. For local autonomy, see especially Michael Zuckerman, *Peaceable Kingdoms: The New England Towns in the Eighteenth Century* (New York, 1970). My endorsement of Zuckerman's thesis does not extend beyond the point made in this paragraph. See the critique by John Murrin in his review of several town studies, *History and Theory,* 11 (1972): 226–274. For immigration, see Clifford K. Shipton, "Immigration to New England," *Journal of Political Economy,* 64 (1936): 275–289.

4. For example, Elisha Cooke, Jr., head of the popular faction in the 1720s and 1730s, was supported by three of his brothers-in-law, Oliver Noyes, John Clarke, and William Payne. But Clarke was also the brother-in-law of Cotton Mather, who consistently opposed Cooke. Elizabeth Clarke, John's sister, married Elisha Hutchinson, that family's patriarch in the eighteenth century. All the Hutchinsons except William supported the prerogative faction after Joseph Dudley became governor in 1703. One of Cooke's uncles, Nathaniel Byfield, was also a brother-in-law of Dudley who turned against him in the last year of his administration. After 1740, with the exception of the Otis, Hutchinson, and Bowdoin kinship networks, few prominent political figures were related.

5. I do not find Stephen Patterson, *Political Parties in Revolutionary Massachusetts* (Madison, 1973), pp. 258–265, and Robert Zemsky, *Merchants, Farmers, and River Gods* (Boston, 1971), pp. 312–320, persuasive that sectional alignments existed. Patterson makes too much of slightly differing ratios in the number of Land Bankers per capita, and of an index of local versus cosmopolitan towns in Van Beck Hall's *Politics Without Parties: Massachusetts, 1780–1791* (Pittsburgh, 1972) drawn from a later period. Zemsky does not provide lists of towns and, at any rate, there are too many exceptions to each of his categories. Some correlation exists between support for the prerogative faction and county seats and suburban towns (usually the first few towns in

any county listed in Table 1 in the Appendix), and between the popular party and subsistence farming communities; see definitions of Edward M. Cook, Jr. in *The Fathers of the Towns: Leadership and Community Structure in Eighteenth Century New England* (Baltimore, 1976). But even here, exceptions are numerous and many towns had extremely variable voting records.

6. See Thomas Hutchinson to the Earl of Dartmouth, 1 October 1773, State Papers, 12: 77–97, Frederick Lewis Gay Transcripts, MHS, for a table of salaries on the eve of the Revolution. A justice of the county courts earned about £20 Massachusetts per annum. Only the province secretary and treasurer (£300), four superior court justices (£200), and one sheriff (£50 to £750), judge of probate (£70), and registrar of probate (£120) per county could make sizeable amounts in government service. (Sheriffs' salaries varied greatly according to the volume of business in each county.) These offices required a great commitment of time, and whether the wealthy individuals who usually held them earned more than in private life is questionable. After 1750, one pound Massachusetts money equalled .75 pounds sterling.

7. The prerogative faction did not necessarily support the governor; Governors Belcher and Pownall sided informally with the popular party. Bernard remained neutral, sometimes favoring one side, sometimes the other, early in his administration.

8. Periods of war are defined in this work as occasions when Massachusetts undertook major expeditions against the French and Indians or considered its survival in serious danger. Between 1722 and 1725, the province launched minor military campaigns against Indians in Maine; between 1759 and 1763, Massachusetts continued to aid Britain's war effort although its previous sense of urgency had gone. Similarly, brief periods of respite or scaled-down conflict occurred during some periods termed "war."

9. See especially John A. Schutz, *William Shirley: King's Governor of Massachusetts* (Chapel Hill, 1960), for stability, and Robert E. Brown, *Middle-Class Democracy and the Revolution in Massachusetts, 1691–1780* (Ithaca, 1955), for perpetual discordance.

10. Jack N. Rakove, in *The Beginnings of National Politics* (New York, 1979), has used a similar approach in describing politics within the Continental Congress. He argues that preexisting class, sectional, regional, etc. animosities mattered less than the flexible, independent responses of the members to alternative courses of policy as the pressures of warfare and organizing a government made themselves felt.

# THE END

# OF PURITAN

# POLITICS

# 1676–1694

## PRESERVING THE CHARTER: 1676–1686

*J*N THE eighteenth century a united Massachusetts led the mainland colonies in four great wars and the American Revolution. But why was Massachusetts so unified internally? Why did it possess the missionary zeal to attack Canada repeatedly? New York, an equally exposed province, could hardly defend its own frontier.

Massachusetts' century of Puritanism made possible its century of war. Unlike few other seventeenth-century settlements, the Bay Colony achieved a stable social and political order within a few years. Disorders such as Bacon's Rebellion in Virginia, Leisler's uprising in New York, or the West Indian struggles among planters, pirates, indentured servants, and slaves were conspicuously absent. When England tried to reform colonial government late in the seventeenth century, imperial troubleshooters could count on significant local help in Virginia and New York—the other mainland royal colonies. But quarrelling factions in Massachusetts discovered that internal differences mattered little in the face of an external threat.[1]

The people of Massachusetts remained more united than most colonists because they resisted the commercial world of seventeenth-century England. In the Puritans' eyes, the age of exploration and expansion had produced disorder, immorality, extravagance, and cruelty both at home and in the colonies. Despite the appalling mortality rates of Virginia and Plymouth, the Puritans liquidated their estates and businesses to escape the universal corruption. They hoped to establish a "true Israel," a "community of saints," to herald and hasten the second coming of Christ.[2]

To keep their land pure, the settlers excluded the disorderly and ideologically deviant. They then went on to limit full church membership to those accepted by an established congregation. As a third line of defense, only such people could vote or hold office. Massachusetts maintained itself as a self-selecting community by making life uncomfortable, if not impossible, for dissidents who did not relish martyrdom.[3]

New England's rocky soil perfectly suited the colonists' religious fervor and passion for order. Prosperity, even survival, depended on hard work, cooperation, and conformity. Subsistence farming, fishing, or marketing local products abroad required hard work. Communal open-field agriculture compelled cooperation. Dependence on the community for land grants mandated conformity. Few men came to Massachusetts to get rich quickly at their neighbors' expense.

After establishing an insular Christian society, Massachusetts enforced a variety of laws that checked social unrest. Settlers had to live in a town. No one could live far from a meeting house. People had to remain with their families until they married. Even those unworthy of communion had to attend church services and adhere to a strict moral code based in part on the Old Testament. The Puritans knew full well that disorder arose when single adults left their communities and pursued careers for personal gain.

Yet despite nearly ideal preconditions for political stability, seventeenth-century Massachusetts did not remain free of strife. The Puritans disagreed among themselves over who deserved to participate in and govern the holy experiment. Disputes over church membership (and hence, political power) in the 1630s forced Anne Hutchinson and Roger Williams into exile. Ministers John Davenport and Thomas Shepard left voluntarily. By eliminating deviants and creating an accepted orthodoxy among those who remained, Massachusetts' rulers ensured internal differences would not jeopardize survival.[4]

But Massachusetts' saints limited their popular base too severely. Within a generation, they transformed themselves from a majority ruling by consent to a privileged minority. During the 1640s and '50s, fewer settlers confessed their salvation and joined the churches. Whether from disinterest in religion, rigorous requirements, or the scrupulous consciences of younger people unwilling to feign conversion, church membership declined. Ministers lamented "declension" from the heroic age of the founders.[5]

Many of the second generation thus could not obtain full citizenship. Their long-lived parents monopolized land and political power until late in the century. By the 1680s no more than 1,800 men, about 25 percent of the adult male population, voted for councillors. In Boston itself, which had about one thousand adult males, Samuel Sewall never recorded over one hundred ballots in any town election before the 1690s. As the seventeenth century progressed, religious and political power became concentrated in relatively few hands.[6]

The Half-Way Covenant brought the controversy between "ins" and "outs" to a head. Many congregations only baptized full communicants who were likely to receive saving faith. But then did the sons and daughters of the baptized who had never been admitted to the Lord's Supper, the "half-way" members, merit baptism? The full communicants, for the most part, did not think so. However, the clergy disagreed. Plagued by shrinking constituencies, they insisted that half-way membership would prepare larger numbers of people for communion, dispel contention, and foreshadow a revived piety. But churches throughout Massachusetts defied their ministers. They refused to baptize the children of half-way members as the covenant of 1662 permitted.[7]

In general, the legislature's upper house, called either the assistants or magistrates, supported the clergy on the Half-Way Covenant. The lower house, the deputies, favored the church members. The alignment of magistrates and ministers versus deputies also carried over into the debates on tolerating Baptists and Quakers and resisting royal government. The deputies favored toleration and implacably defied the crown, whereas the clergy and upper house opposed toleration. They urged accommodation with England on practical grounds, considering appeasement the only alternative to destruction. However, many exceptions could be found among all three groups. Alignments were not hard and fast; individuals followed their own courses on the three major issues.[8]

In 1664, during the Half-Way Covenant quarrel, King Charles II sent a commission to investigate complaints of the Puritans' intolerance and disobedience to royal authority. The commissioners accomplished little, but they inspired discontented people to petition the crown in 1666 for the religious, political, and economic freedom they claimed their rulers had denied them. The maritime towns of Boston, Salem, Newbury, and Ipswich supplied 167 signatures. This number equalled perhaps 20 percent of the colony's freemen. Only 31 signers were merchants; the rest were craftsmen, retailers, physicians, or untraceable; 77 were freemen, 90 were not; 126 had lived in

Massachusetts for at least seven years. Clearly opposition to the Puritan commonwealth was by no means limited to either the unfranchised or a handful of upper class merchants.[9]

Throughout the last half of the seventeenth century, aggrieved men in towns throughout Massachusetts protested the saints' minority rule. Local historians have found increased conflict in Springfield, Suffield, and Northampton in the Connecticut Valley, and Dedham, Sudbury, Boston, and Andover, to say nothing of Salem, in the east. Strife also occurred between an urban minority and the rural majority. Since the 1630s Boston had fought the rural towns in the General Court. And within the capital itself, the behavior of merchants and well-to-do inhabitants offended the more pious, less wealthy church-going set. But in general, dissension spread itself among different issues, and failed to take on hard-and-fast alignments based on economic or regional interests. Internal strife did not therefore prove insurmountable in the face of a common peril.[10]

King Philips' War (1675–1676) at least achieved a united front against the Indians, but it failed to reconcile the opposing factions. The war destroyed half of New England's towns, severely damaged most of the rest, ruined the economy, cost £100,000, and produced the highest casualty rate of any war in American history (in proportion to the population). But everyone began blaming each other for a catastrophe regarded by all as God's judgment. The preachers censured the General Court for tolerating Baptists and Quakers, whose strictness appealed to many of the communicants. Somewhat inconsistently, they also criticized the legislature for permitting drunkenness, swearing, Sabbath-breaking, and other forms of immorality. The deputies, for their part, viewed the war as a punishment for the apostasy of the Half-Way Covenant itself.[11]

Immediately following King Philip's War, Massachusetts faced another challenge. In 1676, England sent Edmund Randolph to investigate the colony and recommend changes in its government. Resistance to the Navigation Acts, defiance of royal power, and refusal to tolerate Anglicans headed the complaints home authorities had been receiving. Determined to make his career in the colonial service, Randolph did everything he could to transform Massachusetts into a royal colony.

But Randolph's efforts to win the hearts of disgruntled elements in Massachusetts failed. Instead, nearly everyone opposed him. Adoption of the Half-Way Covenant and church membership both rose after 1675, indicating renewed enthusiasm for the colony's ideals and the establishment's need to expand its base. Randolph's heavy-handed means of imposing English rule ensured that even those who supported him did so halfheartedly. Dislike of Randolph meant that political division from 1676 until the Glorious Revolution was spirited but superficial. In the General Court, if not all the towns, factionalism based on class, generational, and religious tensions declined. Leaders differed over the means, but not the end, of diffusing the impact of a disastrous war and an overzealous administrator. Ten years later they discovered enough of a common heritage to oppose Sir Edmund Andros's dominion of New England almost to a man.[12]

To be sure, Randolph pretended that the majority supported him. He did so primarily to bolster his case with the English authorities. But he overestimated the number and misrepresented the nature of his adherents, called the moderates by historians. Even they regarded the royal control he espoused with mixed feelings. The most prestigious among them—the colony's perennial Governor Simon Bradstreet, his brother-in-law Joseph Dudley, and Dudley's brother-in-law William Stoughton—had no desire to alter the colony's frame of government in accordance with Randolph's wishes. Instead, they read the handwriting on the wall, realized total autonomy could not be retained, and sought to turn the inevitable changes to their own and the colony's advantage. For example, Bradstreet won Randolph's praise for his fruitless efforts to enforce the Navigation Acts. However, the governor thereby hoped to prevent rather than introduce more stringent controls over colonial trade. Stoughton, for his part, served as agent to England to save the charter. He did not blame the loss of the colony's self-government on its unruly behavior as Charles II and James II indiscriminately revoked local charters throughout the empire to eliminate resistance to royal power. Even Dudley, another emissary, did his best to preserve the old constitution. When it was lost, he successfully convinced Randolph that "His Majesty should at first betrust the government wholly to persons among us." Nevertheless, these moderates set themselves against the old-charter faction that favored uncompromising resistance.[13]

The moderate/old-charter division anticipated the limited sort of political conflict which prevailed in Massachusetts until the 1760s. Neither faction constituted a distinct socioeconomic class. Leading merchants and land speculators, many of them personal friends and relatives, supported opposing sides.[14] The split also lacked a firm religious basis. The province's Anglican and Anglicized merchants supported the moderates, but most merchants were not Anglicans and most moderates were not merchants. The ministry, angered at the General Court's resistance to the Half-Way Covenant, in general supported the moderates, who favored it. But there were notable exceptions. Among the clergy, Increase Mather of Boston's Second Church urged on the diehards. On the other hand, old-charter leader Thomas Danforth (Massachusetts' lieutenant-governor for most of the 1670s and 1680s), could not gain admittance to a church until 1690. Samuel Nowell, a third leader of the irreconcilables, eloquently defended local self-government using the rights of Englishmen rather than the rights of Puritans.[15]

The moderates displayed the loose cohesion that hampered any real party development in Massachusetts outside Boston before the revolutionary crisis. They did not consistently support Randolph or each other, but exercised their independent judgments as issues arose. For instance, in 1682 the moderate upper house voted down the deputies' bill creating a local naval office to enforce the Navigation Acts and thereby circumvent Randolph's authority. However, Nathaniel Saltonstall, John Richards, and Bartholomew Gedney, whom Randolph considered well-disposed, joined with his opponents.[16]

Many of the moderates enjoyed the political confidence of the electorate. Governor Bradstreet and Councillors John Pynchon and Nathaniel Saltonstall usually polled one thousand votes out of twelve hundred, as many as Danforth or Nowell. Even Dudley and Stoughton, who failed of a majority in 1684 and 1686, were elected during the rest of 1680s.[17]

The image of the moderates as a handful of elite merchants who openly welcomed royal government must therefore be modified. They disagreed with the old-charter leaders primarily over whether England's campaign against the colony should be resisted or appeased. The limited factional animosity during the final decade of Puritan rule explains why both groups worked together so easily against Sir Edmund Andros. Appearances to the contrary, the British challenge ensured that Massachusetts became more, not less, united after 1675.

REVOLUTION AND COLLAPSE: 1686–1691

In 1685, after a decade of procrastination, England finally revoked Massachusetts' charter and imposed a royal government. The new regime, which officially took power in New England on 14 May 1686, embodied more extreme reforms than the moderates had expected. Some of them had sought an assembly elected by freeholders worth £400 instead of church members. But the new constitution abolished the deputies entirely.[18] Randolph soon quarrelled with acting Governor Joseph Dudley and his appointed advisory council over how far the changes should go. The collector complained that they failed to enforce the Navigation Acts and had engrossed frontier land. They in turn insisted that Randolph wanted some free tracts for himself and hoped to monopolize the authority (and hence the fees) for enforcing customs regulations.[19]

Dudley also adopted conciliatory policies toward the old-charter faction, which infuriated Randolph. He appointed Increase Mather, that "bellows of sedition," President of Harvard College.[20] He refused to levy taxes without an assembly or to promote the Church of England. The governor allowed most elected militia officers to retain their places and appointed prestigious people to the new office of justice of the peace regardless of previous ties. Dudley's government may have been royal in form, but it was quasi-Puritan in substance.

Randolph soon turned the tables on his erstwhile allies when Dudley's successor, Sir Edmund Andros, arrived late in 1686. Andros wasted no time offending moderates and diehards alike by imposing heavy taxes and instituting Anglican services. He required everyone in the colony to confirm their landholdings with new and costly deeds. This was unreasonable because many titles rested on undocumented local grants. Andros dealt with his opponents by prosecuting them before packed juries.[21]

Andros's tactics alienated his native supporters almost to a man. When Nathaniel Saltonstall and ex-Governor Bradstreet refused even to serve on the council, the governor charged them with sedition and attempting to alienate the affections of the people. Andros refused to endorse the moderates' land schemes and angered the merchants by enforcing the Acts of Trade. Five of his own councillors—William Stoughton, Wait Winthrop, Samuel Shrimpton, Bartholomew Gedney, and William Browne—headed the list of prominent inhabitants demanding his abdication on 18 April 1689.[22] A sixth, Richard Wharton, joined a veritable Massachusetts' government-in-exile seeking to have him removed. Between 1687 and 1690, Increase Mather, Samuel Nowell, Samuel Sewall, Elisha Cooke, Thomas Oakes, and Sir William Phips—all of whom figured prominently in the province's politics over the next quarter century—journeyed to England to negotiate a more favorable constitution.[23] Andros indeed faithfully represented King James II: he united the old-charter and moderate factions against him as effectively as his royal master's excesses provoked a union of Whigs and Tories at home.

While Massachusetts' agents abroad endeavored to restore its self-government, the people took more direct action. Informal news that William of Orange had invaded England reached Massachusetts in

4 April 1689. As word spread, Andros could no longer hold together the militiamen he led against the rebellious Indians of Maine. The men deserted and marched on Boston. In response, a bipartisan committee of ministers and leading citizens, "surprised with the people's sudden taking of arms," formed an interim government to prevent violence.[24] The new authorities then took Andros and his followers into custody for their own safety.

Although Randolph charged that "the ministers of religion were at the head of this revolt," the new government's insistence that it had acted to protect Andros is undoubtedly correct.[25] Increase Mather's overly optimistic account of his negotiations in England raised hopes that even King James was about to remove the governor.[26] Since leading inhabitants had good cause to believe they might have been rid of Andros legally, it is improbable that they would have risked rebellion to hasten the process.

Unfortunately, the new government, originally a self-selected Council of Safety, proved even less successful than Andros in maintaining order. The Glorious Revolution brought England's friendship with France to an abrupt halt. It thereby suddenly transformed New England's cold neutrality toward New France into open war. For the first time, the Maine tribes received extensive moral encouragement from Jesuit priests and material support from Count Frontenac in Quebec. The first two years of King William's War (1689–1697) reduced Massachusetts to chaos. The Abenakis and Norridgewocks destroyed the colony's settlements in Maine, which had extended a hundred miles up the coast and into the interior. The colony was reduced to a precarious foothold in the region's southern tip.[27]

Although the Council of Safety consisted of a broad coalition of ministers, old-charter men, moderates, and Anglicans, it failed miserably. The people "openly disowned the power of the government and refused to pay rates and estate taxes." In Boston, no one even paid the poor tax; Benjamin Bullivant, Andros's attorney-general, wrote that "the poor people are ready to eat one another. The soldiers that were returned from the eastward . . . were disgusted at receiving no pay," and "spoke very insolently to their new masters, crying publicly in the streets: God Bless Sir Edmund Andros, and damn all pumpkin states!" It proved nearly impossible to enlist soldiers. Randolph commented that "they have no officers fit to command them, so the soldiers prefer to lie in gaol" rather than serve.[28]

As if the war in Maine were not trouble enough, the new regime decided to conquer Port Royal and Quebec the following year. Sir William Phips, who had returned from England, persuaded the assembly which had supplanted the Council of Safety in June 1689 to undertake the expedition. Increase Mather had told Phips that only such an unprecedented demonstration of loyalty could restore the old charter. Commanded by Phips, Massachusetts' army seized Port Royal. But sickness and delays made a major assault on Quebec itself impossible. The fleet had to return before the St. Lawrence River froze. To finance the campaign, and in the opinion of some to "cheat the men who served on it," the colony issued paper money for the first time. The bills immediately depreciated 25 to 50 percent. Boston merchant Francis Brinley wrote that "we are stopping the mouths of the soldiers with a new mint of paper money. Not many will take it and those that will scarce know what to do with it." Taxes increased to over thirty times their prewar level. Andros's attorneys in England answered charges that he had oppressed the people by showing that his successors "found the tax imposed by Sir Edmund so much too small that they have levied not one [pence], but seven pence half pence in the pound."[29]

The taxes might have been bearable had the government proven minimally competent. But while the troops marched off to Canada, the province could not even guard its frontiers. For the first and only time, to excuse itself from defending the settlers, the council echoed the arguments of royal attorneys that Massachusetts had no legitimate title to Maine. When "the people begged for help, Mr. Danforth asserted that Jesus Christ was king of earth as well as heaven, and that if Jesus Christ did not help them, he could not." Bullivant reported that "the common people now wish Sir Edmund Andros were back again."[30]

The government that replaced Andros never possessed any legitimacy. People refused to serve in its armed forces, recognize its courts, pay its taxes, or even accept its money. Governor Bradstreet tried to dismiss this chaotic situation as a "false report" spread by Andros's cronies. But in the same letter to England he himself admitted that "we have endeavored to check [the Indians] but very ineffectually" and that "the whole [Canada] expedition has been borne by a few private persons, there being no public treasury." In May 1691, Massachusetts' magistrates admitted their own impotence by asking the king to settle a new government.[31]

Complete self-government would have died even if the agents' negotiations had succeeded in restoring it. Between 1689 and 1691, the interim rulers sought to bolster the tottering regime in a manner that abolished forever a community of saints. To broaden popular support, they permitted ex-moderates and Anglicans like Shrimpton and Wharton to enter the inner circles of government. King's Chapel, the Anglican church in Boston, functioned peacefully. In two years' time, the colony admitted 738 new freemen, an increase of between a third and a half. It even adopted Andros's institution of a standing army and his court system, replete with justices of the peace, to preserve order.[32] But it was not enough. As early as October 1689, an observer noted that "all parties long for orders from England to settle us, and indeed they are wanted, for the people grow very divided under the present constitution and this terrible Indian invasion." An anonymous letter of December 1690 went so far as to claim that "our present extremity is such that any order from the king will be acceptable."[33]

The chaos of 1689 to 1691 forced even the staunchest adherents of the old constitution to admit that it was dead. Massachusetts could not protect its inhabitants from the French and Indians nor even keep internal order unless it secured legitimacy and material assistance from England. All possible basis disappeared for a faction that seriously desired a return to the pre-1685 situation. Massachusetts repudiated the old Puritan regime to the extent that only one-eighth of those who served in the General Court of 1685 reappeared in 1692.[34] The factions that emerged under the new charter concerned themselves over who would rule within its framework, not over the validity of the charter itself. Under the pressure of warfare, Massachusetts found itself courting the very royal authority it had resisted so tenaciously in the past.

### INSTALLING A ROYAL GOVERNMENT: 1691–1694

The old-charter and moderate factions failed to create a viable government in Massachusetts. The colony's four remaining agents—Increase Mather, William Phips, Elisha Cooke, and Thomas Oakes—did just as badly in Britain. As early as February 1689, King William's Privy Council rejected a petition that the charter be restored. Denying the agents' claim that Massachusetts had lost it through Stuart tyranny, the council insisted that the colony well deserved its fate. William then stipulated that he would appoint a royal governor although taxes would not be levied without an assembly. He ordered the Lords of Trade to prepare "a further establishment as may be lasting and preserve the rights and privileges of the people of New England and yet reserve . . . a dependence on the Crown of England."[35] Despite two years of feverish activity, the agents never got a better offer.

# The End of Puritan Politics

Instead of trying to negotiate the best possible charter within this framework, Mather and his colleagues wasted their time trying to restore the old constitution through incessant lobbying and pamphleteering.[36] Only in April 1691, when sixty-one prominent and wealthy New England merchants asked the king to "take the colony into his immediate care and protection," did they face reality and begin serious negotiations.[37] This petition marked the first collective political action explicitly taken by a large number of merchants in Massachusetts' history. All except three of the signers appear to have played no significant role in politics before the inter-charter period,[38] but in 1693 and 1694 the towns elected six of them to the house of representatives. The merchants had had enough of incompetence at home and abroad. Their election to the assembly demonstrated that they had considerable popular support.[39]

The new constitution represented a compromise between the agents' and the crown's original positions.[40] The royal governor could appoint the judiciary with the council's consent, veto laws, and command the militia. However, the house of representatives, in conjunction with the outgoing council, elected the new upper house. The towns continued to elect the deputies annually. Each community could send one representative, two if it had over forty houses. Boston, in imitation of London's parliamentary representation, could send four. All adult males worth £40 sterling or possessing a freehold valued at 40 shillings annually could vote for deputies. This established a very broad suffrage.[41]

Such a charter created a precarious balance. It failed to settle the constitutional balance among the governor, council, and assembly. Rather, none of the three branches could act alone, and all had to consent to legislation. Stalemate resulted when any used its full powers of obstruction. Thanks to the necessities of war, such deadlocks occurred rarely before the 1720s except during the brief and disastrous regime of William Phips. Phips's troubled administration (1692–1694) failed to unite the province as nearly everyone had hoped.

Phips began well. With the interim government on the verge of collapse, the population was overjoyed that Andros and Dudley were not returning to execute their opponents. The legislature unanimously thanked King William for Phips's appointment. Even a good friend of Joseph Dudley, Salem's Reverend John Higginson, expressed the consensus that "our good Mr. Mather did good service to God and his people in procuring Sir William Phips to be our governor rather than some others."[42]

19

# The End of Puritan Politics

Phips and Mather made every effort to convince Massachusetts that while the form of government had changed, its substance had not. The governor told the assembly that greeted his arrival that "God had sent him there to serve the country, and he would not abridge them of any of their ancient laws and customs, but all privileges, laws, and liberties as was practical in the days of old should be as they were before." The legislature's first act, which Phips approved, continued all existing statutes until further notice. The governor even announced that "nothing grieved him so much . . . as that he had the government by commission." Phips sanctioned the creation of a provincial naval office with sole power to enforce the Acts of Trade, and thereby to supplant the royal collector. New Hampshire's Lieutenant-Governor, John Usher, maintained that Phips publicly announced that goods from anywhere in the world could be brought into the province "on land or water without any entry or clearing." The intent of the Naval Office Act was plain. Phips and the legislature designed it to quiet the anxieties of those merchants who favored a royal government to maintain law and order but feared the rigorous enforcement of commercial legislation.[43]

However, most of sixteen statutes passed in 1692 were designed to placate the Puritans. Harvard College obtained a charter that excluded the royal governor from any role in its administration. The Fellows of the College—the ministers of Boston and the tutors appointed by them—had total control. The province's court system omitted King's Bench and Exchequer which functioned without juries. The legislature instituted only county courts and a Superior Court of Common Pleas to handle civil and capital criminal offenses. Nor were the courts confined to common-law restraints: they could adhere to Puritan jurisprudence. The General Court confirmed existing land titles but made no effort to secure the King's Woods, which pleased land speculators and lumbering men. In effect from 1692 until disallowed by the Privy Council in 1695, the new laws not only restored nearly complete autonomy, but all the major political interests—the old-charter faction, the moderates, the merchants, and the Puritans—ought to have been satisfied.[44]

However, the initial harmony was short-lived. A government headed by Sir Edmund Andros himself could hardly have made more enemies in so brief a time. Phips refused to create the broad basis of support any new regime needed to survive. Instead, Increase Mather—to whom King William had given the right of appointing the first governor and council—excluded all his political opponents from power. Elisha Cooke and Thomas Oakes—who had opposed the new constitution and suggested legal action to restore the old—could not even secure the lowly office of justice of the peace, let alone the seats on the council for which their public services obviously qualified them. Excluded members of both the old charter and moderate factions fumed for the very reason Cotton Mather exulted: "all the councillors of the province are of my father's nomination; my father-in-law, and several related unto me, and several brethren of my church. The governor of the province is one whom I baptized, one of my dearest friends."[45] The Mathers' choice of officers ensured rapid dissipation of the new government's widespread support. Phips's regime appeared as their personal instrument rather than a satisfactory solution to the province's disorder.

Most of the opposition came from the old-charter faction. But Mather's procrastination in negotiating a new charter, the resulting two years of confusion, and the quarrel among the agents severely modified former political alignments. The composition of the new council reveals the extent to which previous factions had changed. Mather chose nine ex-moderates who had been selected for Andros's council, although three had refused to serve. All had participated in the interim government that replaced him. On the other hand, Mather also selected four of the old charter councillors who had opposed the Dominion of New England, and five political newcomers. The remaining ten members consisted of men who had made their political debuts during the inter-charter period. Thus Mather, the former spokesman for the old-charter faction, picked only four of his former cohorts for the twenty-eight man body.[46]

Mather's selection of the hopelessly incompetent Phips to execute his program also proved counterproductive. A rough and ready ship's carpenter and sea captain, Phips had obtained wealth and a knighthood in 1687 by recovering a sunken treasure ship in the West Indies. The Mathers had thereafter spent a good deal of their considerable energy trying to transform him into a God-fearing Puritan. The only native New Englander other than Dudley with sufficient prestige at home to obtain the governor's chair, the inexperienced Phips would be their personal instrument. He seemed like a good investment; he was only forty-one years old in 1692 and had a fair prospect of governing for decades.[47]

He did not. Observers described the new governor as totally unfit for his post. Critics claimed that "he cannot yet read a letter, much less write one"; that the council was "ashamed of his behavior"; and that he selected his associates from "out of the mob . . . amongst whom noise and strut pass for wit and prowess." Within a year of Phips's arrival both the former old-charter and moderate factions within Massachusetts detested him. Moreover, the royal navy, the customs service, and the other royal governors on the North American continent had buried their differences to assist each other in removing him.[48]

One example of Phips's unwillingness to uphold royal authority was his brusque treatment of Captain Richard Short of H.M.S. *Nonsuch.* His conduct here displayed a comic flair sadly lacking in Massachusetts' political history. Phips and Richard Short first quarrelled over the prize money for a French ship they captured. Exercising his Vice-Admiralty authority, the governor deprived Short of the profits. Their spats continued when they reached Massachusetts, and culminated on 4 January 1693, in Phips's physical assault "with all imaginable violence" on his antagonist. He then imprisoned Short amidst "witches, wizards, injuns, and negroes," denied him habeas corpus or even visitors, and finally shipped him back to England to stand trial for insubordination. However, Short managed to escape the governor's clutches. Phips made the mistake of putting him aboard a ship owned by Nathaniel Byfield, the Speaker of the House of Representatives and a good friend of Joseph Dudley. Instead of taking Short to England, Byfield arranged to deposit him in the safekeeping of New Hampshire's Lieutenant-Governor John Usher. Upon discovering Byfield's duplicity, Phips sent some men to kidnap Short. When Usher arrested them, Phips made a personal attempt to retrieve Short. Byfield and Usher eagerly communicated Phips's behavior to Joseph Dudley—waiting patiently as Chief Justice of New York to be restored to his old post—and the colonial administration.[49]

Phips treated the customs service with equal disdain. He "laid aside" and threatened to imprison Lawrence Hammond and Jahleel Brenton, whom the Treasury entrusted to register cargoes, search for contraband, and collect duties. When on 25 May 1693, Brenton seized a sloop carrying illegal goods, Phips led a mob of fifty persons to recover it. He then treated his constituents to another brawl on the waterfront. Phips and Massachusetts' Naval Officer Benjamin Jackson granted their own clearances so indiscriminately that Brenton "looked upon the governor's clearance to be no more than if it had been from an Indian." The governor had good reason to fear Brenton and Hammond. John Usher estimated that during Phips's brief administration he netted £9,000 in underhanded trading ventures, notably a mysterious £1,000 in "Arabian gold got from pirates."[50]

Phips's relations with the navy and customs officers, although undignified, did not pose a major threat to the security of the English colonies in North America. His behavior toward his fellow governors did. Lieutenant-Governor Usher only obtained military assistance for his fledgling province when Phips was in Maine and Lieutenant–Governor William Stoughton acted in his stead. Phips ignored Usher's complaints that Indians he had presumably pacified continued to attack New Hampshire.[51] Three months after Phips left the province, the Massachusetts assembly pleaded with the king for assistance in suppressing the very same Indians.[52]

Even more serious, Phips would not cooperate with his colleagues to the south. When New York's Governor Benjamin Fletcher requested assistance against the French, Phips replied "I will not send a man nor a farthing of money to the assistance of New York and 'tis a monstrous thought to suppose I should." He even refused to attend a conference on prospective quotas. Fletcher had his revenge. He plotted with Virginia's Lieutenant-Governor Francis Nicholson (another victim of Phips's temper) to withhold a very important letter. It informed Phips that an English fleet requiring provincial assistance was to arrive in Boston in the spring of 1693. Nevertheless, even though Phips somehow learned of this new Canadian expedition, he still did nothing to prepare for it. When Sir Francis Wheeler and his forces arrived in mid-June, the fleet decimated by smallpox, Phips was a bundle of excuses. He could not, he claimed, mobilize the militia without the assembly's consent. It was not sitting and he refused to call a special session. He also maintained that it was too late in the season for a campaign, and if the troops were allowed to land the province might be infected with smallpox.[53] Phips may have been trying to save his fellow inhabitants' money and lives, but neither Wheeler, the other governors, nor the English colonial administration saw it that way. Few governors in the history of the empire so alienated their fellow civil servants.

## OUSTING A ROYAL GOVERNOR: 1692–1694

It might well be imagined that a governor so unpopular with imperial authorities would have been idolized by the stubborn Puritans of Massachusetts Bay. But this was not the case. All parties agreed that Phips did more than challenge their respective interpretations of Anglo-American relations. He also threatened the minimal standards of decency and competence that had to be maintained if the empire were to survive in North America.

Paradoxically, the most humane and intelligent act of Phips's administration embroiled him in his first major domestic quarrel. When he returned from a summer campaign against the Indians in 1692, he found "many persons in a strange ferment of dissatisfaction" from the witch trials then under way in Salem. Phips immediately censored all discourses "that may increase the needless disputes of the people upon this occasion," halted the executions, and obtained a royal order that "the greatest moderation and all circumspection be used" in future prosecutions. These moves saved lives and eliminated a potential source of social disruption. But they also made Phips an implacable enemy, Lieutenant-Governor Stoughton, who had "hurried on these matters with great precipitancy." Thereafter, the furious Stoughton quarrelled with Phips about his treatment of Short and Brenton, tried to enforce the Navigation Acts despite his superior's wishes, and compiled the evidence used against Phips at his trial.[54]

Moreover, a number of unlikely candidates had joined Stoughton in supporting the witch trials enthusiastically. Phips's disbanding of the tribunal rebuked the "persons of the best prudence" in the province, his criterion for appointing them in the first place. The nonpartisan tribunal included four former moderates and four former old-charter men.[55] In retrospect, Phips's decision to end the trials appears noble and sensible. Pragmatically, it alienated the leaders of both factions.

Like the new charter itself, the trials had given the province an opportunity to reintegrate itself. Merchants and Puritans, or pro- and anti-Phips factions, no longer had to blame each other for the province's distresses. The loss of the old charter, Indian warfare, and financial problems could simply be dumped in the Devil's lap. It is possible to account for the outbreak of witchcraft by localized class conflict in Salem[56] or Andover (where seven of the victims came from, as opposed to eight from Salem and four from the rest of the province),[57] or the actual practice of the black arts.[58] The repressed anti-maternal feelings of Puritan teenagers may also have played a role.[59] But what really needs explaining is why someone like Stoughton—a political trimmer who served in the inner circles of the five previous regimes—so suddenly became an uncompromising zealot. The most plausible reason is that the trials provided the government's politically flexible leaders with an opportunity to convince themselves that they truly believed in their religious and political ideals. Phips's sudden dismissal of the tribunal, although necessary given increasing popular discontent, turned the province's principal men against him.

Phips treated the General Court with even less tact. Three of the major legislative disputes that emerged in the next century occurred for the first time: control of spending, the governor's salary, and the assembly's choice of its speaker. Although materials describing these controversies are scanty, enough remains to show that the governor's professed devotion to the province's liberties went only so far. He did not balk at violating the charter or tampering with the membership of the General Court if it suited his politics or profited him financially.

Quarrels over taxation and expenditures broke out immediately after Phips's arrival. Shortly before, the interim government had levied a £30,000 tax. The inhabitants had to pay a poll tax of 10 shillings per head and personal property was taxed at 25 percent of assessed value. This money had been used to pay for past war expenses, and Phips found the treasury empty when he took office. Nevertheless, without any authorization from the house, he added to the distress in the summer of 1692 by building a fort at Pemaquid in Maine. This move increased the debt by £20,000. Angered by this flagrant violation of the charter right of taxation, assemblymen complained that "they could have no account of the country's money when required, nor any reason why the country was so much in debt." Several representatives suspected Phips's "whole management was crooked, being much more to his own interest than the good of the people."[60]

To cover Phips's extravagances, the deputies were obliged to tax estates at one-fourth their annual income. They also introduced an import tax on wines, molasses, sugar, and logwood. These taxes were originally intended to meet only the "great charges . . . in defending and securing Their Majesties' subjects." But like so many other levies in history, they proved sufficiently lucrative to be made permanent. In light of Phips's arbitrary expenditures, the assembly understandably rebuffed his requests for a contingency fund to meet government charges during its recess. The deputies also refused to vote him any salary at all for the first two years of his administration. This prompted him to write privately to the king asking for a fixed income independent of their will.[61]

Within six months of Phips's arrival, nearly everyone detested him. Samuel Sewall recorded the names of those present when in November 1692, Elisha Cooke returned home and kept a "Day of Thanksgiving" to celebrate his arrival. Former moderates Wait Winthrop, Governor Bradstreet, and Samuel Shrimpton joined Cooke's supporters John Richards, Thomas Oakes, Thomas Danforth, and Elisha and Eliakim Hutchinson. The Mathers did not appear. The new government so alienated the province's leading men that even Mather's handpicked council turned against him. When it chose the province's first Superior Court on 6 December, Stoughton received all fifteen votes and Danforth was runner-up with twelve. The three remaining seats went to

## The End of Puritan Politics

Wait Winthrop, an ex-moderate, and John Richards and Samuel Sewall of the old-charter faction.[62] All had celebrated Cooke's return.

Phips's difficulties mushroomed when a new General Court met in May 1693. the appointed council had to stand for election. Even though most of the members probably voted for each other, the house was so angry that it rejected eleven of the twenty-eight incumbents. Former Governors Thomas Hinckley of Plymouth and Simon Bradstreet of Massachusetts went down to defeat. In their stead, the legislature added Cooke and Danforth. Eleven of the thirteen representatives Phips had appointed justices of the peace lost their seats as well. The tallies obtained by former moderates and old-charter men reveal that within the anti-Phips faction, popularity depended more on individual prestige than former political allegiance. Sewall headed the list with seventy-seven votes from the twenty-eight councillors and approximately fifth representatives present. Danforth and Nathaniel Thomas of the old-charter faction and ex-moderates Wait Winthrop and John Richards each had sixty or more. On the other hand, Stoughton and Cooke obtained only thirty-one each. They squeezed in on a subsequent ballot in which fewer votes were cast. Unlike most of the others, they were controversial figures in their own right. Phips showed his displeasure at the election by vetoing Cooke.[63]

Confronted with nearly universal opposition, Phips attempted to counter his rivals by purging them from the house of representatives. A caustic observer remarked that these "were gentlemen principally of Boston who were too near Sir William to think well of him." The new house for 1693 contained at least six Bostonians serving as deputies for other towns. All had petitioned for a royal government in 1691, and had compelled Increase Mather to begin serious negotiation for a new charter. The house had elected one of them, Nathaniel Byfield, its speaker. Hoping to eliminate his enemies at one stroke, Phips proposed a bill requiring all deputies to live in the town for which they served. When this failed, he dissolved the house in July and ordered new elections for November. When the new assembly met, he took the precaution of "deposing" Speaker Byfield. On 21 November, he somehow persuaded the house to choose a new speaker on the grounds that Byfield was ineligible because he had served on a house committee. Seven days later, the residency law passed twenty-six to twenty-four in the assembly and nine to eight in the council. This narrow margin determined that the assembly would consist mostly of rural deputies who voted on issues presented by the house's leaders, instead of a politically motivated group of interested coastal representatives. (Paradoxically, future governors would have been happy to receive prominent Bostonians serving for country towns. They complained the assembly was too large and blindly followed the opposition.) Immediately after the act passed the council, Phips rushed into the assembly's chamber and personally evicted the Bostonian non-residents.[64]

The following May, the new house expelled five representatives elected in defiance of the law. Phips threatened to turn them out physically if the house did not. On their behalf, Byfield wrote to Joseph Dudley to "let not the governor's treatment of the assembly die" and to use his best efforts to have the measure disallowed. Thanks to Phips's extreme tactics, Dudley found himself in the novel position of defending the assembly's rights against the governor's intrusions.

Phips finally secured a pliant assembly in 1694, but it was too late.[65] Byfield, Stoughton, Dudley, and others had communicated word of his misdeeds across the Atlantic. The Lords of Trade recalled him in January 1694 to answer for his conduct. They empowered Stoughton and the council to gather depositions against him, which they did thoroughly. Phips tried to thwart them, in vain, remaining in Boston until mid-November, doing "all he could to hinder the proof, . . . sometimes threatening the witnesses their ears ought to be cut off and sometimes barring (as he called it) others from swearing." While in England, Brenton sued the unfortunate governor for assault and required him to post bail of £20,000. But Phips eluded his enemies by his sudden death on 18 February 1695.[66]

Counting Phips, between 1686 and 1694 Massachusetts underwent no fewer than six changes of government and an equal number of factional realignments. The moderates triumphed temporarily over the old-charter faction in 1685 when Britain revoked the charter. Joseph Dudley's brief administration (1686) then witnessed the moderates' attempt to conciliate their opponents. This, in turn, alienated Edward Randolph and the English authorities, who retaliated with the arbitrary government of Sir Edmund Andros (1686–1689). At this time the moderate and old-charter factions cemented their unity against his "usurpations," as they termed them. However, once they had overthrown him, they soon lost the confidence of the general population. The interim government (1689–1692) lacked the ability to manage the war provoked by the Glorious Revolution. All parties then looked to England to settle a recognized government. However, when the mother country finally acted, Increase Mather's quarrel with Cooke and Oakes, his choice of the incompetent Phips as governor, and his refusal to appoint members of all factions to the council produced a nearly unanimous reaction. But opposition did not form against the royal government itself, only against those entrusted with its execution.

In the midst of this instability, one fact became overwhelmingly clear. By 1694, nearly everyone in Massachusetts regarded British authority—dreaded by the old-charter and moderate factions alike as late as 1686—as necessary for survival. The colony could not withstand the dual strain of disastrous warfare and internal political strife. A new stability and unity, based on general acceptance of royal government, could easily have been established with the new charter. However, because of Phips's eccentricities, it had to wait until Lieutenant–Governor William Stoughton assumed the chair. Phips's truly bizarre conduct set his regime apart from that of every wartime governor before the Revolution: he failed to achieve greater cooperation between the factions in Massachusetts and between the colony and England.

# *Notes to Chapter II*

1. For a general description of political violence and instability in the seventeenth century, see in James Morton Smith, ed., *Seventeenth Century America: Essays in Colonial History* (Chapel Hill, 1959), introduction by Oscar Handlin, and Bernard Bailyn, "Politics and Social Structure in Virginia"; for Puritan Massachusetts as an exception to the rule, see Robert E. Wall, *Massachusetts Bay: The Crucial Decade, 1640–1650* (New Haven, 1972), esp. pp. 232–233; T. H. Breen, *The Character of a Good Ruler: Puritan Political Ideas in New England, 1630–1730* (New Haven, 1970), esp. p. 83; and T. H. Breen and Stephen Foster, "The Puritans' Greatest Achievement: A Study of Social Cohesion in the Seventeenth Century," *Journal of American History*, 60 (1973): 5–22. Authorities in Massachusetts scrupulously enforced orderly behavior even when it was not to the colony's advantage. Edward Randolph could not obtain effective compliance with the Navigation Acts, but he could walk the streets of Boston unmolested at a time when Massachusetts' self-government was at stake. Those who tried to obstruct him physically were punished. See Michael G. Hall, *Edward Randolph and the American Colonies, 1676–1703* (Chapel Hill, 1960), pp. 61–62.

2. See especially Darrett Rutman, *American Puritanism* (Philadelphia, 1971) for this interpretation. Good refutations of the notion that economic hardship in England was primarily responsible for the Puritan migration appear in Thomas Hutchinson, *The History of the Colony and Province of Massachusetts Bay* (Cambridge, 1936), 1: 41, and Samuel Eliot Morison, *Builders of the Bay Colony* (Boston, 1930), pp. 379–386.

3. See, for this and the next two paragraphs, Stephen Foster, *Their Solitary Way: The Puritan Social Ethic in the First Century of Settlement* (New Haven, 1971); Rowland Berthoff, *An Unsettled People: Social Order and Disorder in American History* (New York, 1971), pp. 3–124; Bernard Bailyn, *The New England Merchants in the Seventeenth Century* (Cambridge, 1955); Edmund S. Morgan, *The Puritan Family: Religion and Domestic Relations in Seventeenth Century New England* (New York, 1966); Roy H. Akagi, *The Town Proprietors of the New England Colonies: A Study of Their Development, Organization, Activities, and Controversies, 1620–1770* (Philadelphia, 1924). For the extent of political participation, see B. Katherine Brown, "Freemanship in Puritan Massachusetts," *American Historical Review*, 59 (1954): 865–883, for a

# Notes to Chapter II

generally accurate summary of changing voting qualifications. She is incorrect, however, in stating that the law of 1664 required that non-freemen possess ten shillings worth of property, rather than pay ten shillings in taxes, to vote in country-wide elections. See Stephen Foster, "The Massachusetts Franchise in the Seventeenth Century," *William and Mary Quarterly*, 3rd. ser. 24 (1967): 613–623, for corrections. In addition to the taxpaying qualification, non-freemen had to be certified as orthodox by a local minister. See also Richard C. Simmons, "Freemanship in Early Massachusetts: Some Suggestions and a Case Study," *William and Mary Quarterly*, 3rd. ser. 19 (1962): 422–428, and "Godliness, Property, and the Franchise in Puritan Massachusetts: An Interpretation," *Journal of American History*, 55 (1968): 495–511; T. H. Breen, "Who Governs: The Town Franchise in Seventeenth-Century Massachusetts," *William and Mary Quarterly*, 3rd. ser. 27 (1970): 460–474; Robert E. Wall, Jr., "The Massachusetts Bay Colony Franchise in 1647," *ibid.*, 136–144, and "The Decline of the Massachussets Franchise, 1647–1666," *Journal of American History*, 59 (1972): 303–310; B. Katherine Brown, "The Controversy Over the Franchise in Puritan Massachusetts, 1954 to 1974," *ibid.*, 33 (1976), 212–241; and an exchange of letters between Brown, Wall, and Simmons, *ibid.*, 25 (1968): 330–339. All of these scholars except Brown agree that the province franchise was restricted by mid-century to about a third of the population. In 1664, a certificate of orthodoxy from one's minister plus payment of a ten-shilling tax extended the franchise but does not appear to have greatly increased participation.

4. Good accounts of early Massachusetts include Edmund S. Morgan, *The Puritan Dilemma: The Story of John Winthrop* (Boston, 1958), and Perry Miller, *Orthodoxy in Massachusetts, 1630–1650* (Cambridge, 1933).

5. Edmund S. Morgan, *Visible Saints: The History of a Puritan Idea* (New York, 1963), pp. 112–138, has suggested that the children of the founders took their obligations too seriously; Perry Miller, "The Half-Way Covenant," *New England Quarterly*, 6 (1933): 676–715, stresses a decline in fervor; Robert G. Pope, *The Half-Way Covenant: Church Membership in Puritan New England* (Princeton, 1969) has confirmed the decline in church membership.

6. For the second generation's limited political opportunities, see Robert E. Wall, Jr., "The Membership of the Massachusetts General Court, 1634–1686," (Yale University, Ph.D. diss., 1965), esp. pp. vi, 248; for ministers' decreasing prospects, see David Hall, *The Faithful Shepherd: A History of the New England Ministry in the Seventeenth Century* (Chapel Hill, 1972), p. 185. Theodore B. Lewis and Linda M. Webb, "Voting for the Massachusetts Council of Assistants, 1674–1686: A Statistical Note," *William and Mary Quarterly*, 3rd. ser. 30 (1973): 625–634; Samuel Sewall Diary, ed. M. Halsey Thomas (New York, 1973), 1: 95, 98.

7. Pope, *The Half-Way Covenant*; Hall, *The Faithful Shepherd*, chs. 8–9.

8. In addition to Hall, *The Faithful Shepherd*, ch. 10, see Richard C. Simmons, "The Founding of the Third Church in Boston," *William and Mary Quarterly*, 3rd. ser. 26 (1969): 241–252; Paul R. Lucas, "Colony or Commonwealth: Massachusetts Bay, 1661–1666,", *ibid.*, 3rd. ser. 24 (1967): 88–107; Breen, *The Character of a Good Ruler*, chs. 2–3; E. Brooks Holifield, "On Toleration in Massachusetts," *Church History*, 38 (1969): 1–13.

9. Theodore B. Lewis, "Massachusetts and the Glorious Revolution, 1660–1692" (Ph.D. diss., University of Wisconsin, 1967) p. 29. The petition itself is in the *Danforth Papers*, *MHSC*, 2nd ser. 8: 105–107. I am much indebted to Lewis's thorough study for my treatment of this period.

10. Kenneth Lockridge, *A New England Town: The First Hundred Years [Dedham 1636–1736]* (New York, 1970); Claude Fuess, "Witches at Andover," *MHSP*, 70 (1950–1953): 8–20; Philip Greven, *Four Generations: Population, Land and Family in Colonial Andover* (Ithaca, N.Y., 1970); Paul Boyer and Stephen Nissenbaum, *Salem Possessed: The Social Origins of Witchcraft* (Cambridge, 1974). For general treatments

of increasing discontent on the local level in the seventies and eighties see Rhys Isaac, "Order and Growth, Authority and Meaning in Colonial New England," *American Historical Review*, 76 (1971): 728–737; a paper delivered by T. H. Breen at the conference of the Organizations of American Historians, 8 April 1977, "Crisis of Authority: Local Factions and Collapse of the Massachusetts Government, 1686–1692"; Ronald K. Snell, "Freemanship, Officeholding, and the Town Franchise in Seventeenth Century Springfield, Massachusetts," *New England Historical and Genealogical Register*, 133 (1979): 163–179; Hall, *The Faithful Shepherd*, pp. 132–133; Pope, *The Half-Way Covenant*, pp. 194.

11. For King Philip's War see David Hall, *The Faithful Shepherd*; Pope, *The Half-Way Covenant*; and Richard Slotkin and James K. Folsom, eds., *So Dreadfull a Judgement: Puritan Responses to King Philips' War* (Middletown, Ct., 1978).

12. The best discussions of support for and opposition to Randolph may be found in Lewis's "Massachusetts and the Glorious Revolution," pp. 411–436, which analyzes the wealth, occupations, and connections of those whom Randolph identified as his supporters. See also Michael Hall, *Edward Randolph*, pp. 21–128; David S. Lovejoy, *The Glorious Revolution in America* (New York, 1972), pp. 122–159; Bailyn, *The New England Merchants in the Seventeenth Century*, ch. 7; Richard S. Dunn, *Puritans and Yankees: The Winthrop Dynasty of New England, 1630–1717* (Princeton, 1962), pp. 212–228; and Foster, *Their Solitary Way*, pp. 182–189. All except Lewis and Foster emphasize the merchants who favored Randolph.

13. Bradstreet asked Randolph to persuade the king to "pardon what is past," since a continuation of the present constitution "would conduce as much to His Majesty's honor, dignity, profit, and satisfaction as the sending over a governor." Simon Bradstreet to Edward Randolph, 8 December 1684, *Mather Papers, MHSC*, 4th ser. 8: 532. William Stoughton to Joseph Dudley, August 1683, quoted in Dean Dudley, *The History of the Dudley Family* (Wakefield, Mass., 1886), p. 167. Joseph Dudley to Cotton Mather, 6 May 1689, *Dudley Papers, MHSC*, 6th. ser. 3: 502.

14. For example, Samuel Nowell of the old-charter faction married the widow of Hezekiah Usher, the brother of the moderate John Usher; John L. Sibley, *Biographical Sketches of Those Who Attended Harvard College* (Cambridge, 1873–    ), 1: 339. Moderate merchant Nathaniel Byfield, a relative of Joseph Dudley, was also the brother-in-law of old-charter stalwart Elisha Cooke; G.B. Warden, *Boston: 1689–1776* (Boston, 1970), p. 92. Major General Daniel Dennison, another leading moderate and kinsman of Dudley, was also related to the Hutchinsons, who supported the old charter; Lewis, "Massachusetts and the Glorious Revolution," p. 420. See Bailyn, *The New England Merchants*, p. 136, for a genealogical chart linking moderates like the Dudleys, Shrimptons, Whartons, and Winthrops with the Hutchinsons, Stoddards, and Scottows of the old-charter faction. For friendly relations between the groups, see Sewall, *Diary*, 1: 76, 85.

15. Lewis, "Massachusetts and the Glorious Revolution," esp. pp. 92–95; Kenneth Murdock, *Increase Mather: The Foremost American Puritan* (Cambridge, 1925), p. 152. For Danforth, see an anonymous letter to John Usher, *CSP*, 13, #1309; for Nowell, see T. H. Breen, *The Character of a Good Ruler: A History of Puritan Political Ideas, 1630–1730* (New Haven, 1970), pp. 117–122.

16. Edward Randolph, "Articles of High Misdemeanors exhibited against a faction," 28 May 1682, and Randolph to [Commissioners of Customs], 25 May 1682, in Robert N. Toppan, ed., *Edward Randolph: Including His Letters and Official Papers. . .* (Boston, 1898–1909), 2: 265–268.

17. Locations of all available council returns are listed in Lewis and Webb, "Voting for the Massachusetts Council"; easily accessible votes are in Sewall, *Diary*, 1: 61, 111, 114, and Samuel Sewall, *Letter Book, MHSC*, 6th. ser. 1:1.

18. Edward Randolph to Samuel Shrimpton, 18 July 1684, *Mather Papers, MHSC*, 4th. ser. 8: 525.

# Notes to Chapter II

19. See Hall, *Edward Randolph*, pp. 98–107; Lewis, "Massachusetts and the Glorious Revolution," pp. 183–184; and Viola F. Barnes, *The Dominion of New England* (New Haven, 1923), pp. 47–70, for Dudley's policies described in this and the following paragraph, and for differences between Dudley and his successor Sir Edmund Andros.

20. The phrase "bellows of sedition" is Randolph's. See his letter to Sir Robert Southwell, 19 August 1683, in Toppan, ed., *Edward Randolph*, 3: 263.

21. Such criticisms may be found in the "Declaration of Grievances," 18 April 1689, in Charles M. Andrews, ed., *Narratives of the Insurrections* (New York, 1915), pp. 175–182; "An Account of the Late Revolutions in New England by A.B.," in William H. Whitmore, ed., *The Andros Tracts*, (Boston, 1868–1874), vol. 2, pp. 191–202; William Stoughton et. al., "A Narrative of the proceedings of Sir Edmund Andros and His Complices . . ." *ibid.*, 1: 135–147; and Joseph Dudley to Cotton Mather, 6 May 1689, *Dudley Papers*, MHSC, 6th. ser. 3: 501–502.

22. Nathaniel Saltonstall to Edmund Andros, 23 September 1687, *Saltonstall Papers*, MHSC, 80:181; Lovejoy, *The Glorious Revolution*, pp. 179–195; Lewis, "Massachusetts and the Glorious Revolution," ch. 10; Hall, *Edward Randolph*, pp. 107–117; "Declaration of Grievances," in Andrews, ed., *Narratives of the Insurrections*, p. 182.

23. Richard Wharton to Wait Winthrop, June 1688, *Winthrop Papers*, 7, MHSC, 6th. ser. 5: 18. The most detailed accounts of the New Englanders in England are in Murdock, *Increase Mather*, chs. 13–14, and in Lovejoy, *The Glorious Revolution in America*, pp. 222–234, 340–353.

24. This paragraph is heavily indebted to Lewis, "Massachusetts and the Glorious Revolution," p. 293; quotation from "Declaration of Grievances," in Andrews, ed., *Narratives of the Insurrections*, p. 182.

25. Edward Randolph to Lords of Trade, 5 September 1689, *CSP*, 13, #407.

26. See, for example, Joshua Moody to Increase Mather, 4 October 1688, *Mather Papers*, MHSC, 4th. ser. 8: 366. Moody wrote that "your acceptance with His Majesty, and the great friends to stand by you, with the large promises made to you, make us like men that dream."

27. The council soon called for new elections and provisionally reinstated the old-charter government. See Lewis, "Massachusetts and the Glorious Revolution," ch. vii. In general, moderates and those unconnected with the old regime favored waiting for royal orders. The old-charter men wanted to resume the former constitution. Most members of both groups however, worked together once the government was settled.

28. Sir William Phips had to dismiss some enlisted men for want of arms. In Braintree, Colonel Edmund Quincy told the governor and council that "by the reason of bad counsel by some evil persons—out of thirteen men impressed there is not but two or three which will go." Edward Randolph to Lords of Trade, 5 September 1689, *CSP*, 13, #407; Journal of Benjamin Bullivant, *ibid.*, #885. See also Quincy to governor and council, 6 July 1689, Josiah Quincy, Jr. Papers, MHS.

29. Letter to John Usher, Phips Papers, 1: 95, MHS; Journal of Benjamin Bullivant , *CSP*, 13, #885; Letter from New England, 2 February 1691, *ibid.*, #1313; Answer of Sir Edmund Andros to charges of the Massachusetts Agents, 24 April 1690, *ibid.*, #844; Michael G. Hall et. al. eds., *The Glorious Revolution in America* (Chapel Hill, 1964), p. 55; Bullivant to Usher, July 1690, *CSP*, 13, #906.

30. Samuel Myles, the Anglican minister in Boston, wrote the Lords of Trade that "the people cannot conceive of what becomes of all the money taken from them unless it is sent to Mr. Mather to procure the charter." Benjamin Bullivant to John Usher, July 1690, *CSP*, 13, #906. Samuel Myles to Lords of Trade, 2 December 1690, *ibid.*, #1239.

# Notes to Chapter II

31. Supporters of the regime expressed similar thoughts privately. Samuel Sewall implored Increase Mather to obtain some ships from the navy to guard the colony's beleaguered coastline and shipping. Fitz Winthrop, who commanded the land forces of the Canada expedition and was tossed ignominiously in jail by New York's rebel Governor Leisler, complained that the "lazy methods" taken against the Indians prepared "us for destruction on every hand." Simon Bradstreet to Lords of Trade, 26 October 1689, *ibid.*, #513; Samuel Sewall to Increase Mather, 29 December 1690, Sewall, *Letter Book, MHSC*, 6th ser. 1:115; Fitz-John Winthrop to Wait Winthrop, 7 June 1690, *Winthrop Papers, 5, MHSC*, 5th ser. 8: 304; Council of Assistants to King William, 8 May 1691, State Papers, 7: 73, Frederick Lewis Gay Transcripts, MHS.

32. Richard C. Simmons, "Freemanship in Early Massachusetts: Some Suggestions and a Case Study," *William and Mary Quarterly*, 3rd. ser. 29 (1962): 424; John M. Murrin, "Anglicizing an American Colony: The Transformation of Provinicial Massachusetts" (Yale University, Ph.D. diss., 1966), pp. 64–69, 164–167.

33. Governor Henry Sloughter of New York was just visiting Boston for a week in February 1691, when several people applied to him to save them from "the arbitrary usurpations of persons in power." Letter to Lords of Trade, 24 October 1689, *CSP*, 13, #509; Henry Sloughter to Earl of Nottingham, 10 February 1691, *ibid.*, #1373; Letter from New England, *ibid.*, #1313.

34. John M. Murrin, Review Essay of New England town studies, *History and Theory*, 11 (1972): 260.

35. Determination of the Privy Council, 22 February 1689, Phips Papers, 1: 21–22.

36. See Cotton Mather's account of his father's agency, *Mather Papers, MHSC*, 1st. ser. 9: 244–250.

37. Petition of "Merchants and others," Phips Papers, 1: 117–123. Thirty-six of these men explicitly identified themselves as merchants or captains. Merchants intervened collectively in Massachusetts politics only occasionally: in 1714, 1733, and 1740 on the currency issue, in the 1750s over high taxation and war, and during the Revolution. In general, merchants were found on either side of any major issue.

38. The exceptions were John Pynchon, Nathaniel Clark, and William Browne.

39. Still, another six months were required until a charter agreeable to both parties could be framed. Originally, the agents wanted to deny the royal governor a veto, the right to appoint the council or the province judiciary, and the control of the armed forces. The Privy Council and Lords of Trade sought to preserve all these powers and thereby render Massachusetts' constitution indistinguishable from the other royal colonies. The agents' counterproposals attempted to restore the old charter in all but name. Draft of charter, 8 June 1691, *CSP*, 13, #1570; agents' answer, 30 June 1691, *ibid.*, #1600.

40. The charter is reprinted at the beginning of volume one of Abner C. Goodell and Ellis Ames, eds., *The Acts and Resolves of the Province of Massachusetts Bay* (Boston, 1869–1922)—hereafter cited as *A&R*. For the essentials of the final draft, see *CSP*, 13, #1806.

41. Robert E. Brown, *Middle-Class Democracy and the Revolution in Massachusetts: 1691–1780* (Ithaca, 1955), p. 80. Even in Boston in 1760, over two-thirds of male householders probably owned £40 sterling in property. Great Fire Manuscripts, Ms. Am., Boston Public Library.

42. Francis Foxcroft to Francis Nicholson, 26 October 1691, *CSP*, 13, #1857; letter to Nicholson, 15 November 1691, *ibid.*, #1875; William Phips to Earl of Nottingham, 29 May 1692, *ibid.*, #2246; John Higginson to John How, 1 August 1694, *Saltonstall Papers, MHSC*, 80: 214.

43. Letter from New England, 1 November 1694, Phips Papers, 4: 93; John Usher to Lords of Trade, 31 January 1693, *ibid.*, 2: 53.

# Notes to Chapter II

44. *A&R*, 1: 35–60.

45. Cotton Mather, *Diary* (Boston, 1911–1912), 1: 147.

46. William H. Whitmore, *The Massachusetts Civil List, 1630–1774* (Albany, 1870).

47. The best account of Phips' early career is Viola F. Barnes, "The Rise of William Phips," *New England Quarterly*, 1 (1928): 271–299.

48. In his more introspective moments, Phips himself admitted that "he has not wit enough for the government." Letter from New England, 1 November 1694, Phips Papers, 4: 85; Richard Short to James Sothern, 20 April 1693, *ibid.*, 3: 39; Childley Brooke to Benjamin Fletcher, 2 August 1693, *ibid.*, p. 72; John Higginson to John How, 1 August 1694, *Saltonstall Papers*, MHSC, 80: 214.

49. This paragraph represents the distillation of numerous letters and depositions in the Phips Papers. See especially 2: 19–22, 42–46, 89–93, 140–144; 3: 42–46; 5: 70–85. Quotations from deposition of John March, 4 January 1693, 2: 44; Richard Short to Lords of Admiralty, 24 April 1693, 3: 42.

50. Phips Papers, esp. 3: 52–56; 4: 4–13, 111–137; quotations from John Usher to Lords of Trade, 31 January 1693, 2: 52; and same to same, 13 February 1695, 4: 39–40.

51. See the exchanges of letters between Phips, Stoughton, and Usher, 12–15 October 1692, and July–August, 1694, Phips Papers, 2: 31–43; 4: 41–53; *CSP*, 14, #1306.

52. Phips had obtained a personal monopoly of the New England fur trade on the pretext that "many persons who only studied their own profit without considering the benefit of the public took advantage of the ignorance and necessity of the Indians." He himself "took advantage of their ignorance and necessity" to the sum of £2000 in one year. William Phips to [King William], 1693, Phips Papers, 3: 121–123; "Phips' Accounts," in John Usher to Lords of Trade, 7 September 1964, *ibid.*, 4: 39–40; Petition of the General Court, 13 February 1965, *ibid.*, 71.

53. Childley Brooke to Benjamin Fletcher, 2 August 1693, *ibid.*, 3: 70; Fletcher to William Phips, 31 August 1693, *ibid.*, p. 99; Phips to Fletcher, 18 September 1693, *ibid.*, p. 94; John Usher to Earl of Nottingham, 31 January 1693, *ibid.*, 2: 61; Josiah Brodbent to Francis Nicholson, 21 June 1692, *ibid.*, 2: 16–17; Francis Wheeler to Phips, 8 June 1693, *ibid.*, 3:55; Phips to Wheeler, 8 June 1693 and 27 June 1693, *ibid.*, pp. 58, 67; Nottingham to Phips, 31 January 1693, *ibid.*, 2: 75–76; Phips to Nottingham, 11 September 1693, *ibid.*, 3: 80; Robert Fairfax to James Sothern, 12 April 1693, *ibid.*, p. 36.

54. Stoughton had advocated the acceptance of spectral evidence—arguing that a person's image could be seen by others only if he or she were in league with the Devil. Phips directed that such evidence be disregarded. Shortly thereafter, when Phips abolished the witchcraft court itself, Stoughton "was enraged and filled with a passionate anger and refused to sit upon the bench in a Superior Court." William Phips to William Blathwayt, 12 October 1692, *ibid.*, 2: 28; Order of King in Council, 26 January 1693, *ibid.*, p. 50; William Phips to Earl of Nottingham, 21 February 1693, *ibid.*, p. 15.

55. Whitmore, *Civil List*, p. 75; William Phips to William Blathwayt, 12 October 1692, Phips Papers, 2: 38.

56. Paul Boyer and Stephen Nissenbaum, *Salem Possessed: The Social Origins of Witchcraft* (Cambridge, 1974).

57. Claude Fuess, "Witches at Andover," *MHSP*, 70 (1950–1953): 8–20.

58. Chadwick Hansen, *Witchcraft at Salem* (New York, 1967).

59. John Demos, "Underlying Themes in the Witchcraft of Seventeenth Century New England," *American Historical Review*, 75 (1970): 1311–1326.

# Notes to Chapter II

60. Legislative Records of the Massachusetts Council, 6: 297 (hereafter cited as Council Records), State House, Boston; William Phips to Earl of Nottingham, 20 February 1693, Phips Papers, 3: 113; John Usher to Lords of Trade, 31 January 1693, *ibid.*, 2: 54.

61. Childley Brooke to Benjamin Fletcher, 2 August 1693, *ibid.*, 3: 70; Nathaniel Byfield to Joseph Dudley, 21 June 1694, *ibid.*, 4: 23-26; Letter from New England, November 1694, *ibid.*, p. 84; William Phips to King William and Queen Mary, 3 April 1693, *ibid.*, 3: 1; *A&R*, 1: 30, 92, 174, 188. Phips finally received £1000 in 1694–1695 after he had "purged" the house.

62. Sewall, *Diary*, 1: 300–301.

63. *Ibid.*, pp. 309–310; John M. Murrin, Review Essay of New England Town Studies, *History and Theory*, 11 (1972): 254.

64. Letter from New England, November 1694, Phips Papers, 4: 84–94; Childley Brooke to Benjamin Fletcher, 2 August 1693, *ibid.*, 3: 70; Nathaniel Byfield to Joseph Dudley, 21 June 1694, *ibid.*, 4: 23–26; Sewall, *Diary*, 1: 311, 314–315; Council Records, 6: 304–309. Customs Collector Jahleel Brenton and his brother Ebenezer also sat in the house. The same sources support the next paragraph.

65. Letter from New England, November 1694, Phips Papers, 4: 94.

66. Determination of the Lords of Trade, 19 January 1694, Phips Papers, 3: 130–131; Customs Commissioners to Lords of Trade, 4 January 1694, *ibid.*, 2: 124; Lords of Trade to William Stoughton, 2 February 1694, *ibid.*, 4: 12. The depositions gathered fill about two hundred pages in Volumes 4 and 5 of the Phips Papers.

# III

---

# FORGING

# PROVINCIAL

# UNITY

# 1694–1713

*F*ROM 1689 to 1713, Europe and America shared the same problem: Louis XIV and his twenty million Frenchmen. England, Austria, Prussia, and various minor states united to oppose the Sun King's efforts to dominate the European continent. The titanic struggle spilled over into the New World where Canada's Governor-General Count Frontenac proved a worthy representative of his royal master. Supported by only a few thousand habitants and some small Indian tribes, he not only defeated Massachusetts' invasions, but terrorized the New York and New England frontiers for a quarter of a century.

But France provided an example as well as a threat. The highly efficient, centralized administration Louis had forged suggested a means of defeating him. If he could hold both Europe and English America at bay, the logical remedy for his rivals was to attain a comparable degree of unity. But internal disorders hampered both England and its North American colonies. The conflicts of the Glorious Revolution had been settled only provisionally. In England, the battle between Whigs and Tories, the latter including a fair number of Stuart sympathizers, undercut England's contribution to the War of the Spanish Succession (1702–1713), called in America "Queen Anne's War." The colonies' own dissensions prevented them from mounting a united defense. The key province of New York was plagued with dissension between supporters and opponents of Jacob Leisler's brutally suppressed rebellion. England tried to unite the northern colonies under the Earl of Bellomont, but his valiant attempt to become the English Frontenac killed him. Outside of Massachusetts, no one would cooperate with him.

If England, New York, and the southern colonies had to confront domestic crisis in addition to military threats, Massachusetts feared only the latter. The limited, quickly resolved conflicts during the quarter century following the Glorious Revolution eloquently testified to the unity Massachusetts had already achieved. Old animosities still lingered, to be sure, but they had rearranged themselves to the point where they could not be the basis of future factional alignments. Massachusetts thus became a bulwark of, rather than an obstacle to, the imperial system.

## CONSOLIDATION: 1694–1702

Massachusetts' heavy commitment to King William's (1689–1697) and Queen Anne's (1702–1713) wars abated political controversy considerably. Lieutenant-Governor Stoughton and Governors Bellomont and Dudley encountered only ineffective opposition from the legislature on political and military issues. To be sure, during Stoughton's administration Massachusetts' politicians diverted their factious propensities into a far less consequential dispute over Harvard College. Bellomont and Dudley also confronted problems with some of their more extravagant demands. But too much can be made of these episodes. The crucial point is that these governors had to manage extensive military campaigns. The court and country factions had to subordinate their pursuit of power to the essential issue of survival.

Disastrous warfare marked the first three years of Stoughton's administration. Massachusetts' summer expeditions to Maine failed to engage the Indians. Meanwhile, the Abenakis and Norridgewocks raided the frontier with impunity by sidestepping the relatively immobile garrisons. In the summer of 1697, just before the Peace of Ryswick brought the province's sufferings to an end, a French force destroyed the new fort at Pemaquid. Indian raiders penetrated to the town of Haverhill within the province itself. So many people fell into debt from high taxation and economic hardship that the province forbade imprisonment for sums under £10.[1] Under these circumstances the assembly, for the first time in 1696 and 1697, voted taxes at the very beginning of its sessions instead of quibbling over the amount. Supplementary grants passed as needed. The legislature gladly entrusted Stoughton with total power to restore fortifications and mobilize troops. It could ill afford disputing such matters at this time.[2]

Emergency measures passed without difficulty. In 1695, an additional £5,000 in Bills of Credit augmented the £30,000 issued in 1689. To feed the frontier refugees and compensate for decreased production, the General Court prohibited the exportation of food. It also interdicted the shipment of silver currency abroad—the money had to pay for defense. The legislature forbade inhabitants to desert the frontier without permission. But the situation worsened. In 1696 Samuel Sewall's brother Stephen wrote that hundreds of men not only left the new towns, but "tired out with watching [for Indians] and paying great taxes, went running . . . to South Carolina and other places." To encourage volunteers, the legislature placed a bounty of £50 on the scalp of every hostile Indian whether man, woman, or child. To give an idea of the province's desperation, it paid Increase Mather the same amount for an entire year's service as President of Harvard![3]

Massachusetts recognized that it needed English assistance. On 15 August 1695, the General Court petitioned for frigates and powder while asking that its neighbors be required to take a more active part in the war. Simultaneously, the province used its own tribulations to excuse its failure to help New York. It also requested that Nova Scotia (Acadia) *not* be restored to France in the event of a peace settlement, since Massachusetts bore the brunt of defending it. With a good deal of nerve, the province still asked for the right to distribute all the land in Maine up to the Gulf of St. Lawrence. It prayed that Customs Collector Jahleel Brenton be removed for charging "unnecessary and unreasonable fees" and causing "delayings, vexations, and expense" to the province's trade. Although unwilling to cooperate with English commercial policy, Massachusetts had to seek the mother country's protection.[4]

Such inconsistent pleas fell on deaf ears. The Board of Trade considered Massachusetts the richest, most refractory, and most undeserving colony in North America. According to their Lordships, the province could not only defend itself quite well but ought to have helped its neighbors. Massachusetts considered its plight so desperate that when word of the negative reaction arrived, some inhabitants gladly offered to surrender their liberties to save the province. Stephen Sewall warned that "if the king does not speedily put a stop to these things [intercolonial quarrels] by unifying several of the governments together, or rather by sending a viceroy over all that may command all in this difficult time of war, I tremble to think what the end will be." A group of merchants echoed his remarks and asked for a strong governor at the head of one thousand regulars to "prevent the total loss of the colonies."[5] Instead of being angered when its requests were rejected, Massachusetts offered to trade increased regulation for military support.

Massachusetts' difficulties kept the political coalition that had ousted Governor Phips from falling apart. Stoughton's amiability also helped. He regarded himself as a caretaker preserving the province from total collapse until a successor arrived. He did nothing to undermine local autonomy. Stoughton complied as minimally as possible with the royal instruction to inform the Board of Trade about events in Massachusetts. He forwarded only the minutes and acts of the assembly and council accompanied sometimes by descriptions of Massachusetts' pitiable state. The Customs Commissioners also complained that although "a good scholar," Stoughton was "not suited to enforce the Navigation Acts."[6] Heading the faction that hoped to reinstate Joseph Dudley as governor, Stoughton's moderate course convinced many representatives that Dudley (who had been imprisoned in 1689 for his refusal to abandon Sir Edmund Andros) no longer posed any threat to self-government.

The cohesion of ex-moderates and old-charter men appears in the council elections from 1695 to 1697. In March 1695, the council chose Elisha Cooke as clerk of the Superior Court with twenty of twenty-five votes. In May, the legislature reelected him to the upper house with sixty-nine of eighty-two votes. Stoughton's own tally rose from thirty-one in 1693 to seventy-one by 1695. Old-charter stalwart Elisha Hutchinson and moderate Bartholomew Gedney increased theirs from thirty-seven and forty-nine to seventy-eight and seventy-four, respectively. The two new councillors chosen in 1695 were Elisha Hutchinson's son Eliakim and Edward Randolph's old crony Samuel Shrimpton.[7] Members of both factions thus supported each other's candidates.

Despite the pressures of war and Stoughton's conciliatory policies, some factional strife did erupt during the mid-1690s. In 1695, word arrived that the Privy Council had disallowed most of the laws passed by the General Court in 1692. When the hectic summer campaigns of 1696 ended, the representatives overreacted by petitioning "for the restoration of the ancient privileges of the colonies of Massachusetts and New Plymouth." When the upper house rejected this resolve unanimously, the "General Court [was] full of contention." New Hampshire's John Usher did not miss the irony that the assembly attached yet another request for military assistance to its remonstrance: "the representatives, though they send to the king for ships and men, yet address him at the same time for their old charter. That is their onions and garlic."[8] A year later, to replace the province's own Naval Office, the Customs Commissioners sent four new royal officials to Massachusetts to suppress illegal trade. Joseph Dudley selected them all. Stoughton appeared guilty by association.[9]

The Privy Council also disallowed the Harvard College Charter as the royal governor had no power to visit the college and supervise its operations. From 1696 to 1701, the representatives sought to circumvent this restriction. But instead of restoring an autonomous college corporation, the house itself hoped to share the visiting rights with the executive. The Dudley faction, the clergy in general, and President Increase Mather favored compliance with the royal instruction. They preferred the anticipated pro forma regulation by the governor to the certain meddling of the deputies. The majority of the council took a third position: *they* should share the visiting rights with the governor.[10]

After considerable wrangling throughout 1696, the representatives capitulated and approved a new charter granting visiting rights to the governor and council. They deprived Boston's ministers of financial control, denied President Mather a seat on the corporation, and required him to reside at Cambridge to pursue his teaching responsiblities more actively than in the past. Stoughton, a personal friend of the discredited Mathers, vetoed the charter in 1696 but acquiesced when it passed the following year. The Fellows and Corporation of the College also surrendered,[11] leaving Increase and Cotton Mather as the only recalcitrants. But the Privy Council also rejected the second charter because the governor did not possess sole visitation rights.[12]

When he finally arrived from New York in 1699, the new Governor Richard Coote, the Earl of Bellomont, compromised the matter to almost everyone's satisfaction. The General Court had refused all along to budge on visitation rights and had recently added the proviso that only Congregationalists or Presbyterians could teach at or govern the college. Bellomont, however, assured his constituents that while *he* could not consent to these demands, Massachusetts could reasonably expect the king to grant both points. On 6 July 1700, the legislature approved his plan. Bellomont recommended the new instrument to the Board of Trade and asked Sir Henry Ashurst to wait upon the Board to ensure its approval.[13] However, by this time the representatives and council were so at odds with each other and disgusted with Mather (who hated to teach and disliked those who substituted) that they refused to vote Ashurst the necessary funds. In May 1701 he complained that "as to your charter I could have got" it, but "I am neither your agent nor had any money to get it."[14] Thereafter the college functioned without royal sanction.

Even before arriving in Massachusetts, Bellomont had become embroiled in its factional turmoil. In 1695 King William appointed him governor not only of Massachusetts but also of New York and New Hampshire (which shared a governor with Massachusetts until 1741) expressly to organize a coordinated defense against the French and Indians. The Privy Council had wearied of a bevy of governors more interested in fighting each other than the enemy. Nevertheless, Bellomont did not arrive in New York until April 1698 or in Massachusetts until 1699. While he stayed in New York, Elisha Cooke, Wait Winthrop, and other leading Massachusetts politicians opposed to Dudley and Stoughton courted him. Temporarily swayed, Bellomont refused to swear in Dudley's protégé Nathaniel Byfield as Judge of Vice-Admiralty until he actually arrived in Massachusetts, giving Ashurst time to replace Byfield with Winthrop. By favoring Stoughton's enemies, Bellomont undermined his lieutenant's efforts to deal with the college controversy. Expecting he would favor them, in November 1698, Cooke and Danforth persuaded the council and house to urge that His Lordship come to Boston "as soon as possible."[15]

They soon regretted their decision. Bellomont's behavior contrasted sharply with his predecessor's. Stoughton had no plans to make Massachusetts obey royal authority and simply devoted himself to holding the line against the Indians. But from the moment he arrived in 1699, Bellomont presented the General Court with ambitious proposals to put Massachusetts in a decent defensive posture, eliminate piracy, and end violations of the Navigation Acts. He did not accomplish all this, but he succeeded to the extent that he alienated his erstwhile friends in the country faction. Conversely, he won over the court party. Bellomont soon termed its leaders, Stoughton and Provincial Secretary Isaac Addington, "men of business and integrity."[16]

Even more important, Bellomont won the affections of the General Court and the population. He explained his success in a letter to the Board of Trade: "I reprove them with temper and not with passion, and I endeavor to reason with them, and I flatter myself much if I have not a good interest with the people of all sorts and ranks." Bellomont's methods achieved notable results in military policy. When he first came to Boston, he complained that this "rich" country would not even build a fort at the mouth of Boston harbor. Within a year, inspired by his eloquent plea to the Board of Trade to match the province's funds, the deputies approved construction of Castle William. He also obtained the first bill punishing mutiny and desertion with death.[17]

Bellomont obtained equally dramatic results regulating piracy. This required two years. At first, the legislature rejected the death penalty for pirates and refused to permit their trial before the Vice-Admiralty Court. Many merchants and some legislators, it was rumored, did a land office business with the buccaneers. Local courts rarely punished them. When the governor suggested "it would be best if the laws respecting piracy were made to have a conformity with those of England," three or four of the councillors "asked with some warmth what the laws of England had to do with them and one of them said they were too much cramped in their liberties already." But in 1700 the legislature made piracy a capital offense. Undoubtedly, the presence of the notorious Captain William Kidd in Boston at this time aided Bellomont's efforts.[18]

The council turned Bellomont's arguments concerning the laws of England against him with respect to the Navigation Acts. But even here he did better than his predecessors. When he suggested compliance, the upper house "alleged they were as much Englishmen as those in England, and thought they had a right to all the privileges that the people of England had," especially the right (so they claimed) to trade freely. Still, Bellomont did persuade the General Court to create a new provincial judiciary, while removing the objectionable features that caused the Privy Council to veto the Act of 1692. The legislature tacitly recognized the Vice-Admiralty Court's right to exist by dropping a clause requiring jury trials in all cases.[19]

All in all, Bellomont obtained forty acts in a little over a year. New laws regulated trade with the Eastern Indians, prevented settlers from fleeing frontier towns under penalty of losing their lands, made military desertion a perpetual offense, and permitted impressment to raise armed forces. Bellomont also persuaded the council to allow him to nominate civil officers instead of merely approving them after their election.[20] Bellomont's good relations with the province must be attributed in part to repeated rumors of Indian attacks and news of some real skirmishes, which constantly reached Boston during the uneasy truce between King William's and Queen Anne's Wars. As the new governor noted, the past war had cost £100,000, accomplished nothing, and resulted in a thousand families leaving the province. Thanks to Bellomont's preparations, Massachusetts could counterattack the French and Indians under his successor Joseph Dudley.[21]

Bellomont's personal popularity and tact undoubtedly contributed to his success. He obtained a salary of £1,000 (Massachusetts money) each of the two years he stayed in Massachusetts and an additional present of £500 in 1700. No executive received this much until late in the 1720s, when the deputies used a high annual salary to bribe governors not to insist on a permanent one. Bellomont's grant, on the other hand, had no ulterior motive. When complaining that his salary fell short of the £1200 sterling he had expected from all his provinces combined, Bellomont blamed only the other colonies. He considered Massachusetts' payments an honor "because they used to give their governor in the time of the old charter but £100 a year." He registered his appreciation by urging that Harvard College be granted a charter guaranteeing local control as the people "have an extaordinary zeal for their religion" and argued eloquently for toleration on principle. The Puritans probably would not have extended this line of reasoning to others.[22]

To be sure, Bellomont did not achieve all his goals, and encountered considerable opposition from the country faction because he asked for so much. He failed to raise fees for Vice-Admiralty officials, and consequently could "get nobody to accept of the place that is honest." Local intransigence effectively stymied John Bridger, appointed in 1698 first Surveyor-General of His Majesty's Woods to halt the destruction of timber suitable for naval masts. Nevertheless, Bellomont reserved his harshest strictures for New York, which had responded to a similar program by drawing up a thirty-two-count indictment to impeach him. He also rebuked the Board of Trade, lamenting more than once that "I am under all the trouble and discouragement imaginable for want of orders from your Lordships and the rest of the ministry." Despite ill health, he wrote eight extremely detailed dispatches while in Massachusetts and received in return "no letter. . .except three or four lines." He felt he could have accomplished still more with some evidence to contradict the colonists' assertions that " the king and his ministers have no sort of care or value for these plantations, not minding whether they fall into French hands or not."[23]

Declaring "that I would rather govern four provinces such as this . . . than that of New York," Bellomont completed the process begun during the inter-chater period. Compelled to acknowledge that they needed British protection, the leading men of Massachusetts found in Lord Bellomont a disinterested, fair-minded executive. Despite his objections to their constitution, he accepted it and tried to work within it. The province realized that royal power had advantages that the more deeply factionalized New Yorkers, scarcely over the bloody retribution for Leisler's Rebellion, could not appreciate.[24]

Although he was well-received by the province as a whole, Bellomont's success devastated the anti-Dudley faction. Within a month of the governor's accession, Samuel Sewall tried to persuade Nathaniel Higginson—an influential East India merchant who had not set foot in

New England for almost thirty years—to return home and nominate himself for governorship. Ashurst, too, blamed the governor's ingratitude for the General Court's failure to pay for his agency. Wait Winthrop suggested that Ashurst should therefore use his influence to select a new governor.[25]

By associating themselves with the popular new governor, Dudley's partisans carried everything before them in the assembly during 1700 and 1701. The deputies elected John Leverett Speaker of the House and prevented Ashurst from being rehired. Puzzled that men who had once supported Sir Edmund Andros dominated the assembly, Wait Winthrop attributed their success to "standard fair speeches and pretences upon our honest country representatives, who many of them are new every year and have not knowledge of the old intrigues." But past animosities mattered less than present defense. Regardless of Winthrop's prejudices, his analysis was correct. The country faction, the "popular" party, had become most unpopular.[26]

Upon Bellomont's death, Stoughton acceded. He once again tried to pursue uncontroversial policies that would unite both factions and lead to the appointment of Dudley or himself as governor. He expressed his sorrow at Bellomont's death, while pleading that one of His Lordship's more unpopular instructions be retracted: he argued that the province could ill afford to construct forts in Maine because it had "expended many thousands of pounds in the assistance of His Majesty's subjects [in other colonies] during the late war, and we are not reimbursed any part thereof." Britain had failed Massachusetts, not the reverse. The assembly petitioned King William that Stoughton himself be appointed governor, although the council, dominated by Cooke, Danforth, and Winthrop, refused to concur. The deputies set a precedent and transmitted the petition on their own. However, Stoughton died in July 1701, only three months after Bellomont.[27]

In the absence of a governor or lieutenant-governor, the charter empowered the council to act collectively as chief executive. It divided the several offices held by Stoughton among members of the anti-Dudley faction and dismissed Increase Mather as President of Harvard.[28] The upper house also petitioned the king to restore the Charter of 1629 and selected Wait Winthrop to join Sir Henry Ashurst to solicit the request. The pro-Dudley assembly refused to concur. The project horrified Ashurst when he learned of it in November. He warned Winthrop: "I wish they were your friends that were for sending you out of the way to be agent. I am sure they were Mr. Dudley's friends." At the same time, Ashurst begged for money "to oppose taking away the *new* charter by Act of Parliament," and concluded that "whoever ordered the addressing for the old charter had a mind, in my opinion, to ruin your country." For Ashurst, naturally, the only possible culprit was Dudley.[29]

He was wrong. Two months before Ashurst and Mason learned that Parliament was considering revoking all colonial charters, Dudley himself had written to Cotton Mather that the province would be wise to defend itself on this count. Dudley was by no means disinterested. He informed his patron William Blathwayt that he had tipped off the Mathers because he hoped to use their influence to facilitate his appointment as governor. They had been excluded from political power since the death of Phips, driven from Harvard, and challenged by the erection of the hostile Brattle Street Church in Boston. The Mathers' international prestige greatly exceeded their local influence. Dudley presented himself as the most palatable candidate to head the new government, claiming that his long absence gave him "a true value of . . . the religion and virtue" to be found in Massachusetts. He pleaded with the Mathers to persuade Ashurst not to oppose his nomination.[30]

But the Mathers helped Dudley even more than he expected. Cotton Mather responded with an unqualified endorsement insisting "that the most considerable people of New England (so far as I see) are united in their opinion that your succession here would be a blessing almost too great for to be expected." Dudley later displayed this note to silence King William's fears that the people disliked him. Covering all possible bases, he also obtained petitions from the ministers of New England and the New England merchants in London. Finally, he procured a letter from the assembly itself, stating that Ashurst no longer spoke for Massachusetts. When in July 1701 the representatives received news of Dudley's appointment, they ignored Ashurst's and Mason's cries to contest the nomination. They submitted instead a perfunctory address to the king requesting that he continue the present charter and chose Constantine Phips, a supporter of Dudley, over Ashurst to present it.[31] Given Bellomont's vigorous administration and rumors of even further regulation, Dudley seemed the most plausible hope of saving at least some provincial liberty while not abandoning measures needed for defense.[32]

To attain the governorship, Dudley presented himself to his American supporters as a defender of their rights. To the Board of Trade, however, he promised that his prestige and local connections could succeed where even Bellomont had failed. The Board instructed the new governor to protect the Church of England and the surveyor-general, obtain a fixed salary, enforce the Acts of Trade, permit only "men of estates and well affected to the government to sit on the council,"[33] and create an effective defense establishment capable of assisting the other colonies. The Board really asked Massachusetts to subordinate its interests completely to those of England whenever the two clashed.

### COUNTERATTACK: 1702–1713

During his brief regime, Bellomont had provided Massachusetts with the sinews of a defense establishment. He had also seriously weakened the opponents of a strong provincial government. Under Dudley, Massachusetts could once again muster its resources for expeditions intended to eliminate the French menace forever. Despite their failure, Dudley effectively used the continued military emergency to stifle the country faction.

When Dudley arrived in Boston in June 1702, he possessed a considerable reservoir of good will. His opponents were weak and discredited. However, he soon began to deplete that reservoir by trying to carry out his instructions inflexibly and by restricting patronage and influence to those who shared his views. Weak support from the Board of Trade caused Dudley to shelve his plans to increase royal authority. However, the increasing seriousness of Queen Anne's War, which broke out less than a month after he arrived, also caused him to subordinate reform to defense. Between 1702 and the unsuccessful Port Royal expedition of 1706, he overcame his initial difficulties and obtained the cooperation of the General Court through his efficient conduct of the war.

At first, instead of seeking a broad basis of factional support, Dudley indentified himself with the smallest group possible: the Anglicans, latitudinarians, and overseas merchants dependent on their British connections. Within a month of his arrival, he had reshuffled the courts' personnel to an extent unprecedented before the revolutionairies ousted the loyalists. He unseated three of the five Superior Court judges, two Inferior Court judges in Suffolk, and one judge in each eight of the province's other nine counties. Only the governor's firm supporters held office. Not one opponent, including men as prominent as Cooke, Winthrop, ex-agent Thomas Oakes, or Andrew Belcher (one of the province's wealthiest merchants and Commissary-General) secured even the lowly post of justice of the peace. Rather than reconciling the opposition in the manner of his successors, Dudley, like Phips, anticipated the spoils system of William Marcy and Andrew Jackson.[34]

Dudley completed his removals in May 1703, when he vetoed the legislature's choice of five councillors — Elisha Cooke, Peter Sergeant, Thomas Oakes, John Saffin, and William Bradford. For a while, the representatives debated whether to choose another set of men to replace them. But as Samuel Sewall informed his brother Stephen, "if the deputies, according to the charter, decline proceeding this year next year the governor may negative eighteen or twenty-one and allow only ten or seven most pliable to his designs."[35] Had the deputies made the veto a constitutional issue, they would in effect have surrendered the right to choose the council.

Dudley also alienated the men to whom he owed his job. When Cotton Mather warned him not to repeat Phips's disastrous partisan appointment policy, Dudley instead visited his friends Byfield and Leverett, told them that Mather had suggested that he desert them, and understandably "inflamed them unto an implacable rage." The governor then refused to name one of the Mathers President of Harvard, their expected reward for supporting his nomination. Vice-President Samuel Willard continued to officiate. By 1703 the Mathers had launched a campaign to unseat their erstwhile protégé.[36]

Finally, Samuel Sewall, whose son had recently married the governor's daughter, became disenchanted as well. The major rift between them occurred in January 1706 after two carters had disputed the right of way with the governor and his son William on the Boston–Roxbury road. Each party blamed the other for the ensuing scuffle. Justice Sewall bailed the men on a misdemeanor instead of directing that they be tried for high treason, as the governor would have preferred. Dudley "was very hot and hard" on Sewall, and complained "that he might be run through, trampled on, and no care taken of him."[37]

However, Dudley's relations with the General Court were generally less one-sided than with many of the province's leading men. Whereas he offended the latter almost without exception, his political flexibility and astute management of the war eventually won over the deputies. True, Dudley and the house complained to the Board of Trade about the illegality and unreasonableness of each other's behavior. But where colonial and imperial interests coincided, they could not have been on better terms. Consequently, as Dudley conceded or compromised most of the controversial issues by 1705, he emerged in a strong position to repel his enemies' redoubled efforts to unseat him in 1706. He thereby forged an alliance with the assembly, whose members supported him rather the country faction's leaders.

Dudley confronted the representatives almost immediately about his salary. He constantly remonstrated with the Board of Trade and Secretaries of State that he performed "the hardest service of any of Her Majesty's governments" but received "the least support." The annual grants, averaging £500 sterling throughout his administration, did not meet "the fifth part of the necessary expenses" of maintaining a dignified household. At every session of the assembly from 1702 until 1705 he urged that fixed salaries be settled on himself, Lieutenant-Governor Thomas Povey (who would have been paid nothing at all had not Dudley appointed him commander of Boston's new harbor fortress, Castle William, at £100 a year), and the Superior Court (which periodically threatened to resign unless each judge received more than £50 annually.) He also hoped to remodel the council and courts so that he could appoint and remove their members at pleasure.[38]

However, when the energetic governor found as little support for his reforming efforts in England as in the province itself, he gave up the struggle. The Board of Trade answered his frequent and detailed letters occasionally, briefly, and discouragingly. In 1704 and again in 1706, it informed him that the crown would neither settle a salary upon him nor use any threats to compel the province to do so. Dudley then dropped the whole issue. Similarly, he received little encouragement for his efforts to enforce the Navigation Acts. He finally won a small triumph when in 1706 he seated Nathaniel Byfield on the Vice-Admiralty bench. Byfield condemned some cargoes, but the situation was hopeless. Four salaried officials could not police New England's forty harbors.[39]

Other quarrels between Dudley and the General Court previewed the sort of constitutional conflicts that paralyzed the government for years in future decades. But the exigencies of war ensured that none of these crises endured more than a few weeks. For instance, in November 1703, the representatives flatly refused to rebuild Pemaquid on the grounds that it would cost £20,000 and no settlers lived within one hundred miles. They then declined to attend a conference proposed by the council to iron out the issue. When the board voted the refusal "a great infringement upon their rights and privileges," and Dudley backed it up by threatening to dissolve the house, a very unenthusiastic conference followed. No fort was built, but the whole affair ended within a few days.[40]

Another serious but brief dispute occurred in 1703. In July's supply bill, the deputies refused to permit the governor and council to spend money during a recess of the lower house. The council protested, and Dudley obtained a compliance by holding the assembly in session for two weeks until it dropped the restrictive clause. Twenty years later, in the absence of military necessity, the same issue took a decade to resolve.[41]

# Forging Provincial Unity

In 1705, Dudley provoked another quarrel by questioning the house's right to choose its own speaker. On 31 May, it replaced John Converse, a man of "estates and loyalty" in Dudley's estimation, by that "Common Wealth's man" Thomas Oakes, whom the governor described as "never quiet," and "so very poor, that sometime since he begged off his tax to the government upon the head of poverty." When Dudley disallowed the choice, the assembly claimed "to be sole judge of their elections." The council agreed with the lower house. Dudley then surrendered because "the pressing affairs of war, that demand a sudden dispatch" did not permit long debates. He would not "delay the affairs necessary for the security of the province." Neither side agreed to use Dudley's acquiescence as a precedent until the Board of Trade gave its opinion. It ruled in favor of the governor, but Dudley in effect conceded by refraining from vetoing Oakes when he was reelected. Who moderated in the house mattered little if it approved necessary military policy.[42]

The General Court had to bury most issues to fight Queen Anne's War.[43] The first years went badly. In 1704, Indians destroyed Deerfield for the second time and attacked Haverhill again. Dudley responded by posting two thousand men on the frontiers in summer and six hundred in winter. These massive deployments cost the province £40,000 a year in 1704 and 1705, an average tax of £5 per family. Dudley also obtained more effective militia laws that gave officers power to muster the most suitable men in their communities. He pushed through a law theoretically ending corruption in the military. It forbade officers or anyone besides the provincial Commissary General to supply the troops. The Massachusetts assembly backed him up, and, in Dudley's own words, voted money and soldiers with "zeal" and "cheerfulness." A steady stream of congratulatory addresses passed from Dudley to the assembly, vice versa, and from both to the imperial administration, praising each other's devotion to the province's best interest. The governor repeatedly petitioned for ammunition and funds, called attention to excessive burdens, and convinced the home authorities to back Massachusetts' expeditions to Port Royal in 1706 and to Quebec in 1709, 1710, and 1711.[44]

Dudley blamed his difficulties with the assembly on a faction—"ill-minded men that would be glad to see all things in confusion, and to that end would create misunderstandings and prejudices in the minds of Her Majesty's subjects against her own government." He discovered "methods taken in the choice of assemblymen that no such should be chosen as had shown obedience." [45] But he was mistaken. Dudley's success in managing the opposition shows that they dominated the house only when imperial and provincial interests obviously clashed. Here the deputies would surely have opposed Dudley anyway. When he dropped his unrealistic demands for salaries and the fort at Pemaquid, Dudley's enemies found themselves without a following.

The popular party's exaggerated assaults on Dudley's character in 1706 and 1707 arose from the realization that he commanded the respect they lacked. Shortly after Massachusetts' expedition of 1706 to conquer Port Royal in Acadia had failed miserably, the General Court accused five merchants of "wickedly managing and carrying on an illegal trade and traffic with the subjects of the King of France" in Port Royal.[46] For nearly two years, Dudley's enemies, headed by Cotton Mather and Samuel Sewall, tried to implicate the governor. They argued that he had supplied the French with the food and weapons that had enabled them to defeat the Massachusetts expedition.

No evidence supports these charges. The illegal trade was discovered in June 1706. When the Superior Court argued that it could not hear the case because the crimes had been committed outside the province's boundaries, Dudley suggested that the General Court itself try the men.[47] The "parcel of resolute rustics" in the house, according to Wait Winthrop, preferred an indictment for high treason to a misdemeanor. But even Sewall, who kept the issue alive more than anyone, was glad that the men were not tried for their lives. Both the assembly and the council immediately declared rumors of Dudley's involvement "utterly false and without the least color of truth," and thanked him for his "utmost readiness and forwardness . . . to detect and discover such illegal traders."[48] The trial ended 25 August 1706. The Court imposed sentences of several months in jail and fines ranging from £50 to £1,000. Dudley represented the proceedings to his superiors as both necessary and just, although technically illegal.[49]

No formal accusations against Dudley appeared until June 1707, a whole year after the affair appeared to have ended. In the interval, Sewall had intimated that the governor may have been bribed by the accused to try them before the legislature, knowing full well the trial would be disallowed in England.[50] But it remained for Sir Henry Ashurst and Cotton Mather, in a pamphlet entitled *A Memorial of the Deplorable State of New England*, to accuse Dudley of treason. They blamed the governor for mismanaging the war, collaborating with Jesuits in stirring up the Indians, and practicing bribery to such an extent that "there is no justice to be had without money." At the same time, a number of London and New England merchants presented a petition to the queen requesting Dudley's removal on these very grounds.[51]

Copies of both the pamphlet and the petition arrived in Boston on 1 November 1707. The council immediately and unanimously voted the charges "scandalous and wicked" despite Sewall's effort to obtain a careful consideration of the matter. The house launched a more thorough investigation, but it uncovered only a pass signed by Dudley permitting Vetch and his friends to carry some knives, nails, and forks with them, and several councillors testified that the quantity of nails mentioned had been altered to incriminate the governor. Dudley remarked that "the house of deputies is out of humor, though after all their search all is as white as chalk, as clean as the driven snow." On 31 November, the assembly concurred with the council in clearing Dudley.[52]

The Mathers had not finished. They claimed that Dudley's vindication had been obtained "when many of the most prudent men of the assembly were gone." The governor then "over-persuaded the remainder . . . the flexible, honest men, perfectly worried and wearied out of their lives by three weeks' altercations." Cotton Mather termed the method by which Dudley was vindicated "barbarous" and "ridiculous . . . [displaying] attempts of our councillors to blanch Ethiopians." In particular, he accused the governor of appointing a "sow gelder" justice of the peace in return for his vote. (The man in question, Nehemiah Jowett, had been prominent in provincial politics since the days of Andros and had served as speaker of the house several times).[53]

Historians have disputed Dudley's culpability on three counts: did he have knowledge of the illicit trade, was he a silent partner, and did he coerce the representatives to clear him? Those who judge him guilty have emphasized a "Memorandum of the Board of Trade" stating he was "highly suspected to be concerned in this illegal trade and (as 'tis said) artfully complied with the assembly's desire of trying these people. Knowing that several in the assembly suspected him, he had friends enough in that house to prevent them asking such questions as might touch him."[54] However, the Board drafted this note shortly after Ashurst's pamphlet and Higginson's petition appeared. It summarized the charges against the governor. Had the Board really considered Dudley guilty, could he have remained governor very long? Finally, Dudley could not coerce a house of representatives into doing anything.[55] For three years he had unsuccessfully tried to obtain fixed salaries, rebuild the fort at Pemaquid, and enforce the Navigation Acts. Could his powers have increased astronomically at the height of his vulnerability? The Council Records and Sewall's *Diary* indicate that the house searched for evidence against the governor, but could find nothing. Dudley survived his enemies' attacks because the province's experience of his administration ran counter to such charges of corruption and treason.

Dudley still had difficulties in 1708. The General Court left out "three of the principal gentlemen of the council of best estates and approved loyalty" in the May election. That July the house drafted a list of six grievances. It charged the governor with making unauthorized expenditures, and criticized Harvard's new president John Leverett for continuing to sit as justice of probate and justice of the peace. When the council objected that the sums spent were trivial or necessary for defense, the assembly sent a memorial off to the queen. Dudley's salary was also reduced from £500 to £400, less than Commissary-General Andrew Belcher's.[56]

But factional strife vanished suddenly in 1709. Aside from a brief dispute over the province agency in 1710, Dudley enjoyed five years of almost completely harmonious relations with the legislature. This transformation may be attributed to the great announcement with which he opened the General Court on 26 May 1709: "I lately humbly addressed Her Majesty for such a strength of shipping and land forces to be sent hither, that might destroy these nests of robbers [in Canada]. She has resolved to send such a strong force . . . as will be able to reduce these colonies of France to the obedience of Great Britain." By representing the forthcoming expedition as both his personal idea and the direct consequence of his influence, Dudley united the entire province. No complaints appeared that he had already assembled the troops, despite the charter's stipulation that the General Court had to approve all military movements outside the province. In short order, the legislature approved the muster of twelve-hundred men. It quickly gathered provisions for four or five months, placed embargoes on overseas grain shipments to ensure sufficient food for the soldiers, and issued £30,000 in Bills of Credit to pay for the campaign. Not only did the Court pardon Samuel Vetch, the commander, for illegal trading, but granted him £60 for his efforts to bring about the campaign. Once more, military necessity rendered other issues insignificant.[57]

For all the province's zeal, British bungling brought Massachusetts' massive efforts to naught. No fleet to transport the soldiers up the St. Lawrence arrived in 1709. In 1710, the vessels finally appeared, but so late in the year that the provincials had to console themselves with capturing Port Royal. In 1711, a third expedition finally reached

Canada, but it failed to take Quebec because of the monumental incompetence of Admiral Sir Hovenden Walker and General Sir James Hill. Massachusetts raised nine-hundred men for the two latter expeditions even though, as Dudley informed his superiors, the public debt mounted to £120,000 and men deserted the province to avoid military service. Both Vetch and Dudley argued that Massachusetts had sacrificed much of its trade to supply the campaigns and exerted itself "more than all the other governments." When taxation and borrowing on future levies could not fund the 1711 expedition, thirty-five merchant partnerships voluntarily loaned £40,000 in specie and supplies. After Hill and Walker left America blaming their failure on Massachusetts' refusal to cooperate, Dudley joined the legislature in writing letters and preparing accounts to place the blame where it belonged. Following the expedition of 1711, he asked for a third attempt on Canada in 1712. But the province was exhausted. The final two years of the war brought a return to guarding the frontiers against Indian raids.[58]

If war united the province internally, King William's and Queen Anne's Wars caused many of the same problems with Britain that poor military cooperation engendered after 1740. The regulars' arrogance and incompetence angered Massachusetts. Their swearing, drinking, and lax observance of the Sabbath did not help. On at least two occasions, officers assaulted inhabitants in Boston. In 1711, a controversy in Charlestown over a borrowed horse led to a full scale riot involving at least twenty soldiers and many townsfolk. Bostonians complained that the army failed to pay them for provisions and services. Samuel Vetch added to the difficulties by buying a house and evicting the tenants. In 1715, the General Court, with the permission of the country faction's Lieutenant-Governor William Tailer, relieved the accumulated frustration and sued the absent Vetch for £20,000. The legislature claimed that he had misused the province's funds by failing to mount effective campaigns in 1709 and 1710.[59]

War involved many provincials in imperial politics in spite of themselves. They had to pay exorbitant taxes and endure long terms in the field. The garrison at Port Royal during the winter of 1710–1711 suffered even more drastically than that at Louisbourg in 1745—scarcely one-fifth of the thousand men returned in good health.[60] Warfare also provoked crowd activity in Boston. Violent opposition to the impressment of colonials into the navy arose in the early 1690s. In 1702 Lieutenant-Governor Povey had to order the gunners at Castle William to fire on a man-of-war to prevent its captain from escaping with a number of Bostonians.[61] Grain shortages in 1709 and 1713 from supplying the expeditionary forces caused crowds to restrain merchants sending much-needed food to the West Indies, where it could be sold more profitably. Provincial authorities did everything in their power to redress the grievances, placing embargoes on exportation until the shortages subsided. Boston also constructed a public granary to prevent future crises.[62]

During the final years of Joseph Dudley's administration, he won over almost nearly all of his old enemies. He eventually reconciled Sewall, Winthrop, the Mathers, Sir Henry Ashurst's brother William—who became the province agent in 1710—and even old Elisha Cooke.[63] But Queen Anne's War ended two years before Dudley's administration. At the age of seventy he faced new issues and confronted new opponents. His final two years in office marked a transition from one era of factionalism to the next. A new generation emerged—Dudley's son Paul, the province's new agent Jeremiah Dummer, Elisha Cooke, Jr., Oliver Noyes, and Jonathan Belcher—men born in the 1670s and '80s rather than the forties and fifties. The older statesmen had created a functioning government out of the chaos of the intercharter period and had ensured its survival over two decades of incessant warfare. The younger men who became prominent after 1713 had to deal with the problems (such as an inflated and unstable currency) and opportunities (such as opening more of Maine to settlement) caused by war. For their elders, military necessity subordinated factional animosity to political administration. No such emergency imposed similar restraints on the younger men. For nearly three decades, Massachusetts' monetary and frontier problems combined with British attempts to bolster royal authority to spark a series of bitter constitutional disputes between the governor and the assembly.

## Notes to Chapter III

1. For military events in King William's War see Philip S. Haffenden, *New England in the English Nation* (London, 1974), pp. 72–120; Samuel Adams Drake, *The Border Wars of New England* (New York, 1887); *A&R*, 1: 226, 330. Imprisonment for debt was justified on the grounds debtors tended to be fairly well-to-do people with hidden assets who would not otherwise disgorge them. Massachusetts' acts for the relief of debtors suggests severe economic hardship became an increasing reason as well.

2. Legislative Records of the Massachusetts Council, 6: 445, 465, 467, 474, 475, 483, Massachusetts Archives, State House, Boston; *A&R*, 1: 237, 277, 306, 310.

3. Council Records, 6: 503, 509, 572; Stephen Sewall to Edward Hull, 2 November 1696, *CSP*, 15, #358. For other fears that the colonies were about to be lost, see Edward Huston to Board of Trade, 1 February 1697, *ibid.*, #651; Samuel Sewall, *Diary*, ed. M. Halsey Thomas (New York, 1973), 1: 363.

# Notes to Chapter III

4. General Court to King William, 15 August 1696, State Papers, 8: 62–65, Frederick Lewis Gay Transcripts, MHS.

5. Opinion of the Board of Trade, *ibid.*, 70; Stephen Sewall to Edward Hull, 2 November 1696, *CSP*, 15, #358; Petition of Merchants to King William, 18 April 1696, State Papers, 8: 54–58.

6. See the following dispatches to the Board of Trade: *CSP*, 15, #196 (24 September 1696); #483 (10 December 1696); #694 (8 February 1697); #1,354 (30 September 1697); *CSP*, 16, #191 (25 January 1698); #348 (12 April 1698); and #462 (16 May 1698); Commissioners of Customs to Board of Trade, 6 November 1696, *ibid.*, 15, #390.

7. The legislature elected no new councillors in 1696 and 1697, although the tallies for leaders of both factions fell slightly. Stoughton slipped from seventy-seven votes in 1695 to sixty and sixty-four. Cooke's totals for the three years were sixty-nine, seventy-two, and fifty-seven. The province's Major General Wait Winthrop, an ex-moderate who had joined Cooke and Danforth, fell from seventy-four votes in 1695 to fifty-eight and fifty-four the next two years. But the degree of cooperation was still considerable. Sewall, *Diary*, 1: 327, 333, 336, 373.

8. Council Records, 6: 489–490; John Cotton to Roland Cotton, 10 December 1696, Miscellaneous Bound Manuscripts, MHS; John Usher to Board of Trade, 23 October 1696, *CSP*, 15, #341.

9. Nathaniel Byfield was appointed Judge of Vice-Admiralty with authority to try customs violators without a jury. Former collector Lawrence Hammond was to register incoming and outgoing cargoes. Henry Franklin (Brenton's former assistant) was entrusted with the actual searching and seizing. Thomas Newton, the province's attorney-general, could prosecute illegal traders before Byfield. Edward Randolph to Lords of Admiralty, 31 July 1696, *CSP*, 15, #120; Commissioners of Customs to Board of Trade, 24 February 1697, *ibid.*, #359. For a description of the new vice-admiralty courts and the simultaneous creation of the Board of Trade, the best account is Charles M. Andrews, *The Colonial Period of American History*, vol. 4, (New Haven, 1938), chs. 8 and 9. See also Carl M. Ubbelohde, *The Vice-Admiralty Court and the American Revolution* (Chapel Hill, 1960), pp. 3–22.

10. A clear and concise account of the Harvard College charters and their fate is found in Samuel Eliot Morison, *Three Centuries of Harvard* (Cambridge, 1936), p. 46. A new charter had been required in 1692 because the revocation of the Old Charter in 1685 had automatically disallowed other charters granted by Massachusetts.

11. Petitions of the President and Fellows of Harvard College, December 1696, and 6 January 1697, Miscellaneous Bound Manuscripts; Council Records, 6: 487, 526, 535, 616; Sewall, *Diary*, 1: 362.

12. Increase Mather to William Blathwayt, 28 March 1698, State Papers, 9: 19; Sewall, *Diary*, 1: 394; William Popple to Solicitor General, 4 August 1698, *CSP*, 16, #725.

13. An influential dissenting member of Parliament who had assisted Mather during his agency, Ashurst had served as the province's agent since 1692 and had secured Bellomont's appointment. William Bassett to [John Cotton], 14 June and 23 June 1699, Miscellaneous Bound Manuscripts; Earl of Bellomont to Board of Trade, 18 July 1699 and 15 July 1700, *CSP*, 17, #657; 18, #641; see also Council Records, 6: 364, 415; 7: 124, 129. For Ashurst's role in appointing Bellomont, see Wait Winthrop to Henry Ashurst, 25 July 1698, *Winthrop Papers*, 6, MHSC, 5th. ser. 8: 533.

14. Council Records, 8: 46; Henry Ashurst to Wait Winthrop, 5 May 1701, *Winthrop Papers*, 7, MHSC, 6th ser. 6: 85.

15. Memorial of the Lords Justices, 16 July 1695, *CSP*, 14, #1964; Sewall, *Diary*, 1: 392; Wait Winthrop to Henry Ashurst, 25 July 1698, *Winthrop Papers*, 6: 533. Assembly and Council of Massachusetts to the Earl of Bellomont, November 1698, State Papers, 9: 11.

16. Council Records, 7: 5–6; Earl of Bellomont to Board of Trade, 15 July 1700, CSP, 18, #641. Bellomont continued to allow his new opponents, the country faction, to sit in council as part of his conciliatory program.

17. Ibid., Earl of Bellomont to Board of Trade, 28 August 1699, 20 April 1700 and 22 June 1700, CSP, 17, #746; 18, #345, #580, #584A; A&R, 1: 438.

18. Earl of Bellomont to Board of Trade, 28 August 1699, CSP, 17, #746; 20 April 1700, ibid., 18, 354.

19. Same to same, 28 August 1699, ibid., 17, #746; 18, #641 (15 July 1700); #890 (24 October 1700); #963 (28 November 1700).

20. A&R, 1: 367–445; Earl of Bellomont to Board of Trade, 23 April 1700, and 2 January 1701, CSP, 18, #354; 19, #3.

21. Same to same, 28 February 1700, ibid., 18, #167; #619 (9 July 1700); William Stoughton to Board of Trade, 20 December 1700, ibid., 18, #1046.

22. Council Records, 7: 32, 120, 134; Memorial of the Lords Justices, 16 July 1695, CSP, 14, #1964; Earl of Bellomont to Board of Trade, 28 April 1699, 22 June 1700, and 15 July 1700, ibid., 17, #746; 18, #580, #641. The Board of Trade instructed Bellomont to obtain a fixed grant but refused either to threaten the colonies or pay him itself.

23. Articles of the New York Assembly and Council against the Earl of Bellomont, 11 March 1700, CSP, 18, #115; Bellomont to Board of Trade, 9 July 1700, ibid., 18, #619.

24. Same to same, 15 July 1700, ibid., 18, #641.

25. Sewall, Diary, 1: 411; Henry Ashurst to Wait Winthrop, 5 February 1701, Winthrop Papers, 7: 81; Winthrop to Ashurst, 29 April 1701, ibid., 84.

26. Noting that Dudley, Stoughton, and Leverett were all "ministers that left preaching for the sake of worldly interest," Winthrop lamented "that the ruin of the ancient liberty of this country is instrumentally owing to the pride, ambition, and avarice of some" who "are fast to their own interest, but I know not to what else." Wait Winthrop to Henry Ashurst, August or September 1699 and 29 April 1701, Winthrop Papers, 7: 47–50, 83–84.

27. William Stoughton to Board of Trade, 10 April 1701, CSP, 19, #315; Isaac Addington to William Popple, 23 April 1701, ibid., 19, #361; Massachusetts Assembly to King William, 18 April 1701, ibid., 19, #347; William Stoughton to Board of Trade, 3 June 1701, ibid., #500.

28. Council Minutes, 16 July, 23 July, and 8 August 1701, ibid., #648, #687, #714; Henry Ashurst to Wait Winthrop, 5 May 1701, Winthrop Papers, 7, 84; William H. Whitmore, The Massachusetts Civil List, 1630–1776 (Albany, 1870), p. 77; Council Records, 7: 242.

29. Council Records, 7: 202, 215, 220, 223, 235–239; Wait Winthrop to Fitz-John Winthrop, 7 July and 11 August 1701, Winthrop Papers, 7: 87, 97; Henry Ashurst to Wait Winthrop, 7 November 1701, ibid., 100–102. Stephen Mason, a London merchant and correspondent of Elisha Cooke, seconded this opinion. Stephen Mason to Elisha Cooke, 7 July 1701, Saltonstall Papers, MHSC, 80: 167.

30. Joseph Dudley to Cotton Mather, 10 May 1701, Curwen Papers, 2: 41, American Antiquarian Society; Dudley to William Blathwayt, 22 July 1701, Dudley-Blathwayt Papers, MHS. In late July and early August, Dudley badgered Blathwayt about the governorship every three or four days.

31. Cotton Mather to Joseph Dudley, 25 August 1701, in Kenneth Silverman, ed., Selected Letters of Cotton Mather (Baton Rouge, 1971), pp. 55, 65–66; Joseph Dudley to William Blathwayt, 26 July 1701, Dudley–Blathwayt Papers; Thomas Hutchinson, "Hutchinson in America," Egremont Manuscripts, #2664, 46, British Museum (microfilm at MHS); Henry Ashurst to Wait Winthrop, 10 July 1701, Winthrop Papers,7: 87–89; Council Records, 7: 243, 245, 248.

32. Despite Dudley's diverse support, Ashurst put up a furious one-man battle against Dudley, which delayed the new governor's commission from July to December. When he failed, Sir Henry wrote a disappointed Wait Winthrop that "if Mr. Dudley does not please you, you may thank yourselves . . . I am so troubled to think that so good a people should be accessory to their own ruin; that what their ancestors with so many hazards planted there, their successors should sell their birthright for a mess of pottage." Henry Ashurst to Wait Winthrop, 25 March 1702, *Winthrop Papers*, 7: 109–110; Joseph Dudley to William Blathwayt, 22 July 1701, Dudley–Blathwayt Papers; for Dudley's commission see Dudley to Board of Trade, 12 November and 1 December 1701, *CSP*, 19, #1001, #1066.

33. Joseph Dudley to William Blathwayt, 29 July and 22 August 1701, Dudley–Blathwayt Papers; for Dudley's instructions see *CSP*, 19, #1067.

34. The council resisted some of Dudley's appointments. Nathaniel Byfield and Nathaniel Thomas, nominated for the Superior Court, had to be content with posts in Bristol and Plymouth counties. Samuel Legg, William Brattle, and Nathaniel Oliver did not meet the council's approval for the Suffolk bench; only the governor's fourth and fifth choices proved acceptable. Dudley also removed sheriffs and registrars and justices of probate throughout the province. Anglicans Charles Hobby, William Tailer, and John Nelson joined Dudley's friends and relatives Nicholas Paige, Edward Bromfield, William Brattle, and the governor's son Paul, the province's new attorney-general, as justices of the peace. See Whitmore, *Massachusetts Civil List*, under appropriate courts and dates. Hobby, Tailer, and Nelson signed a petition criticizing the province's hostility to Anglicans on 4 February 1706, *CSP*, 23, #76. Dudley identified Bromfield as a friend in a letter to his wife, 6 May 1696, *Dudley Papers*, *MHSC*, 6th. ser. 3: 514.

35. Although some of these men were as wealthy as any in the province and Oakes and Cooke had served as province agents, Dudley justified his vetoes on grounds of their poverty and their unwillingness "to serve Her Majesty." When the Board of Trade questioned him about removing Peter Sergeant, a cousin of Sir Henry Ashurst and the husband of the widow Phips, the governor replied that if "Ashurst would have his kinsman sit at the board to contradict Her Majesty's commands . . . I hope he will be alone in that opinion." Council Records, 7: 333; Board of Trade to Joseph Dudley, 4 February 1706, *CSP*, 23, #85; Dudley to Board of Trade, 15 June 1706, *ibid.*, #236; Samuel Sewall to Stephen Sewall, 3 June 1703, Curwen Papers, 1: 3. The councillors who replaced these five included at least two close friends of Dudley—Edward Bromfield and Samuel Legg.

36. Excerpt from Cotton Mather, *Diary*, *MHSC*, 1st. ser. 4: 131; Council Records, 7: 366; Sewall, *Diary*, 1: 472; Cotton Mather to Earl of Nottingham, 23 November 1703, in Silverman, ed., *Selected Letters of Cotton Mather*, p. 67. This time, the Mathers linked their fortunes to Colonel Charles Hobby, whom Dudley had appointed to command the Boston militia in 1702. An Anglican, "a gay man, a free liver, and of very different behavior from what would have been expected would endear him to the clergy of New England," Hobby proved an even greater disappointment than Dudley. From 1704 until 1709, Henry Ashurst periodically reassured the Mathers that Hobby was about to succeed Dudley as governor. But in 1709, Francis Nicholson and Samuel Vetch gave Hobby a command in the Quebec expedition. He returned to Massachusetts a partisan of Dudley once again. Thomas Hutchinson, *The History of the Colony and Province of Massachusetts Bay*, (Cambridge, 1936), 2: 114; Henry Ashurst to Wait Winthrop or Increase Mather, 16 September 1704, 2 February 1706, 21 May 1706, 17 July 1707 and 10 October 1709, *Winthrop Papers*, 7: 133–209, *passim*. For Hobby's reversal, see Ashurst to Increase Mather, 10 February and 10 May 1710, *ibid.*, 215–218.

37. Sewall began to support Nathaniel Higginson's candidacy once again, but Higginson never expressed any interest and actually favored Hobby. Sewall, *Diary*, 1: 533–547, *passim*; Samuel Sewall to Nathaniel Higginson, 16 October and 21 October

# Notes to Chapter III

1706, and 10 March 1708, Sewall, *Letter Book, MHSC*, 6th. ser. 1: 319, 322, 361–362; Cotton Mather to Stephen Sewall, 11 October 1706, in Silverman, ed., *Selected Letters of Cotton Mather*, p. 72.

38. Joseph Dudley to Earl of Nottingham, 15 October 1702 and 10 December 1702, *CSP*, 20, #1046; 21, #30; Dudley to Board of Trade, 5 September 1703, 19 December 1703, 13 July 1704, 1 November 1705, 1 February 1706, and 2 October 1706, *ibid.*, 21, #1094, #1398; 22, #451, #1472; 23, #65, #511; Henry Ashurst to Wait Winthrop, 16 September 1704, *Winthrop Papers*, 7: 133.

39. As late as 1709, Dudley had to remind the Board of Trade that he did not, in fact, appoint the Massachusetts Council! Board of Trade to Joseph Dudley, 16 February 1704, 4 February 1706, *CSP*, 22, #11; 23, #85; Dudley to Earl of Nottingham or Board of Trade, 25 August 1702, 20 October 1702, 10 May 1703, 13 July 1704, and 1 March 1709, *ibid.*, 20, #810, #1073; 21, #673, #697; 22, #455; 24, #391.

40. Council Records, 7: 329, 337, 347; 8: 11; Joseph Dudley to Earl of Nottingham, 10 December 1702, and 4 April 1703, *CSP*, 21, #30, #543.

41. Sewall, *Diary*, 1: 487; Council Records, 7: 312–356, 402–416, *passim*; 8: 11–14.

42. Joseph Dudley to Board of Trade, 25 July 1705 and 1 November 1705, *CSP*, 21, #1372, #1422; Board of Trade to Dudley, 4 February 1706, *CSP*, 23, #85; Council Records, 8: 115–118; Sewall, *Diary*, 1: 523; Massachusetts Archives, 107: 30.

43. For example, after Dudley approved Oakes as speaker, Sewall noted that "he wished us [the General Court] well with our work." Sewall, *Diary*, 1: 524.

44. For an account of the military aspects of Queen Anne's War, see Haffenden, *New England in the English Nation* (Oxford, England, 1974), pp. 204–290, and Drake, *Border Wars* (New York, 1897), *passim*; Joseph Dudley to Board of Trade, 13 July 1704, *CSP*, 22, #455; Dudley to Secretary of State Charles Hedges, 10 March 1705, and 1 February 1706, *ibid.*, 22, #947; 23, #70; Dudley to William Popple, 9 April 1702, *ibid.*, 20, #321; Dudley to Board of Trade, 10 October 1704, *ibid.*, 21, #690; Council Records, 7: 292, 430; 8: 180, 183; House of Representatives to Queen Anne, 12 July 1704, *CSP*, 22, #451; *A&R*, 1: 499, 532. For earlier militia laws, see *ibid.*, 1: 129–142, 146, 268.

45. Council Records, 7: 363; Joseph Dudley to Earl of Nottingham, 10 May 1703, *CSP*, 21, #673.

46. Council Records, 7: 208, 218–220. One of the accused traders, Samuel Vetch, later commanded the 1709 and 1710 Canada expeditions.

47. Sewall, *Diary*, 1: 547; Council Records, 8: 220–225.

48. Samuel Sewall to Nathaniel Higginson, 16 October 1706, Sewall, *Letter Book*, 1: 333; Wait Winthrop to Fitz-John Winthrop, June 1706, *Winthrop Papers*, 6: 335; Council Records, 8: 208.

49. Council Records, 8: 225, 237–242; Joseph Dudley to Board of Trade, 8 October 1706, *CSP*, 23: #525.

50. Samuel Sewall to Nathaniel Higginson, 16 October and 21 October 1706, Sewall, *Letter Book*, 1: 333–337.

51. [Sir Henry Ashurst], *A Memorial of the Present Deplorable State of New England* (London, 1707), reprinted in Sewall, *Diary, MHSC*, 5th. ser. 6 on starred pages. A reply by Paul Dudley follows. It is noteworthy that both here and in the governor's own exchange of letters with the Mathers in 1708 (*MHSC*, 1st. ser. 4: 126–130), the Dudleys responded moderately and temperately to their opponents' accusations. The deponents in the affidavits collected by Ashurst and Mather do not swear that Dudley was involved in the trade, but only that "it is reported" that he was. The petition is in Hutchinson, *History*, 2: 145.

52. Council Records, 8: 318, 325–333; Sewall, *Diary*, 1: 574, 590. Sewall had second thoughts about his vote of 1 November and published his reasons for believing Dudley was guilty. He noted that the governor did not really design "to hurt the province, but [only] to gratify grateful merchants." Sewall was especially irked by the condemnation of his friend Higginson's petition as "scandalous and wicked." Such censures would "discourage persons of worth and interest" to undertake the redress of grievances in the future. Dudley retorted that Sewall "valued Mr. Higginson's reputation more than his [Dudley's] life." *Ibid.*, 1: 577–580. Sewall's reply is in the Massachusetts Archives, 20: 111.

53. The Mathers' anger was probably motivated by Dudley's successful maneuvers to have his friend John Leverett elected President of Harvard College at this time. Leverett received eight votes from the corporation as against one and three, respectively, for the younger and elder Mather. Although Leverett's anti-Calvinist theology was unpopular with the representatives, Dudley persuaded them to grant his protégé a salary by reintroducing the Charter of 1650 which permitted the General Court to supervise the president and corporation. Sewall, *Diary*, 1: 570, 573, 581; Council Records, 8: 325, 344–345; Cotton Mather to ?, 8 October 1707, Miscellaneous Bound Manuscripts; Cotton Mather, *The Deplorable State of New England* . . . (London, 1708), in Sewall, *Diary*, *MHSC*, 5th. ser. 6: 117\*, 127\*; Mather to Stephen Sewall, 13 December 1707, in Silverman, ed., *Selected Letters of Cotton Mather*, pp. 74–76; Whitmore, *Massachusetts Civil List*, p. 132. Thorough analyses of the illegal trade controversy, replete with picturesque quotations, may be found in Perry Miller, *The New England Mind: From Colony to Province* (Cambridge, 1953), p. 275; T. H. Breen, *The Character of a Good Ruler: Puritan Political Ideas in New England, 1630–1730* (New Haven, 1970), pp. 234–236; Kimball, *The Career of Joseph Dudley* (New York, 1911), pp. 180–190; and Richard Bushman, "Corruption and Power in Provincial America," in *The Development of a Revolutionary Mentality: Library of Congress Symposium on the American Revolution* (Washington, 1972), pp. 63–91. Bushman makes the good point that the charges of bribery and corruption were designed more for English than American consumption, since pecuniary corruption was a real possibility in England although not in Massachusetts. Bushman also argues, as I do, that such charges were rare. Dudley, Henry Ashurst, and Cotton Mather were the only authors of political tracts concerning Massachusetts from the Glorious Revolution until the Land Bank of 1714, when three more appeared. And the 1707–1708 tracts were published in London.

54. George M. Waller, *Samuel Vetch: Colonial Enterpriser* (Chapel Hill, 1960), p. 89, and Breen, *The Character of a Good Ruler*, p. 234, use the memorandum to implicate Dudley, as do G.B. Warden, *Boston: 1689–1776* (Boston, 1970), pp. 63–64, and John Gorham Palfrey, *A Compendious History of New England*, (Boston, 1856–1890), 4: 278. Everett Kimball, *The Career of Joseph Dudley*, pp. 116–119, and Thomas Hutchinson, *History* 2: 115–116, exonerate the governor.

55. Besides the four historians cited above in n. 54, Bushman, "Corruption and Power in Provincial America," p. 74, argues that even though the governor was probably not guilty, "Sewall's implicit rebuke of Dudley probably spoke more truly for the feelings of the house than the resolution clearing him of corruption," since Sewall was reelected to the council with ninety-eight of ninety-nine votes the following year. But twenty-two of the twenty-seven incumbents who disagreed with him were reelected as well.

56. Joseph Dudley to Board of Trade, 10 July 1708, *CSP*, 24, #33; Council Records, 8: 378–379, 408.

57. Council Records, 8: 429, 442, 452–455; 9: 2–3.

58. Samuel Vetch to Earl of Sunderland, 2 August and 12 August 1709, *CSP*, 24, #437; Vetch et. al. to Sunderland, 24 October 1709, *ibid.*, 24, #488; Joseph Dudley to Board of Trade, 11 November 1710 and 17 October 1711, *ibid.*, 25, #482; 26, #123;

Dudley to Viscount Bolingbroke, 29 October 1712, *CSP*, 27, #116; Council Records, 9: 65, 123, 134–140, 144–145, 153, 193.

59. Suffolk Inferior Court of Common Pleas, Extended Record Books (1706, 385; 1712, 141; 1714, 277, 291, 303, 324; 1715, 158), New Court House, Boston. I am indebted to John Murrin for calling my attention to the riot in Charlestown, which is described more fully in Chapter 8. Middlesex Court of General Sessions (1686–1688 and 1692–1723), 269–270, Middlesex Files, Folio 49X, Middlesex County Courthouse, Cambridge.

60. Joseph Dudley to Board of Trade, 17 October 1711, *CSP*, 25, #123.

61. Josiah Brodbent to Francis Nicholson, 21 June 1692, Phips Papers, 2: 12, Frederick Lewis Gay Transcripts, MHS; Thomas Povey to Lords of Admiralty, 8 August 1702, *CSP*, 20, #768.

62. Carl Bridenbaugh, *Cities in the Wilderness: The First Century of Urban Life in America*, 2nd. ed., (New York, 1955), pp. 196, 353–354. Gary Nash, *The Urban Crucible* (Cambridge, 1979), pp. 58–65, has an excellent account of the war's economic impact.

63. Sewall, *Diary*, 1: 583, 716; Joseph Dudley to Wait Winthrop, 11 February 1708, *Winthrop Papers*, 7: 163; Jeremiah Dummer to Joseph Dudley, 19 February 1711, Miscellaneous Bound Manuscripts, MHS; William Ashurst to Increase Mather, 10 August 1714, reprinted in Worthington C. Ford, "The Governor and Council of Massachusetts Bay, 1714 to 1715," *MHSP*, 2nd. ser. 15: 327.

# IV

---

## PARALYSIS

## 1713-1730

$\mathcal{A}$FTER the French and Indian War, Britain undertook to reform the colonial government in response to the Americans' poor showing. No comparable effort followed Queen Anne's War despite the provinces' pathetic record outside of Massachusetts. The Board of Trade did its best, but it did not control Parliament. The English cabinet could hardly worry much about the colonies when the Jacobite Rebellion of 1715 demonstrated the need to forge a stable political system at home.

The Duke of Newcastle, Secretary of State for the Southern Department and hence the colonies from 1724 to 1748, and Sir Robert Walpole, England's first "prime minister" from 1721 to 1742, turned to patronage to reconcile their opponents. The colonies became an important source of posts for the relatives and friends of men whose loyalty the ministry required. The cabinet did not regard overseas territories as a means of expanding the empire's wealth and power, as they had before and would again after 1740. Instead, the Newcastle–Walpole era traded incompetence and instability in the provinces for political harmony at home.

Between Queen Anne's and King George's Wars, two styles of politics prevailed in British North America: paralysis and procrastination. Governors who conscientiously tried to maintain their authority confronted surly provincials who knew they would suffer little for resisting them. In these instances, government came pretty much to a halt. Assemblies and executives disputed their powers until either sur-

61

# Paralysis

rendered or a compromise was reached. On the other hand, many governors delayed performing duties that offended their constituents. They tried to maintain the good will of the legislators they depended upon for their incomes. Occasional written rebukes from overseas could be disregarded if one had the proper connections. Under the procrastinators, government also did little. In either instance, governors had to worry more about displeasing influential colonists with their own British connections than about faithfully performing their duties.

Massachusetts experienced both sorts of administration during the inter-war period. Before 1730, executives tried for the most part to check an assembly testing its strength. Thereafter, Jonathan Belcher played a double game, and sought to persuade both the assembly and the ministry that he championed its cause.

During the inter-war period, the popular party literally lived up to its name for the only time before the American Revolution. Most deputies followed Elisha Cooke and the other leaders of the newly created Boston Caucus. The Board of Trade played into their hands by compelling the province's unhappy governors to insist that the assembly settle fixed salaries on the executive, grant the governor and council the power to spend money appropriated by the representatives, and curtail the money supply. These offensive royal demands, combined with inflation, and settling the Maine frontier, guaranteed that peace proved to be a mixed blessing for Massachusetts.

## THE POPULAR PARTY EMERGES: 1714–1723

In 1714, currency suddenly became a controversial issue in Massachusetts. There were two reasons for the emergence of this problem, which vexed the province until 1750. From the beginning of Queen Anne's War, taxes payable in gold or silver could not provide the necessary funds. Beginning in 1703, the General Court annually issued tax anticipation notes. These circulated as money because people needed them to pay their taxes in subsequent years. Until 1707, all bills fell due the following year. But by then economic hardship caught up with Massachusetts. Overseas trade declined because the province put so many men and resources into the war. New York and Philadelphia began to assume more of the middle and southern colonies' carrying trade. These factors reduced Massachusetts' ability to import specie. For the rest of the war, bills became redeemable at longer and longer intervals as people lacked the means to pay their taxes on time. Notes issued after 1710 could remain outstanding for six years. Wartime expenses and a declining international trade thus presented Massachusetts with severe postwar inflation.[1]

While the war lasted, fiscal policy remained uncontroversial. Everyone agreed that Massachusetts needed more money quickly. Reporting on the province's economic problems, Governor Dudley explained that "the returns for England pass through so few hands, that many if not most have no share in them and so have not the wherewithal to pay for goods." He recommended that an export trade, such as shipbuilding for the royal navy, be encouraged to bring in money. Meanwhile, he approved wholeheartedly of a paper substitute: "without it I could never have sustained nor clothed the forces that have defended and secured the colony." Dudley spoke for a province that realized that inflation, war, and economic decline had formed an inseparable trinity.[2]

By 1714, Massachusetts' economic health had grown so bad that Dudley reluctantly postponed taxes due that year until 1719. Although recognizing the delay might well increase inflation, he was persuaded by the General Court that the people simply could not pay, even though circulating currency had nominally increased from £6,431 in 1703 to £173,970 in 1713.[3] But the province unanimously complained of a "scarcity of bills" because specie had vanished. People were reluctant to accept the depreciating province bills for private transactions, which further accelerated the "decline of trade."[4]

Wartime consensus that government notes best solved these monetary problems disappeared in 1714. As the bills declined in value, two rival schemes surfaced. Each had its own interpretation of the crisis. Supporters of the province bills (public bankers) blamed popular extravagance and over-importation of luxuries. This theory neatly excused the government for any wrongdoing, and shifted the blame onto the general public. If only people would control their excesses, Massachusetts' overseas deficit and post-war hardships would vanish. Those favoring a private bank disagreed. They focused resentment on the hoarding and oppression by a small class of wealthy international traders. They then identified these tyrants with the Dudley faction. Since most private bankers belonged to the opposition, their currency scheme served their political aspirations. In 1714, Massachusetts' monetary theorists failed to go beyond ad hominem explanations for the province's woes. In the 1720s and '30s they would begin to analyze economic forces.

The private bankers fired the opening salvo. Their plan allowed people to mortgage their property to the directors for bills worth up to two-thirds their estimated value. The mortgagees had to pay five percent interest on their loans. The principal became due in five years. Shareholders, who had to buy stock in blocks of £50, supplied the notes, governed the company, and received the profits after deducting a portion for the province. The bank received widespread support in the Boston merchant community and—unlike future Land Banks— virtually nowhere else: 180 traders petitioned for it. The instigators were known political opponents of Governor Dudley: John Colman, Elisha Cooke, Jr., his brothers-in-law William Payne and Oliver Noyes, Lieutenant-Governor William Tailer, and Nathaniel Byfield who had enraged Dudley by being an ineffective admiralty judge.[5]

The private bank never got off the ground. On 20 August 1714, as the directors prepared to implement their plan, the council decreed it improper for "private persons to presume to proceed upon a project without the knowledge and leave of government." A group headed by the governor's son Paul and including Andrew and Jonathan Belcher, the Hutchinson family, and Samuel Sewall successfully proposed an alternative plan to the legislature. The government itself, represented by five trustees, would issue bills in sums of £50 to £250 on good security at five percent. The public bank thereby substantially duplicated the private except for the all-important matter of who controlled it. Although the legislature instructed the trustees to reserve a proportion of the bills for the inhabitants of each town, the trustees did business only in Boston, which indicated that the bill was written primarily to placate the Boston merchants who had agitated for the bank.[6]

To strengthen the bills' value, the legislature finally made counterfeiting punishable by death, a measure both Bellomont and Dudley had previously failed to obtain. Clearly, the General Court agreed with Paul Dudley that the Land Bank was "a very effectual way to enslave this country" since in a short time "this private government . . . would have the people's estates themselves." The Land Bankers' insistence that "the tendency of a public bank to . . . unite the power of the country and cash together" would "bring all the people into a servile dependency upon the court interest and render them subject and servile" proved ineffective.[7]

Even though rural support was needed for the bank to pass, Paul Dudley's arguments revealed an underlying conflict between the Bostonian merchants and the country towns over the causes and remedies of economic decline. Dudley ingeniously papered these over. In practical terms, he gave the merchants the bank they asked for. But to get the measure through, he blamed them for the "loss of the province's silver" by importing "from abroad more than we could pay for." He also condemned the "great extravagance of the people in their purchases, buildings, farms, expenses, apparel and . . . above all, the excessive consumption of rum and wine."[8] By giving the merchants the substance and the farmers the rhetoric, Dudley succeeded in uniting everyone except his father's more stubborn opponents behind the public bank.

The matter would probably have rested there, at least until new problems with the public bank arose. But Queen Anne died on 1 August 1714. Her death provoked a succession crisis that led to the Jacobite uprising and the decline of Dudley's patrons, the English Tories. Despite its willingness to cooperate with Dudley for the past several years, the assembly had little affection for the crusty old man. Sensing that political changes in England had undone the governor, the house refused to support a council vote requesting his continuance. With Dudley's departure impending, the Land Bankers saw the possibility of obtaining a royal charter to legalize their operation. To that end, Nathaniel Byfield sailed for England; he also hoped to become governor himself. Thus, the queen's death prolonged factionalism based on the Land Bank.[9]

When he arrived in England, Byfield learned that a Colonel Elizeus Burgess (a man indicted for murdering two men in duels and described by an acquaintance as "the most immoral man in the world") had been chosen to succeed Dudley. Despite Burgess's unsavory reputation, Byfield supported him in the hope (false, as it turned out) that he would obtain a charter for the Land Bank. Actually, Byfield had no other choice. Province agents Jeremiah Dummer and William Ashurst, firm adherents of Dudley, wrote back in horror that a "gentleman of a very profane, irreligious conversation" was about to leave for Boston. They were joined by Jonathan Belcher, who had been sent to London by his father and authorized to spare no expense to oppose the Land Bank. All three persuaded Viscount Barrington, head of the dissenting interest in Parliament, to recommend his brother Colonel Samuel Shute for the governorship. Belcher and Dummer placated Burgess by repaying the £1,000 he had spent to obtain his commission. They termed this "the best money ever laid out. New England does not know the unspeakable happiness that will come by this change." Shute acceded in June 1716. Dummer predicted that he would govern New England for life.[10]

During the interval between Dudley's removal in October 1715 and his successor's arrival on 4 October 1716, the Land Bankers weakened their already precarious position. Burgess and Byfield had arranged for the commission of Lieutenant-Governor William Tailer, a private banker, to be renewed. Immediately after succeeding Dudley, Tailer reshuffled the province judiciary, most notably in Suffolk County, where he replaced Jeremiah Dummer, Sr., and Penn Townsend with his cousin Edward Lyde and Adam Winthrop. He also removed the Dudley brothers, William and Paul, as sheriff and registrar of probate, and vetoed the legislature's reelection of the younger Dummer as agent. Since the Land Bank had lost, Tailer's measures further hurt Dudley's opponents. When he permitted the assemblymen to elect the attorney general, they revealed their opposition to his policies by choosing Paul Dudley. (Tailer somehow deluded himself that only "Dudley's family assisted by an inconsiderable party opposed him.") To accompany Shute, the agents made certain that Whitehall chose a new lieutenant-governor: Jeremiah Dummer's twenty-seven-year-old brother William, a son-in-law of Joseph Dudley.[11]

Shute's appointment insured that Dudley's supporters kept their predominance. The new governor's amiable personality, combined with the general revulsion against the Land Bankers, guaranteed that he encountered little trouble at first.[12] In 1717 and 1718, the Boston Town Meeting replaced Cooke, Oliver Noyes, and William Payne with Edward Hutchinson, a trustee of the public bills, Habijah Savage, and Joseph Wadsworth. The new representatives, in company with Samuel Thaxter of Hingham, appointed a justice of the peace by Joseph Dudley in 1713, and Jonathan Remington of Cambridge, Jonathan Belcher's closest friend, dominated the assembly.[13] Delighted that an "agreement as to the public interest and so little of a party spirit" prevailed, Shute found the "unanimity" of both houses "praiseworthy."[14] The province appeared well on its way to the long and peaceful administration Jeremiah Dummer had predicted.

But while Shute and his political allies won the battle over the Land Bank, they lost the war over Massachusetts. The governor's mishandling of the other major problem arising from the war, settling the frontier, undid his success on currency matters. Shute made the mistake of supporting Surveyor-General John Bridger's attempts to preserve the King's Woods in Maine and New Hampshire. To insure a sufficient supply of masts for the navy, Parliament had passed a law that protected pine trees greater than two feet in diameter on ungranted land. Bridger arrived in Massachusetts in 1698 and had proven ineffectual for two decades. Inadequate to his job, he had to patrol the entire lumbering region (southern Maine and the inhabited part of New Hampshire) with the aid of one or two deputies hired out of his own salary. Even if he caught a violator, he could not prove anything. Logs were logs, and there was no way of telling if they came from public or private lands, or once milled, what their size had been. Until 1711,

## Paralysis

Bridger also had to prove his cases before local juries and the Massachusetts Superior Court. They had flatly refused to protect the woods because no province law specified how to enforce the Act of Parliament. Despite his best efforts, Governor Dudley could not obtain one. In 1711, the vice-admiralty judge finally obtained jurisdiction over the King's Woods, but both Nathaniel Byfield and his successor, John Menzies, were financially interested in logging themselves.[15]

In 1710, Dudley abandoned a hopeless situation and gave up on Bridger, who had never obtained evidence to convict anyone. The ludicrous nature of the surveyor's efforts appears most clearly in a letter he wrote to the Board of Trade in 1713. With an air of triumph he boasted of at last having obtained three convictions. In addition to his other failings, Bridger was personally corrupt. He sold rights to fell trees he should have protected and tried to hinder legitimate logging. It is difficult not to agree with Joseph J. Malone's conclusion that Bridger was "a scoundrel, whose dishonesty cost his government vast sums of money, and whose egotism and foolishness proved more costly still."[16]

Bridger's political impact, however, overshadowed his personal corruption. During Queen Anne's War, he had little effect because the province founded few new towns from 1698 and 1711. Maine had been reduced to three towns in 1713, but five new ones were founded immediately after the war. Eighteen communities were set up in the rest of the province between 1712 and 1720. (See Table 8.) A newcomer to the province, Shute took his instruction to prevent the wasting of the woods seriously. He supplied Bridger with moral support and armed guards. To strike back at Shute, the private bankers, headed by Elisha Cooke, Jr., suddenly launched an all-out campaign against Bridger. Early in 1718, Cooke presented a memorial to the house claiming that the surveyor was "strenuously endeavoring by wrong insinuations and threats to compel the inhabitants . . . to pay him forty shillings for each team they sent to cut and get timber." Cooke's first effort to stir up things failed. With Hutchinson, Thaxter, and Wadsworth dominating the house, it simply turned the matter over to the governor and council. Nothing happened to Bridger, but Shute responded by vetoing Cooke's election to the council in May 1718. On 25 June the politically unemployed Cooke reiterated his charges. But this time, he spoke on behalf of the Maine representatives. He thereby obtained an investigatory committee that, after listening to local complaints, had to conclude that Bridger had accepted bribes and invaded private property. Cooke had paved the way for the investigatory committee's findings by personally visiting the frontier and insinuating to the settlers that all of Maine was exempt from Bridger's jurisdiction. He argued that because Massachusetts had purchased the region from the heirs of Sir Ferdinando Gorges in 1677, it belonged to the province as *private* property. Shute countered once again, dismissing Cooke as Clerk of the Superior Court with the consent of four of the five judges, the exception being Land Banker Addington Davenport. A number of "rude, injurious, and reflecting" remarks about the governor Cooke made several times while drunk exacerbated matters.[17]

Cooke struck back at the governor and recovered his power by creating the Boston Caucus, America's first political machine. Some background on Boston politics is necessary to understand this innovation. Between the Glorious Revolution and 1719, the town of Boston had vacillated between supporting and opposing the governor. Although the political allegiance of all the representatives cannot be positively known, many can be identified because of three tightly fought elections in the late 1690s for which Samuel Sewall recorded the votes. (See Table 10.)[18]

Before 1719 the Bostonian factions were about equally balanced. It is difficult to say whether voters elected representatives on factional lines or chose distinguished inhabitants out of personal respect, since they usually voted for members of both court and country. The 1703 election, which Sewall described as "the most unanimous election that I remember to have seen in Boston," appears to have ended with a deal whereby each faction voted for the other's candidates. This compromise lasted until 1715, when a complete Land Bank ticket was elected. Two years later, supporters of Shute and the public bank replaced the private bankers. But in 1719 and 1720 the Bostonians restored Cooke, Noyes, and Payne to their seats by narrow margins.[19]

The country faction's renewed vigor can be attributed to the new political organization it created: the Boston Caucus. Thomas Lechmere reported unusual activities in 1719. "To the surprise of all the great ones," a town meeting unanimously chose Cooke moderator on 14 March. A later one elected him selectman by a great majority of the "mobility," or lower classes.[20] In 1727, the first issue of the *New England Weekly Journal* poked fun at a "Brahmin Club" consisting of several Harvard graduates, that is to say, Cooke and his cohorts.[21]

The Caucus's rule did not go unchallenged. In 1720, about 400 voters showed up again. A pamphlet written to support Cooke explained that someone, probably Paul Dudley, tried to hinder an "expected vote":[22]

## Paralysis

A certain gentleman (or rather mere R[asca]l) having placed himself on the bench and assumed an uncommon air of impudence, he began to dictate to his superiors [the people]. [He proposed] that all the inhabitants of the town should have the oaths of allegiance and abjuration tended to them, before they were allowed to vote[23] . . . as if he should undertake to prove to a demonstration, that lawyer and liar are synonymous terms, till the moderator was forced to exert his authority to still his unruly harangue. . . . This [speech] extremely exasperated the town, to be challenged by such a d[amne]d D[udley?], where perhaps there are not 400 more true and loyal subjects in the king's dominions; 'tis generally supposed he came (as a tool) to hinder the *expected vote*.

Dudley's effort failed. While no statistics survive for 1720, in 1721 only 247 voters appeared; between 223 and 235 voted the Caucus slate.

How did the Caucus function? We can only rely on descriptions from a later period and conjecture that its methods remained the same. The Reverend William Gordon, writing around 1780, maintained that "more than fifty years ago, Mr. Samuel Adams's father and twenty others . . . used to meet, make a caucus, and lay their plan for introducing certain persons into places of trust and power. When they settled it, they separated, and each used their particular influence within his own circle."[24]

The leading members of the Caucus had three potent means influencing the voters: money, alcohol, and medicine. Several were fabulously wealthy. Cooke and Noyes, respectively, left fortunes of £63,000 and £17,000. William Clarke owned the largest private wharf in Boston. According to loyalist Peter Oliver, Cooke, "the Catiline of his era," spent £9,000 in bribes.[25] Alcohol may have been another important medium of persuasion. Clarke and Cooke drank notoriously.[26] There were almost a hundred houses and taverns licensed to sell liquor in Boston, a town with a population of about 12,000. (Cotton Mather, for once in his life, did not exaggerate when he claimed that "this town has an enormous number of them.") Bribery may have taken liquid form. Third, Cooke, Noyes, and Clarke were physicians who could easily circulate among the electorate. And, unlike the court politicians, they did not sue their fellow inhabitants for small amounts in the Suffolk Court of Common Pleas. All in all, several methods were used to obtain the 200 or so votes needed to win most Boston elections.[27]

# Paralysis

Yet the Caucus never controlled Boston completely. It selected most, but not all, of the representatives from 1719 until the late 1730s. For example, the voters chose one Isaiah Tay between 1717 and 1719 and again from 1722 to 1725. According to Thomas Hutchinson, Tay was "one of those persons who serve upon a pinch, when a favorite candidate cannot be carried by either party."[28] This assessment seems accurate because Tay usually received a number of votes that differed strikingly from his colleagues. In 1717 and 1719 he outpolled all the other candidates by a sizeable margin, while from 1722 and 1725 he was either third or last in the total. The 1726 and 1727 elections indicate the Caucus's limited control even more strongly. Elisha Cooke had been in England for much of the previous two years. When he returned he served on the council, where he exerted much less influence than in the house. The province had been forced to accept the Explanatory Charter, and Cooke's tactics as agent had jeopardized the original charter as well. To retaliate, the Bostonians elected Joseph Wadsworth—who had served from 1717 and 1718 as a prerogative man, John Ballantine, and Nathaniel Greene to represent them. Contests during these two years, atypically for the 1720s, were closely fought. (See Table 10.)[29]

Although the Caucus was controlled by upper-class men previously active in politics, it helped to expand political consciousness in Boston. Beginning in 1721, the town meeting began to instruct its representatives almost annually. Unlike the locally-oriented mandates passed elsewhere in Massachusetts before the Stamp Act, Boston called upon its deputies to defend the people's liberties.[30] Boston alone developed an organization linking town and provincial politics. In the 1760s, the Caucus enabled the town to mobilize popular opposition to British policies.

By enabling the popular party to win consistently in Boston, the Caucus set the stage for the events of 1720. That year, according to Thomas Hutchinson, "the contests and dissensions in the governments rose to a greater height than they had done since the religious feuds in the year 1636 and 37."[31] By identifying Shute with Bridger, the Caucus ousted the governor's leading Bostonian supporters from the house. The situation appeared as desperate for the court faction as it had for the country faction only two years earlier.

From 1720 until his precipitous departure on New Year's Eve, 1723, Shute quarrelled constantly with the assembly. Each side made unprecedented incursions on the other's hitherto unquestioned powers. Shute increased the already considerable tension when the assembly met in 1720. First he approved, then he disallowed, Elisha

Cooke's election as speaker. The governor cut off the budding debate over whether he in fact possessed such a power by dissolving the legislature.[32] The country members had made a useless trip to Boston only to be confronted by duplicity and an assault on their rights.

The new house, which met on 3 July, gave Shute just as much trouble. It took three ballots to elect a speaker. Cooke still headed the field, but after a long altercation, the house chose Timothy Lindall of Salem, a member of Cooke's faction who proved acceptable to Shute. However, the governor then dissolved this assembly when it made more trouble in eleven days than he had seen in four years. First, the deputies ignored his proposals to placate the increasingly restless Norridgewock Indians of Maine. Instead, they spent most of their time arguing that Shute had no right to veto the speaker. They refused to build truckhouses to centralize and monitor the Indian trade on the grounds they would "occasion fears and animosities." The representatives also denied any appropriations for the soldiers guarding the Maine outposts unless they, rather than the governor, directed the placement and movement of troops. Finally they cut Shute's salary from £1,200 a year to £1,000 and reduced Lieutenant-Governor Dummer's from £50 to £35. Dummer refused to accept this sum as beneath his dignity.[33]

Debates over the frontier and the governor's powers plagued the General Court for the next two years. When open war with the Maine tribes broke out in the fall of 1720, the house refused to send troops to seize Sebastian Ralle, the Jesuit priest responsible for the trouble. It only placed a reward of £200 on his head and directed the sheriff of York County to capture him. The deputies also insisted on directing the disposition of troops with such minuteness that they could launch no effective campaign. With a handful of easily defeatable Indians on the warpath, the governor and house bickered for two years over the control of troop movements. A new quarrel erupted in December 1722 when the house accused Colonel Shadrach Walton, commander of the forces, of padding muster rolls and not paying his soldiers their due wages. The deputies wanted to remove him immediately. Shute, however, forbade him to appear before them except in the governor's presence and insisted on retaining Walton until the charges were fully proven.[34]

In the 1720s, military policy had become a political football. It only affected Maine and did not compel factional cooperation. The war itself became a pawn in the debate over the governor's prerogatives.

Wartime exigencies also did not stop Governor Shute from complaining about reduced salary. In 1721, for the first time in five years, he mentioned that he had been instructed to obtain a permanent, fixed grant. The timing of this message reveals that Shute had never really expected a fixed salary. But by raising the issue at this point he sought to woo the deputies away from those who attacked him as an enemy of their liberties. He wanted to show the house that he had been most accommodating in not insisting on the full perquisites of his office. The assembly remained unmoved. It responded by terming £1,000 a year an "honorable allowance," and continued to pay him that sum for the rest of his administration.[35]

Shute also had to defend his charter power to adjourn the legislature. During the smallpox epidemic of 1721, the deputies refused to move themselves from Boston to Cambridge as the governor asked. Had they conceded this point, the governor would have established his right to adjourn and relocate the house at will. The assembly only gave in when Oliver Noyes and William Hutchinson, two Boston representatives and Cooke's right-hand men, died of the disease. Even then the deputies held out until Shute agreed not to use his action as a precedent.[36]

In addition to directing the assembly's quarrel with Shute, the popular party launched the first major barrage of political literature in the post-1689 period. Aside from the three pamphlets written by Paul Dudley, Henry Ashurst, and Cotton Mather in 1707 and 1708, another three debating the Land Bank of 1714, and two short tracts concerning local Boston politics in 1715, political writing had previously been limited to theoretical tracts such as election sermons.[37] But at least a dozen works appeared in 1720 and 1721 debating the merits of Elisha Cooke's defense of provincial liberty. Most also discussed the effects of a depreciating currency on Massachusetts.

The battle commenced with Cooke's own *Just and Seasonable Vindications*. Here he defended his partisan behavior with tongue in cheek. He took credit for preventing Bridger from making "shameful havoc of trees for masting His Majesty's royal navy, by selling liberty for persons, for filthy lucre, to cut, fell, and carry out as many trees as their private occasions call for." Cooke then passed over his "ill-treatment" of the governor as purely "personal." He contended that he "had done everything that could be expected to remove all misunderstandings." But at the end of the essay he became serious. To concede any substantive point "would have been very criminal in me . . . and [I would] ever after be ranked among those despicable wretches that would sacrifice their country to serve themselves."[38]

## Paralysis

Cotton Mather, a good friend and advisor of Shute, responded with his customary vigor. Mather's *News from Robinson Crusoe's Island* presented affidavits showing that Cooke had tried to prevent Bridger from exercising even his legitimate authority. Mather also dismissed Cooke's assertion that the province would be reduced to slavery if the house compromised on the speaker. The minister's opening lines compared the province to "the island now known by the name of Insania" that threatened to sacrifice its charter by a too rigorous construction of a few small points.[39] Cooke's followers answered Mather's arguments with ad hominem barbs. They condemned him in the most scurrilous terms as one whose "Scribendi Catholicus [writing about everything] has made him famous on both sides of the Atlantic, whose brain is so overcharged with so great a variety of news." They compared him to the "the great Don Dago [the Pope]," and taunted him that he "had represented a loyal and peaceable people as factious, turbulent, and worse than the savage monsters of Africa."[40]

The popular party took advantage of its quarrel with Shute to reintroduce the Land Bank. Other signs appeared propitious. The province bills and £50,000 of the loan of 1714 had failed to stem the triple tide of inflation, currency shortage, and general economic decline. The loan, which had to be obtained in Boston, soon angered the rest of the towns, as did the high minimum amount: £50. In response, the house decentralized subsequent distribution. County commissioners handled the £100,000 issued in 1716. Significantly, the General Court chose Elisha Cooke and Oliver Noyes, who favored the private bank, as two of the five Suffolk trustees. In 1720, the legislature entrusted the towns themselves with a new £50,000 loan. A final £60,000 public loan of 1728 even required that, to facilitate payment of taxes, each community distribute its share among taxpayers in proportion to their assessments. The law of 1716 and all future acts also reduced the amount each individual could subscribe to ten shillings instead of £50. The Boston merchants may have considered the 1714 loan sufficient, but it apparently supplied little circulating money to their hard-pressed country cousins. When in 1720 the General Court appointed a committee of six leading Bostonians—including Thomas Hutchinson, Addington Davenport, and Jonathan Belcher, three trustees of the 1714 loan—to assess the currency crisis, they reversed their earlier position and argued that it "will be greatly for the service and benefit of the public not to emit any more bills on loan." By 1720, dissatisfaction with the public bills gave the Land Bankers the courage to try again.[41]

However, having lost badly the first time, none of the popular leaders within the legislature openly endorsed the Bank. Instead, John Colman, a merchant in constant legal and financial trouble who led the Land Bankers again in 1740, advanced their proposals in three acerbic pamphlets. However, a "gentleman," probably Oliver Noyes, and the anonymous author of another tract supporting Elisha Cooke backed Colman up.[42]

For the first time, advocates of both public and private bills presented sophisticated theories accounting for Massachusetts' economic hardships. Jonathan Belcher and clergyman Edward Wigglesworth defended restricted issues of public bills. Belcher blamed the province's idleness and conspicuous consumption for its plight. "The needless multitude of retailers, petty shops, hucksters, and forestallers of the market" received special censure. He urged moral reformation as the province's only hope, exhorting the people to work hard and practice "peace, love, and unity." To these arguments, Wigglesworth added that far from declining, the countryfolk found in Boston "sumptuous buildings, gallant furniture, costly clothing . . . and great and scandalous expense at taverns." The root of all evil was overimportation and overextension of credit. The way to remedy it was simply to "leave off trusting"—stop buying foreign commodities on credit—and encourage manufactures. He also suggested in passing that the province keep its currency stable by burning many of the bills in existence, exchanging those that remained for silver, and forbidding the exportation of specie to keep it in the country. Wigglesworth thus reintroduced the notion, which gained increasing support throughout the thirties and forties until it triumphed in 1749, that Massachusetts should resume a silver currency.[43] In short, the public bankers tried to maintain the pleasing illusion that Massachusetts had complete control over its destiny if only people would be less extravagant.

In reply, Colman and the Land Bankers argued in terms of economic forces. They condemned their opponents for talking like men "utterly unacquainted with trade." To abandon credit or consumption, or to take up manufacturing would destroy what little commerce remained. Far from finding Boston idle and luxurious, Colman insisted that "this town is as industrious a place as any, if they have work to do; if they stand idle, it is because no man will hire them." The high price of foreign commodities could be attributed to scarcity, not to excessive demand. The shortage of bills arose from the decline of the province's fishery and West India trade that had previously provided money to pay for the imports. Colman suggested removing whatever import duties remained to stimulate the economy, but he stressed increasing the money supply as far more important. By fostering trade and enabling people to pay off their debts, a large supply of paper money would give the province some goods of its own to exchange. Far from too much paper being extant, the Bankers insisted £200,000 hardly sufficed for some hundred towns. Colman even advanced the somewhat heretical notion that paper money was vastly superior to silver, for the government could regulate its quantity to suit economic needs.[44]

The private bankers insisted that only their scheme could reap the full advantages of paper money. By postponing redemption of public notes whenever money became tight, the General Court had depreciated its own bills and driven them out of circulation. A private company could not enjoy such a luxury upon pain of bankruptcy. Colman also maintained that a scarcity of bills benefited the wealthy merchants and public officials who controlled the government. He noted that "every term four or five hundred writs (perhaps more) are given out against good, honest housekeepers, who are as wealthy to pay their debts as their credit would be, and have wherewithal to pay, but can't raise the money." The people were "squeezed and oppressed to maintain a few law and other officers of the courts, who grow rich on the ruins of their neighbors." He coupled his proposals with the suggestion that the voters rid the assembly of sheriffs and lawyers, most of whom supported public bills or a reduced currency. Predicting rebellion if the high and mighty did not mend their ways, Colman concluded his plea:

> The rich, great, and potent with rapacious volume blow down all before them, who have not wealth or strength to encounter or avoid their fury . . . so must a flourishing province fall a sacrifice to the rage, ambition, and avarice of a few, who aspire at nothing short of being lords, and long to be glutting themselves with the blood of the victim, and trampling on the just rights of the people.[45]

However, efforts to convert the hostility against the prerogative faction and public bills into support for the Land Bank failed. Colman's collaborators in the house of representatives did not even bring up the Bank. He gained only a three-month prison term for his intemperate remarks until he apologized for insulting the country and its officials. Even the Boston Town Meeting did not approve the Bank. But by prudently refraining from publicly supporting the Bank, the country party lost none of its popularity.

# *Paralysis*

The General Court acted on the arguments of Colman's opponents. It increased the supply of public bills through the loan of 1720 and permitted taxes to be paid in kind for the first time in the province's history. In a gesture more symbolic than substantive, to attack both overimportation and usless expenditures, the Court curtailed "luxurious" and "extravagant" funerals by outlawing gifts of imported scarves and rings to mourners. It also forbade private lotteries and limited credit to two years. In 1722 the legislature further enhanced the accessibility of money by issuing one-, two-, and three-penny denominations of paper in circular, square, and hexagonal shapes, respectively.[46] Although these measures did little to stem the inflationary tide, the Land Bank idea remained dormant until the late 1730s.

A little over a year after the Land Bank had run its course, Governor Shute—possibly frightened by an assassination attempt—fled Massachusetts on 31 December 1722.[47] Trapped between the criticisms of his superiors for laxness and his constituents for tyranny, Shute resolved to present his case in person to the royal administration.[48] The Massachusetts house's final assault on his powers strengthened his resolution to depart. It did nothing less than create a new constitutional body to supplant him as commander in chief of the armed forces! On 6 December, the deputies proposed a Committee of War composed of seven deputies and four councillors to meet biweekly and arrive at military decisions. The committee would then "lay the same before His Excellency for his approval and consent." This plan would have reduced the governor to a rubber stamp of the house because the committee was to decide by majority vote. The council and governor naturally rejected it.[49]

During Samuel Shute's troubled administration, the prosecution of a war was a major political issue. However, the pressure of mere frontier skirmishes could not pacify the legislature itself. Shute's regime began a period of Massachusetts factionalism that consisted largely of internal struggles among the branches of the General Court. It also marked the maximum limit of the house's demands—future struggles consisted only of resistance to specific royal instructions. But for more than a decade no governor could claim that "all things [were] quiet" and "nothing material has happened," as Samuel Shute did in 1717.[50]

### CRISIS AND COMPROMISE: 1723–1728

Three periods of factionalism marked Lieutenant-Governor William Dummer's term (1723–1728) as acting executive. First, he

spent two years settling the quarrels and ending the war that he had inherited from his predecessor. He thereby achieved a relative calm. In
1725, worried that Samuel Shute's complaints might revoke the
charter, disgusted with Elisha Cooke's pitiful defense of the province
in England, and pleased with the lieutenant-governor's complaisant
personality, the deputies approved the Explanatory Charter.[51] They
thereby conceded the governor's powers to adjourn the house and veto
the speaker. But in 1727 the popular faction recovered its strength
because Britain tried to reduce drastically Massachusetts' money supply.

Initially, the representatives wasted no time pouncing on Dummer.
Two days after he had assumed office, they declared Colonel Walton
"obnoxious to this government" and removed him without pay.
Ironically, while condemning Walton for his failure to destroy a newly
erected French fort at Penobscot, the assembly simultaneously "protested against carrying on the war in an offensive manner at present"
unless Dummer gave it a free hand. Its only positive action placed a
bounty of £100 on Indian scalps. It rejected a bill suggested by the
council forbidding trade with the French.

But Dummer and the council found a way out of the impasse. During recesses of the assembly in 1723 and 1725, Dummer utilized a
broad construction of his charter power as commander in chief to
launch successful expeditions that defeated the Indians decisively and
recaptured Penobscot. Although lasting peace finally came to Maine,
the house refused to pay the participating soldiers' back wages. The
men in turn retaliated by deserting their garrison posts. Dummer's
decisive though unconstitutional action showed how easily the Indian
nuisance could have been eliminated at any time during the past five
years. But the popular party and representatives ignored the practical
benefits of his actions and regarded them only as they affected the
house's privileges.[52]

The assembly also struck back at Dummer by dismissing his brother
Jeremiah as province agent. His replacement was none other than
Elisha Cooke. Cooke sailed for England in December 1723 to refute
Governor Shute's charges that "this house [was] attempting to en-
croach upon the royal prerogative, or coming into some things, they
had no right to under the present happy constitution." During 1724
and 1725, all eyes focused on Elisha Cooke in England, where the fate
of this "happy constitution" would be irrevocably decided.[53]

Massachusetts had been in sporadic danger of losing its charter
since the days of Ashurst and Bellomont. Impressed with the ability of
France's sparsely populated Canada to defeat the populous but

disunited English colonies, the Board of Trade and Secretaries of State changed most of the proprietary and charter colonies to royal governments between 1702 and 1720. Massachusetts avoided more stringent regulation thanks to the assiduous efforts of Jeremiah Dummer. Most notably, his famous *Defence of the New England Charters* (1721) insisted that these documents had the status of fundamental law outside of Parliament's jurisdiction. He also maintained that the broad liberties allowed the settlers served as inducements to loyalty rather than independence.[54]

However, the Massachusetts house viewed Dummer primarily as a partisan of Shute or Dudley rather than a spokesman for the whole province. He had made himself unpopular by warning that Cooke's attacks on the governor and the surveyor-general compromised his efforts to save the charter. Dummer insisted that "in the present situation of our affairs, the governor's friends are the true friends of the country." The deputies fired him in 1721, rehired him the following year when they learned that Shute had sent home "false insinuations, unjust, unreasonable remarks and animadversions," and fired him again in 1723 to make room for Cooke. Nevertheless, the faithful Dummer informally assisted his erstwhile opponent.[55]

The appointment in 1724 of the Duke of Newcastle as Secretary of State for the Southern Department helped Cooke enormously. Unlike his predecessors, Newcastle viewed the colonies only as sources of patronage posts that he distributed to obtain parliamentary majorities.[56] Whereas Cooke's formal appearances before the Board of Trade were disastrous,[57] Newcastle assured him that under no circumstances did the ministry "intend to vacate the charter or hurt the people in their rights." Even if the Board of Trade forced the issue into Parliament, Newcastle predicted that "the House of Commons would be very tender of the privileges of the people."[58]

Nevertheless, Cooke still had to surrender the house's rights to choose its speaker and to adjourn itself without the governor's consent. He would have had to give up even more, but he convinced the Board of Trade that all the other disputed points (notably the guarantee of an "honorable support" for the governor, the right of the council and governor to spend money appropriated by the house, and the control of the King's Woods) had already been conceded! Governors Burnet and Belcher would soon discover Cooke had been lying.

Cooke's shifty maneuvering made his agency a success. However, John Colman, Henry Newman, Jeremiah Dummer, and other correspondents had written back that the charter owed its preservation to Shute's and Dummer's efforts rather than to Cooke's clever ruse and

Newcastle's apathy. Unsavory tales of Cooke's tavern brawls and drunkenness also filtered back to Massachusetts.[59] As a result, both the town of Boston and the General Court turned against the popular faction in 1725 and 1726. For the only time between 1719 and 1738, the prerogative faction elected two of four Boston representatives. (See Table 10.) In 1726, only one member of the popular party (Ezekiel Lewis) ranked among the house's six leading committee members. Although Cooke returned home in time to oppose the very charter he had negotiated, in January 1726 the house approved it forty-eight to thirty-two and the council nineteen to four. Many who favored the charter had opposed surrendering these powers all along. Only with difficulty did the council persuade the deputies to "accept of" rather than "submit to" it. Debate grew so heated that for the first time a roll call appeared in the *House Journals*. Previously published to reveal what the house did collectively, for this issue the *Journals* became the means for constituents to learn how their representatives voted and to remove or reelect them accordingly. The roll call does not seem to have made much difference. The following May, seventeen deputies voting for the charter and twelve opposing reappeared.[60]

If the Explanatory Charter displeased the representatives, they were even more angry at the popular faction for nearly losing the whole constitution. A rare council ballot survives for May 1726. Of the four councillors who opposed the charter, Nathaniel Byfield obtained 77 out of 114 votes, and John Clark and Thomas Palmer could not even gain election on the first ballot. In contrast, many of the nineteen favoring the Explanatory Charter were reelected on the first ballot, eight of them with one hundred votes or more.[61]

But the house's willingness to cooperate with Dummer and the court faction ended abruptly in 1727. When the General Court opened in May, the lieutenant-governor read a new instruction insisting that the £100,000 loan of 1716 be called in as scheduled within a year. All further emissions would require a suspending clause except for each year's necessary government expenditures. Led by Cooke, the house employed a number of stratagems to get around this. It insisted that one assembly could not be bound by the decisions of its predecessors to redeem bills on time. When Dummer remained adamant, the deputies offered to call in the old notes only if a further £60,000 were emitted. When all else failed, they took advantage of the loophole in Dummer's instructions permitting bills necessary for government expenses. The lieutenant-governor had casually suggested that the province's fortifications needed repairs. The assembly responded by offering to loan £62,000 to the port towns, including £30,000 to Boston, for defense. This sum greatly exceeded the required amount and would have delivered the bulk of the money to the popular party through the Boston Town Meeting. Dummer rejected these subterfuges. He dissolved one General Court and held another in session an unprecedented 165 days to compel the house to draw in the £100,000. But his adversaries had greater powers of endurance. The lieutenant-governor finally consented to retire only £40,000 when the council advised him to disregard his instructions. This was the last major action of his administration.[62]

Dummer's first years in office provided a brief respite from the factional strife which plagued Massachusetts from 1720 to the mid-1730s. But his final days augured poorly for the future. Once again the Board of Trade had saddled an executive with an unworkable directive that gave the popular party a ready-made issue to dominate the assembly. When William Burnet, a no-nonsense, dedicated administrator, succeeded Dummer in 1728, the Board hoped that he could repeat his success as Governor of New York.[63] Instead, he faced a resurgent country faction.

STALEMATE: 1728–1730

William Burnet arrived in Massachusetts in July 1728 with orders to obtain a guaranteed minimum salary of £1,000 sterling per annum. If he failed, he had to decide immediately whether it would be necessary to send a company of regulars as "the only means of bringing these people to have a respect for their government." However, the Board of Trade secretly told him that such a request, if forthcoming, would never be granted. The Board reasoned that the mere threat "will put these people in fear, and make them most complying in other things in order to prevent it."[64] Burnet's instruction set a pattern for the next decade. Presenting governors with impossible tasks, the Board simply withdrew or modified them when they could not be executed. It thereby implicitly rebuked the men who had striven to carry them out. Such irresolution played right into the hands of Elisha Cooke. Although the assembly had to accept the Explanatory Charter and later surrender the right to supervise accounts, the country faction successfully persuaded the house that British threats could be safely ignored.

Burnet spent nearly all of the fifteen months of his remaining life trying to obtain his permanent grant. The messages of the governor and the assembly became longer and longer and more and more vituperative.[65] Each faction resorted to unprecedented steps to outwit the other. One of Burnet's innovations included moving the General Court from Boston to Salem to remove the pernicious influence of the Town Meeting and Caucus. He hoped to punish the town by depriving it of the usual profits from housing and feeding the rural deputies. He also refused to accept any non-perpetual salary, vetoed the representatives' own wages until they paid him, and to wear down the deputies he kept them sitting for 184 days in 1728. They responded by refusing to do any business at all. Burnet then attempted to alienate the representatives from the people by informing the towns that the deputies' conduct was certain to provoke revocation of the charter.[66]

The representatives, for their part, pioneered new methods to counteract Burnet's. They offered him one-year grants of £1,700, £3,000, and finally £6,000 Massachusetts money (the last equal to about £2,000 sterling) to violate his instruction. The assembly arranged for Burnet to lodge with Elisha Cooke while his mansion was under repair. But the doctor's well-known persuasive powers failed to have the desired effect. Finally, when the council refused to join the house in selecting agents to protest Burnet's behavior, the assembly chose its own spokesmen. Jonathan Belcher, an immensely wealthy merchant who had twice been left out of the council for his staunch adherence to the governor, abruptly changed his stance and accepted the agency in company with his London business partner, Francis Wilkes. When the council refused to vote Belcher any expense money, the assembly appealed directly to the towns. However, only ten towns out of 120 provided the sum of £1,800 (about £600 sterling). Even the Boston Town Meeting refused 161 to 91 to contribute, but voted 169 to 121 to circulate a subscription among the inhabitants. Five-sixths of the agency's funds came from wealthy Caucus members.[67]

Abundant disturbances marked Boston politics during 1729 and 1730. In July 1729, the conjunction of a food shortage, the governor's threats, and the landing of Irish immigrants to settle property claimed in Maine by prominent Bostonians triggered a riot.[68] The Bostonians attempted to convince other towns to instruct deputies on the governor's salary, but only three or four followed suit. Burnet considered Boston's interference in non-local matters as "dangerous to the constitution" and was glad it did not become a precedent.[69]

In June 1730, the governor's friends ran their own candidate, Anglican merchant George Craddock, for Boston representative to weaken the Caucus's influence. The effort failed—the people cried "popery was coming in upon them in a torrent" and "they were to be devoured by the scarlet whore." Elisha Cooke moderated the election: "he refused some votes and scrutinized others well qualified, but passed all who voted against Mr. Craddock." In both 1729 and 1730, the voters elected the straight Caucus slate of Cooke, Thomas Cushing, Ezekiel Lewis, and Samuel Welles. The least any of them polled was 184 votes out of 192 in 1729, and 465 of 474 in 1730. The town apparently agreed overwhelmingly with one Benjamin Walker, who described Burnet as "arbitrary . . . and breaking into our laws, which he seems not to value at all, nor anything or person in the province but his own interest."[70]

The governor's threats thus met with two reactions: indifference in most of the country, defiance in Boston and the house itself. Massachusetts had grown weary after years of such futile threats. Councillor John Cushing remarked that "no evil happened" when the province had refused to fix salaries before. His only fear was that "an easy compliance" would encourage future royal demands.[71] Britain had cried wolf once too often.

Burnet had to deal with more than the expected resistance from the Massachusetts house. Belcher's and Wilkes's influence over the Duke of Newcastle further undermined his efforts. They accused him of harrassing the assembly, collecting unreasonable and illegal fees, and refusing to allow the deputies to supervise treasury appropriations. Jeremiah Dummer came out of retirement to testify on the house's behalf. In consequence, Newcastle ordered Burnet "not to throw the province into a passion or put a stop to the public business." He told the hapless governor "not to exact or demand any other fees than what are legal, or have not been customarily taken by the governors of the province." Publicly, Newcastle approved Burnet's conduct and accused the assembly of trying "to throw off their dependance on the crown." Privately, His Grace asked Burnet to use his "best endeavor that a stop may be put to any parliamentary inquiry" of the sort proposed by the Board of Trade.[72]

As part of his conciliatory program, Newcastle backtracked on the governor's instructions. Less than a year after Burnet's arrival, he was permitted to accept a salary merely for the duration of his administration. But the house turned down even his proposal, fifty-four to eighteen. Burnet did not like this compromise either. The bill's supporters had trouble convincing him that they had not betrayed him.[73] Unlike Newcastle, Burnet realized only too well that concessions would be interpreted as capitulation.

Mercifully, Newcastle's rebuke of Burnet's conduct did not arrive until after his death. His successor, Jonathan Belcher, faced the task of restoring harmony between the house and the governor and between Massachusetts and Britain. Unlike the upright Burnet, the unscrupulous Belcher achieved this feat by persuading his superiors that on some issues Elisha Cooke had been right all along.

## Notes to Chapter IV

1. Joseph B. Felt, *An Historical Account of Massachusetts Currency* (Boston, 1839), pp. 56–63; Curtis P. Nettels, *The Money Supply of the American Colonies Before 1720* (Madison, 1934), p. 267; Leslie V. Brock, *The Currency of the American Colonies, 1700–1764* (New York, 1975), pp. 591–592; Andrew M. Davis, *Currency and Banking in the Province of Massachusetts Bay* (New York, 1901), 1: 88, 443; Gary Nash, *The Urban Crucible* (Cambridge, 1979), pp. 62–65, 112–113.

2. Joseph Dudley to Board of Trade, 1 March 1709 and 1 December 1713, *CSP*, 24, #391; 27, #509. A brief controversy had arisen in 1705 when the representatives tried to depreciate province bills to eight shillings per ounce of silver rather than six as mandated by the governor's instructions. This measure chiefly affected foreign exchange and Dudley withheld his consent. Joseph Dudley to Board of Trade, 25 July 1705, *CSP*, 22, #1274. An earlier private bank, proposed by Englishman John Blackwell in 1686, received bipartisan endorsement from Acting Governor Dudley and William Stoughton of the moderates and Elisha Cooke and Elisha Hutchinson of the old-charter faction. Andrew M. Davis, *Colonial Currency Reprints* (Boston, 1910), 1: 70.

3. Legislative Records of the Massachusetts Council, 9: 382, 392, Massachusetts Archives, State House, Boston.

4. Brock, *The Currency of the American Colonies*, pp. 591–592 is the source for estimates of currency in circulation.

5. These men signed a pamphlet supporting the Bank: Davis, *Currency Reprints*, 1: 312; Felt, *Massachusetts Currency*, pp. 63–68; G.B. Warden, *Boston: 1689–1776* (Boston, 1970), pp. 68–79, gives a good account of the Bank. He views it as the culmination of a plan by this group of Bostonian merchants to dominate the province's economic life. Their ventures included a salt monopoly, rights to develop the Boston Neck Road, wharves, land speculation, and lumbering. See also Davis, *Currency Reprints*, 1: 34–44. For Byfield's defection, see Thomas Hutchinson, *The History of the Colony and Province of Massachusetts Bay* (Cambridge, 1936), 2: 158.

6. Council Records, 9: 417; *A&R*, 1: 750; 2: 42. The names of the trustees are in Hutchinson, *History*, 2: 156.

7. See Davis, *Currency Reprints*, 1: 247, 254, 258, 282, 285, and 301 for these and similar arguments.

8. *Ibid.*, 1: 251.

9. Council Records, 9: 414. For an account of the succession crisis in England and its relation to Massachusetts politics, see Worthington C. Ford, "The Governor and Council of Massachusetts Bay, 1714 to 1715," *MHSP*, 2nd. ser. 15: 327–361.

10. The documents describing the maneuvering in England are found in the William Tailer Letter Book, MHS; and Albert C. Matthews, "Colonel Elizeus Burgess," *PCSM*, 19 (1916–1917), pp. 360–372.

11. William H. Whitmore, *The Massachusetts Civil List, 1630–1776*, (Albany, 1870); William Tailer to Thomas Sanford, 20 December 1715 and 3 June 1716, Tailer Letter Book MHS.

12. The province ministers, especially Benjamin Colman and Cotton Mather, praised the new governor as "incomparable," "a father," and wrote their English correspondents that if they had a choice, "the whole people, almost to a man, would choose him for their governor." Mather invited nearly a quarter of the House of

# Notes to Chapter IV

Representatives to a conference at his home and successfully dispelled any "hazard of disorder and confusion and iniquity in our General Assembly by reason of three violent men [Cooke, Noyes, and Payne]." The deputies responded by voting Shute £800 in six months, more than Joseph Dudley had ever been paid for an entire year. Address of the Ministers of Christ, 30 May 1717, *CSP*, 29, #589; Benjamin Colman to Viscount Barrington, 5 June 1717, Colman Papers, MHS; Cotton Mather to Barrington, 4 November 1718, *MHSC*, lst. ser. 1: 105; Kenneth Silverman, ed., *Selected Letters of Cotton Mather* (Baton Rouge, 1971), p. 221; Cotton Mather, *Diary* (Boston, 1911–1912), 2: 382; *Journals of the House of Representatives of Massachusetts Bay*, (Boston, 1919–    ) 7: 160 (hereafter cited as *House Journals*).

13. Whitmore, *Civil List*, p. 136; Lucius Paige, *History of Cambridge* (Cambridge, 1879), p. 639; Remington and Belcher even insisted on being buried in adjoining tombs.

14. *House Journals*, 2: 7.

15. The documents relating to Bridger are scattered throughout the *CSP*. See especially his instructions of 19 December 1705, 22, #1517; his complaints that the laws could not be enforced, 23 July 1711, 26, #41; 31 August 1711, 26, #85; 2 February 1712, 26, #271. Joseph J. Malone, *Pine Trees and Politics* (Seattle, 1964), chs. 2–4.

16. Early in his career, Bridger had to require armed guards from Governor Dudley to protect himself. The inhabitants accused him of preventing them from cutting timber on their own lands and of permitting some people to cut trees reserved for the navy upon payment of a bribe. The situation was made difficult because Maine at the time consisted of an unintelligible patchwork of conflicting proprietary claims based on overlapping and vaguely defined Indian titles. Furthermore, the settlers claimed that all lands within townships were granted and hence exempt from Bridger's authority, whereas the surveyor insisted that only land belonging to individuals was immune. Dudley's anger with Bridger appears in his letter to the Board of Trade, 3 February 1710, *CSP*, 25, #107. Bridger described the convictions in a letter to the Earl of Dartmouth, 10 January 1713, *ibid.*, 27, #247. For his difficulties with the Vice-Admiralty Courts, see his letter to William Popple, 21 May 1711, *ibid.*, 25, #846; for the colonists' complaints and the surveyor's responses, see John Bridger to Board of Trade, 14 July 1718, *ibid.*, 30, #616, and Malone, *Pine Trees and Politics*, p. 71.

17. Malone, *Pine Trees and Politics*, esp. pp. 57, 79: *House Journals*, 1: 130, 222; 2: 43, 47, 108. Samuel Sewall, *Diary*, ed. M. Halsey Thomas, (New York, 1973), 2: 916; Samuel Shute to a Mr. Penhallow, 2 February 1719. Pepperrell Papers, MHS. For towns founded in Maine, see Charles E. Clark, *The Eastern Frontier: The Settlement of New England, 1610–1763* (New York, 1970), p. 122.

18. Figures in Table 10 are taken from Sewall, *Diary*, vol. 1, and W.H. Whitemore, ed., Boston Record Commissioners' *Reports*, vols. 8, 12, 14, 16, 18 (Boston, 1880–1902). (Hereafter cited as *Boston Records*.) Francis Foxcroft and Theophilius Frary are questionable. Foxcroft definitely favored Dudley in the early 1690s; his name appears on the list of sixty-one merchants in 1691, he was a non-resident representative in 1693, and he corresponded with imperial officials in favor of royal government. Frary was removed as commander of Castle William in 1701 by a council hostile to Dudley in favor of Elisha Hutchinson. Yet neither man was appoined a J.P. in 1702 and it would have been foolish for the group supporting Dudley to have run five or six candidates. G.B. Warden's analysis of Bostonian politics at this time in *Boston: 1689–1776* (Boston, 1970), pp. 51–59, is erroneous. He describes Byfield as a partisan of Cooke, and Belcher as a supporter of Dudley even though it is inconceivable a man of Belcher's importance—Commissary-General, one of the province's wealthiest merchants—would not have been appointed to some office in 1702 if he favored Dudley. Warden's interpretation of town politics as pitting "merchants" against "people" is puzzling: nearly all the main figures were merchants or men related to them with other sorts of wealth. John White is identified as pro-Dudley based on Thomas Hutchinson, *The History of the*

*Colony and Province of Massachusetts Bay* (Cambridge, 1936), 2: 188. All the Hutchinsons except William were prerogative men at this time: *ibid.*, 2: 188; Thomas Hutchinson, "Hutchinson in America," Egremont Manuscript #2664, 46, British Museum, (microfilm at MHS).

19. The number of voters decline to two or three hundred in the 1720s, given the absence of partisanship.

20. Thomas Lechmere to Richard Lechmere, 14 March 1719 and 4 May 1719 *MHSC*, 6th. ser. 6: 388. One cannot definitively say that the machine Cooke created was the Caucus, but this was the only name applied to Boston's local political organization. Cooke surely created the Caucus's immediate ancestor if not the club itself.

21. Cited in Warden, *Boston*, pp. 94–95.

22. Andrew M. Davis, *Colonial Currency Reprints* (Boston, 1910), 1: 115. My emphasis. The pamphlet, published in July 1720, is entitled *Reflections upon Reflections of More News from Robinson Crusoe's Island.* Dudley was one of the few lawyers in the province. Samuel Sewall also noted that "the people were under a great ferment" at this time; *Diary*, 2: 952.

23. A hint that the behavior of Cooke and his followers threatened to overthrow the government.

24. William Gordon, *The History of the Rise, Progress, and Establishment of the Independence of America* (London, 1780), 1: 105.

25. Peter Oliver, *The Origin and Progress of the American Rebellion* (Stanford, 1961), p. 25. See Clifford K. Shipton, *Biographical Sketches of Those Who Attended Harvard College* (Cambridge, 1873–    ), 4: 260–263 and 369–371 for Noyes and Cooke; and Oliver O. Roberts, *The History of the Ancient and Honorable Artillery Company* (Boston, 1854), 2: 260–262, 316–318, for all three. Warden asserts that many office holders in Boston during the 1720s "were not merchants, the economic leaders of Boston, nor even from well-established families." *Boston*, pp. 94–95. But the top leadership clearly came from this group.

26. John Colman to Benjamin Colman, 10 May 1724, and 18 May 1724, Colman Papers, MHS, wrote that Cooke, during his agency in England, drinks "very hard, and when the wine or rather the punch works, there is nobody or order of men escapes his censures." Colman also explained that Cooke once passed out in a tavern and injured his head. On another occasion he tried to pick someone's pocket as a prank.

27. Warden, *Boston*, p. 96; Cotton Mather, *Magnalia Christi Americana* (Boston, 1855, 1853), 1: 100. Lawsuits by Cooke, Noyes, and Payne tended to be for large amounts. The Dudleys and Samuel Shute, on the contrary, frequently sued inhabitants over small sums. Suffolk Court of Common Pleas, 1703: 78, 104, 108; 1706: 323; 1713: 185; 1714: 334; 1720: 223, 336, 338; New Court House, Boston.

28. Hutchinson, *History*, 2: 178.

29. Samuel Sewall notes that Thomas Fitch, who had been appointed a J.P. by Dudley, also received "many votes" in 1727. Letter to Cotton Mather, 25 April 1727, Sewall, *Letter Book*, vol. 2, MHSC, 6th. ser. 2, 224.

30. For a thorough discussion of instructions in provincial Massachusetts see Robert Dinkin, "Provincial Massachusetts: A Deferential or a Democratic Society" (Ph.D. diss., Columbia University, 1968), ch. 5, which supercedes Kenneth Colgrove, "New England Town Mandates," *CSMP*, 21 (1920), pp. 411–449.

31. Hutchinson, *History*, 2: 174.

32. *House Journals*, 2: 228–233; fragment from Samuel Sewall's *Diary*, *MHSP*, 2nd. ser. 6: 388. Several councillors who strongly supported Shute received lower totals than most of the others, although still enough to be elected: Edward Bromfield (67), Thomas

# Notes to Chapter IV

Palmer (70), Jonathan Belcher (64), and Paul Dudley (59), as against 103 for Nathaniel Byfield and 110 for John Clarke whom Shute vetoed.

33. Sewall, *Diary*, vol. 2, p. 953; *House Journals*, vol. 2, pp. 236, 245–247, 258–266.

34. *House Journals*, 2: 267–268, 328–329; 3: 63, 79, 126–128.

35. *Ibid.*, 2: 352.

36. *Ibid.*, 2: 129, 134, 205; Hutchinson, *History*, 2: 188, 204.

37. For a discussion of the pamphlets on Boston's incorporation, see Warden, *Boston*, pp. 73–79. Satirical tracts, such as Cotton Mather's *Political Fables* (1692) and theoretical treatises such as John Wise's *A Vindication of the Government of the New England Churches* (1717) were occasionally published as well.

38. Elisha Cooke, *Mr. Cooke's Just and Seasonable Vindications* (Boston, 1720), pp. 6, 8, 10, 16, 20, Evans, #2109. The following description of Cooke's attempt to reach an understanding with the governor appears in the Council's Executive Records, 8: 141: "Colonel Shute was out walking and Mr. Cooke, having only his nightshirt, cap, and slippers on, came up to the governor in the middle of the street and proposed calling a conference on the speaker question. The governor told Cooke he did not think himself upon a foot with him, at which point the doctor turned away and said he would take his own measures."

39. Cotton Mather, *News from Robinson Crusoe's Island* (Boston, 1720), 1: 7–10, Evans, #39730.

40. Davis, *Currency Reprints*, 2: 118, 134. All the relevant pamphlets except Cooke's and Mather's are in this collection.

41. *A&R*, 1, 2: 61, 189, 470; Felt, *Massachusetts Currency*, p. 73.

42. Davis, *Currency Reprints*, 2: 10, 113. For some lawsuits involving Colman, see Suffolk Court of Common Pleas, 1711, 9, 10, 11, 53, 63; 1712, 86, 126, 151; 1713, 268, 295; 1714, 6, 54, 55, 74, 78; 1720, 176; 1721, 268; 1721, 18; 1722; 202, 282.

43. *Ibid.*, 1: 355–356; 2: 140, 150–151.

44. *Ibid.*, 2: 68, 73, 76, 88–89, 234–238.

45. *Ibid.*, 1: 409; 2: 229, 234; John M. Murrin, review of town studies, *History and Theory*, 11 (1972), p. 250–251, estimates that civil suits equal to one-fifth the number of adult males in Suffolk County were annually filed at this time.

46. Davis, *Currency Reprints*, 1: 397; *A&R*, 2: 104, 149, 229, 231.

47. Hutchinson, *History*, 2: 217; Peter Oliver, *Origin and Progress of the American Rebellion*, p. 27.

48. The Board of Trade accused Shute of gross negligence and permissiveness in the performance of his duty. "A lover of ease and diversions," he had sent only four letters of about half a dozen lines each to the Board of Trade until he received a complaint in 1719 that he had not complied with his instruction to "transmit regularly" accounts of expenses and acts of the legislature. Whitehall asserted that is had only been told of John Bridger's troubles by the surveyor himself, and found "many things relating to your government printed in the public newspapers here of which you had given us no account." The Board especially rebuked Shute for consenting to a Massachusetts law which instituted a policy of reverse mercantilism by taxing goods from England at one percent. Hutchinson, *History*, 2: 218; Samuel Shute to Board of Trade, 29 September 1718, and 11 January 1719, *CSP*, 30, #700; 31, #1; Board of Trade to King George II, 24 April 1719, *ibid.*, #160; Board of Trade to Shute, 4 June 1719, *ibid.*, #217.

49. *House Journals*, 3: 130.

50. Elisha Cooke maintained that "the royal charter will sufficiently maintain such a procedure, . . . [the General Court] being fully empowered to make, ordain, and establish all manner of wholesome and reasonable orders that they shall judge to be for the good and welfare of this province." In a message of 20 December, the house accused the governor of not prosecuting the war as it had directed and of countenancing Walton's corruption. A Committee of War "would have a tendency to prevent like mischievous practices in the future," and merely required "some alteration" in the governor's power. *Ibid.*, pp. 146, 161; Samuel Shute to Board of Trade, 27 February 1717, and 23 July 1717, *CSP*, 29, #402, #666.

51. Hutchinson, *History*, 2: 219.

52. The house also reduced the governor's contingency fund to £500 for each recess of the General Court. Previously, all money left in the treasury when the representatives were not in session could be disposed of by the council and the executive. *House Journals*, 4: 176–215; 5: 7, 68ff., 214; 6: 9.

53. *House Journals*, 3: 195; 5: 233–280.

54. For the assault on the charters, see I.K. Steele, *The Politics of Colonial Policy: The Board of Trade in Colonial Administration, 1696–1720* (Oxford, 1968), ch. 8.

55. Jeremiah Dummer to [Edmund Quincy], 25 April 1721, Miscellaneous Bound Manuscripts, MHS; *House Journals*, 3: 44; 4: 63; 5: 233, 280. For a fine account of Dummer's activities, see Charles L. Sanford, "The Days of Jeremy Dummer," (Harvard University, Ph.D. diss., 1952).

56. James Henretta, *"Salutary Neglect": Colonial Administration Under the Duke of Newcastle* (Princeton, 1972).

57. Lord Townsend accused Cooke of trying to supplant the king with the House of Representatives, of playing a "bold game" and offering nothing but "trifles" in his defense, and of having forfeited the charter "over and over." Accounts of Cooke's agency are in the Belknap, Pepperrell, and Cushing Papers, MHS, and Elisha Cooke to ?, 5 July 1725, *Saltonstall Papers*, *MHSC*, 80: 352–355.

58. Cooke also received help from Samuel Shute, of all people. Shute's hostility was only directed at a handful of factious leaders in the house whom he blamed for misleading the deputies and town of Boston. While complaining about the assembly's intrusions on his powers, he simultaneously insisted that "the whole clergy of the province as well as the generality of the people are zealously affected to Your Majesty's person and government." New Englanders in England at the time praised the "zeal the governor shows for preserving our charter." Henry Newman to Samuel Penhallow, 3 June 1725, Belknap Papers, MHS; John Colman to Benjamin Colman, 27 March 1724, Miscellaneous Bound Manuscripts MHS.

59. See letters in the note immediately preceding and John Colman to Benjamin Colman, 10 March 1724, 26 March 1724, and 4 February 1726, Colman Papers, MHS. Cooke spent much time intriguing with Samuel Vetch in an effort to make the latter governor: see Vetch to King George, 22 January 1724, *CSP*, 24, #21 and Thomas Lechmere to John Winthrop, 23 May 1723, *MHSC*, 6th. ser. 6: 404.

60. Materials relating to the Explanatory Charter are in the *House Journals*, 7: 450ff; see also Massachusetts Archives, 20: 248–249. Many smaller towns rarely reelected representatives and such a large turnover was typical. Of the twenty men serving on five or more committees in the house, twelve favored the charter and seven opposed it; one did not vote. Only three voting yes and two no were not reelected.

61. See *The New England Courant*, 22 January 1726, and Albert C. Matthews, "The Acceptance of the Explanatory Charter," *PCSM* (1913), pp. 389–400. See Boston Public Library, Manuscript Collection, for the list of councillors. The list is dated

"about 1729" but the only year all the councillors listed served is 1726. One name was omitted, that of Elisha Cooke, whom Dummer had permitted to sit on the council since 1724.

62. *House Journals*, 7: 229; 8: *passim*, esp. pp. 140, 163. Dummer, like Shute before him, was rebuked by the Board of Trade for his leniency. Alured Popple to William Dummer, 26 June 1727, *CSP*, 25, #615. Dummer and the council favored Thomas Hutchinson, Sr.'s, scheme to provide a currency by importing gold and silver. For Hutchinson's project, see John Alford to Stephen Sewall, 15 May 1725, Curwen Papers, 4: 2, American Antiquarian Society, and Josiah Willard to Josiah Cotton, 7 March 1727, Curwen Papers, 3: 12. In 1717, one Massachusetts pound was worth £2.25 sterling; in 1723 the exchange ratio was 2.7:1; in 1727, 3.4:1. Davis, *Currency and Banking*, 1: 443.

63. See Patricia Bonomi, *A Factious People* (New York, 1971), pp. 111–124, for Burnet's career in New York.

64. Instructions to William Burnet [1727], *CSP*, 35, #849. Burnet formally requested forces on 31 March 1729, in letters to the Duke of Newcastle and the Board of Trade, *ibid.*, 36, #340, #341.

65. Burnet based his speeches on voluminous research in English law detailing how Parliament had consented to grant the king a salary for life. He argued that the king's loyal subjects in America should follow Parliament's example. The governor also cited examples from previous *House Journals* showing that because Shute's and Dummer's salaries were withheld until they had signed all of the assembly's acts, they had been reduced to either dependence or poverty. The house, for its part, stressed the power of the purse given to them in the charter. Since Parliament had voted the monarch a permanent salary voluntarily, any similar measure in Massachusetts should also be optional. *House Journals*, 8: 251–435, *passim*, 9: 1–81, *passim*.

66. To maintain himself while the debate went on, Burnet became the first governor to collect fees on clearance passes from vessels leaving Boston harbor and raised the other fees of his office to a level comparable to New York's. By these measures he obtained some £200 sterling. William Burnet to Board of Trade, 13 September 1729, *CSP* 36, #387; 30 September 1729, *ibid.*, #404; 23 January 1729, *ibid.*, #571; *House Journals*, 8: 362, 394, 435; 9: 73, 76, 86.

67. *House Journals*, 8: 251, 323, 337, 390; 9: 30, 50, 52. For a discussion of the house's efforts to raise money, see Robert Dinkin, "Massachusetts: A Democratic or a Deferential Society?," p. 135, and *Boston Records*, 8: 10; 9: 283. Burnet's back salary was denied his widow and children until Belcher and Wilkes were paid £3,000 as well. The council refused this bill until Belcher himself returned as governor. The nine other towns contributed the following sums: Newbury, £100; Gloucester, £50; Haverhill, £50; Plymouth, £50; Dedham, £40; Middleborough, £22; Duxbury, £16; Wenham, £12; Kingston, £10. Belcher's business correspondence with Wilkes is in Volume I of his Letter Books, MHS; for his political about-face, see *An Account of the Rise, Progress, and Consequences of the Two Late Schemes, Commonly called the Land Bank or Manufactory Scheme and the Silver Scheme* (Boston, 1744), in Andrew M. Davis, *Colonial Currency Reprints*(Boston, 1910-1911), 4: 238–249, esp. 333–334; and David Dunbar to Duke of Newcastle, 4 February 1730, *CSP*, 37, #49.

68. Councillor John Cushing linked the politicians opposed to Burnet with the disturbance:

> There are a great many worthy persons there (as well as those that think themselves so), but when men of a pretty good deal of money, a little wet, and a great deal of will set up for politicians and rule the roost, the world must needs turn topsy-turvy and nothing can stand before them. I don't wonder that public town-meetings do prosecute the methods agreed upon

in private clubs, where they become hot, and talk big and fast—all things would live but when the mobs get the clubs in their hands . . . when the people have once begun to knock one another in the head there will be no end of it.

[John Cushing] to ?, 22 August 1729, Miscellaneous Bound Manuscripts, MHS; Carl Bridenbaugh, *Cities in the Wilderness: The First Century of Urban Life in America, 1625–1742*, 2nd. ed., (New York, 1955), p. 383.

69. William Burnet to Board of Trade, 26 October 1729, *CSP*, 36, #429.

70. David Dunbar to Alured Popple, 5 June 1730, *ibid.*, 37, #274; Diary of Benjamin Walker, *CSMP*, 28: 243.

71. An anonymous letter to the Board of Trade insisted that the province "would much rather that the Parliament of England should revoke their charter than the assembly should pay the least regard to His Majesty's instructions, for if the charter does not make them independent of the crown it is not worth keeping." Agent Belcher encouraged this attitude: he wrote from London that "if we must be compelled to fix salaries, doubtless it must better be done by the supreme legislature than to do it ourselves: if our liberties must be lost, much better they should be taken, than we be in any manner accessory to our own ruin." David Dunbar to Alured Popple, 10 October 1729, *CSP*, 36, #1018; [John Cushing] to ?, 8 August 1729, Miscellaneous Bound Manuscripts; ? to Board of Trade [1729], *CSP*, 1729, Davis, *Reprints*, 3: 333–334.

72. Agents' memorial to the king, 1729, *CSP*, 36, #921; Duke of Newcastle to William Burnet, 26 May 1729, *ibid.*, #792, #793; Jeremiah Dummer to Newcastle, 7 October 1729, *ibid.*, #925; Board of Trade to Newcastle, 8 October 1729, *ibid.*, #927; Order of Privy Council, 23 October 1729, *ibid.*, #949.

73. William Dummer to Duke of Newcastle, 15 September 1729, *ibid.*, #904; Benjamin Prescott to John Chandler, 23 June 1729, Ms.C. 2041, New England Historic Genealogical Society. Prescott, representative from Groton, congratulated Chandler, deputy from Woodstock, on his unanimous election to the council despite his known friendship for Burnet. Prescott asked Chandler to "remove the ill opinion His Excellency may have of me," as he voted for the temporary salary.

# V

# PROCRASTINATION
# 1730 - 1741

*I*N Jonathan Belcher, Massachusetts acquired a governor wise in
the ways of British and colonial politics. He had traveled twice to
England on political business. The first time he helped make Samuel
Shute governor. On his second trip, he persuaded the Duke of
Newcastle to revoke William Burnet's most objectionable instructions.
In Massachusetts he had acquired a reputation for trimming his sails
to catch the wind, served repeatedly on the council, and defended
public bills of credit. Belcher was a politican above all else: he wanted
to be Governor of Massachusetts, and stopped at nothing in his efforts
to attain and then retain that post. He flattered his wealthy and
powerful English connections in hundreds of letters. He vehemently
denounced and plotted against his enemies in the province. Most of
all, he compromised, usually in devious ways, the issues that had undone his predecessors. Had not his opponents proven equally
resourceful, he might well have governed Massachusetts for far longer
than twelve years.[1]

Belcher's administration went through three phases. Between 1730
and 1735 he resolved the old business of the governor's salary, the
Maine frontier, and the supply of the treasury. He thereby laid potential groundwork for long-term, peacetime political harmony. He encountered little opposition until 1739. But when Britain tried to force
the province to reduce its money supply, Belcher's personal enemies

used a new Land Bank crisis to overthrow him. Despite his earlier achievements, Belcher could not avoid the fate of every other peacetime governor. His administration ended in turmoil when he could no longer dodge the perennial issues of currency inflation and imperial regulation. By trying to keep on good terms with the province and the administration, he lost the respect of both.

### NEUTRALIZING THE CAUCUS: 1730–1735

Belcher applied for the governorship a few hours after news of Burnet's death reached England. He persuaded the Duke of Newcastle and the Board of Trade that the disputes with Burnet had "become almost entirely personal" and that he could convince the assembly to grant a fixed salary. His Grace agreed, conveniently ignoring Belcher's past letters urging Massachusetts to continued defiance. Belcher's informal influence greatly outweighed his known opposition to the very policies he had to implement. As he wrote Benjamin Colman, the king's remembrance of his visit to Germany nearly thirty years earlier played a crucial role in securing the appointment.[2]

The imperial administration saddled Belcher with rigid instructions exceeding even Burnet's. In addition to obtaining a guaranteed £1,000 per year, he had to require that the governor and council alone disburse money in the treasury. Belcher barely managed to talk the Board of Trade out of instantly abolishing all New England bills of credit! Instead, it required liquidation by 1741. After that, Massachusetts could issue only £30,000 annually to cover routine government expenses. Even that had to be redeemed the following year. The Board of Trade took Belcher at his word that the disputes with Burnet were "personal." If for some reason he could not obtain total compliance "immediately," he had to return to England. Then the province's charter would be brought before Parliament.[3]

Whether Belcher really expected to accomplish all this is questionable. Surveyor-General David Dunbar noted that everybody in Massachusetts considered his demand for a fixed salary mere dissimulation. Dunbar gave most credence to a report that Belcher intended to "spin out three years in his government by promising that next year's assembly will comply."[4] Dunbar underestimated the number of years by nine.

When Belcher arrived in Massachusetts, respect for royal authority was very low. Several leading members of the court faction—including Paul Dudley, Jonathan Remington, John Stoddard, Thomas Fitch, and Addington Davenport—failed to be reelected to the council in 1729 and 1730.[5] But Belcher developed a simple method for accomplishing the impossible. On every major issue, he worked openly (when possible) or covertly to insure a favorable outcome for the province. He opposed Dunbar's efforts to survey the woods and settle a colony of Scotch–Irish in Maine; he thwarted attempts to enforce the Acts of Trade; acting as Governor of New Hampshire, he did everything in his power to prevent that province from defending itself in a boundary dispute with Massachusetts; he permitted the house to elect the attorney general beginning in 1733; he temporized on his instruction to reduce the supply of paper money; and he achieved a satisfactory compromise on the question of a fixed salary.

Belcher's unscrupulous but practical program appeared most strikingly in his innovative patronage policy. He faced a problem here. His agency had been supported by the popular faction and its leaders in the Boston Caucus. But how could he appoint these men to office and leave out those who supported royal instructions? He avoided the dilemma by choosing members of both factions. Elisha Cooke, Nathaniel Byfield, and William Brattle of Cambridge—who had been removed as a justice of the peace by Governor Burnet—became justices. But the Court of Common Pleas for Suffolk County, which only had four members, proved an obstacle. Most politically influential people, several of whom aspired to this body, lived in that county. Since the Belchers had been feuding with the Dudleys over some land in Milton, the governor removed William Dudley, a councillor and former Speaker of the House, and Edward Hutchinson to make room for Elisha Cooke and old Nathaniel Byfield. (Byfield had been reappointed judge of vice-admiralty in 1728.) Belcher also permitted Caucus members Ezekiel Lewis, Thomas Cushing, and William Clarke to sit on the council. Cooke himself, however, had learned his lesson. He preferred to stay in the house where he could exercise more power.[6]

But Belcher's appointments created problems for Cooke in the Boston Town Meeting. Aware of the governor's efforts to implement policies they mutually supported, Cooke at first joined his camp. But he thereby lost favor in the Caucus because Belcher's formal speeches to the General Court manifested a much harder line—as they were obliged to for British consumption—than his informal negotiations with the Duke of Newcastle. Cooke's preferment gave the appearance that he had sold out. The election returns of 1732 through 1737 reveal that though he continued to dominate Boston politics, the court faction contested more elections. Two or three times as many voters appeared as in the 1720s. It frequently took a second or even a third ballot to elect the town's fourth representative.[7]

The unstable nature of the Caucus's influence in the 1730s appeared in the widely fluctuating totals for Cooke and Samuel Welles. At first, Welles outpolled Cooke and had begun to replace him as the primary author of the house's belligerent replies to the governor's speeches.[8] But after his poor showing in 1732, Cooke reversed his policy of supporting Belcher. He then drafted an appeal to the House of Commons protesting the governor's instructions for the supply of the treasury. Welles, however, considered this move extremely dangerous, since it requested the Commons to rebuke the king for issuing instructions the province disliked. Welles's prudence cost him votes in 1733.[9] The following year, after the Commons condemned the house instead of supporting it as Cooke had predicted, both Cooke and Welles barely squeezed into office.[10] Belcher's double game had forced the Caucus to be just as flexible, with disastrous results.

The Cooke–Welles quarrel and Cooke's death in 1737 revolutionized Boston town politics. Except for 1726 and 1727, the inhabitants had chosen only one supporter of the prerogative faction as town representative from 1719 to 1736. Habijah Savage, appointed a justice of the peace by Burnet, squeezed into office in 1732 by a margin of 9 votes out of 655. But in 1737, twenty-six-year-old Thomas Hutchinson managed to win election on the third ballot. Hutchinson, who would shape provincial politics for three decades, staunchly favored the prerogative faction. In 1738, three of his associates joined him. Until the 1760s, court and country factions closely contested Bostonian elections.[11]

The Caucus, which had functioned with remarkable success in opposing the governor, could not survive a governor who agreed with its policies. To support him would compromise the leaders, who would be reduced to minions of the executive. But how could an issue be found to oppose him? One bizarre solution to this dilemma appeared in 1733 when Cooke tried to replace Belcher with arch-imperialist Surveyor-General David Dunbar—while simultaneously instigating the provocative address to the House of Commons that insisted on the assembly's right to supervise appropriations. Although Belcher surely had no intention of breaking up the Caucus, his effort to conciliate it insured that it had to sacrifice either its power or its principles. For over twenty years thereafter it functioned ineffectively, for it had lost both.

The inability of the Caucus to respond successfully to Boston's increasing economic problems also undermined its influence. Taxes rose, and trade and inhabitants departed beginning in the 1730s. The Bostonians turned increasingly to prerogative men such as Hutchinson and Andrew Oliver. To be sure, the inhabitants did not approve of their anti-democratic proclivities. They sought to abolish the Town Meeting in favor of a self-selecting corporation, and they lived much of the time in the surrounding countryside as aspiring country squires. But they compensated with administrative competence and plans to aid the troubled economy. They proposed town markets to relieve congestion, noise, and overpricing, and they tried to introduce manufacturing to employ increasing numbers of poor people. Following Cooke's death the ineptitude of Caucus politicians such as James Allen and John Tyng helped the court faction to compete on an equal basis with the opposition.[12] Belcher's unintentional weakening of the Caucus thus helped to launch the court politicians who guided Massachusetts' destinies until the Revolution deposed them.

## PLACATING THE ASSEMBLY: 1730–1735

Belcher handled the house of representatives as astutely as the Caucus. But it took several years to settle the deputies. The governor could not violate his instructions too blatantly or he might well have been recalled.

Early in his administration, Belcher pretended he wanted the fixed salary. Unlike Burnet, who argued that as the king's representative he could press any instructions he chose, the new executive admitted that the province was well within its rights resisting this edict. But he warned that the practical consequences of asserting them would be disastrous. Belcher explained to the legislature that "I did everything in my power consistent with honor and justice for preserving and lengthening the peace of this province." Massachusetts had no alternative except capitulation.[13]

Belcher's public about-face provoked an immediate reaction. Some people wanted to "spit in his face" and the "mob threatened to pull down the houses of any of the representatives" voting the fixed salary. The Caucus termed Belcher's acceptance of his appointment a betrayal, and Dunbar claimed that many men "of the first rank" were sufficiently angered to trade the instruction for a new governor.[14]

Belcher was confident he could weather the storm. He dissimulated freely to the Board of Trade. On 2 October 1730 he promised a "dutiful and reasonable return" within ten days even if the house did not "come up to the terms" of the instructions. But the deputies treated him exactly like Burnet. They voted large sums of money with no hint that they would be made perpetual. Within three weeks of his arrival, the deputies offered Belcher £3,000 plus £1,500 compensation for his agency. He could not understand their recalcitrance, and expostulated that "you are differing in trifles, for you have long ago come up to the quantity the king requires." To no avail he dissolved the General Court and ordered new elections.[15]

Belcher used verbal belligerency, however, as a ploy. All along he tried to persuade Newcastle and the Board of Trade to modify their instruction. He refused to return home in 1731 as ordered if he failed. He argued his way out of that by insisting that if *he* could not obtain a permanent grant, no one could.[16] Persuaded by Newcastle and Walpole, the Board fell right in with Belcher's plot. Beginning in 1731, it allowed him to accept an annual support if it did not serve as a precedent. Theoretically, Belcher still had to enforce his instruction, but merely to save face. In June 1735, when he once again asked the Board of Trade for permission to accept an annual salary, it reversed its stand of over thirty years and recommended that "the said article of the governor's instruction should be repealed, because we apprehend it cannot be supported by any construction of the clauses in the charter granted to Massachusetts Bay!"[17] It thereby accepted an interpretation put forth by Elisha Cooke and repudiated the directions that had made life miserable for every governor since Joseph Dudley.

To be sure, the Board added that it expected the assembly to pay the governor at least £1,000 sterling annually. But Belcher only obtained £3,000 in paper currency, no more than £600 sterling, for the rest of his administration. His successor William Shirley also frequently failed to obtain the required sum. The value of Massachusetts' money remained sufficiently debatable until the province adopted a specie currency in 1750 that the salary could fall short of the required amount. Still, thanks to Belcher's machinations, the province secured an acceptable compromise that permitted it to regulate the wages of each governor. The house no longer waited until the governor signed its acts and resolves at the end of each session, but voted his grant when it first met each May session. The salary was used no longer to intimidate the executive to approve laws with which he disagreed.[18]

On the other hand, the governor and council won an unconditional victory on supplying the treasury. In April 1731, after the coffers had been nearly empty for six months, the house, "with the greatest reluctance," voted £17,000 to be disbursed at the direction of the executive and upper house. But then resistance hardened and the province had no money until November 1733. After two years, Belcher complained that soon "there will be no government at all."[19]

Unlike the salary issue, the supply of the treasury not only pitted Massachusetts against Britain, but also set the house against the council.[20] This matter, too, might have been compromised to the assembly's satisfaction. But to convince his adherents that he had not sold out to Belcher, in June 1732 Elisha Cooke persuaded the assembly to appeal to the House of Commons. The deputies pleaded that "a compliance with His Majesty's royal instruction will endanger if not wholly subvert and destroy the necessary essentials of government; vizt: the power of legislation or divest the General Court of a power of making reasonable and wholesome laws."[21] Never before had Massachusetts so boldly denied the king's right to instruct the governor.

Instead of vindicating the house, as Cooke had predicted, the Commons turned the matter over to the Privy Council. The king's advisors replied that Massachusetts had manifested "great undutifulness to the crown," had attempted to "assume to themselves all the executive power of government," and had revealed "a determined tendency to throw off their dependence on Great Britain, which is so necessary to be maintained for their own preservation." Immediately after the reply arrived in October 1733, the frightened deputies, who had refused to enact the instruction by a vote of fifty-six to one the previous year, approved it fifty-five to twenty-five. As with the Explanatory Charter, the General Court respected an extraordinary exercise of royal authority more than routine instructions to governors.[22]

With some help from the overzealous Cooke, Belcher settled the two major constitutional issues he inherited. He experienced little further trouble until 1739.[23] Changing leadership in the General Court during Belcher's administration solidified the shift from hostility to cooperation. Between 1730 to 1733, the seven or eight most active members of the court, with the exception of John Chandler of Woodstock, either belonged to the Caucus or were allied with them—Benjamin Lynde, Jr. of Salem; Edward Shove of Dighton; and William Brattle. When Welles and Brattle changed sides in 1734, the situation reversed itself until 1739. Although Boston's Cooke and Thomas Cushing, Jr., continued to be extremely active, John Stoddard of Northampton, John Choate of Ipswich, Robert Hale of Beverly, Samuel Danforth of Cambridge, Benjamin Prescott of Groton, and Richard Saltonstall of Haverhill joined Chandler. In 1737 and 1738, Boston itself began to elect prerogative men. In 1738, Belcher legitimately boasted that "the heats and broils they were in before my arrival seem at present to be pretty well laid."[24]

# Procrastination

Despite his successes, Belcher had brushed aside, rather than solved, two problems. First, he owed his good relations with the Massachusetts assembly to compromising royal power. As a result, Belcher had to defend himself continually for not supporting the province's admiralty and customs officers. He alienated the very officials who counted on the executive for support. Second, he still had to retire £375,000 in paper money by 1741.[25] His halfhearted efforts in that direction gave rise to the Land Bank debate. Belcher thus disposed of one sort of opposition only to confront another.

Belcher's most persistent opponent, David Dunbar, was already on the scene when the governor arrived. As Surveyor-General of the King's Woods, he had to enforce John Bridger's hopeless instructions to preserve the forests. To add to his unpopularity, he also had to settle a colony of Scotch–Irishmen in a region within the District of Maine. It would be named Georgia, after King George II, and then be detached from Massachusetts.[26]

The proposed colony raised a storm in Massachusetts. A crowd formed in Boston in 1729 to prevent the Scotch-Irish from landing. The new colony would instantly confiscate much property claimed by the inhabitants. People of all classes used land speculation as a road to wealth or a means to provide inheritances for their children. As Jonathan Peagrum, Surveyor of His Majesty's Customs, reported in 1736: "they are not much inclined to learn manufacturing. But their chief aim is to procure tracts of land, though there is no use arising from their possession, then to sell them at high prices to persons to settle." Dunbar reported that his settlements enraged the Massachusetts speculators by threatening to depreciate their carefully acquired holdings.[27]

Dunbar encountered opposition from both Belcher and the Caucus. He complained that the governor actually planned to destory Fort Frederick, the principal site of the new colony, and periodically accused him of plotting with the Indians to that end.[28] Numerous people in Massachusetts presented Dunbar with deeds claiming ownership of his land and filed hundreds of lawsuits against him for damaging their property. His enemies included Elisha Cooke, Nathaniel Byfield—before whom Dunbar had to obtain convictions in the Vice-Admiralty Court—and one Samuel Waldo, a Boston merchant in partnership with Cooke.[29]

By supporting Cooke and Waldo, Belcher temporarily gained Cooke's friendship at the beginning of his administration. He wrote home that Dunbar had "threatened to murder the king's subjects and to enter upon them with fire and faggot" and to "tie people to trees and whip them and burn the fruits of their honest labor." In short, Dunbar generally treated the settlers "like French slaves."[30]

In 1730 Cooke and his associates sent Samuel Waldo to England to have Dunbar and his Irishmen removed. First, Waldo obtained an order forbidding Dunbar to proceed with the settlement while the case was being disputed. In 1734, the Privy Council finally ruled that the lands in fact belonged to Massachusetts and that Dunbar had no business being there.[31] Having at last viewed the governor's salary from Elisha Cooke's angle, Britain also accepted his interpretation of property rights in Maine. But with typical inconsistency, the Privy Council had appointed Dunbar Lieutenant-Governor of New Hampshire three years earlier to show the crown's resentment at Belcher's opposition to the new colony.[32] Dunbar remained a thorn in Belcher's and Massachusetts' side when he assumed his new post.

The two men next quarrelled bitterly over the New Hampshire–Massachusetts boundary. Belcher did everything in his power to prevent New Hampshire from winning its case, including dissolving its assembly whenever it deigned to consider the matter. He thought New Hampshire too insignificant to be a separate province and lobbied to annex it to Massachusetts.[33] Dunbar, on the contrary, supported New Hampshire's efforts to have its own governor, assuming he would be a likely candidate. When the two provinces failed to compromise, a royal commission consisting of councillors from New York, Rhode Island, and Connecticut and the contending parties met in 1737. Since the other provinces also were engaged in boundary disputes with Massachusetts, the decision went entirely in favor of New Hampshire. The smaller province's triumphant assembly promptly submitted a memorial to the crown condemning Belcher's partiality. Dunbar sailed for England to oust his rival. The Massachusetts representatives, who had even rebuilt the fort at Pemaquid to prove their interest in protecting the disputed region—something Belcher boasted no other governor had obtained for forty years—responded with an address vindicating the governor.[34]

Thus, Dunbar's activities helped Belcher ingratiate himself with the assembly and people of Massachusetts. But they also gave Elisha

Cooke and Samuel Waldo an excuse to attack the governor in 1733, and an opportunity to recover their influence in the assembly. As the agent for the royal mast contractor Ralph Gulston, Waldo shared with Dunbar an interest in protecting the woods from spoilage through private lumbering.[35] He could easily show that Belcher had failed to protect Dunbar, especially after 1734 when a crowd assaulted him near Exeter, New Hampshire. With Dunbar obliged to abandon Georgia, Waldo himself began to care for the Irish in Maine. Belcher warned him against trespassing on lands guaranteed to the Penobscot Indians. Waldo in turn accused Belcher of instigating native attacks on his settlement.[36]

However, Dunbar was not fated to replace Belcher. That honor went to William Shirley, an impoverished English lawyer. Shirley had arrived in Massachusetts in 1731 supported only by his wits and an intelligent wife related to the Duke of Newcastle. Belcher at first praised Shirley as "an ingenious, sober, modest gentleman, and rather too much of the latter for one of his profession." The governor appointed him Advocate-General of the Vice-Admiralty Court. Personally ambitious and angered by Belcher's acquiesence in illegal trade, Shirley soon turned against the former governor.[37] In 1738, Shirley and Samuel Waldo consummated the alliance that ousted Belcher. Shirley had the connections but not the money to obtain the governorship; Waldo and his supporters—including wealthy Boston merchants such as the Faneuils, Allens, and Christopher Kilby—had nearly infinite financial resources but no personal ties with men like Newcastle and Walpole. Shirley and Waldo agreed to a deal where the former would be appointed governor and use his influence to make the latter his lieutenant. Shirley said he did not plan to stay in office long. He would leave within three or four years, after "establishing a good interest," since "except upon first coming into the government," he could not expect "above £500 sterling annually." Shirley thus led Waldo to believe that he would govern only briefly and then turn over the chair.[38] Aided by Mrs. Shirley, Waldo obtained Newcastle's promise that Shirley would be appointed if Belcher were removed.[39] But Newcastle gave no sign that Belcher's days were numbered.

Belcher's enemies fabricated, or as Shirley put it, "with the help of new evidence worked up," all sorts of complaints against him. They accused him of supporting an inhabitant of Maine, Charles Frost, in his appeal against Deputy-Surveyor Charles Leighton over the seizure of some logs. Belcher's alleged hostility to the Church of England and partiality to Quakers and Baptists did not go unnoticed, nor did his laxity in enforcing the Acts of Trade. Shirley and his coconspirators also unjustly accused Belcher of doing nothing to raise volunteers for an expedition to the West Indies when the War of Jenkins' Ear broke out with Spain in 1739.[40]

Belcher, however, was a formidable antagonist. He used his son Jonathan Jr., his brother-in-law Richard Partridge, and province agent Francis Wilkes as personal representatives in Britain. He himself deluged Newcastle, Walpole, First Lord of the Admiralty Sir Charles Wager, Clerk of the Privy Council Jonathan Sharpe, and prominent dissenting religious figures with accounts of his successful administration and treacherous enemies. Shirley complained to Waldo that "although I doubt not of his [Newcastle's] promise in case Belcher is out, yet I am afraid he is not very willing that he should go out."[41]

Yet patronage and intrigue neither ousted nor preserved Belcher. As Thomas Hutchinson (in England from 1740 to 1742 as a triple agent to have the Land Bank outlawed, to have Belcher retained as governor, and to have the disputed New Hampshire lands returned to Massachusetts) noted: "I had it from the Lord President's [of the Board of Trade] own mouth that Belcher's security for some time had been his steady conduct in the affair of money."[42] Without the Land Bank crisis Belcher might well have governed Massachusetts for the rest of his life.

### THE LAND BANK: 1739–1741

Belcher could not temporize as successfully on currency as he had on other issues. He did his best, though. Instructed in 1730 to retire £335,000 of outstanding notes by 1741, he permitted the legislature to finance expenditures so the sum still stood at £326,000 in 1740. Much of Rhode Island's and Connecticut's paper circulated in the Bay Colony as well. Between them, the two colonies increased their circulating medium by some £400,000 in the 1730s. Massachusetts' merchants also issued £110,000 in private notes in 1734 (reduced to £76,000 in 1736 and £44,000 in 1740). Faced with Parliamentary liquidation of its official bills, Massachusetts prepared by using several substitutes. As one pamphlet praising Rhode Island's obliging emissions commented: "hungry persons will be tempted to eat trash, if they can't get wholesome food."[43]

Belcher and the General Court sought to solve the currency problem using public bills of credit. They obtained dispensations from the Board of Trade to issue more than £30,000 annually because that sum could not meet government expenses. The governor remonstrated that "to tell the people the government must be supported and the charge of it paid without letting them have wherewithal to do it, I could really expect no other answer from the assembly but that I was an Egyptian taskmaster and required them to make bricks without straw."[44]

Belcher also persuaded the house to adopt a currency scheme proposed by Thomas Hutchinson, Jr., and Sr., in 1737. The province printed a new sort of bills, called "new tenor" at the time but subsequently known as "middle tenor" to distinguish them from a third type of bills issued in 1742. Worth three times old tenor bills of the same denomination, Massachusetts loaned them to persons who promised repayment in silver and gold at 6s. 8d. per ounce, rather than the going rate of 27s. Up to £60,000 could be subscribed. Belcher praised the law as the "best of its kind" ever passed. It corrected "the errors of bills made for above twenty years past," and would soon bring Massachusetts money within thirty percent of sterling. The Hutchinsons personally subscribed £6,000 of the initial issue of £32,000, confirming the younger Thomas's pledge to "engage for as large a sum as my estate and circumstances will admit of." But the plan failed. Since the bills could only be redeemed in silver after ten years, people hoarded them.[45]

Even the Board of Trade and British merchants—who, as the Reverend Benjamin Colman complained, "are a legislature for us"— sought to relax the £30,000 instruction, indicating it was only a threat to induce Massachusetts to halt its depreciation.[46] In October 1739, Belcher received a new set of instructions permitting increased sums of money. They had to be redeemed at three, six, and ten year intervals at the fixed value of 6s. 8d. per ounce of silver.[47] Although the house rejected this proposal (its practical effect would have been similar to Hutchinson's scheme), it illustrated that all parties were striving for a solution. As the younger Thomas Hutchinson wrote from England in 1741, "it is not unlikely that the instruction to the governor will be relaxed. What they want here is some proposals for bills that will keep up their value."[48] But while the parties were converging, they did not reach consensus in time.

When reforming the public bills came to naught, private persons took matters into their own hands. The first attempt, the Merchants' Notes of 1734, failed for the same reason as the middle tenor bills. Although redeemable in specie, possessors had to wait five years, which guaranteed hoarding. The General Court stopped issuance of these bills after £110,000 had been placed in circulation. Belcher predicted that they "bid fair to ruin this country," since they merely added another currency to the variety in existence.[49]

But Belcher did not dislike the notion of a private bank *per se*. In 1737 John Colman sounded him out on the possibility of reviving a Land Bank. Belcher recommended it to the Board of Trade the following year, although qualifying his recommendation for the same reason he had opposed the Merchants' Notes: "provided such a one can be projected as would practically maintain the value from time to time of the bills that go from it."[50]

Arguments about Massachusetts' money supply came to a head in 1739. For the first time the assembly refused to supply the treasury at all rather than reduce the supply of bills. On 28 June, the deputies advertised for "any scheme or proposal from any persons whatsoever for the furnishing of a medium of trade," to be submitted to a committee during the recess of the court.[51] Two projects appeared. In December, John Colman proposed a Land Bank again. The directors would loan £150,000 in bills at three percent interest to anyone who mortgaged land or property to guarantee repayment in bank bills or commodities in twenty annual installments. The Bank received support throughout the province, from husbandmen and traders as well as twelve Boston merchants who had favored the Merchants Notes. Eventually 1,253 people subscribed. Early in 1740, Edward Hutchinson and about 106 merchants, mostly from Boston, advanced a rival Silver Bank. They planned to issue bills in the course of their commercial transactions redeemable in silver after fifteen years.[52]

Both the Land and Silver banks developed elegant theoretical defenses. Hugh Vans stood at the head of the Land Bankers. Like his predecessor and colleague John Colman, he was a merchant in constant legal and financial trouble—he went bankrupt at the height of the French and Indian War. Vans first introduced the economic writings of John Locke into a Massachusetts political debate. He maintained that labor and its fruits constituted the sole source of exchange value. All currencies—gold, silver, paper, or whatever—derived their worth from common consent, "which can give a comparative, commutative value to things that had little or none before." A "natural or market pound" determined the value of each nation's money. It varied with the quantity of money in existence relative to the amount of goods, services, and trade. The nominal number of bills in circulation had nothing to do with the depreciation of Massachusetts' notes, which Vans attributed to "the [declining] trading circumstances of the community and wholly influenced by them." Too little, not too much money circulated. Massachusetts once had enjoyed £90,000 *sterling* whereas the bills outstanding only amounted to £45,000. The word sterling is the key: precisely because money had lost so much of

its value, Massachusetts needed more to meet its trading requirements. Only paper based on landed security sufficed, since a
silver currency would simply be shipped overseas to pay for imports.[53]

The Silver Bankers disagreed. Thomas Hutchinson, future governor
of the province, first entered politics as a champion of the silver interest. Dr. William Douglass, a Scottish physician who had opposed
Cotton Mather on the smallpox inoculation in 1721, and later became
a principal critic of Governor Shirley's military expeditions, proved
even more vocal. Unlike Vans, they insisted that silver and gold had
instrinsic value and that the large quantity of bills depreciated them.
Hutchinson maintained that "the universal trading part of the world,
as one tacit confederacy have fallen into some general rules which by
custom of merchants are become as fundamental: one of these is a
silver medium of trade."[54]

During the currency debate, the Land Bankers and their supporters
declared American independence of European economic theory.
"General" customs and "universal" usage did not bind America, as the
Silver Bankers insisted. Adopting Lockean arguments, Vans declared
that the only true standard of value came from the consent of each
community. These arguments would be transferred from the
monetary to the political plane thirty years later.

At the same time, Hutchinson and Douglass decried the extravagance of the common people. They reiterated Paul Dudley's and
Edward Wigglesworth's old arguments that idleness, debt, and over-
consumption lay at the heart of Massachusetts' difficulties. Douglass
remarked that "Boston never was more extravagant and gay than at
present, but never was more in debt," while "the husbandmen in the
country spend many idle days in their rum taverns."[55] Massachusetts'
false prosperity depended on exploiting the Bostonian and European
merchants who supplied it with goods.

The Land Bankers, however, attributed whatever prosperity remained in Massachusetts to its very use of paper money. They argued
that if paper so injured the merchants, why did they not only continue
to trade, but grow wealthy to boot? As the anonymous author of "A
Modest Apology for Paper Money" boasted:[56]

> Let us compare the present condition of this province with
> what it was thirty years ago. Tell the new towns and
> parishes; observe the buildings, the furniture, the habit and
> diet of the people in general. . . . In my opinion we owe
> more to paper money than any people on earth except the
> Dutch.

In this debate too, the germ of a future revolutionary controversy
appeared. Like some future loyalists, the Silver Bankers regarded

America as the spoiled brat of the world, living off the bounty of Europe and the competence of a select merchant class. But the Land Bankers insisted that America's very uniqueness and rejection of European values accounted for its remarkable growth.

These arguments initially came to little. During its final session, the assembly elected in 1739 "strictly forbade" both banks to issue any bills until a new house met in May. At the same time, the deputies gave qualified support to the silver scheme, terming it "serviceable, unless a better medium of commerce may be found." But they condemned the Land Bank notes. They were based "upon a slender foundation," insuring that "the circulation of them among the people of this province may have a great tendency to depreciate the bills of credit already circulating."[57]

The house of representatives had taken its cue from Governor Belcher, who first opposed both schemes unequivocally. On 14 April 1740, he informed the Board of Trade that these "bubbles" would cost British creditors "perhaps ten shillings in the pound of their just debts," and recommended "an Act of Parliament forbidding on severe penalties the government and all private companies from pressing to such extreme expedients."[58] However, Belcher soon changed his mind about the Silver Bank when its directors agreed to make their bills payable in silver immediately on demand. He then wrote that "these bills not only do honor to the government, but [are] of service to the people as a medium in commerce, for they are truly and really equal to silver and gold." There would be no need to hoard them, which had been the downfall of previous silver schemes. But the "iniquitous" Land Bank bills had no fixed value and left the ratio at which they could be exchanged for commodities "*ad libitum* to the directors." People might mortage their entire estates to obtain the bills and then find themselves unable to pay them back if the directors chose to be arbitrary. In addition, the Bank's charter did not limit the quantity of bills the directors could issue.[59]

The province disagreed with Belcher. In 1740, the new assembly refused to outlaw the Land Bank by a vote of fifty-nine to thirty-seven. The governor nevertheless persuaded the council to issue a proclamation warning the people that the notes "tended to defraud men of their substance, and to disturb the peace and good order of the people." The house retaliated by voting forty-two to twenty-eight on 21 January 1741, to investigate and report on the governor's and council's proclamation.[60] Belcher prorogued the assembly before the committee could report. Between November 1740 and April 1741, he also dismissed sixteen justices of the peace and one judge of the Inferior Courts (George Leonard) for supporting the Bank. In addition, he urged judges to prohibit Land Bankers and their attorneys from appearing before the provincial courts.[61]

Belcher's measures provoked an equally extreme response from the Land Bankers in the 1741 elections to the General Court. The Bank acted as a province-wide political lobby to elect sympathetic delegates. A hard money man like William Douglass regarded this electioneering as "imperium in imperio," an effort to establish an unconstitutional political body, but his arguments had little effect.[62] Of the forty-three men who opposed the Land Bank or an investigation of the council's proclamation, only eleven retained their seats, whereas thirty-three of the sixty-three who favored it did so. Unknowns replaced house leaders such as Thomas Lee and Benjamin Brown of Salem. Even prestigious John Chandler of Worcester went down to defeat. He had voted in favor of the Land Bank, but he did not subscribe, and he was a close friend of Governor Belcher.[63] Only the roll calls after 1765 met with such a profound popular reaction.

The "Land Bank House" proceeded to give Belcher a taste of his own medicine, and removed thirteen councillors who agreed with him. When he refused to approve their replacements the council's membership remained for a year at fifteen instead of the statutory twenty-eight. Belcher's conduct inspired the Bankers to threaten a march on Boston to force their opponents to accept the Bank notes.[64] But then word arrived that William Shirley had replaced Belcher; he assumed the chair on 17 August 1741. Belcher's enemies in England had played their ultimate card. They had somehow persuaded his brother-in-law, Richard Partridge, a "person devoted entirely to his interest," to speak in favor of the Land Bank.[65] Despite his opposition to the Bank, Belcher was actually removed for supporting it!

Although it engendered a virulent controversy at the time, the Land Bank produced no lasting political divisions. By the elections of May 1742, little factional strife remained in the province. This harmony owed much to Governor Shirley, who managed both to disband the Bank and to solve in short order the seemingly impossible dilemma of liquidity or depreciation. But he needed the cooperation of the Land Bankers themselves, who supported him because he ingeniously united most of the Bankers with their opponents by minimizing the hardship when Parliament outlawed the Bank.

Commitment to the Bank proved less absolute than support for any viable currency. Before Belcher polarized the province with his harsh reaction, currency had created, the governor wrote, "*many* parties and factions."[66] For instance, the 1739 assembly refused fifty-three to nineteen to redeem any more province bills before 1742,[67] which might suggest at first glance that most members of the assembly were inflationists and hence Land Bankers. But this very house passed the restraining order against the Bank. Of the fifty-three men voting against redemption in 1739, thirty-one were reelected and voted on the Land Bank roll calls in 1740. Nineteen approved of the Bank, but thirteen opposed, which roughly corresponds to the entire assembly's division (fifty-seven to thirty-nine, forty-two to twenty-eight) on these issues. Of nineteen "anti-inflationists" in 1739, fourteen were reelected and voted on the Land Bank: nine opposed but five favored it. In short, no definite correlation exists between representatives who favored or opposed province bills or the Land Bank. Alignment on the Land Bank and various other monetary schemes displayed a flexibility that indicates groping for a solution within a wide framework, defined by staunch paper money advocates like Vans on the one hand and silver currency men like Douglass and Hutchinson on the other.[68]

Similarly, at least fifteen of the Land Bankers had been involved in various monetary proposals and agreements limited to wealthy men in the Boston area throughout the 1730s. Samuel Adams, like eleven other Bankers, supported the Merchants' Notes and agreed to to accept Rhode Island bills in 1733, as had John Colman himself. Robert Hale of Beverly, a Land Bank director, and four others subscribed to both the Land and Silver Banks. Clearly they viewed the Land Bank as by no means the only way to combat uncontrollable inflation without eliminating the province's money supply.[69]

The Bank also collapsed with little trouble because during the brief period of its operation, it began to suffer from the very difficulties its opponents had predicted. Some of the directors issued too many bills on insufficient credit (they later became the "delinquent" partners). Others refused to accept the depreciating bills. Plans emerged for local, county Land Banks to compensate for the parent Bank's failure. As Andrew M. Davis has concluded, "it can hardly be doubted that the Land Bank could not long have been maintained even if the government had not undertaken to suppress it."[70]

Although the Land Bank itself did not produce long-lasting factional disputes, it left enduring bitterness. Lawsuits and efforts to make the delinquent partners pay continued until 1767, ruining Samuel Adams, Sr., among others.[71] To be sure, specifically connecting revolutionary antagonism with the Bank is difficult. For instance, of the nine Bank directors, George Leonard's and Robert Auchmuty's sons became loyalists; Silver Bankers Edmund Quincy and James Bowdoin fathered prominent revolutionaries, while the families of their co-directors Andrew Oliver and Edward Hutchinson remained loyal. But warfare in the 1740s and 1750s aggravated the economic problems that had provoked the Bank crisis in the first place.

# *Notes to Chapter V*

1. I have deliberately refrained from emphasizing Belcher's nasty but amusing letters, which are amply quoted in John A. Schutz, *William Shirley: King's Governor of Massachusetts* (Chapel Hill, 1961), chs. 1–2, and "Succession Politics in Massachusetts, 1730–1741," *William and Mary Quarterly*, 3rd. ser. 15 (1958), pp. 508–520; and Robert Zemsky, *Merchants, Farmers, and River Gods* (Boston, 1971), ch. 5. These works are especially good on personal opposition to Belcher and give full accounts of the efforts to remove him. I stress his accomplishments of settling the salary and treasury disputes.

2. Surveyor-General David Dunbar was horrified at the selection of a man who "was always a declared enemy to all governors except Mr. Shute, who was of his own religion," and was so virulent against the Church of England that he made his prospective son-in-law Byfield Lyde convert to Congregationalism. Jonathan Belcher to Benjamin Colman, 17 February 1730, Colman Papers, MHS. Belcher had first taken the superfluous precaution of making certain that his old friend Samuel Shute had no desire to return. Board of Trade to Privy Council, 12 November 1729, *CSP*, 36, #969; David Dunbar to Duke of Newcastle, 4 February 1730, *ibid.*, 37, #49.

3. Instructions to Jonathan Belcher, 20 March 1730, *ibid.*, #59.

4. [William Winslow] to [Daniel Ayrewell?], 22 September 1729, Miscellaneous Bound Manuscripts, MHS; David Dunbar to Alured Popple, 21 September 1730, *CSP*, 37, #449. On 12 January 1731, Dunbar wrote Newcastle that "notwithstanding any assurances he may give to the ministry, everybody tells me that his pretences are only to spin out time and keep the affair out of Parliament." *Ibid.*, 38, #12.

5. Belcher realized the difficulty of his task: "I must walk very circumspectly lest the king's ministry should imagine I am not zealous enough for the honor of the crown, and lest the House of Commons should think I bear too hard on the privileges of the people. I'll endeavor to steer as nicely as I can between them." Belcher insisted over and over again, as he wrote to Sir Robert Walpole, that "the interest of Great Britain and the liberty of the British plantations are very compatible and to be pursued as one interest." Salem's representative Benjamin Lynde, Jr., a future Chief Justice of the Superior Court, and David Dunbar both commented on the deputies' replacement of six prerogative councillors in 1730 and five in 1731: see *Diaries of Benjamin Lynde and Benjamin Lynde, Jr.*, ed. Fitch E. Oliver (Boston, 1880), p. 134; and David Dunbar to Alured Popple, 5 June 1730, *CSP*, 37, #274. Jonathan Belcher to Richard Partridge, 11 November 1731, *Belcher Papers*, *MHSC*, 6th ser. vol. 6 and vol. 7, vol. 1, p. 42; Jonathan Belcher to Sir Robert Walpole, 20 November 1731, *ibid.*, 1: 57.

6. Belcher appointed Byfield Chief Justice of the Suffolk Court, which involved a demotion for Thomas Palmer, with Cooke's son Middlecott (who unlike his father and grandfather never took any interest in politics) as its clerk. William H. Whitmore, *The Massachusetts Civil List, 1630–1774* (Albany, 1870), p. 77; for Middlecott Cooke's appointment, see *Belcher Papers*, 1: 48. For enmity between Belcher and the Dudleys, see Jonathan Belcher to Richard Partridge, 1 November 1731, *ibid.*, 1: 38; Belcher to Sir Robert Walpole, 1 January 1740, *ibid.*, 2: 264–265; and David Dunbar to Alured Popple, 12 January 1731, *CSP*, 38, #12. That Cooke and almost no other politician in the eighteenth century would not leave the house for the council illustrates that most officeholders considered prestige and deference more important than political power in a modern sense.

# Notes to Chapter V

7. See Table 10.

8. Thomas Hutchinson, *The History of the Colony and Province of Massachusetts Bay*, (Cambridge, 1936), 2: 263. Hutchinson remarked that Welles' prolix messages could be distinguished from Cooke's short, blunt drafts.

9. *Journals of the House of Representatives of Massachusetts Bay* (Boston, 1919–    ), 10: 172.

10. Whitmore, *Civil List*, p. 77. On 7 April 1735, Belcher wrote to his son Jonathan Jr. that "the Doctor [Cooke] continues very poor. I have hope Mr. W[elles] will be able to hold it, though I have had much difficulty to silence his enemies, who are the more numerous from their supposing him to be a friend of the governor." *Belcher Papers*, 2: 200. Belcher dropped Cooke from the Suffolk Court in 1733 (Byfield's death spared him a similar fate) and reinstated William Dudley. Welles, who no longer held a majority in the town after 1734, was regularly elected to the council (and approved by Belcher) beginning in 1735. Belcher appointed his son-in-law Byfield Lyde as clerk of the court to replace Middlecott Cooke. *Belcher Papers*, 1: 519.

11. Hutchinson, *History*, 2: 198. See Table 10.

12. These themes are treated in detail in my forthcoming article with Ralph Crandall, "Metropolitan Boston Before the American Revolution: An Urban Interpretation of the Imperial Crisis," which discusses the future loyalists' estrangement from the populace through Anglicanism, intermarriage, unwillingness to invest in the Boston economy, and personal success during a war which harmed their countrymen. Yet they retained considerable political power, even in the Boston Town Meeting, until the early 1760s.

13. Belcher compared Massachusetts' risking of Parliamentary intervention to the legendary Roman Cato:

> The fame of Cato's wisdom reflected honor on old Rome, while he made so brave a stand for the liberties of his country, but when Caesar shut him up in his little Utica, and offered him terms of honor, his murdering himself rather than submit to a power he could no longer rationally resist, has left a lasting brand of infamy on the memory of that great patriot.

The analogy was unfortunate: as Thomas Hutchinson remarked, Belcher presented himself thereby as enforcing "a mere exertion of power." *House Journals*, 9: 238, 240; Hutchinson, *History*, 2: 282.

14. David Dunbar to Alured Popple, 29 August 1730, CSP, 37, #402; same to same, *ibid.*, 38, #12.

15. Jonathan Belcher to Board of Trade, 2 October 1730, *ibid.*, 37, #474. *House Journals*, 9: 263–264, 339, 365.

16. As early as April 1731, Belcher asked leave to accept annual grants as he had received "the most public and solemn assurances of an honorable support." Was it reasonable that he should "go on to support the king's honor in the chair of government at the expense of his own estate"? Besides, he had obtained more from the assembly "than any other governor has been able to." "With great deference and submission," Belcher questioned whether it was "exactly agreeable to the honor and dignity of the crown to be urging on an assembly what they have so often and publicly denied." For Belcher's requests to have the instruction dropped, see his letters to Duke of Newcastle, 26 April 1731, CSP, 38, #157; to the Board of Trade, 19 October 1731, *Belcher Papers*, 1: 14; 8 January 1733, CSP, 40, #7; 2 June 1734, *ibid.*, #158; and to Martin Bladen, 30 December 1731, *Belcher Papers*, 1: 92. The Board of Trade agreed to a one-year grant on 10 August 1731, CSP, 38, #350.

17. Jonathan Belcher to Duke of Newcastle, 9 June 1735, *ibid.*, 41, #589; Board of Trade to Privy Council, 26 August 1735, *ibid.*, 42, #82.

18. On 18 June 1736, Belcher wrote Newcastle that he would try to have his salary "as near £1000 sterling a year as I can possibly persuade them to"; *ibid.*, #337. For Shirley's difficulties, see the following chapter. The house justified paying lower salaries by their interpretation of exchange rates with pounds sterling, although neither Belcher or Shirley protested terribly. After 1750, rates remained constant, which straight-jacketed the deputies on this point.

19. Belcher noted in his speeches the ironic fact that the deputies nevertheless continued to pay themselves and commented that "it will look mean and dishonorable in the eyes of the whole world, that you have . . . taken effectual care for the payment of your daily service in the General Court, but have . . . entirely neglected the pay of the garrisons." *House Journals,* 10: 415; Jonathan Belcher to Duke of Newcastle, 19 May 1733, *CSP,* 40, #170.

20. The house accused the council of "extravagantly" misusing the public funds at various times in the past, and blamed this mismanagement, rather than its own failure to vote funds, for the empty treasury. The assembly claimed it would bring "the province into ruin and destruction, by putting their estates in the hands of a very few persons." The council had a quorum of seven, four of whom made a majority. *House Journals,* 10: 104, 123, 256.

21. *House Journals,* 11: 67. Belcher, for his part, commented that "all the struggle in this matter is for power. They that have control of the money, will certainly have the power. I take the single question on this head to be, whether the king shall appoint his own governor, or whether the house of representatives shall be governor of the province." Jonathan Belcher to Duke of Newcastle, 26 December 1732, *CSP,* 39, #285.

22. William Brattle, a deputy from Cambridge who had been in the forefront of the opposition's leadership, reversed his stand and delivered a key speech to procure the final vote. One Gyles Dulac Tidmarsh, who had earlier received the thanks of the house for assisting Agent Wilkes in defending the province, assaulted Brattle at the Bunch of Grapes Tavern for his remarks. *House Journals,* 11: 73, 93, 278, 309.

23. Advocate-General William Shirley noted "the House of Commons has treated Dr. Cooke's late memorial to them against His Majesty's instruction . . . with dire resentment and indignation, which sounds like a thunderclap in the ears of his mob." Belcher praised the assembly which settled the treasury issue as "the best to the honor of the king and his governor of any since my arrival" and issued periodic reports to his friends in London and New Hampshire gleefully recounting the drastic decline of "old Toper [Cooke] and his clan." William Shirley to Duke of Newcastle, 1 October 1733, *Correspondence of William Shirley,* ed. C.H. Lincoln (New York, 1912), 1: 4. Jonathan Belcher to Richard Partridge, 13 November 1733, *Belcher Papers,* 1: 515; Belcher to Duke of Newcastle, 1 June 1734, *CSP,* 41, #34. Jonathan Belcher to: Richard Waldron, 16 November 1733, *Belcher Papers,* 1: 415; Samuel Willard, 4 January 1734, *ibid.,* p. 520; Richard Waldron, 6 September 1734, *ibid.,* 2: 121, in which he remarked: "old Toper is shrunk into a mushroom and dies over and over every day"; and Henry Sherborn, 11 April 1737, Belcher Letter Book, vol. 5, MHS.

24. Belcher wrote letters to Chandler and Stoddard requesting their presence in the General Court: *Belcher Papers,* 1: 504; 2: 455, 457; he identified Shove twice as a "natural enemy" in letters to Richard Partridge, 19 December 1732, *Belcher Papers,* 1: 224, and Andrew Belcher, Jr., 27 December 1732, *ibid.,* p. 492. Burnet ousted Lynde as justice of the peace in 1729 for his opposition to the fixed salary; in 1736 Boston's Thomas Cushing nominated him for the council in an effort to replace the elder Lynde, the Chief Justice of the Superior Court. He only received 34 votes of 124, but the following and subsequent years the house elected him nearly unanimously. Belcher did not object. *Lynde Diaries,* pp. 72, 144, 148, 154, 156.

25. Jonathan Belcher to Duke of Newcastle, 23 May 1738, *CSP,* 44, #234. Leslie V. Brock, *The Currency of the American Colonies, 1700–1764* (New York, 1975), pp. 591–592.

26. For Dunbar's instructions and documents relating to Georgia, see *CSP*, 36, #627-631 (14 March-21 March, 1729).

27. Land speculation provided for children who could not conveniently farm their fathers' original holdings: Charles S. Grant, "Land Speculation and the Settlement of Kent, 1738-1760," *New England Quarterly*, 28 (1955), pp. 51-71; Report of Jonathan Peagrum, 30 April 1736, *CSP*, 42, #297; David Dunbar to Alured Popple, 9 August 1737, *ibid.*, 43, #438. Thomas Hutchinson wrote that later many people opposed the annexation of Canada because new territory depreciated existing land values. Hutchinson to William Bollan, 14 July 1760, Massachusetts Archives, 25: 17. References to this collection are to the typescript copy prepared by Catherine Barton Mayo at the MHS.

28. David Dunbar to Alured Popple, letters of November 1730, *CSP*, 38, #528-540; same to same, 9 August 1737, *ibid.*, 43, #438.

29. Dunbar was unimpressed by the titles. Most of their claims rested on a purchase of 1674, and "the Indian who put his mark on the deed" was only "one of a tribe and had no more power to sell that or any other land than the Governor of Boston has to sell the entire province." The surveyor also reported having seen "no less than three such titles from different Indians" to approximately the same tract and argued that if Waldo were to be confirmed in possession of everything for which he had a title, then the crown would have to surrender all of Maine and Nova Scotia. Letters of David Dunbar to various officials, October 1729, *ibid.*, 36, #500-556; David Dunbar to Alured Popple, 25 May, 5 June, 16 June, 29 August, 15 September, 21 September, and 17 November 1730; 4 June 1731; *ibid.*, 37, #254, 274, 288, 402, 438, 452, 533; 38, #217. For Waldo's deed, see 28 March 1728, Henry Knox Papers, MHS.

30. Jonathan Belcher to Board of Trade, 29 October 1731, *Belcher Papers*, 1: 19; 23 February 1732, *ibid.*, p. 100; Jonathan Belcher to Duke of Newcastle, 1 July 1734, *CSP*, 61, #230.

31. Alured Popple to David Dunbar, 11 February 1731, *ibid.*, 37, #49; order of Queen in Council, 10 August 1732, *ibid.*, 39, #346.

32. Board of Trade to King George, 4 November 1731, *ibid.*, 38, #467.

33. Jonathan Belcher to Richard Waldron, 24 May 1737, Belcher Letter Book, vol. 5, MHS.

34. Edmund Quincy was dispatched as a special agent to change the verdict but he died on the voyage over. In 1740, as a private agent for the Massachusetts proprietors of the boundary lands, Thomas Hutchinson tried in vain to accomplish the same end. For Quincy's choice, New Hampshire's complaint, and Massachusetts' answer, see *House Journals*, 15: 120; 16: 160-173. For the rebuilding of Pemaquid, see Jonathan Belcher to Richard Partridge, 13 November 1733, *Belcher Papers*, 1: 515. For Dunbar's voyage, see the succession of letters beginning with same to same, 24 December 1736, Belcher Letter Book, vol. 5. For Hutchinson's agency, see Thomas Hutchinson to Josiah Willard, 31 July 1741, Massachusetts Archives, 25: 1-2.

35. Gulston complained to Newcastle, who complained to Belcher on 3 October 1734, *CSP*, 41, #332.

36. See depositions and letters of the settlers, dated 1738, in Knox Papers, vol. 50. See also David Dunbar and Benjamin Pollard to Elisha Cooke, both 1 October 1733; and Middlecott Cooke's letters to his father, 2 November 1734; 17 April and 24 April 1735; all in Cooke Family Papers, 9, Q-T, *Saltonstall Papers*, *MHSC*; Samuel Waldo to Alured Popple, 9 July 1736, *CSP*, 42, #355.

37. Shirley turned down the admiralty judgeship itself in 1733 on the death of Nathaniel Byfield since it paid barely £15 a year. The new judge, Robert Auchmuty, was initially a friend of Belcher's as well. However, their salaries depended on seizures of illegally imported cargoes. The incomes of Belcher and his merchant friends—

including Richard Waldron, Secretary of New Hampshire, and Richard Partridge, the governor's brother-in-law and agent in London—depended on smuggling. Jonathan Belcher to Edward Onslow, 29 October 1731, *Belcher Papers*, 1: 20; Belcher to Richard Waldron, 24 September and 22 October 1739, *ibid.*, 2: 205, 223. William Shirley to Duke of Newcastle, 1 October 1733, *Shirley Papers*, 1: 2.

38. The eager Waldo deeded Shirley one-fiftieth of his frontier lands and advanced the £1,500 required for Shirley's commissions to pass the seals. In return, Shirley assured his coconspirator that he was "not at all afraid of being turned out of the government, if it should fall my lot to have it . . . a family interest, my personal acquaintance with the Newcastle family, and several friends in Parliament" were a guarantee of impregnability. See William Shirley to Samuel Waldo, 15 April 1739, a long and extremely revealing letter that proves Shirley's intentions in obtaining the government were at first purely financial and self-seeking. Further letters of 21 April, 7 May, 21 May, and 9 June, are also helpful. Waldo's deed to Shirley is dated 3 July 1738. All in Knox Papers, vol. 50.

39. Duke of Newcastle to William Shirley, 5 April 1740, *Shirley Papers*, 1: 18.

40. Belcher raised ten companies for the expedition, six more than required, but was obliged to dismiss the extra men when there were no transports or weapons for them. *House Journals*, 18: 103. Belcher refused to allow Shirley to assist in mustering the men. Shirley claimed Belcher "slept ten weeks" while he did all the work. Jonathan Belcher to William Shirley, 12 July 1740, *Belcher Papers*, 2: 360. Shirley to Duke of Newcastle, 4 August 1740, *Shirley Papers*, 1: 24–26.

41. Other correspondents included Thomas Coram and Henry Newman, who were active in New England missionary work. See *Belcher Papers* and Letter Books. Belcher's efforts were seconded by those of the Reverend Benjamin Colman: see his letters for 1735–1740 in Colman Papers; Colman turned against Belcher during the Land Bank crisis. See his letter to the governor, 6 January 1741, Colman Papers, MHS.

42. Schutz, *Shirley*, p. 42; Thomas Hutchinson to Benjamin Lynde, Jr., 17 August 1741, *Lynde Diaries*, p. 222.

43. Leslie V. Brock, *The Currency of the American Colonies, 1700–1764* (New York, 1975), pp. 591–592; Andrew M. Davis, *Colonial Currency Reprints*, (Boston, 1911–1912), 3: 9.

44. Jonathan Belcher to Board of Trade, 1 November 1737, *CSP*, 43, #565.

45. Davis, *Currency and Banking*, 1: 139–140; Davis *Reprints*, 3: 151–160, quote at p. 160; Jonathan Belcher to Francis Wilkes, 11 July 1737, Belcher Letter Book, vol. 5; Belcher to Board of Trade, 11 July 1737, *CSP*, 43, #372.

46. Benjamin Colman to Francis Wilkes, 19 November 1739, Colman Papers.

47. *House Journals*, 17: 105–143.

48. Thomas Hutchinson to Benjamin Lynde, 12 August 1741, *Lynde Diaries*, p. 222.

49. Jonathan Belcher to Richard Waldron, 20 April 1734, *Belcher Papers*, 2: 43; *House Journals*, 17: 49, 77, 181.

50. *An Account of the Rise, Progress, and Consequences of the Land Bank* (Boston, 1744), in Davis, *Reprints*, 4: 240; Jonathan Belcher to Board of Trade, 20 December 1738, *CSP*, 44, #550.

51. *House Journals*, 17: 29. The house also antagonized Belcher by electing his arch enemy Paul Dudley their speaker. Dudley had been vetoed as a councillor for two consecutive years. *House Journals*, 17: 5.

52. Good descriptions of both banks are found in Davis, *Currency and Banking*, vol. 2. For lists of members, *ibid.*, pp. 292–313, and Davis, "Boston Banks and Those Who

Were Interested in Them," *New England Historical and Genealogical Register*, 57 (1903): 279–281. The best account of the division over the Land Bank is Cathy Mitten, "The New England Paper Money Tradition and the Massachusetts Land Bank of 1740," (Columbia University, M.A. thesis, 1979) which shows supporters included not only the well-to-do bankers George A. Billias, *Massachusetts Land Bankers of 1740* (Orono, ME, 1959) found, but also more obscure people of various social strata. She also takes due account of the shifting and unstable divisions on the currency issue in the late thirties, an approach stressed here. See also Nash, *The Urban Crucible*, (Cambridge, 1979) pp. 136–139, 212–216.

53. For Vans's legal trouble, see Suffolk Court of Common Pleas, 1727, 167, 261, 295, 314, 363; 1729, 93; 1731; 7, 57, 521, and so forth, New Court House, Boston; *A&R*, 4: 107. See Davis, *Currency Reprints*, 3: 191, 203, 391–415 for the crux of his arguments.

54. Davis, *Currency Reprints*, 3: 152, 232–233; 309, 327–329; 4: 57 for the essence of Douglass's and Hutchinson's case.

55. *Ibid.*, 3: 234.

56. *Ibid.*, 3: 11.

57. *House Journals*, 18: 260.

58. Jonathan Belcher to Board of Trade, 14 April 1740, *Belcher Papers*, 2: 503.

59. Same to same, 17 November 1740, *ibid.*, p. 348.

60. *House Journals*, 18: 47–48; 185–186.

61. Massachusetts Archives, 102: 86–108, 475; Executive Council Records, 10: 480, State House, Boston.

62. Davis, *Reprints*, 4: 78.

63. *Lynde Diaries*, p. 162.

64. Massachusetts Archives, 102: 163–168. The Bankers probably never intended to march; little tangible evidence of planning was discovered. The Bank was advanced when exchange rates were stable at roughly five to one with sterling, indicating that it did not coincide with severe economic distress. William Douglass, *A Summary, Historical and Political . . . of British North America*, (London, 1715) 2: 494. Still, Belcher found a "malignant spirit" which "*very near*" at last broke out in a riot of insurrection." Jonathan Belcher to Thomas Hutchinson, 11 May 1740, *Belcher Papers*, 2: 388 (my emphasis). The Lowell Family Papers, 1657–1830, MHS, contain the council tallies for 1740 and 1741, see Table 14.

65. Davis, *Reprints*, 4: 274; Hutchinson to Benjamin Lynde, 8 August 1741, *Lynde Diaries*, pp. 222–223, notes that Partridge's appearance in favor of the Bank was taken as proof that Belcher supported it.

66. Jonathan Belcher to Richard Partridge, 26 November 1739, *Belcher Papers*, 2: 248. My emphasis.

67. *House Journals*, 17: 256–258.

68. Mitten, "The New England Paper Money Tradition," pp. 3–4.

69. Davis, "Boston Banks," pp. 279–281.

70. Davis, *Currency and Banking*, 2: 155–157.

71. Mitten, "The New England Paper Money Tradition," ch. 3.

# VI

## CRUSADERS AND CRITICS

## 1741–1756

$\mathcal{I}$N THE 1740s, the sleeping British lion awoke with a roar. Men like the Duke of Bedford and Earl of Halifax entered the cabinet, and forced the lackadaisical Newcastle to raise his sights.[1] They pursued colonial expansion and war to increase national power. Between 1740 and 1763, Britain fought two world wars and conquered a new empire in India. But like the "enlightened despots," their continental counterparts, the imperial visionaries had plans for internal reorganization as well. They sought a refurbished, centralized colonial system that subordinated the provincials' interests to the mother country's. When they tried to implement this half of their program, the American Revolution resulted.

Just as Jonathan Belcher had proven Massachusetts' perfect representative for an empire of "benign neglect," his successor William Shirley embodied the new aggressive imperialism. A man of energy, intelligence, and ambition, Shirley persuaded Massachusetts to take the lead among the colonies and almost singlehandedly launched King George's War in the northern provinces. He urged a colonial union, stabilized the currency once and for all, and in 1755, rose to be commander in chief of the North American forces when General James Braddock met his death in Pennsylvania.

Like his British superiors, Shirley can be judged in either of two ways. He deserves praise for restoring energy and unity. He united a province split by the Land Bank and the Great Awakening, and led it in a great crusade.[2] He thereby enabled the prerogative faction to dominate for two decades. On the other hand, Shirley bought success at a high price. The governor's enemies mocked his "golden dream of being happily arrived at a new era of justice," and complained of "the many burdens the oppressed inhabitants of the province labor under," the "distinguishing marks of our boasted new era."[3] Shirley's military expeditions produced widespread dissatisfaction, not only with him personally, but with British policy. To Shirley's credit, he liquidated the Land Bank quickly and prevented it from producing further tensions. But his campaigns, and the lack of cooperation from the home authorities, undid his intelligent handling of the Bank.

Government did not pose a direct threat to the common man's well-being during the two decades of peace before 1740; but war took a tremendous toll in lives and money. Except for a few brief outbursts of enthusiasm, Shirley had to cajole and threaten the assembly to vote funds and men. His policies directly involved unprecedented numbers of people in Anglo-American politics as soldiers, taxpayers, and members of mobs resisting impressment. The number of men who participated actively in the house increased severalfold to manage the war. (See Table 4.) Shirley and his cohorts resorted to unsavory tactics to overcome the opposition: politically motivated prosecutions, expulsion of dissident assembly members, and direct defiance of legislative resolves. His opponents, among them young Samuel Adams, retaliated by developing the ideology of resistance that destroyed the first British Empire two decades later. At the same time, British administrators began to consider colonial reform in response to the other colonies' reluctant participation and Massachusetts' own surliness toward those soldiers and sailors sent to defend it.[4]

UNFINISHED BUSINESS: 1741–1745

Shirley's administration began auspiciously. He was determined not to let the Land Bank ruin him, and here an act of Parliament inadvertently helped. The law abolished the Land Bank and united the province. Had it simply declared the notes null and void, all would have been well, but it required any partner to redeem personally *all* outstanding bills at face value from whomever presented them. Any subscriber would be liable in court for treble damages for notes unredeemed by 29 September 1741. Even the elder Benjamin Lynde, a councillor removed by the Bankers, condemned the act's severity. So did Hutchinson and William Douglass, who had preferred gradual to sudden, drastic reductions in the money supply.[5] Christopher Kilby, a Boston merchant who had opposed the act and helped Shirley become governor, assured his friend and partner Thomas Hancock that "the attempt against it [the Bank] was being levelled not merely at the project, but the whole province, in special against the house."[6]

Everyone thus had an interest in discovering a workable manner to enforce Parliament's decree. The major obstacle was that the partners were collectively responsible for the entire sum of money. Noteholders could select any of the thousand-odd subscribers from whom to obtain redemption. Some individuals bought up large sums to press legal actions against their enemies. Shirley complained that his opponents threatened Bankers who were friendly to him with lawsuits unless they changed their allegiance.[7] But his own followers were not blameless, either. Thomas Paine of Boston attempted to corner £20,000 of the notes to sue Robert Auchmuty, who had sought the province agency to oppose Shirley.[8]

The logical remedy, which Shirley induced the General Court to adopt, limited the quantity of bills for which each subscriber had to answer to his initial investment. This measure reversed political alignments: instead of Land Bankers confronting their opponents, now the nondelinquent partners (supported by the government) could sit securely. The small number of delinquents who had overextended their credit bore the full burden. By January 1743, Shirley estimated that only £7,000 out of £49,000 the Bank had circulated remained at large, and only 125 of the 800 subscribers who had taken out bills had defaulted.[9]

Shirley reaped great political rewards due to his handling of the Bank's liquidation. He could now count most of the Land Bankers among his staunch adherents. They proved no real friends to inflation and supported his plans for maintaining the value of the province bills. As a pamphlet written in 1744 to defend Shirley from Belcher's attempts to regain his post remarked, "it must be a very extraordinary change indeed, if it could be wrought so suddenly on them as to bring them from espousing the worst scheme of notes, and almost as bad a supply bill, to . . . [enact] greater legislation toward regulating the province currency than the best composed assembly in the province had done for thirty years."[10] By 1742, harmony prevailed.

The legislature's willingness to forget the Bank appears most strikingly in the elections for councillors. Of the fifteen men the "Land Bank" House had removed in 1741, twelve returned by 1744 and the other three had died. On the other hand, only two of the thirteen Land Bankers chosen to replace them ever sat in the council again: Otis Little in 1743 and John Otis (grandfather of the famous James) from 1747 to 1757. The ex-Land Bankers immediately resumed the tradition of electing councillors for administrative rather than partisan reasons. Some representatives removed for opposing the Bank such as William Browne, John Chandler, and Thomas Hutchinson, also returned in 1742.[11]

Shirley's success in finding a currency to replace the Land Bank notes completed his liquidation of the Bank. Before permitting the house to supply the treasury in 1741, he persuaded it to adopt Hugh Vans' scheme requiring that all debts contracted after March 1742 be readjusted to account for depreciation. The General Court was to determine the rate of depreciation twice yearly. If it failed to agree, the eldest councillor from every county would meet and determine the rate. If they too refused to handle this hot potato the Superior Court could fix rates.[12] The act proved "very unpopular," and in practice the Superior Court handled the matter.[13] But an acceptable currency had been created, and laws stood upon the books to convince Britain that the province upheld its currency's value.[14]

Shirley further increased financial and political stability by persuading the Board of Trade to remove two of its instructions. They no longer required suspending clauses to issue more than £30,000 in bills of credit yearly—Shirley noted that merely mentioning this infuriated the house. Second, after Massachusetts began participating in King George's War in 1744, no impediments remained to issuing whatever sums provincial defense required.[15] By 1749, approximately £1,900,000 in bills circulated, valued at less than one-tenth that sum in sterling.[16] As so often in history, military exigencies supplanted the most pressing peacetime concerns.

Despite Shirley's financial acumen, strife was not totally absent. He renewed his predecessors' efforts to acquire a settled salary, pressing his demands in the poorly attended winter sessions after the house had passed his currency reforms. Despite the greater proportion of court members, he failed. Furthermore, Shirley did not even obtain the £1,000 sterling per annum, still written into his instruction, in the first year of his tenure. Rather than accept the £750 and (after his protest) the £950 sterling offered for 1741–1742, he at first refused any salary at all. The house spent most of the January and March sessions disputing the size of his grant. Shirley obtained his full £1,000 sterling the following two years and continued to hold out hopes for a permanent salary. But he never obtained one and failed to maintain his previous income level when the war became unpopular.[17]

Shirley also had some difficulty with timber barons and the Boston merchant community.[18] Determined to enforce the White Pine Laws and Acts of Trade, he even obtained the first provincial act to protect the King's Woods. When his proclamations proved of little value here, he sent his son-in-law, the new admiralty advocate William Bollan, to Maine and appointed several justices of the peace to preserve the forests.[19] At the same time, Shirley and Bollan attempted to curtail the "large" illegal trade in Boston, conducted by men "of the greatest fortune." Only one vessel was condemned during Shirley's first year. But he did his best, even while realizing only significant structural changes in maritime justice could make a difference.[20]

Despite difficulties stemming from Shirley's excessive zeal, the first part of his administration was a definite success. The General Court worked effectively to take the currency question, the last unsolved problem faced by past executives, out of politics. Good will between Shirley and the legislators accounted for their initial enthusiasm for his vast military projects. But the war's progress undid much of Shirley's achievement.

LOUISBOURG AND BEYOND: 1745–1748

Massachusetts' experience during King George's War (1744–1748) differed radically from those of the other mainland colonies. The thanks or blame must be attributed almost entirely to William Shirley. Before February 1745, when he persuaded the General Court to undertake the Louisbourg expedition, no one expected anything of importance to occur in the North American theater. This campaign and its successor, the abortive Canada-Crown Point expedition, achieved a short-term crusading spirit at the expense of increased long-term Anglo-American conflict.[21] Opposition to British measures widened from struggles between the house and the governor—although these continued—to mass protests against naval impressment and general dissatisfaction with the mother country's incompetence and lack of concern. King George's War both precipitated imperial efforts to reform the colonies and altered provincial perceptions of British policies.[22]

As soon as Britain formally declared war on 31 March 1744, Shirley quarrelled with the assembly over the imminently expected hostilities. On 10 April, he asked for advance approval of all war expenditures the council might pass during the deputies' recess. The house refused, and feared this "dangerous precedent" might impose "upon the province a very large expense." Shirley may well have already hinted at some ambitious project.[23]

When a new house met on 31 May 1744, Shirley immediately convinced it to defend the English fort at Port Royal, Nova Scotia. The representatives complied, but without enthusiasm. They later replied halfheartedly to Shirley's message praising them for saving the garrison: "this success in some measure alleviates the difficulties we have laid ourselves under, in parting with so many men, and advising to a considerable sum for their encouragement and supply."[24] Shirley could not at first obtain any men or money to protect Fort Dummer, originally built by Massachusetts but given to New Hampshire by the Boundary Commission of 1737. Only in June 1745, after he implied that defending it might induce Britain to return it to Massachusetts, did the assembly change its mind.[25] The governor also began in the first year of the war to criticize the house for voting very light taxes and financing most expenditures with paper money.[26]

Shirley next adopted an extremely broad interpretation of a royal instruction to "take all opportunities, as far as depends on you, to distress and annoy the French."[27] In January 1745, the house went into secret session to vote £50,000 and enlist 3,000 land and sea volunteers to "attempt the reduction of Cape Breton to its former obedience and subjection to the crown."[28] As with most important measures in Shirley's administration, the deputies proved reluctant. Thomas Hutchinson wrote that it passed by one vote. Even twenty years later, he still thought it a foolish expedition that succeeded by mere chance: "considerate persons . . . could not . . . avoid gratefully admiring the favor of divine providence in so great a number of remarkable incidents which contributed to the expedition's success."[29]

While the General Court by no means unanimously favored the expedition, enthusiasm soon swept the entire province. New Lights like Jonathan Edwards, and Old Lights like Charles Chauncy joined Anglican revivalist George Whitefield to link the campaign with the universal battle against Popery and the Antichrist. Whitefield persuaded William Pepperell to bury his animosity against Governor Shirley and lead the troops.[30] Three-thousand New Englanders participated, all volunteers (as the assembly stipulated) except two-hundred sailors who had to be pressed into service.[31]

Massachusetts' overwhelming enthusiasm for both King George's and the French and Indian Wars cannot be explained simply by self-interest or the desire to be rid of the French once and for all. In the latter conflict the province raised approximately six times as many men in proportion to its white population as Virginia—its closest competitor—and fought the former virtually by itself.[32] Unlike several other colonies, Massachusetts suffered no attacks on its own frontiers, and enlisted men for offensive expeditions to Nova Scotia, New York, and Canada. Furthermore, Massachusetts' purpose transcended most other provinces. While the Great Awakening spread throughout the colonies, Kerry Trask and Nathan Hatch have shown that Massachusetts' religious zeal remained especially high. The crusading spirit continued unabated through both wars, and added fuel to the American Revolution as well.[33]

Massachusetts' increasing economic woes and social tensions help to explain its militant enthusiasm.[34] Hardship did not fall equally on all, but mostly on young men and in the overcrowded older settlements of eastern Massachusetts and the Connecticut River Valley.[35] As an index, we may examine the 165 soldiers enlisting in two companies for the Cartagena Expedition of 1740 who recorded their ages, occupations, and birthplaces: 121 were under thirty, and the median age was twenty-five. Eighty-one of the men gave their occupations as husbandmen, but significantly over half were either laborers (32) or artisans (52). The enlistment profiles illustrate the conjunction of urban distress in Boston and other seaports with the inability of sons to inherit farm land in the shrinking acreages of the older settlements. Many men were in debt; the General Court had to forbid the imprisonment of soldiers for this offense. And while 28 of the 165 were immigrants, most of the rest were caught in a temporary unemployable situation between adolescence and adulthood.(Fred Anderson has shown the same pattern held in the French and Indian War.)[36] They did not necessarily constitute a permanently impoverished group. Heavy casualty rates and the expansion of the frontier after both wars—Massachusetts even apart from Maine, added sixteen towns between 1751 and 1754, and another forty-five between 1759 and 1768—undoubtedly eased the situation temporarily.[37]

The lure of military pay, plunder, promotion, and adventure thus helped Massachusetts solve a threatening social problem. From the 1740s onward, writers included "boys" or young people when describing threats to law and order along with the more traditional categories of servants, seamen, strangers, and Negroes. (Many in the first three of these groups were young as well.) For instance, Thomas Hutchinson's minister, William Welsteed of the New Brick Church, condemned "the rudeness and dissoluteness of manners manifestly prevalent among our children and youth." Fifteen years later, Hutchinson himself commented that "a refractory, disobedient child has become so common among us as scarce to be noticed." The General

Court itself passed a stricter Riot Act in 1753 to discourage violence at the annual Pope's Day Celebration on 5 November. Its justification was that "instead of encouraging an abhorrence of disorder and forming a spirit of loyalty in the youth of the town, the aforesaid practices have been attended with horrid profaneness and other of the greatest immoralities, and have raised a mobbish and tumultuous spirit in the children and youth." Some condemnations linked restlessness among people to their "idleness"—that is to say, unemployment. Commenting on the numbers of war widows with dependents flocking to Boston, the *Boston Evening Post* lamented the increasing number of children "clothed in rags and brought up in ignorance and idleness."[38] Massachusetts' great enthusiasm for the mid-century wars therefore stemmed not merely from the glory, profits, and public esteem leading court politicians hoped to obtain, nor from the sermons of ministers anticipating the Second Coming. On the grass roots level, Massachusetts was full of young people with no place to go and nothing to do. War took care of them—in both the literal and colloquial senses—during the forties and fifties. In the sixties and seventies they turned to revolution.

From the beginning, Massachusetts presented the Louisbourg Campaign, which attained its objective on June 17, 1745, as undertaken for British rather than provincial benefit. Such declarations sought to pry financial compensation out of the reluctant British Treasury. The legislators stressed that "notwithstanding their utter inability to support the charges of such an undertaking, [they] have hazarded on the proposed expedition and petition . . . His Majesty's favor and compassion to the province, in relieving them from such part of the expenses and burden as to his wisdom should seem reasonable." As a writer noted in the *Independent Advertiser* on 4 July 1748, Massachusetts had imprudently attacked Cape Breton without either assured support from the British fleet or guaranteed compensation from the Treasury. He wrote that the First Lord of the Treasury had told Agent Bollan "that whatever we received on account of the expedition, we must look upon as a bounty, as we made the expedition without order."[39]

By becoming a suppliant for the Louisbourg reimbursement, Massachusetts only exacerbated its problems. For once the representatives made themselves dependent on Britain for financial compensation, Shirley could then extort further grants of troops and money. He threatened that if they did not proceed with great vigor, Britain might think twice about paying for Louisbourg. On 31 May 1746, Shirley proposed to conquer Canada by way of Crown Point in New York.

The governor warned that "a wrong step in the affair will endanger our being disappointed in our expectations [of compensation]." That July, when he impressed men enlisted for frontier duty into the expedition contrary to the house's resolves, the representatives refused to pay them. Shirley warned that if he had to use money from the British treasury, he would explain to his superiors why this was necessary. But the Canada expedition never got under way. The assault on Crown Point was unsuccessful. Despite the king's promises, Massachusetts received no reimbursement for this mobilization.[40]

Most of the tension between Shirley and the assembly concerned the placement and command of soldiers, and the duration of their service. First, some troops who had volunteered or been impressed for one theater of war were then transferred to a less attractive post. Others enlisted to obtain a more favorable post, necessitating impressments to fill the vacated commands. The house protested in vain that "we have always looked upon the impressing of men even for the defence of their own inhabitants as a method to be made use of in cases of great necessity only." The governor also held provincial soldiers on garrison duty long after their enlistments had expired. He kept some men at Annapolis in Nova Scotia from mid-1744 until January 1746. The entire 3,000-man Louisbourg contingent (of whom more than nine hundred died from exposure and disease) remained at Cape Breton from June 1745 until a long-awaited British garrison arrived in April 1746. The assembly complained that such extended service reduced "due confidence in the promises of government."[41]

After the Crown Point expedition failed in October 1746, Shirley obtained men and supplies only with difficulty. The house rejected his proposal to permit Negroes to enlist. Throughout 1747, he tried for a renewed Crown Point or Canada expedition, arguing that otherwise the Iroquois and Massachusetts' other Indian allies would "look upon us as a weak and contemptible people." But in June 1748, the house protested that it could not raise taxes because of "the difficult circumstances and disadvantages this people labor under." The province's expenditures had risen to an annual £400,000 in its depreciated currency, some £40,000 sterling. Moreover, "many thousands" had either been killed, impressed into the navy, or deprived of contributing to the economy by their long service in the army. The house indicated its opinion of Shirley's military strategy by voting him a salary of only £1,900 Massachusetts money in 1748, which barely equalled £190 sterling. It then condemned the whole war: "it affords us a very melancholy reflection when we consider the extreme heavy burden brought upon the people of this province, and the small prospect there is of any good effect from it . . . we have been the means of effectually bringing distress, if not ruin upon ourselves."⁴²

In addition to quarrels between the governor and deputies over the scope of military operations, King George's War provoked mutual contempt between the provincials and the British forces. In particular, the people regarded the impressment of American seamen into the navy as a gratuitous insult to His Majesty's most loyal subjects. Britain itself only justified this illegal practice by military necessity. Mobs formed to resist press gangs in Boston in 1741, 1745, and 1747. Except for the Charlestown riot in Queen Anne's War, these incidents marked the first time since the Glorious Revolution that crowd violence had been directed against British power. In every instance, the entire province united against the outrages: the Boston Town Meeting and General Court protested, the populace rioted in the streets, and leading citizens such as Thomas Hutchinson seconded the crowd's demands. In the final protest, the celebrated Knowles Riot of December 1747, the town of Boston held British officers as hostages to ensure the return of some impressed men. Commodore Charles Knowles replied by threatening to bombard the town. Knowles ultimately returned most of the men, but with very ill grace.⁴³

Not only did impressment provoke Anglo-American conflict, but each side became disgusted with the other's handling of the war. Knowles, who succeeded Admiral Peter Warren as commander of the West India squadron, considered Cape Breton useless and wanted it returned to France. He found the Massachusetts garrison "of so obstinate and licentious a disposition that not being properly under military discipline there was no one among them in any order."⁴⁴ The provincials were equally bitter. Thomas Hancock, though a personal friend of Knowles, expressed the general sentiment that "such a blundering ministry we never had. . . . Everything fail, and had it not been for that glorious affair of Cape Breton, we should have nothing to boast of." Josiah Quincy, Sr., in England at the time, was even more caustic. He complained of the ministry's unconcern with the northern colonies. Most members of Parliament, he wrote, subordinated "the interest of the nation," to considerations of "how much more will the P[rime] M[inister] give me for my vote and interest than another at my Ele[ctio]n? The consequence of which must be in time the ruin of this kingdom."⁴⁵

Quincy did not exaggerate. Sixty years later, old John Adams recalled how as a boy he had listened to his father discuss the Cape

Breton expedition "and I . . . received very grievous impressions of Great Britain." Adams also remembered that critical discussions of British military policy at the house of Colonel James Putnam of Worcester County in the 1750s "gave me such an opinion and such a disgust of British government, that I heartily wished the two countries were separated forever."[46]

As long as the province vigorously pursued the war, factional opposition to Shirley remained latent. It appeared mostly when the assembly tried to reduce the war to fit the province's capabilities. But in the winter of 1747–1748, peace negotiations began. With rumors circulating that Britain would return Cape Breton and not compensate the province for its exertions, Shirley's enemies could no longer contain themselves. They founded a newspaper and wrote a number of pamphlets introducing the ideology that twenty years later justified the American Revolution. The six years of peace between King George's and the French and Indian Wars (1748–1754) also witnessed a prolonged struggle over the means of stabilizing the province's war-inflated currency. Massachusetts' pent-up resentment at the costs and conduct of war ensured that political strife succeeded military hostilities.

## SAMUEL ADAMS AND REVOLUTIONARY IDEOLOGY
### 1748–1749

Within two months of the Knowles Riot, a group of men including twenty-five year old Samuel Adams, Jr., and the printer Daniel Fowle launched a new sort of newspaper in Boston, *The Independent Advertiser*. Unlike the existing weeklies, it did more than reprint official documents, publish advertisements, or keep the populace up to date on the latest European developments. It became the vehicle for a philosophical critique of Governor Shirley's administration. Adams and his colleagues introduced the "Old Whig" political ideas of John Locke and the "New Whig" variant of William Trenchard and John Gordon into Massachusetts.[47]

Whig ideology only became relevant to Massachusetts and vital to the opposition during Shirley's regime. Previously, the principal quarrels between the governor and house disputed the limits of royal instructions and the provincial charter. Other major quarrels, under Dudley and Shirley, related to the practical problem of running a war.

Shirley's administration, however, presented a novel phenomenon. The house of representatives was conducting an unpopular and costly war. Not only were many individuals disgruntled but—as some of the deputies' messages made perfectly clear—they only kept up the fight to obtain reimbursement from Britain. It therefore became necessary for the opposition, for the first time, to detach itself from the assembly. Once the house itself became an instrument of oppression, an appeal had to be made to a higher standard that explained how the people's own representatives had betrayed their constituents.

Whig ideology fit the Massachusetts situation perfectly. *The Independent Advertiser* cited the "Old Whig" Locke to condemn a government that failed to protect the inhabitants' "lives, liberties, and estates." It argued that by forcing men to fight, impressing them illegally into the navy, and taxing them excessively, the state could legitimately—even violently—be opposed. The writers then used Trenchard's and Gordon's "New Whig" ideas to explain that only a morally and financially corrupted government would so betray its people. Furthermore, only an equally depraved populace without "republican virtue" or public spirit would tolerate such oppression. *The Advertiser* blamed the war on representatives with military commissions bribed by Sir Plume (Governor Shirley)[48] and his chief adviser Alexander Windmill (Thomas Hutchinson).[49] The paper charged that men accepted these posts to obtain illicit profits from supplying and paying their men. But the *Advertiser* directed most of its complaints of corruption against Shirley personally, alleging that he had made an enormous sum of money raising a royal regiment of colonials to garrison Louisbourg.[50]

A twofold remedy existed for these evils. Adams, Fowle, and their colleagues enjoined the populace to reject placemen or "tools" as deputies. Such injunctions had rarely appeared in Massachusetts. I have found only three earlier exhortations, dating from 1707, 1721, and 1742.[51] Second, and more significantly, mob violence, short of revolution, emerged as the legitimate response to lawless acts of nominally lawful authorities. *The Independent Advertiser* treated the Knowles Riot as collective self-defense: a government unable to protect the citizens from Knowles's illegal press gang reduced them to a state of nature, in which they could defend themselves by any means if the state failed to do so. As Thomas Hutchinson noted, "some of the higher spirits" in town termed Governor Shirley's temporary departure from Boston at the height of the riot "a desertion or an abdication." *The Independent Advertiser* later insisted that where the government failed to do its duty, the people "have an undoubted right to use the powers belonging to that state [of nature]." The final issue of the paper found it "notorious, that the sober sort, who dared to express a due sense of their injuries, were invidiously represented as a rude, low-lived mob."⁵²

Little in *The Independent Advertiser* hinted that the French and Indians really menaced Massachusetts. Governor Shirley and the Boston Anglicans' "popish" refurbishing of King's Chapel threatened it far more.⁵³ Anonymous writers constantly denounced England as a den of incompetence and corruption that did little to help the province defend itself. The most extreme critique occurred upon the restoration of Louisbourg:

> Why is the security of the brave and virtuous . . . given up to purchase some short-lived and precarious advantages for lazy [damned?] f[oo]ls and idle All[ie]s? The security was purchased with the blood of the former and sacrificed to the indolence of the latter. The first won it by bravery; the latter forfeited it by Tr[e]ach[e]ry and Cow[ar]dice. As if our Min[i]stry . . . had determined to counteract the essential laws of equity, as much as possible, as they have done the rules of policy and prudence.⁵⁴

The new political activism represented by Adams and Fowle supplemented a more elite, personal opposition against Shirley. Sir William Pepperrell,⁵⁵ Christopher Kilby,⁵⁶ Dr. William Douglass, Samuel Waldo, and James Allen—all of whom except Allen had previously staunchly supported the governor—now joined forces to remove him. All but Douglass journeyed to England by 1749. Shirley followed them to defend himself. Before the governor left, however, he initiated lawsuits against Waldo and Douglass and arranged to expel Allen from the assembly.

Shirley sued Douglass for £10,000. The province's only European-trained physician had done much to earn the governor's wrath. He criticized the unsanitary conditions at Louisbourg, which claimed the lives of nine-hundred men during the winter of 1745. (Only one-hundred men had been injured in the assault itself.) An uncompromising opponent of paper money, he was angry that Shirley had issued more bills in eight years than all his predecessors combined over the previous fifty. In his monumental *Summary, Historical and Political . . . of North America*, published serially in the *Boston Gazette* beginning in 1747, Douglass roundly attacked Shirley's military strategy and "governors in general, who may by romantic (but in perquisites profitable) expeditions, depopulate the country." His criticisms of Admiral Knowles and mass impressment induced Shirley and Knowles in 1749 to initiate their suit. Douglass countersued and won: the final verdict awarded him £750 plus costs. Both sides appealed to the Privy Council, but all trace of the ultimate verdict is lost.[57]

The governor's suit against Waldo was even greater: £12,000. To be compensated for the Canada expedition of 1746, Massachusetts had to prepare detailed accounts. Shirley entrusted this task to Waldo, who had commanded the troops, but Waldo denied receiving such an instruction. Shirley then blamed Waldo's theft of the soldiers' arms and money for his negligence and sued the general for damages.[58] Whether Waldo was guilty or not, Shirley clearly hoped to palm off responsibility for the province's failure to be reimbursed. These tactics met with popular resentment. In 1749 the Bostonians expressed their opinion of Shirley's policies by choosing Waldo to represent them over Speaker of the House Thomas Hutchinson by a margin of 539 votes to about 200.[59] Waldo soon sailed for England, where he hoped to remove the man he had made Governor of Massachusetts.

James Allen also met a new form of counterattack. Another unsuccessful competitor for the supply of Louisbourg, he served as Boston's representative from 1738 to 1742 and again from 1748 to 1754 (in the interim Hutchinson's brother-in-law Andrew Oliver outpolled him).[60] Allen celebrated his return in 1748 by accusing the governor of trading with the French, a charge echoed in *The Advertiser*.[61] On 12 November 1748, the house suspended Allen until he apologized. When he tried to present his case, Hutchinson, still the speaker, ruled him out of order; on 27 December, a poorly attended session expelled him. Thirty representatives constituted the majority. When Boston reelected him, the deputies refused him his seat again.[62]

After his foes had ousted him, Allen appealed to their constituents to turn *them* out of office. He published both their names and those of the deputies who voted for Hutchinson's plan to establish a silver currency with the Louisbourg conpensation.[63] Whether because of Allen's pamphlet or for other reasons, fifteen of the forty towns that favored Hutchinson's plan in 1749 voted to pass an inflationary monetary bill negating it two years later. On the other hand, Allen did not produce the immediately expected turnover of personnel. Thomas Hutchinson and Robert Hale met defeat, but eighteen of the thirty men who voted to expel him and twenty-six of the forty who supported hard money, both average proportions, did not.

Allen's lists indicate a shift in factional allegiance during the first eight years of Shirley's administration. Fourteen of the thirty towns that voted for Allen's expulsion had favored the Land Bank in 1740, as did eighteen of the forty that voted for Hutchinson's currency scheme. Allen was right about placemen being loyal to the governor, at least on this vote: twenty-five of thirty who voted to expel him and thirty-two of the forty who supported the currency bill served either as militia officers or justices of the peace.

Although all Shirley's enemies worked in concert, their efforts proved ineffectual. The governor had befriended Thomas Hutchinson by supporting his plans to retire the province's supply of paper money. From 1748 to 1753, the principal issue in Massachusetts politics was the ability of the anti-inflationists to hold the line. With Hutchinson acting as "prime minister" during Shirley's absence, their fight succeeded.[64]

### A SPECIE CURRENCY: 1748–1753

Governor Shirley wrote to the Duke of Bedford that Massachusetts would never have established a silver currency without Thomas Hutchinson. Hutchinson planned the act sinking the paper money "alone" and "all measures . . . [were] settled by his extraordinary abilities and uncommon influence with the members [of the General Court]."[65] While the governor sojourned in England and France from August 1749 to August 1753, Lieutenant-Governor Spencer Phips nominally ruled Massachusetts. But the real power rested with Hutchinson and seasoned legislators such as John Choate of Ipswich, Robert Hale of Beverly, the house's new speaker, Thomas Hubbard of Boston, and James Otis, Sr., of Barnstable. In Shirley's absence, they prevented the deputies from reestablishing low taxes, reintroducing paper money, and depleting the province's silver reserves. This was no easy task. However, once the house had established a specie currency, the prerogative could outlast the country party. The hard money advocates simply waited until the winter legislative sessions, when many of the rural inflationists had departed, to obtain tax bills perpetuating their new coinage. Additionally, the court's domination of the council enabled it to defeat inflationary supply measures, forcing the house to go along with hard money if the government were to function at all.

In 1748, Hutchinson first advanced the notion that Massachusetts should use the reimbursement from Louisbourg to redeem some £2,000,000 in inflated currency. On 3 February, Shirley also warned the General Court that money had "sunk so low" it would "in a very little time bring many good farmers to poverty." He "most earnestly recommend[ed]" a new means of meeting expenses. With currency at an all-time low of under one-tenth sterling, the province received news that Britain was procrastinating approving its Louisbourg expenses. To ensure delivery of the money, Hutchinson convinced the legislature in late February 1748, just before it dissolved, to inform agents Kilby and Bollan that the silver would be used to stabilize New England's finances.[66]

But Hutchinson had won only half the battle. The assembly had indicated that it intended to use the silver to end inflation but had adopted no specific plan. Bollan wrote back of efforts being made to postpone the grant. *The Independent Advertiser* printed a memorial signed by agent Kilby and a number of British merchants arguing that unless paper money were abolished throughout New England the silver would not help Massachusetts, since people could still use Rhode Island bills. Another writer in *The Advertiser* wanted to keep the money in the Bank of England to earn interest. If brought to Massachusetts it would be shipped away to pay for imports.[67]

In November, the house acted to overcome these obstacles. First, it fired Kilby. Then on 20 January 1749, after five weeks of debate, it adopted, forty to thirty-seven, Hutchinson's plan to redeem its current money, known subsequently as old tenor, for silver coins at a ratio of eleven to one. The sum Britain paid for Louisbourg thereby covered the total currency outstanding. To ensure the new money faced no competition, all provincial officials had to take an oath that they would use neither old tenor nor other provinces' bills. Shirley wrote that Hutchinson had "managed and conducted" the law "through the opposition and difficulties it long labored under . . . being almost the whole business of five weeks."[68]

The currency controversy spilled over into *The Independent Advertiser* and brought forth several pamphlets hostile to Hutchinson's program. The three major objections anticipated the opposition to Alexander Hamilton's financial plan of forty years later. First, silver currency would benefit rich creditors at the expense of poor debtors. One writer predicted the merchants would "export all the silver, make remissions for themselves, . . . [and] lodge their estates in England, by which means we shall in a few years have neither silver nor paper, and all be undone, beggars or slaves."[69] Second, current possessors were to redeem the bills at a flat rate of eleven to one. No discrimination would occur between those who had held them when they were considerably more valuable and those who had acquired them recently.[70] Third, a letter from London found its way into *The Independent Advertiser* accusing Governor Shirley, Charles Apthorp, William Bollan, New Hampshire agent John Thomlinson, and one "J.C." of buying up the bills to make a profit.[71] A further parallel between Hutchinson's and Hamilton's plans is that both passed by the narrowest of margins after a couple of legislators altered their stances. Samuel Witt of Marlborough and Samuel Livermore of Waltham decided at the last moment that it would be best to retire the paper all at once rather than gradually.[72]

Thus a legislature with many members absent adopted Hutchinson's program after a long debate. Only a minority of the public favored it at first, and many opposed it strongly. Although Hutchinson had always been elected to the house by narrow margins, usually less than sixty percent of the votes since 1743, he received only about 200 of over 700 ballots in May 1749. He complained to his friend Israel Williams, "they were the principal inhabitants but we are governed not by weight but by numbers."[73] The General Court then elected him to the council, but not overwhelmingly. No returns survive for 1749, but two years later he only polled 70 of 116 votes; his brother-in-law Andrew Oliver had 65. In contrast, twenty-one of twenty-eight other councillors had over 90. Other signs of popular disapproval appeared. When Hutchinson's Boston residence burned down, arson was suspected, but could not be proven. (At the time of the fire, some lower-class spectators called out "let it burn.") The council felt obliged to offer an armed bodyguard, which Hutchinson declined. A strange shakedown scheme in which several members of the council had to pay blackmail upon pain of being kidnapped also occurred at this time.[74]

About this episode in his life, Hutchinson wrote in his unpublished autobiography that eventually he "was as much praised for his *firm* as he had before been abused for his *obstinate* behavior." But it took time. Massachusetts endured acute financial distress for several years as debtors found they had to come up with hard cash, which took time to circulate. Lieutenant-Governor Phips noted "that the bills being mostly called in and the silver not yet circulating . . . a great stagnation of business ensued." Opposition to the new currency appeared in "several tumultuous assemblies in and around Boston." A severe drought during 1749 and a smallpox epidemic which made the rounds of the province between 1752 and 1754, killing several hundred people in Boston alone, added to the economic dislocation.[75] To compensate for the misery caused by the new currency, Phips, speaking for the prerogative faction, introduced two new projects. One encouraged the immigration of foreign Protestants. A second paid bounties to promote the growing of foodstuffs "so we may be able to live more within ourselves and depend less upon our neighbors for the common necessities of life." Despite vigorous support in the newspapers, and efforts by the legislature to entice newcomers, both schemes met with little success.[76]

The court faction's fight to maintain a stable currency constituted the major issue on Massachusetts' political agenda from 1749 to 1753. Signs that popular discontent had penetrated the assembly appeared almost immediately once the money arrived from England. In December 1749, the house made it clear that the province also expected compensation for the Canadian expedition and its diverse expenses defending the other colonies. At the same time it informed Bollan that "it is of great importance to the province that the other governments should be obliged to a speedy and equitable redemption of their respective bills."[77] The agent wrote back that Massachusetts had asked Parliament to set a very dangerous precedent by regulating the colonies' internal affairs. He predicted that by such an act "the constitution of the colonies would have been wholly subverted and a despotic power vested in the crown." But Massachusetts cared more about practical than constitutional issues at this point.[78] As it was, Parliament's Currency Act of 1751 still permitted the New England colonies to issue £30,000 of paper annually and did nothing to abolish the vast sums already in existence.[79]

Paper money advocates in Massachusetts tried several times to abandon the new medium. In 1750, the house voted to pass a light tax and emit a new form of notes to pay most government expenses. But as in 1749 the hard money advocates had greater staying power. On 5 April, at the beginning of the court's final session, a proposal to issue the new bills carried forty-six to thirty-three; on 20 April, it failed thirty-one to twenty-eight. The court party persuaded seven representatives to change their votes and nineteen participants in the first roll call did not show for the second. Trouble threatened again in May 1751. After three weeks' debate, the deputies adopted an inflationary and inadequate supply bill thirty-six to twenty-six. Lieutenant-Governor Phips promptly vetoed it.[80]

Grassroots resistance to the new currency and the taxation also emerged.[81] Despite a law calling for the return of all old tenor notes by 1750, redemption had to be postponed several years because people continued to use them.[82] The transition to hard money shocked a population used to easy access to paper money of various sorts. The blame for the treasury's shortage fell on the tax collectors and, most especially, on Province Treasurer William Foye. Foye must have been doing a good job, since he had been elected routinely since 1736. But in May 1753, the house fired him and questioned his honesty and competence by voting seventy-one to thirteen that the next treasurer had to advance a £30,000 bond to guarantee proper performance of his office. The council defended Foye and replied that this bill "might tend to discourage any gentleman of character and estate from accepting the trust." The board refused to join with the deputies in electing a replacement.[83] Finally, both houses agreed on Harrison Gray of

Boston, who offered to post the bond. Gray must have been extremely competent, since he served without incident throughout the revolutionary crisis until 1774.[84]

The house made one last attempt to undo currency reform by introducing bimetallism. On 11 September 1753, it voted fifty-three to twenty-five to monetize gold and use the new medium to redeem the old tenor paper money still in existence. Accepting Hutchinson's and Andrew Oliver's argument that the cheaper medium would drive out the dearer, the council refused the bill.[85]

The virulence of the currency debate appears from seven roll calls printed on this issue in the *House Journals* from 1751 to 1753. Only four votes had been published before, one relating to the Explanatory Charter and three to the Land Bank. (There were sixteen additional roll calls from 1754 to 1768.) Unlike the constitutional conflicts of the 1720s and 1730s, which manifested nearly universal opposition to the governor's instructions, the fiscal and military issues of Shirley's administration divided the province itself.

## EXCISE AND WAR: 1753–1756

Governor Shirley returned from England in August 1753. While overseas, he wasted a good deal of energy in the futile Paris negotiations to fix the Canadian boundary. He succeeded in keeping his post, although he had applied in vain for the more profitable and less burdensome government of the Leeward Islands.[86] Shirley found little rest in Massachusetts. Financial problems occasioned by the conversion from paper to silver money came to a head in a new debate over the governor's salary and the excise controversy of 1754. The outbreak of war that year and Shirley's appointment to succeed General James Braddock as commander in chief of all the British forces in North America proved even more disrupting.[87] Although Shirley encountered little local opposition, a small group of self-interested men unseated the governor. Including Thomas Pownall[88] and Lord Loudoun, his successors as Governor of Massachusetts and commander in chief, respectively, they succeeded where Samuel Waldo and James Allen had failed.

The excise controversy occupied most of Shirley's first full year back in the province.[89] On 1 June 1754, the house voted a new tax bill differing from the province's long-standing law. It taxed the consumption of liquor by individuals rather than the amount sold by retailers. The excise collectors now had to demand an account "of all and every persons whomsoever in this government, of all the wine, rum, brandy,

and other distilled spirits expended by them (on oath if required)."
The oath was the representatives' revenge for the oath forbidding
public servants from accepting paper money. A penalty of £10 punished false swearing. Although the deputies considered the new act
necessary "to prevent polls and other estates from being over-
burdened,"[90] it met with tremendous opposition from pamphleteers in
Boston. They reiterated all the charges that had defeated Robert
Walpole's proposed British excise in 1733. The Reverend Samuel
Cooper of Boston and the printer Daniel Fowle wrote pamphlets with
colorful titles such as *The Total Eclipse of Liberty* and *Monster of
Monsters*.[91] Fowle and an alleged accomplice, Royall Tyler—who
later became a representative from Boston and a councillor—served
five and two days in jail, respectively, for comparing the debaters in
the assembly to squabbling matrons from ancient Rome. Their imprisonment brought cries that the liberty of the press had ended.
Fowle unsuccessfully sued House Speaker Thomas Hubbard for sending him to jail.[92]

The principal focus of the debate centered on public versus private
rights. Opponents of the excise, who wrote all except one of the relevant tracts, conjured up visions of corrupt excise men ransacking
houses for liquor, pocketing the money collected, and even forcing the
daughters of honest poor men to surrender their virtue to keep their
fathers out of debtors' prison.[93] The one author who supported the
tax retorted that "I perceive no man can have any natural right, in conflict with the good of the country," and insisted that the excise collectors would act responsibly because the General Court selected them.[94]

Much of the excise debate embodied the rural–urban antagonism
that had broken out in Massachusetts in the late 1730s. The opposition centered in Boston. Throughout the fifties, the metropolis complained of overtaxation. The one-fifteenth of the population residing
in the capital paid approximately one-fifth of the province tax. Eva-
sion was common. The Boston selectmen observed that some people
temporarily removed to the country when it was time to pay rates. To
escape high taxes, prominent merchants maintained residences in the
surrounding towns while conducting their affairs in the city.[95]

The interior towns persistently refused to grant Boston tax relief
despite its economic distress. One writer objected that while the
seacoast depended on imported rum and wine, rural farmers manufac-
tured their own alcohol out of corn or made cider, which exempted
them from the tax on purchased liquor. Far from being a luxury tax,
as its supporters claimed, the excise robbed the ports for the benefit of
the interior.[96] The roll call bears out this interpretation. All seventeen

nays came from Boston, Salem, Marblehead, Plymouth, the small towns surrounding them, and Maine.[97]

The excise complicated the factional profile of Shirley's administration. The governor himself opposed the tax, making common cause with the likes of James Allen and Daniel Fowle.[98] But he did not travel the full distance with the anti-excise faction. It would have been foolish to alienate a three to one majority. The governor merely asked that the representatives consult their constituents. If they still adhered to their vote, he would not oppose it. The towns proceeded to vote but the representatives ignored their wishes. The thirty-six towns that expressed a preference on the excise opposed it twenty-six to ten.[99] But the pro-excise faction claimed that "those towns were for the bill that would not . . . meet upon it."[100] This may well have been the case as a nearly equal proportion of representatives favoring (twenty-four of fifty-two) or opposing (eight of seventeen) the tax were reelected.[101] Both the excise and a stamp tax (similar to the one Britain later imposed) lasted only until 1757 when special Parliamentary grants for war expenditures eased the province's burdens.[102]

No sooner had the excise been adopted than the last and greatest of the Anglo-French eighteenth-century wars broke out. Massachusetts again led in intercolonial defense, and requested that Britain find some means of compelling the other colonies to contribute their fair share of men and money in the common cause.[103] At the Albany Congress of September 1754, Pennsylvania's Benjamin Franklin proposed a Plan of Union to accomplish this end. However, none of the colonies favored Franklin's scheme, which the delegates had adopted, because it removed the crucial powers of taxation and raising troops from the local legislatures. Thomas Hutchinson rewrote the measure to reserve these privileges, but even so, Massachusetts was unenthusiastic.[104] The vague motion that "there be a general union of His Majesty's colonies on this continent" passed the house only forty-one to thirty-seven on 14 December. On 27 December the deputies tabled the measure more decisively (forty-eight to thirty-one), until after the representatives had consulted their constituents. Perhaps this last vote was sarcastically directed at Shirley's proposal that the towns consult on the excise, for the deputies repudiated any union at all the very next day.[105]

The variety of political issues during the latter half of Shirley's administration resulted in extremely flexible voting patterns in the house between 1751 to 1756. The number of representatives supporting or opposing the governor's stand not only varied widely on related measures, but even on the same issue. On the Plan of Union, eleven representatives changed their positions within two weeks, ten from aye to nay. Two roll calls in late 1754 and early 1755, the first increasing the grant to Governor Shirley, the second to ex-treasurer Foye, also reveal discontinuity even though Shirley and the council supported Foye. Of the twenty-three members in favor of Foye, all had voted on Shirley's salary: eleven in favor, twelve opposed; thirty-one of the forty-two men who opposed Foye voted on the earlier roll call: twelve supported Shirley, nineteen did not. Thirteen representatives who favored the excise took the governor's side on the Plan of Union; four who opposed it also rejected the plan. Those who favored the excise had opposed increasing Shirley's salary the previous year twenty-one to seven, but even the opposers of the excise had divided five to five on this question. Thus, many representatives treated as separate issues Shirley personally, his military policy, and his fiscal policy. Some went along with war measures even though they disliked the court faction's leadership.

During Shirley's final years in office, he restored the factional harmony absent since the early forties. Military conflict had broken out again, but as the governor remarked to the assembly, "affairs between the English and French on this continent are now in a very different state from what they have been in heretofore; and it is evident that the design of the French is now not to distraught or harrass any part of the British colonies, but to exterminate the whole." For the first time, France mounted the sort of large-scale expeditions against the British settlements that Massachusetts had launched against Canada. Massachusetts responded heroically: in 1755, three-thousand men garrisoned Nova Scotia while forty-two hundred marched in the ill-fated expeditions to Niagara and Crown Point. The following year, the province mustered thirty-five hundred more troops for another futile campaign against the latter post. Massachusetts levied a tax averaging of £80,000 new tenor (about £60,000 sterling) from 1756 to 1760. By 1756, Governor Shirley had to advance the province £30,000 sterling from the regular army's funds to enable it to participate in the second Crown Point expedition.[106]

Under these circumstances, open opposition to Shirley nearly vanished. Proud that its governor had succeeded General James Braddock as commander in chief, the legislature threatened with a libel suit "some evil minded persons" who criticized the war. Only an illegal trade with the enemy marred the province's record. But the legislature responded by embargoing supplies and provisions, and requiring traders to post bond that they would unload their cargoes in the British dominions.[107]

# Notes to Chapter VI

As in King George's War, cooperation with the British proved difficult. Using his Lieutenant-Governor Spencer Phips as a mouthpiece, Shirley pressed the reluctant deputies hard for manpower drafts for the Crown Point expeditions. Naval impressment also hurt Massachusetts: it threatened the survival of the province's fishery in the Grand Banks. Thomas Hutchinson and Agent Bollan argued unsuccessfully that the province charter prohibited impressments as it forbade inhabitants from being sent outside of Massachusetts without the General Court's consent.[108]

Massachusetts' troubles increased when Lord Loudoun replaced Shirley as commander in chief following the disastrous campaigns against Niagara, Oswego, and Crown Point. Loudoun, his assistant Thomas Pownall, Shirley's own second-in-command Sir William Johnson, and old Jonathan Belcher (now Governor of New Jersey) succeeded in having Shirley removed from his government in August 1756. In an attempt to retain him, the General Court showered the departing governor with praise for his "assiduous and unusual application to the public business."[109] Having finally prevailed over local opposition, Shirley was ousted for his failings as a military commander. He could not defend himself against the well-connected people with whom he dealt as commander in chief.

Few colonial governors altered the course of American history to the extent William Shirley did. His military expeditions during King George's War forced Massachusetts and the home authorities to examine seriously each other's role in imperial defense. In this respect, Shirley's administration left two possible legacies. By compelling the province and Britain to depend upon each other, opportunities for both cooperation and conflict increased. King George's War after Louisbourg brought out the negative side: the country faction opposed the war using the Whig ideas it later revived to justify the American Revolution. On the other hand, no major outbursts of discontent occurred in Massachusetts during the first two years of the French and Indian War. More oscillations occurred later in the war.

# Notes to Chapter VI

1. War between Britain and Spain broke out in 1739 (the War of Jenkins' Ear); war between France and Britain began in 1744 (known as King George's War). Massachusetts participated in the former conflict by supplying men for the West Indies expedition of 1740 and furnishing sailors to man the navy. The dates of this chapter are those of Shirley's governorship. They were chosen to facilitate dealing with the historiographical issue of whether and what sort of political stability Massachusetts attained at this time.

# Notes to Chapter VI

2. See especially, John A. Schutz, *William Shirley: King's Governor of Massachusetts* (Chapel Hill, 1960), preface; and Robert Zemsky, *Merchants, Farmers, and River Gods* (Boston, 1971), chs. 6–7. Their interpretations of Shirley recognize stability but also take conflict into account. Stability does not mean Shirley maintained the consistent support of the same people. He entered office with Samuel Waldo and Christopher Kilby among his principal adherents and Thomas Hutchinson as his most effective enemy. By 1748, these positions had reversed. See Jack P. Greene, "The Growth of Political Stability: An Interpretation of Political Development in the Anglo-American Colonies, 1660–1760," in John Parker and Carol Urness, eds., *The American Revolution: A Heritage of Change* (Minneapolis, 1975), for a discussion of criteria for political stability. My definition approximates that of J.H. Plumb, *The Origins of Political Stability: England, 1675–1725* (Boston, 1967), p. xvii: "the acceptance by society of its political institutions and of those classes of men or officials who control them." Shirley and his partisans themselves first drew attention to the unusual nature of his administration. In 1741, he noted that he "entered upon the government of a province, where Colonel Shute quitted the chair, and Mr. Burnet broke his heart through the temper and opposition of the people, and Mr. Belcher in the midst of his countrymen failed of carrying any one of those points, which might have been expected from him." Nine years later, Shirley somewhat untruthfully wrote the Duke of Newcastle that "throughout my whole administration a perfect harmony has ever subsisted between me and the assembly," and "there has never happened the least quarrel, ill-will, or misunderstanding." Province Secretary Josiah Willard, who had accompanied Governor Shute to the province in 1716, agreed that "although we have had none but good governors for the [past] six and twenty years . . . and we might have lived happily with any of them had it not been our own fault," only Shirley achieved the elusive "harmony and agreement between the several parts of the legislature." William Shirley to Duke of Newcastle, 23 August 1741, William Shirley, *Correspondence of William Shirley*, ed. C.H. Lincoln (New York, 1912), 1: 39. (Hereafter cited as *Shirley Papers*.) Same to same, 23 January 1750, *ibid.*, p. 493. See also John Thomlinson to Samuel Waldo, 7 April 1742, Massachusetts Archives, 53: 118, State House, Boston; Josiah Willard to Benjamin Avery, 30 December 1743, *ibid.*, p. 14.

3. *A Letter to the Freeholders and Other Inhabitants of the Province* (Boston, 1742), Evans, #4988, p. 4; *A Letter to the Freeholders and Other Inhabitants of Boston* (Boston, 1749), Evans, #6299, p. 3.

4. For a more detailed discussion of opposition to Shirley's military policies, see John Lax and William Pencak, "The Knowles Riot and the Crisis of the 1740s in Massachusetts," *Perspectives in American History*, 10 (1976): 163–214 and Douglas Leach, "Brothers in Arms?—Anglo-American Friction at Louisbourg, 1745–1746," *MHSP*, 89 (1977): 36–54.

5. *The Diaries of Benjamin Lynde and Benjamin Lynde, Jr.*, ed. Fitch E. Oliver (Boston, 1880), p. 162; Andrew M. Davis, *Colonial Currency Reprints*, (Boston, 1911–1912), 3: 155–355. Douglass wrote "it is to be hoped the Parliament of Great Britain will not use any vigorous, sudden measures, but gives us time . . . to extricate ourselves"; Thomas Hutchinson to Benjamin Lynde, 12 August 1742, *Lynde Diaries*, p. 223.

6. Christopher Kilby to Thomas Hancock, 10 September 1741, Miscellaneous Bound Manuscripts, MHS.

7. William Shirley to Board of Trade, 7 November 1743, *Shirley Papers*, 1: iii. In particular, Beverly's representative Robert Hale, a Bank director, was the target of one Nathaniel Martyn. As a member of the house, Hale was immune from prosecution. Martyn tried to oust him to collect on the bank notes. The house ruled that "for any person or persons to offer any means or rewards to influence any elector in voting for his representative is a high offence, as it is a manifest infraction on the liberty of the subject. . . . Every elector ought to have great freedom of speech and action in the important af-

fair of choosing his representative, provided what he offers with respect to the person or persons to be elected is done with decency, justice, and truth, and the considerations offered to influence the conduct of the electors be generous and rational and suited to the understanding and freedom of men." *Journals of the House of Representatives of Massachusetts Bay,* (Boston, 1919–      ), 20: 407.

8. Thomas Paine to Samuel Stork, 6 January 1743, Robert Treat Paine Papers, MHS.

9. Some difficulties arose implementing this scheme: access had to be obtained to the Bank's records and the relative responsibilities of each participant ascertained. The assembly first passed a bill giving the commissioners chosen to liquidate the Bank power to break into homes and sell the effects of those who could not redeem their notes. No appeal was allowed to the courts. The governor, who in this instance proved more concerned with the personal rights of the inhabitants than did their own representatives, refused to consent to the bill until these drastic clauses were removed. William Shirley to Duke of Newcastle, 15 September 1742, and to Board of Trade, 30 January 1743, *Shirley Papers,* 1: 89–91, 98–99, 108–111; *House Journals,* 19: 4; 20: 63, 156, 180, 199, 236; Davis, *Currency and Banking in Massachusetts,* (New York, 1901), vol. 2, ch. 9.

10. Davis, *Currency Reprints,* 4: 295.

11. William H. Whitmore, *The Massachusetts Civil List, 1630–1774* (Albany, 1870), pp. 56–59.

12. *House Journals,* 14: 105, 111, 174; 20: 219; William Shirley to Duke of Newcastle, 23 January 1742, *Shirley Papers,* 1: 89-90. In 1747 (*ibid.,* 3: 373) the legislature instructed the adjustors not to govern the rate by one or two commodities only, but by the general price of all goods.

13. William Shirley to Board of Trade, 19 March 1743, and Shirley to Duke of Newcastle, 31 January 1749, *Shirley Papers,* 1: 102, 466–467.

14. Shirley also disposed of the bills issued in 1737, known as middle tenor, which unlike regular province bills were redeemable in gold and silver after five years. Although no silver and gold existed to redeem them, the assembly agreed to pay the bill holders (or hoarders, to put it more accurately) 33⅓ percent more than current value in "new" tenor. Shirley claimed that this was "the best I could procure for them, and was obtained with much difficulty." The possessors were satisfied, although one of Shirley's enemies claimed, with considerable exaggeration, that this bill depreciated the people's estates nearly 30 percent. William Shirley to Board of Trade, 24 January 1743, *ibid.,* p. 97; *A Letter to the Freeholders and Inhabitants of the Province,* Evans, #4988, p. 4.

15. William Shirley to Duke of Newcastle, 17 October 1741, 23 January 1742, and to Board of Trade, 10 August 1744, *Shirley Papers,* 1: 76, 80, 140; Board of Trade to Shirley, 9 September 1744, *ibid.,* p. 144.

16. William Douglass, *A Summary . . . Historical and Political . . . of North America,* (London, 1755), 1: 493. Douglass quotes the official rate. However, a bushel of wheat selling for 3.6 shillings sterling required 60 shillings Massachusetts; the ratio varied for different commodities. *Historical Statistics of the United States* (Washington, 1960), p. 771. See also *House Journals,* 22: 57; 24: 238; 25: 12, for the extent of depreciation.

17. *House Journals,* 19: 179–252, *passim*; William Shirley to Board of Trade, 23 June 1742, *Shirley Papers,* 1: 87.

18. A second source of conflict during Shirley's first years stemmed from a small group of Belcher's friends—notably Thomas Hutchinson and James and Jeremiah Allen—who tried to elect a province agent unfavorable to Shirley's interest after the General Court dismissed the aged Francis Wilkes. Two possible successors emerged: Shirley's candidate John Thomlinson, a New Hampshire merchant who had helped him

obtain the governorship, and Eliakim Palmer, Hutchinson's London business partner. Shirley vetoed Palmer's election, but the house chose Robert Auchmuty and Christopher Kilby instead of Thomlinson. Shirley disliked Auchmuty but approved him because he used his followers to defeat Palmer. Auchmuty never went to England, and in February 1744 Kilby became sole agent. *House Journals*, 20: 77; 21: 302, 363; William Shirley to John Thomlinson, 27 February 1742, and 6 April 1743, Shirley–Thomlinson Letters, MHS.

19. Colonel William Pepperrell, whom Shirley described as "king of that country," boasted ineffectually that his money and influence at court would nullify Shirley's campaign. William Shirley to John Thomlinson, 27 March 1742, 6 April 1743, and 20 May 1743, Shirley–Thomlinson Letters, MHS.

20. Bollan commented that the traders "poisoned the minds of all the inhabitants of the province, and matters are brought to such a pass that it is sufficient to recommend any trade to their general approbation that it is unlawful." He complained that until all breaches of trade were cognizable only in the admiralty court, a jury trial "is only trying one illicit trader by his fellows, or at least his well-wishers." "Illegal Trade," collected letters of William Shirley, William Bollan, and Robert Auchmuty, 26 February 1743, Boston Public Library.

21. Full accounts of military events in King George's War may be found in Schutz, *William Shirley*, pp. 80–122, and George A. Wood, *William Shirley: Governor of Massachusetts, 1741–1756* (New York, 1920), pp. 181–359.

22. The Duke of Bedford's and the Earl of Halifax's plans to tighten control of the colonies and promote intercolonial defense can be directly linked to Shirley's complaints that other colonies did little to aid Massachusetts. Alison G. Olson, "The British Government and Colonial Union, 1754," *William and Mary Quarterly*, 3rd. ser. 17 (1960), pp. 22–34.

23. *House Journals*, 20: 410.

24. William Shirley to General Court, 31 May 1744, *Shirley Papers*, 1: 122–124; *House Journals*, 21: 10, 29, 85; 120 men were sent.

25. *House Journals*, 21: 42, 64; 22: 34. Massachusetts was still defending Fort Dummer in 1757; *ibid.*, 33: 417.

26. *Ibid.*, 21: 111–114.

27. Duke of Newcastle to William Shirley, *Shirley Papers*, 1: 122.

28. William Shirley to Duke of Newcastle, 14 January 1745, *ibid.*, pp. 161–166; Resolutions of Massachusetts General Court, 25 January 1745, *ibid.*, pp. 169–170; *House Journals*, 21: 180–190.

29. Hutchinson, *History*, 2: 313.

30. Schutz, *Shirley*, p. 100; John A. Schutz, "Imperialism in Massachusetts during the Governorship of William Shirley, 1741–1756," *Huntington Library Quarterly*, 23 (1960): 222; Nathan O. Hatch, "The Origins of Civil Millennialism in America: New England Clergymen, War with France, and the Revolution," *William and Mary Quarterly*, 3rd. ser. 31 (1974): 417-422; Alan Heimert, *Religion and the American Mind* (Cambridge, 1966), pp. 82-84; Wood, *Shirley* pp. 169–170, 275–276.

31. Hutchinson, *History*, 2: 314.

32. Jack P. Greene, "Social Context and the Causal Pattern of the American Revolution: A Preliminary Consideration of New York, Virginia, and Massachusetts," in *La Revolution Americaine et L'Europe* (Paris, 1979), p. 7.

33. Kerry Trask, "In the Pursuit of Shadows: A Study of Collective Hope and Despair in Provincial Massachusetts During the Era of the Seven Years War, 1740 to 1765" (University of Minnesota, unpublished Ph.D. diss., 1971); Nathan O. Hatch, *The Sacred Cause of Liberty* (New Haven, 1977).

# Notes to Chapter VI

34. Trask, "In the Pursuit of Shadows," explains Massachusetts' crusading mentality as an escape from its problems.

35. Myron Stachiw, ed., *Massachusetts Soldiers and Sailors During the French and Indian Wars, 1722-1743* (Boston, 1979); *Year Book of the Society of Colonial Wars in the Commonwealth of Massachusetts* (Boston, 1899), pp. 80-81, 92-94.

36. *A&R*, 2: 1037; Philip Greven, *Four Generations: Population, Land and Family in Colonial Andover* (Ithaca, 1970); Kenneth Lockridge "Social Change and the Meaning of the American Revolution," *Journal of Social History*, 6 (1971): 403-439; Robert Gross, *The Minutemen and Their World* (New York, 1976), pp. 68-108.

37. See Fred Anderson, "The Experience of Provincial Military Service in Eighteenth Century North America: The Crown Point Expedition of 1756 as a Test Case," unpublished paper, and his forthcoming Harvard University dissertation; Nash, *The Urban Crucible*, pp. 244-245.

38. See Chapter 8; William Welsteed, "The Dignity and Duty of Civil Magistrates (Boston, 1751), p. 57; *Boston Evening Post*, 11 June 1753, both cited in Trask, "In Pursuit of Shadows," pp. 97-100 with other examples; Josiah Quincy, ed., *Reports of Cases Argued . . . Before the Superior Court of Massachusetts Bay* (Boston, 1865), p. 259; *A&R*, 2: 642.

39. *House Journals*, 21: 198; William Bollan to General Court, 27 February 1748, quoted in *The Independent Advertiser*, 4 July 1748. *The Advertiser* noted on 14 November that "the solicitation of reimbursement, we have been taught, did not depend upon the merit of our past services, but upon new capers, new expenses, and new expeditions."

40. *House Journals*, 22: 162, 182; 23: 18, 42, 93-95, 125.

41. *Ibid.*, 22: 207, 246, 252.

42. *Ibid.*, 23: 187, 307-308; 24: 163; 25: 37, 52, 66.

43. For a discussion of impressment, see Lax and Pencak, "The Knowles Riot."

44. Wood, *Shirley*, pp. 338, 367; Letter of Commodore Knowles to Duke of Newcastle, Sparks Manuscripts 43, New England Papers, 2: 62, Houghton Library, Harvard University.

45. Thomas Hancock to [Christopher Kilby], 20 October 1746, Box 7, folder 1, Hancock Papers, New England Historic Geneological Society (hereafter NEHGS); Josiah Quincy, Sr., to Henry Flint, 18 July 1748, Josiah Quincy, Jr., Papers, MHS.

46. John Adams to Skelton Jones, 11 March 1809; John Adams, *Works*, ed. Charles Francis Adams (Boston, 1850-1853), 9: 611.

47. James and Benjamin Franklin made use of "Cato's Letters" in the *New England Courant*, but not to criticize specific policies; see David L. Jacobson, *The English Libertarian Heritage* (Indianapolis, 1965), pp. 1-11. William Douglass in 1738 and Governor Shirley in 1742 had mentioned the "state of nature" and "natural rights" of man in passing, but did not develop their points. Davis, *Currency Reprints*, 4: 24; *House Journals*, 20: 69. (It is somewhat ironical that Locke's doctrine was first introduced to Massachusetts by Shirley and Douglass, two British immigrants. The popular party disliked both of them for their support of hard currency.) The use of "natural rights" was an intellectual necessity for Americans to judge their society and government without reference to British law and tradition, and thus a prerequisite for the Revolution. For a discussion of the staff of *The Independent Advertiser* and quotations from its pages, see Lax and Pencak, "The Knowles Riot."

48. See *The Independent Advertiser*, 21 November 1748. All of Shirley's enemies used this nickname. Jeremiah Allen wrote to Samuel Waldo on 13 November 1749, that "Dr. Douglass is preparing a compound for Sir Plume" with respect to the paper currencies. See also same to same, 23 January 1750, Massachusetts Archives, 53: 440, 478.

49. On Windmill, his plan for magically changing copper into silver, and a satire on his boasts that everything of importance in the history of Massachusetts had been effected by members of his family, see *The Advertiser*, 27 March and 11 April 1748.

50. While condemning misuse of patronage, *The Advertiser* wished more of it had come New England's way. It complained that Shirley and Pepperrell appointed too few inhabitants as officers in their regiment. See, for example, the issues of 31 October 1748, and 21 August 1749. Twenty years later, even Thomas Hutchinson gave the same verdict on Shirley's motives for the campaigns: "he had a fair prospect, in this way, of promoting his private interest." Hutchinson, *History*, 2: 313.

51. For attacks on the assembly, see the issues of 28 March 1748, 2 May 1748, 9 May 1748, 20 June 1748, and 8 May 1749. The previous criticisms of placemen are found in the Mathers' attack on the house for exonerating Dudley; in Davis, *Currency Reprints*, 2: 233, 242; and in *A Letter to the Freeholders* . . . (Boston, 1742), Evans, #4988. Other electioneering pamphlets appeared to aid *The Advertiser's* efforts in 1749 and 1750. They denounced Shirley, placemen, and the governor's monetary policies. See James Allen, *Letter to Freeholders and Other Qualified Voters* (Boston, 1749), Evans, #6344, and *Letter to the Freeholders of the Town of Boston* (Boston, 1750), Evans, #6527.

52. Hutchinson, *History*, 2: 332–333; *The Independent Advertiser*, 8 February 1748 and 5 December 1749.

53. See the issues of 4 January 1748, 1 August 1749, 17 August 1749, and 17 July 1749. Ironically, Shirley's son-in-law William Bollan received the thanks of the house in 1750 for his opposition to an Anglican episcopate; *House Journals*, 27: 32; William Bollan to Thomas Hubbard, 25 August 1750, Miscellaneous Bound Manuscripts.

54. *The Independent Advertiser*, 10 October 1748; see also 14 November 1748.

55. Pepperrell's opposition may be attributed to dissatisfaction with his salary for the Louisbourg campaign. Until 1757 he periodically requested additional grants. He also resented being shunted aside for the rest of the war. Finally, his nephew and heir Nathaniel Sparhawk, and his partner Joseph Gerrish of Newbury did not win the supply of the British and provincial forces at Louisbourg. Thomas Hancock and Charles Apthorp, although competing with each other, eventually arranged an amicable division of the spoils, in part through their willingness to bribe British officers. For the competition to supply Louisbourg, see Zemsky, *Merchants, Farmers, and River Gods*, ch. 8, and Thomas Hancock's letters in his Letter Book, MHS, and the Hancock Papers, NEHGS. See also Nathaniel Sparhawk to Samuel Waldo, 10 November 1749, and Joseph Heath to Waldo, 29 January 1750, Massachusetts Archives, 53: 447, 485; *House Journals*, 33: 452, 468.

56. A good friend and business partner of Thomas Hancock, Kilby proved a hopelessly incompetent province agent. Shirley had to convince the council not to fire him in 1747. Even Hancock complained that he never kept the province properly informed of its interests. The final straw came in 1748 when Kilby—who had been forced to accept Shirley's son-in-law William Bollan as a coequal special agent for the Louisbourg reimbursement—opposed Bollan's efforts to ship the money to Massachusetts as rapidly as possible. Along with twenty-five merchants, Kilby signed a petition reprinted in *The Advertiser*, 21 November 1748, recommending that payment be postponed until Parliament settled the value of all New England currencies. The infuriated representatives immediately named Bollan sole agent. He retained the post until 1763.

See *House Journals*, 22: 89; 25: 130 for Bollan's appointment on 31 July 1745, and Kilby's removal on 17 November 1748. For Kilby's inefficiency and the effort to remove him, see Thomas Hancock to Christopher Kilby, 20 August 1746 and 23 January 1747, Hancock Letter Book, MHS. Shirley's opponents tried to obtain the agency for Benjamin Avery in 1749: they had a narrow majority in the house but the council favored Bollan nineteen to two; Joseph Heath to Samuel Waldo, Massachusetts Archives, 53: 485. Hancock to Kilby, 7 December 1747, Hancock Papers, Box 4, folder 10, NEHGS.

57. John Noble, "The Libel Suit of Knowles vs. Douglass, 1748, 1749," *PCSM*, (1895–1897), 1: 213–240; see Douglass, *Summary*, 1: 315, 336, 348, 501, and *The Independent Advertiser*, 4 July 1748, for the doctor's charges.

58. The Superior Court heard the case on 22 April 1749. Despite Waldo's insistence that "not one of the witnesses sworn for that purpose nor all of them put together supported any one such article or charge," he had to pay £500 plus costs. Waldo suspected that the jury was bribed. A retrial acquitted him. William Shirley to Samuel Waldo, 28 June 1748, 7 July 1748; Waldo to Shirley, 28 June 1748; "The Case of General Samuel Waldo"; "The Case of Waldo vs. Shirley," 22 April 1749, an account of the trial signed by a number of Waldo's friends including the Allen brothers and two future Boston representatives, Harrison Gray and William Cooper; and Waldo to Christopher Kilby, 24 April 1749; all in Henry Knox Papers, vol. 50, MHS.

59. Thomas Hutchinson to Israel Williams, 19 May 1749, Israel Williams Papers, MHS.

60. For Allen's involvement in the supply, see Thomas Hancock to Christopher Kilby, 22 July and 7 August 1745, Hancock Letter Book, MHS.

61. Thomas Hutchinson, "Hutchinson in America," Egremont Manuscript, #2664, 56, British Museum (microfilm at MHS). *The Independent Advertiser*, 29 August 1748.

62. *House Journals*, 25: 116, 148, 150, 157.

63. James Allen, *Letter to the Freeholders and Other Inhabitants of Massachusetts Bay* (Boston, 1749), Evans, #6299.

64. For use of this phrase, see Nathaniel Sparhawk to Samuel Waldo 18 May 1749, Massachusetts Archives, 53: 494; on 1 January 1750, Joseph Heath of Roxbury, another Waldo supporter, wrote him that "Mr. Hutchinson drives all before him"; n.d., *ibid.*, p. 484. Spencer Phips, nephew and heir of William Phips, Lieutenant-Governor of Massachusetts, managed to hold this office from 1733 to 1757 without leaving any significant impression on his contemporaries. The only reference I could find to his character, from Thomas Hutchinson, "Hutchinson in America," p. 65, is mildly complimentary. When Isaac Royall put in to be lieutenant-governor upon Phips's death, Hutchinson wrote "no man could be more unfit than Royall, being inferior in understanding to Phips and wanting some good qualities of which Phips was possessed besides."

65. William Shirley to Duke of Bedford, 31 January 1749, *Shirley Papers*, 1: 467.

66. *House Journals*, 10: 238, 276, 302; the difficulties in obtaining the money are fully recounted in Davis, *Currency and Banking*, 1: 219–232.

67. *The Independent Advertiser*, 28 March and 27 November 1748. See also *A Word in Season to All True Lovers of Their Liberty and Their Country—Both of which are in the Utmost Danger of Being Forever Lost* (Boston, 1748); Davis—*Currency Reprints*, 4: 363. The author of the *Appendix to Massachusetts in Agony*, one "Cornelius Agrippa" (Boston, 1751), in Davis, *Currency Reprints*, 4: 474, and Dr. Douglass favored keeping the silver in England.

68. *A&R*, 3: 430–441; William Shirley to Duke of Bedford, 31 January 1749, *Shirley Papers*, 1: 467. Thomas Hutchinson wrote to Israel Williams on 1 February 1749, that if Williams and the absent representatives from Hampshire County had appeared, he "could have saved three weeks' wrangling," Williams Papers. Hutchinson noted in his *History*, 2: 334–336, that when he first "laid the proposal before the house, . . . it was received with a smile and generally thought to be an Utopian project." He had to overcome not only "the major part of the people, [who] were no sufferers by a depreciating

currency," but those who favored keeping the money in the Bank of England or the provincial treasury and issuing paper money backed by the silver.

69. *A Word in Season*, in Davis, *Currency Reprints*, 4: 360.

70. The author of *A Brief Account of the Rise, Progress and Present State of the Paper Currencies* (Boston, 1749) wrote: "There has been such a confounding of property that it is absolutely impossible to redress what is past." "Everyone who has been a possessor ought to have had his part of the loss made up to him, and not the possessor of the present day run away with the whole." Davis, *Currency Reprints*, 4: 389, 391.

71. *The Independent Advertiser*, 3 April 1749; see also 21 November 1748 for a more general criticism. The letter was attributed by Josiah Quincy, Sr., to Major Otis Little of Pembroke, another of Shirley's opponents then in London. Little himself was alleged to possess £30,000 of the bills. Letter to Edmund Quincy, 30 November 1748, Josiah Quincy, Jr., Papers, MHS. "J.C." was probably John Choate. Isaac Winslow accused James Otis, one of Shirley's lieutenants, of engrossing £12,000 sterling of the bills. Letter to Samuel Waldo, 7 December 1749, Massachusetts Archives, 53: 455. Thomas Hutchinson was speculating in New Hampshire bills ("which made a great noise") in the hope that all the colonies' currencies would be regulated. James Russell (Representative of Charlestown) to James Otis, 8 September 1750, Otis Papers, Columbia University, Box 1.

72. Hutchinson, *History*, 2: 336–337.

73. Thomas Hutchinson to Israel Williams, 19 May 1749, Williams Papers.

74. Hutchinson in "Hutchinson in America," pp. 58–59, was being less than objective when he wrote that "scarce a year had expired after the exchange of the money before the people in general were perfectly satisfied." *Massachusetts in Agony* (Boston, 1749) made reference to the "lust of power, lust of fame, lust of money through envy, pride, covetousness, and violent ambition" of "the great lord of the manor, his gilded equipage, party-colored attire, and himself besmeared with gold, . . . nor should any countryman own one inch of improved land between Boston and the Blue Hills." Davis, *Currency Reprints*, 4: 438–439. The area described is Milton, where Hutchinson had built a house. *A&R*, 3: 474.

75. Joseph Felt, *An Historical Account of Massachusetts Currency* (Boston, 1839), pp. 129–130; Trask, "In the Pursuit of Shadows," pp. 136–137, 167–174.

76. *House Journals*, 26: 86, 217; 27: 7, 153, 158; 28: 111. The governor's renewed insistence on the right to choose an attorney-general was also disputed; *ibid.*, 26: 38; 27: 35–36. Shirley and Phips insisted on this power beginning in 1749. Trask, "In the Pursuit of Shadows," pp. 125–127.

77. *House Journals*, 26: 165.

78. See Bollan's letters to Thomas Hubbard, 12 April and 12 May 1751, Bollan Papers, NEHGS. Bollan commented that "the difficulty of getting the members of Parliament to understand the nature and operations of the bills of credit in the colonies is unspeakably great."

79. For the Currency Act, see Lawrence H. Gipson, *The British Empire Before the American Revolution*, (New York, 1936–1972), 3: 13. The act only applied to New England.

80. James Allen, back as representative for Boston, decided this would be the ideal time to exacerbate the government's financial crisis by putting in a claim to be compensated for the losses to his estate from his father's twenty years' service as the province's treasurer. He was not successful. Phips, too, complained that he could not even obtain the paltry sums (about £300 annually) voted him. *House Journals*, 27: 35, 42, 47, 52, 56, 62, 66, 69, 97, 109, 198, 234.

81. *Ibid.*, 27: 93; 28: 85, 128. Opposition to taxes had appeared previously during the Andros regime and intercharter period. In 1694 (*A&R*, 1: 177) the General Court

admitted two-thirds of the previous years' assessment remained unpaid. Towns on the Rhode Island and Connecticut border—claimed by both Massachusetts and its neighbors—had given constant trouble on this count. I am indebted to John Murrin for these examples.

82. *A&R*, 3: 774.

83. Foye was blamed for all the province's arrears: see Harrison Gray to James Otis, 23 June 1752, Otis Papers, MHS. Both men voted for the bond. *House Journals*, 21: 29.

84. For the bond, see *ibid.*, 31: 176.

85. *Ibid.*, 30: 88; Davis, *Currency and Banking*, 1: 248.

86. William Shirley to Duke of Newcastle, 23 November 1752, *Shirley Papers*, 2: 1–31. For an account of Shirley's activities in England and France, see Schutz, *Shirley*, ch. 8, and Max Savelle, *The Diplomatic History of the Canadian Boundary* (New Haven, 1940).

87. Military events affecting Massachusetts during the French and Indian War are described in Gipson, *The British Empire Before the American Revolution*, vol. 6, chs. 6–7; vol. 7, chs. 4, 7, and 8.

88. Pownall had been Loudoun's secretary and Lieutenant-Governor of New Jersey; his brother John was the Board of Trade's most active member in the 1750s and 1760s.

89. After his arrival, Shirley began to wrangle with the assembly over payment for his services in England. On 19 December 1753 he received £1,400 "in full consideration of his past services," whereas he had hoped to obtain something approximating his full £1,000 sterling a year for each of his three years in Britain. He brought up this demand again in August 1756, just before he left for England, with equally negative results. *House Journals*, 30: 132, 153; 33: 145.

90. *Ibid.*, 30: 43.

91. See Paul Boyer, "Borrowed Rhetoric: The Massachusetts Excise Controversy of 1754," *William and Mary Quarterly*, 3rd. ser. 21 (1964): 328–351.

92. *House Journals*, 31: 63–72; 32: 10, 56–59, 340–353. The council questioned a house bill to spend £1,000 to defend Hubbard; after a large debate, a compromise was arranged to cover the indeterminate expenses. In the eighteenth century, truth was not considered a legitimate excuse to criticize the government. The anti-excise faction invoked standards of free speech which did not become generally recognized until the nineteenth century. See Leonard W. Levy, *Legacy of Suppression: Freedom of Speech and Press in Early American History* (Cambridge, 1960).

93. See especially Samuel Cooper, *The Crisis*, Evans, #7176; and the following anonymous works: *A Plea for the Poor and Distressed Town of Boston*, Evans, #7296; *The Review*, Evans, #7305; and *The Voice of the People*, Evans, #7329. (All: Boston, 1754).

94. [William Fletcher], *The Good of the Country, Impartially Considered* (Boston, 1754), Evans, #7312, p. 32. Fletcher's constituents in Cambridge did not agree and did not return him and William Brattle, who also supported the excise, to the house.

95. For a general discussion of Boston's tax problems, see Warden, *Boston, 1689–1776* (Boston, 1970), ch. 7; John M. Murrin, "Anglicizing an American Colony," (Yale University, Ph.D. diss., 1966), p. 118; *House Journals*, 21: 85; 33: 36, 38, 164, 174; 34: 404.

96. *A Plea for the Poor and Distressed Town of Boston*, pp. 2, 5.

97. *House Journals*, 31: 38.

98. Shirley injected the natural rights argument into the legislative journal for the first time, criticizing the excise as "altogether unprecedented in the English governments"

and "inconsistent with the natural rights of every person in the community." He predicted that "a general discontent throughout the province, and disaffection to His Majesty's government would be the fruit of it." The council too found the tax "without precedent in any of His Majesty's dominions." Samuel Cooper called Shirley "the father of his country" and his praise bordered on blasphemy: "the people were not indeed so impious as to shout on this occasion, it was the voice of God and not of a man, but . . . this speech of our governor was heard like the voice of a kind messenger from Heaven." *House Journals*, 21: 46; Samuel Cooper, *The Crisis*, pp. 11, 13.

99. Robert Dinkin, "Massachusetts: A Deferential or a Democratic Society?" (Columbia University, Ph.D. diss., 1968), p. 143.

100. *Boston Gazette,* 31 December 1754.

101. Several of the house's most important members—John Choate of Ipswich, Robert Hale of Beverly, Chambers Russell of Lincoln, and Samuel Welles of Boston—prudently abstained. An anonymous pamphlet, *The Review*, pp. 5, 7, accused them all of being prime movers of the tax. Shortly after the excise was adopted, grants were passed to Shirley and Agent Bollan. The author of *The Review* commented "perhaps Judge R[ussel]ll, Mr. W[e]lles of B[oston], and other leading men in the house, so zealous for these grants may be able to tell" why they were passed. The implication is that Shirley's consent to the excise, after the representatives approved it a second time, was obtained by bribery.

102. For the Stamp Act, see *House Journals,* 21: 202–203, 283, 288; 32: 83; 33: 294, 304, 307. The bill was adopted on 8 January 1755, and repealed on 2 February 1757.

103. *House Journals,* 26: 165; William Shirley and Governor George Clinton of New York to Board of Trade, 18 August 1753. *Shirley Papers*, 1: 165.

104. Referring to Hutchinson's plan, Sir Henry Frankland, Boston's custom collector, contended that:

> Nothing conscionable in the military war can be done by the colonies
> in their present disunited state. The plan of union, as concerted by the
> committee at Albany, would soon make us a formidable people.
> Disinterested public-spirited men of sense, who are versed in the nature
> of government, do declare that no objection can be made to
> it. . . . The prerogative and the rights of the people are both reserved
> therein without the least infringement upon the other.

Quotation from Diary of Sir Henry Frankland, 17 March 1755, MHS. For a general discussion of Hutchinson's role at the Albany Conference, see Lawrence Henry Gipson, "Thomas Hutchinson and the Albany Plan of Union," *Pennsylvania Magazine of History and Biography,* 74 (1950): 5–35. It is doubtful whether Hutchinson originated the plan, as Gipson claims, but he did revise it in the hope of making it more palatable.

105. *House Journals,* 31: 152–153, 182, 184.

106. *Ibid.,* 32: 17, 84, 116, 153; 33: 26, for the extent of Massachusetts' exertions; for expenditures, see *ibid.,* 32: 99–110; 33: 45, 110, and Gipson, *The British Empire Before the American Revolution,* 7: 159–163, 316–324. Massachusetts' contribution is reflected in the proportion of Parliament's reimbursement given to the province: for 1756, Massachusetts obtained £68,000 out of £115,000 for all the mainland colonies; for 1757, £27,380—only Connecticut was also paid that year; 1759, £62,000 out of £200,000; 1760, £60,000 out of £180,000; 1761, £43,000 out of £133,000; 1762, £45,000 out of £132,000. All told, Massachusetts received approximately one-third of some one million pounds. *Ibid.,* vol. 10, ch. 3.

107. *Ibid.,* 32: 404. For illegal trade, *ibid.,* pp. 87, 93, 249, 305.

108. For army impressment, *ibid.,* 32: 53, 99, 102, 103, 109–110, 141; 33: 45, 110. For navy, *ibid.,* 33:123–124, 164, 179–180, and Thomas Hutchinson to William

Bollan, 9 September 1756, Miscellaneous Bound Manuscripts, MHS; for the fate of Hutchinson's petition see William Bollan to Massachusetts General Court, 1 October 1757, Bollan Papers, NEHGS. Bollan's own memorial, incorporating Hutchinson's, is in folder 14 of his papers. The entire issue is discussed in William Pencak, "Thomas Hutchinson's Fight Against Naval Impressment," *New England Historical and Genealogical Register*, 132 (1978): 25–36.

109. *House Journals*, 33: 116. For Shirley's quarrel with Loudoun, see William Shirley to Earl of Loudoun, 3 September 1756, 13 September 1756, *Shirley Papers*, 2: 528–530, 550–559. Loudoun was angry that the Massachusetts regiments would not permit their officers to be replaced by British regulars; John Winslow to Council of War, July 1756, and Lord Loudoun to Shirley, 2 August 1756, *ibid.*, pp. 493–495. See Fred Anderson, "The Experience of Provincial Military Service in Eighteenth Century North America: The Crown Point Expedition of 1756 as a Test Case," unpublished paper. Loudoun was also upset that although Shirley was recalled in August, he delayed his departure. Loudoun to Shirley, 6 September 1756, *Shirley Papers*, 2: 547. For Shirley's enmity to Johnson, see Shirley to Sir William Johnson, 9 September 1755, Calendar of Shirley Manuscripts, MHS. Shirley complained that Johnson should have captured Crown Point that year as he vastly outnumbered the French; Johnson also had kept Shirley poorly informed. Assessments of the relative guilt of Shirley and his enemies vary. Stanley Pargellis, *Lord Loudoun in North America* (New Haven, 1933), ch. 5, is partial to Loudoun; Schutz, *Shirley*, favors Shirley.

# VII

## THE FRAGMENTATION OF MASSACHUSETTS 1756–1765

$\mathcal{B}$ETWEEN Governor Shirley's removal and the Stamp Act crisis, Massachusetts politics moved through three stages, each accompanying a different phase of the French and Indian War. During Thomas Pownall's first year in office and Lord Loudoun's tenure as commander in chief (1757 and early 1758), little united Britain and Massachusetts except a common enemy. Pownall and Loudoun soon began to fight with each other. Shirley's old supporters generally took Loudoun's side against Pownall, who aligned himself with the country faction. Furthermore, Loudoun's strenuous attempts to weld colonial troops and resources into a united fighting force subordinate to Britain antagonized even his staunchest supporters.

When the ministry replaced Loudoun, strife in Massachusetts abated considerably. General James Abercromby's unfortunate assault on Fort Ticonderoga in July 1758 once again made the French presence on the province's western frontier seem alarmingly close. Thereafter, Generals Jeffrey Amherst and James Wolfe turned the tide of battle. For two years, Massachusetts could bask in the glory of successful joint ventures with Britain for the first time since the capture of Louisbourg in 1745. Louisbourg was retaken in July 1758, Quebec assaulted successfully in September 1759, and the surrender of Montreal in September 1760, to all intents and purposes, ended French rule in Canada. Even Governor Pownall's adherence to the country faction and quarrels with leading court politicians could not hamper the united effort or dampen the general enthusiasm.

Once Montreal fell, Massachusetts found itself in a strange position. In one sense, it was still at war. Conflicts with Indians in the Ohio Valley and the south continued, as did the struggle in the West Indies against France and Spain. The province responded to British requests for troops until 1764. Yet in another sense, the real war was over. Once the French had been driven from Canada, the greatest obstacle to New England's prosperity and expansion no longer existed. The long-suffering province expected victory to bring an end to its tribulations.

Yet Massachusetts' difficulties continued. Beginning in 1760, the legislature once again quarrelled with British generals over embargoes, supplies, and troops. The province undertook further campaigns reluctantly, as its purpose had been accomplished. Nevertheless, it continued to lead the colonies' mobilization. Massachusetts' anger over the Writs of Assistance, trade regulation, the "Anglican bishop," its thwarted plan to convert newly conquered Indians, the Sugar Act, and insufficient reimbursement for war expenditures takes on an added dimension if it is remembered that thousands of the province's men were still in the army. Massachusetts sensed the inconsistency when a Britain that continued to ask for funds and troops also sought to revamp the province's institutions and deny the just rewards of its exertions.

Massachusetts experienced renewed, bitter, and increasingly divisive conflict as "the Great War for the Empire" wound down. Disputes over frontier lands, a college for western Massachusetts, and bimetallism supplemented Anglo-American strife. Until Parliament passed the Stamp Act in 1765, the court and country factions jockeyed for power on approximately equal terms. The Hutchinson and Otis families, respectively, led the prerogative and popular factions. Even Francis Bernard, the province's new governor who took office in July 1760, could not remain above politics despite his conscious effort to keep his life as pleasant as possible.

Massachusetts' difficulties in the 1760s mirrored those of the empire. Victory did not so much solve problems as exchange one set for another. Britain bought its triumphs at the cost of a debt amounting to some £170 million; war taxation had risen to twenty-five percent of income on estates. After the Peace of Paris in 1763 the empire seemed to fall apart. In Asia, the East India Company approached bankruptcy as famine in Bengal killed millions of people. North America, hardly recovered from fighting the French, had to deal with unprecedented numbers of immigrants, religious dissenters, Indian uprisings, land riots, and disputed boundaries. In Britain itself, William Pitt's wartime coalition broke down. Political radicalism added to the instability engendered by six, weak, short-lived ministries during the 1760s. Even before the war had ended, various elements in North America, the West and East Indies, and the British Isles had begun to quarrel over the spoils of victory.

WINDING DOWN THE WAR: 1756–1760

When Governor Thomas Pownall left Massachusetts in 1760 to become the absentee Governor of South Carolina, the General Court lavishly praised his administration. The legislature expressed its deep regret at losing "a governor so perfectly acquainted with the interest of the country and these plantations and so indefatigable and successful in joining in protecting the same."[1] But according to Pownall's hand-picked Lieutenant-Governor Thomas Hutchinson, the deputies were hiding their contempt behind this grandiloquent manifesto. Perhaps they sought to impress Pownall's powerful brother John, Secretary to the Board of Trade. Hutchinson denied Pownall's popularity and claimed that his adherents lost their seats in the assembly. Hutchinson wrote that the new governor associated himself with Shirley's enemies and hurt the war effort by collaborating with the popular party.[2]

Hutchinson's account of the two factions is accurate, but he let his own animosity get the better of him. He overestimated the general dissatisfaction with the governor. Severe moral judgement might be passed upon Pownall's machinations against Shirley, Hutchinson, and British military policy. But as his biographer notes, while in Massachusetts, he was a "Defender of American Liberty," if not a devoted servant of the crown.[3] Pownall staunchly defended the province against the charges and impositions of his erstwhile patron, Lord Loudoun. The truth lies somewhere between Hutchinson's maledictions and the legislature's praises.

However, Pownall did not reach Massachusetts until nearly a year after Shirley left in September 1756. In the interim Thomas Hutchinson acted unofficially much as a Governor of Massachusetts would have. Lieutenant-Governor Spencer Phips was seventy-four years old. Hutchinson remarked that "at his years, vigor and close application cannot be expected." Lord Loudoun directed his important correspondence to Hutchinson instead, who advised Loudoun how to obtain men and money from the reluctant colonies. His Lordship even asked and followed Hutchinson's advice that the reconquest of

Louisbourg was a necessary prerequisite to attack Quebec. Otherwise, the French could have sailed up the St. Lawrence and retaken Canada or raided the colonies using Cape Breton as a base. (The expedition proved disastrous despite the sound advice.) When Phips died in 1757, Loudoun and Pownall both recommended that Hutchinson succeed him.[4]

When Pownall arrived, however, he soon alienated Hutchinson and the court faction over patronage matters. He first sought to replace province Agent William Bollan—his predecessor's son-in-law—with his brother John Pownall. Hutchinson had always supported Bollan, and claimed that he "could not so dishonor himself as to give up his friend." "Coldness" between Hutchinson and Pownall "began soon thereafter."[5]

Pownall erred here, as Bollan had ably and energetically defended the province's interests despite perennial complaints that he was over-worked, underpaid, and in precarious health. Throughout the 1750s, he lobbied to abolish the prohibitory duty on foreign molasses imposed by the Molasses Act of 1733. He also opposed its replacement by a lower tariff designed to raise a revenue.[6] Bollan protested indefatigably against impressment and forcefully presented accounts of the province's great military exertions to pry some of the promised reimbursement out of the treasury. He was a great deal more than the private agent of the "Shirlean faction," as James Otis, Jr., later charged.[7]

But, through little fault of his own, Bollan failed in these endeavors. His reputation for hypochondria and padding his expense accounts helped Pownall's campaign against him.[8] On 12 October 1758, the house voted to dismiss him by a vote of thirty-eight to thirty-four. The division bears out Hutchinson's contention that Shirley's friends generally opposed Pownall and vice versa, although some deputies supported or opposed both governors:[9]

|  | Pro-Shirley Towns | Anti-Shirley Towns |
|---|---|---|
| Towns supporting Bollan | 19 | 13 |
| Towns opposing Bollan | 11 | 19 |

Pownall also quarrelled with the Hampshire County representatives who had furnished Governor Shirley with his most consistent support. In 1758 he appointed one Charles Phelps justice of the peace despite Israel Williams' insistence that "he was obnoxious to the people." All twelve incumbent justices threatened to resign their posts rather than serve with such "a conceited, pedantic, and impertinent person." They insisted that when practicing before the Hampshire Court of Probate, Phelps had stooped to "unworthy methods frequently running into obvious absurdities." The justices only gave in after Hutchinson informed them that Pownall had no compunctions about replacing them all. Hutchinson still continued to support Pownall publicly because he thought otherwise he would have to resign his lieutenant-governorship.[10] But when the new Governor Francis Bernard submitted to the council his nominations for justices in March 1762, the name of Charles Phelps was conspicuously absent.[11]

Unlike Hutchinson, other members of Shirley's faction such as General Timothy Ruggles and Thomas Hancock gladly embraced the new executive.[12] James Otis of Barnstable—who at the age of fifty-five, despite his yeoman service on behalf of Shirley, held no official position greater than justice of the peace—also befriended Pownall.[13] Pownall appointed James Otis, Jr., Advocate of the Vice-Admiralty Court, and reiterated Shirley's promise that the elder Otis would have the next vacancy on the Superior Court.[14]

However, prerogative politicians such as Hancock and Otis made up but a minority of Pownall's following. Most of it consisted of men they had combatted for a decade—Harrison Gray, William and Samuel Cooper, and John Tyng (the unofficial leader of the Bostonian opposition following the death of James Allen in 1754).[15] More illustrious opponents of Shirley and Hutchinson such as Isaac Royall and Sir William Pepperrell also found the new governor a congenial ally.[16]

Pownall won the allegiance of those representatives who opposed the demands Britain obliged him to press. Privately, the governor agreed with the country faction that the mother country's requests were totally unreasonable. For example, Hutchinson related that once at 11:00 P.M. he had to break up a quarrel between Pownall and Loudoun over whether the province should supply 180 rangers for winter scouting. The governor opposed another crucial instruction that the province raise 7,000 men in 1759 on the grounds that 5,500 sufficed. The court faction could obtain an additional 1,500 only with difficulty.[17]

Both house roll calls and Pownall's quarrel with Lord Loudoun confirm his allegiance to the country faction. On 9 December 1757, the deputies voted forty-eight to thirty-two not to draft a portion of the militia for frontier defense to supplement enlistments.[18] Of the twenty-three opponents of this bill present on the roll call to fire Bollan, only six had supported the agent whereas eight of the nine deputies in favor who voted on the earlier roll call wanted to retain him. Most of the governor's supporters opposed British defense policy. Similarly, Loudoun's quarrel with Pownall can only be explained by the latter's halfhearted support of the war. Both His Lordship and Hutchinson agreed that Pownall had frustrated military ambitions. Loudoun described Pownall as "the worst man alive and the wrongest and falsest man I ever met. His plan is to be put at the head of all the colonies in North America." His Lordship foresaw "more trouble to whoever commands in this country from him than from all the people on the continent." And if Hutchinson can be trusted, in 1758 Pownall even withheld a letter to Jeffrey Amherst at Louisbourg containing General James Abercromby's request for reinforcements at Crown Point. When the news of Abercromby's defeat reached him, "Pownall behaved like a man elevated with joy." Pownall apparently thought that his office entitled him to the intercolonial prestige and military commands that Governor Shirley had acquired for it. He failed to realize that his predecessor's triumphs had been personal. By scheming to oust Shirley, Pownall had in fact ensured the governorship would return to its former dimensions.[19]

But disagreements between Massachusetts and British officials over the conduct of the war began before Pownall arrived, and continued after he left. Massachusetts' contribution to the war dwarfed the governor's factional difficulties. The province did not spare itself. From 1755 and 1759 it mustered at least seven thousand soldiers for active service, five thousand in 1760, and three thousand annually until 1763. Taxes rose to the astronomical sum of £100,000 in 1759 and 1760 and remained above £70,000 for the rest of the war. From 1754 to 1762, Massachusetts spent £818,000 on the war: Parliament reimbursed some £352,000 but the province itself had to bear the rest. As late as 1765, even after what Governor Bernard termed "severe taxation" had been in effect for several years, the provincial debt had declined only from a high of £505,000 in 1761 to £387,000. Taxes rose to £500 sterling annually for some merchants; the poll tax in Boston increased from a peacetime rate of three or four shillings to over sixteen shillings. Bernard concluded that Massachusetts had spent "an immense sum for such a small state! The burden of which has been grievously felt by all orders of men."[20]

Although it had determined that current taxation support as much of the war as possible, Massachusetts had to finance most of its expenses through treasury notes issued to government contractors and soldiers. Specie currency had never been entirely adequate—beginning in 1750 £18,400 in notes had to be issued. Hence, Massachusetts' heaviest taxes came not during the war itself, but afterwards. In

# The Fragmentation of Massachusetts

1765—the first year in a decade Massachusetts sent no troops beyond its boundaries—the year Britain implemented the Stamp Act because the colonials supposedly paid insufficient taxes to defend themselves—Massachusetts levied £197,000 to redeem outstanding treasury notes, nearly twice the tax of any year in its history! Taxes remained high several years thereafter—£157,000 in 1766, £125,850 in 1767, £100,000 in 1768, £88,000 in 1769 and 1770, £92,500 in 1771, and £75,000 in 1772 before reaching a bearable £46,000 in 1773.[21] Taxation after the French and Indian War added to the economic hardship provoked by the war itself. During the 1780s, Massachusetts' similar dogged insistence not to burden future generations with the revolutionary war debt provoked Shays's Rebellion. In the 1760s the "corrupt" Tories became the focus of Massachusetts' resentment.[22] But in the 1780s, the revolutionaries themselves were the targets of popular unrest.

Individual economic difficulties appeared most devastatingly in the form of numerous bankruptcies. In 1757 the legislature felt obliged to pass the first major bill reforming the treatment of bankrupts in Massachusetts' history. An alternative now existed for debtors instead of being forced to forfeit their entire estates and go to prison. Persons who advertised in the Boston newspapers, did not try to hide any of their wealth, and permitted their affairs to be investigated by commissioners could begin life with a clean slate. Insolvents able to pay at least half their debts retained five percent of their wealth up to £200; those able to pay two-thirds kept seven and one-half percent up to £250; anyone satisfying three-fourths of the claims against him was allowed ten percent of his estates under £300. The reform proved timely: lists of the financially distressed in the province's journals tempered joyous news of British victories. Forty-two people filed under this act before Britain disallowed it on the formal grounds it failed to contain a suspending clause, although the real reason was it provided a precedent to defraud British creditors. Massachusetts' efforts to solve its pressing economic problems constructively met with imperial hostility.[23]

Bankruptcies continued after the war. In February 1765, the default by war contractor Nathaniel Wheelwright on £120,000 sterling set off a chain reaction. Combined with other causes, Wheelwright's demise produced fifty-eight recorded bankruptcies between March and October 1765, and seventy-seven more by February 1768. Most bankrupts were Boston-based merchants and well-to-do people who had developed extensive lines of credit. For example, those filing in 1757 included Byfield Lyde, son-in-law of former Governor Belcher,

Joshua Loring, commander of the provincial flotilla, Hugh Vans, the firm of Colman and Sparhawk which had competed for the supply of Louisbourg, and Edmund Quincy and Sons.[24] Not only did Massachusetts tax itself to the limit in the common cause; many of its inhabitants literally went bankrupt.

No one questioned the extent of Massachusetts' mobilization. Its quality unfortunately left much to be desired. Britain and the province disagreed over the number, disposition, and ability of the provincial soldiers. The legislature confined Massachusetts' troops to particular posts and enlisted them for limited periods coinciding poorly with military necessity. As Loudoun complained at a meeting of the New England colonies in 1757: "The confining of your men to any particular service appears to me a preposterous measure. Our affairs are not in such a situation as to make it reasonable for any colony to be guided by its own particular interest." Other problems included soldiers sent to the front without arms and men enlisting and deserting several times to collect bounties. Contractors and officers made profits from provisions supplied to their men. The province's insistence that impressment only be used as a last resort ensured that each year's fresh supply of men took several months to be mustered. Recruiting parties met with resistance in Boston and Marblehead. Loudoun also wanted colonial troops to be led by British officers. His insistence that only one provincial officer ranking higher than captain accompany any command threatened local autonomy and insulted the province's military capability.[25]

Military disputes sometimes pitted the entire province against British authorities. This occurred most spectacularly during the quartering episode of December 1757 and January 1758. The province gladly offered to billet regular forces for the winter but insisted on passing its own law to authorize the step. Lord Loudoun, on the other hand, maintained that only the British Quartering Act of 1694, which gave commanders quartering powers in England, was necessary. The assembly could not see the reason for his indignation: "we are really at a loss what steps to take to terminate this affair since His Lordship does not seem dissatisfied so much from the insufficiency of what we have done, as from the manner of its being done by a law of the province." Loudoun, however, argued that if he accepted voluntary quartering "it would throw the whole continent into confusion, from South Carolina to Boston, and turn three-quarters of the troops at once into the streets to perish." Nothing less than the commander in chief's ability to conduct the war apart from local interference was at stake. Loudoun threatened that if the assembly did not comply he would "instantly order into Boston the three battalions from New York, Long Island, and Connecticut, and if more are wanted, I have two in the Jerseys at hand besides those in Pennsylvania." If Massachusetts refused to quarter one regiment voluntarily, the entire army would be lodged in Boston. Loudoun also hinted that Britain would not pay for the province's "very extravagant" war expenses if it failed to house the troops sent to protect it.[26]

Even Loudoun's friend Thomas Hutchinson disapproved of his quartering policy. Brookline representative Jeremiah Gridley, heading a committee of the house, tried to reach a compromise without deciding the limits of provincial and British law. But Hutchinson drew up what he somewhat immodestly termed a "memorable" memorial denying that the Quartering Act extended to the colonies. At least, the memorial was memorable enough to persuade Loudoun.[27]

Like Loudoun, Pownall also learned the hard way that military necessity did not supercede the Massachusetts representatives' traditional privileges. Despite his reluctance to support the British army, Pownall jealously tried to preserve his own powers as governor. He, too, had engaged in disputes with the assembly over the quartering of troops. In another case, Pownall and the legislature had agreed upon the number and disposition of troops for the winter of 1757–1758. However, the governor insisted that by stipulating the size and locations of the garrisons the house violated his charter authority as commander in chief. No governor had tried to exercise this authority since Samuel Shute. When Pownall vetoed the bill, the house briefly refused to vote any troops at all. The exasperated executive protested that "you are resolved to run matters to that extreme, that you will leave the frontier without any provision of defense. . . . There is no difference about the service, the only question is who shall direct it, the house of representatives or the king's governor?" When the house refused to budge, Pownall answered his own question and signed the bill under protest.[28]

Pownall's plan to revamp the province's cumbersome militia system met with equally negative results. Samuel Livermore of Waltham raised the specter of military government and compared the governor to Oliver Cromwell. Livermore's opposition illustrates that beneath the personal factionalism of Pownall's regime the major issue was the extent of Massachusetts' military effort. Livermore led a sizeable body of deputies who believed the province's capabilities had been dangerously overextended and rejected any changes in its traditional mode of government or defense. The house voted nearly all its supply bills under protest.[29] However, most of these disputes occurred before Britain began to win consistently after mid-1758.

But the extent of conflict during Pownall's administration should not be overestimated. Even Livermore and his followers wanted to win the war. Even the prerogative faction knew Britain and the other colonies exploited Massachusetts' generosity, but the popular politicians tried to reduce the burden. Conversely, the court faction opposed impressment, quartering, and limiting provincials to captain's rank.

Pownall's tenure fortunately coincided with the war's climax. This limited the extent to which he could openly lead the country deputies in attacks on royal policy. Similarly, the court faction found itself supporting the governor's instructions regardless of their personal feelings toward him. Pownall's successor, Francis Bernard, was less fortunate. Once Canada had been conquered, the northern colonies' sense of both peril and exhilaration vanished; the people of Massachusetts were free to fight among themselves.

### BERNARD'S BROAD-BOTTOMED SYSTEM: 1760–1765

A confident and cheerful Francis Bernard assumed the Governorship of Massachusetts in July 1760. During his two years as Governor of New Jersey, he had laid to rest the factional quarrels that had plagued his two immediate predecessors in that province, Jonathan Belcher (who died in 1757) and Thomas Pownall. He attributed his success to a "system," which he described as basing "my administration on the broad bottom of the people in general." In his speeches to the General Court and in private letters, Bernard made it his explicit goal to "make a trial, whether party divisions may not be as well removed from this small province as from Great Britain." To achieve consensus he determined "never [to] show the least disposition to deceive or impose upon the people," and to make "openness, integrity, disinterestedness, and affability" the foundations of his conduct.[30] Related to the Shutes and Barringtons (one of his ten children was named Shute), Bernard revealed the same easygoing personality that had at first characterized his predecessor, Samuel Shute. Rumors circulated before he arrived in Massachusetts that "he is not a man of intrigue, that he loves to be quiet himself, and is willing other people should be so too."[31]

For the first half of his administration, Bernard tried so hard to ingratiate himself with the province that he jeopardized his relations with British officialdom. For example, when General Jeffrey Amherst ordered an embargo on colonial shipping in 1762 to prevent illegal trade, Bernard objected that "this public-spirited province can ill afford to lose the small trade remaining to it." In any event, he thought that Massachusetts tolerated no such traffic. But most important of all, the measure would prevent him from maintaining the "good harmony which I have brought about in this province." He also claimed to have no desire to enforce the Acts of Trade, and rhapsodized: "if I could have disposed with this service, I might have enjoyed a continual sunshine of ease and popularity." And when the Board of Trade rebuked Bernard for accepting the grant of Mount Desert Island in return for supporting provincial land claims in Maine, he innocently protested: "I was not a prime mover. . . . I could not consistently with the good understanding which I have hitherto preserved with the General Court have obstructed their proceeding." Bernard pretended to be "amazed that I should incur the displeasure of my superiors by appearing as an advocate for the province," but he deserved it. He at first reduced questions of imperial defense and administration to the course that best pacified his constituents.[32]

Throughout his administration, Bernard defended Massachusetts from overzealous imperial officials. When Amherst complained that Massachusetts' soldiers not only took far too long to enlist but deserted left and right once they had, the governor shot back that it served Amherst right for not paying or releasing them promptly. The volunteers also needed assurances that they would not be shipped off to the southern colonies. In January 1764, Bernard supported Massachusetts' refusal to raise seven hundred men for General Thomas Gage's frontier defenses in the Ohio Valley since neither New York nor Pennsylvania would do so. (He later changed his mind, as did the legislature.) He opposed the two generals' embargoes to prevent sending supplies to the French and Spanish, and repeatedly denied that Massachusetts had an illegal trade. Bernard constantly stressed his province's exertions in the common cause—he used its heavy debt as an argument against the Stamp Act—and remonstrated that "it cannot be a matter of indifference to me that this province should be seen in a worse light than it has hitherto appeared."[33]

Bernard's attitude made him extremely successful in raising troops. His intelligent and persuasive speeches to the General Court are oases in deserts of the *House Journals*. Aware that the province no longer thought itself in immediate danger, he pointed out in 1762 that "you must not think that if the war does not rage at your own doorstep, you may therefore be unconcerned spectators in it. Wherever the battle is fought, the prize [Canada] is in this country." The house promptly voted the thirty-two hundred men he requested. On a later occasion, he obtained another three thousand men by arguing: "you who have so cheerfully borne the heat of the day will not decline serving in the cool of the evening." At every available opportunity, he wrote his superiors in London that the province's supply bills "were the result of free will uninfluenced by any notions except a sense of duty."[34]

Bernard also lobbied powerfully against the Molasses, Sugar, and Stamp acts. He considered the first of these an unenforceable "perpetual stumbling block" to the customs house. If the northern colonies could not import foreign molasses, they would "soon become desperate and they really won't be able to live." Bernard argued that discriminating against them in favor of the islands harmed England as much as Massachusetts, since "the trade of New England is really that of Great Britain." He condemned the Stamp Act because it would drain the province's dearly earned specie and prevent it from discharging its "enormous" war debt. He even called the legislature into special session in October 1764 to draw up a protest. He proposed similar concerted measures by the colonial governors against the Hovering Act, which permitted naval officers to enforce customs regulations, though on the mercenary grounds that it deprived them of their shares of forfeitures.[35]

Even after his behavior during the years following the Stamp Act riots made him persona non grata, Bernard still continued to protect the province and its inhabitants from what he considered invasions of their legitimate rights. He worked out agreements with the navy to prevent the impressment of inhabitants, and enforced them. He continued to argue that the province "can't bear a revenue" act and protested the Townshend Acts. In some respects, Francis Bernard was one of the best friends Massachusetts ever had, but this aspect of his administration has been ignored in favor of his extreme response to the events after August 1765.[36]

Unfortunately, Bernard's greatest strength proved his principal weakness. In his effort to please everybody, he pleased nobody. For the first five years of his regime, he made it his principal object, as he stated, "to place myself on a bottom of my own. When I came here I found the province divided into parties so nearly equal, that it would have been madness for me to have put myself at the head of either of them." On more than one occasion he resolved to "keep myself out of the dispute as well as I can."[37]

But Bernard's attempt at neutrality backfired. Both parties—the pro-Pownall country faction headed by John Tyng, and the anti-

Pownall court group led by Hutchinson—thought he favored its rival unduly. The Otises and Councillor William Brattle began to oppose Bernard when he appointed Thomas Hutchinson Chief Justice of the Superior Court in 1761. The bipartisan distribution of patronage also annoyed Hutchinson and his camp. Hutchinson did not think the Bernard "system" well-designed to make both himself and the province "easy and happy." He argued instead that "a governor in the plantations must support those who are friends to government or they cannot long support themselves." He disapproved Bernard's toleration of "the opposers of government" and predicted he would discover "by experience the truth of Sir Robert Walpole's saying that one expedient makes a great many more."[38]

Bernard solved the patronage problem by trying to give everyone of importance as much as possible. James Otis, Sr., did not get the chief justiceship, but Bernard appointed him Judge of Probate and Chief Justice of the Barnstable County Court when Sylvanus Bourne died in 1763. In consequence, James Otis, Jr., supported the governor's efforts to reinforce General Gage in the Ohio Valley in 1764 and even to pay Thomas Hutchinson a special salary as chief justice in 1765. John Tyng, the fiery Boston representative, became a Justice of the Inferior Court in Middlesex in 1762. As for justices of the peace, Bernard nominated 462 men, or about 1 in every 100 adult males in the province. The last time an entire slate had been selected (by Jonathan Belcher in 1733) the number was 233.[39]

Leaders of both factions found Bernard's generosity counterproductive. Israel Williams complained that "the name of a justice is become very contemptible; by having to do with such people the chief magistrate makes himself of a party." Superior Court Judge John Cushing, who frequently informed Hutchinson about increasing factionalism and lawlessness in Bristol County, went even further:[40]

> A spirit of levellism seems to go through the country and very little distinction between the highest and lowest in office. Whether this may not be a good deal owing to the governor's adhering to persons of neither honor or honesty and so appointing persons in civil and military situations, some scandalous, others wholly unfit, and by that means they and even the office [are] brought into contempt.

The country faction agreed with its opponents' analysis, although it naturally differed as to who was scandalous and unfit. In a letter to Benjamin Prat, a noted attorney and former Boston representative who had been appointed Chief Justice of New York, Oxenbridge

Thacher delectably sketched the major political actors of the early 1760s and Bernard's efforts to keep on good terms with them:[41]

> The expectation of your return occasions great joy among all honest citizens. In truth we have not such plenty of honest and able men among us that we can ship those of this character to an ungrateful people who know not how to price or treat them. We seem to be in the sleep or stupor that Cicero describes his country to be in a year or two before the Civil War broke out. The sea is perfectly calm and unagitated; whether this profound quiet be the forerunner of a storm I leave to your judgment. We daily see many of your predictions accomplished respecting the commotions and disorder of our politicians, caucus men, plebian tribunes, etc. etc. I remember that intimate character you gave me of a certain man [Tyng] who is not of our brotherhood [lawyers] but who attempted to be of it, who had strict connections with the caucus and still keeps them at the same time that he is a sort of prime minister to the government. In the new commission he is appointed a justice; he is a great adversary of Summa [Hutchinson]. Your old client and friend Paulinus [Otis] he that from handling the broadax hath been called to guide the helm of the commonwealth retains his honesty and usefulness. The governor pays him great court, hath made him a justice of the quorum, consults him about affairs of state, and seeks to retain him in his councils as a balance to Summa, for whom sound reason and discretion required him to find a balance if he does not mean to be wholly weighted down himself.

Although committed to an equitable distribution of patronage, Bernard blundered badly by choosing to award the post of chief justice to Hutchinson. Hutchinson's personal collection of offices—chief justice, lieutenant-governor, judge of probate, councillor—had been approximated before. William Stoughton had previously held a similar aggregation, as had Samuel Sewall except for the lieutenant-governorship. But politically prominent inhabitants who deserved rewards had increased severalfold since the beginning of the century.[42] Furthermore, while Hutchinson's own services to Massachusetts justified his personal prominence, it surely did not excuse the presence of his relatives on the county judiciary and the Superior Court.[43] While the number and professional consciousness of lawyers in the province increased, the principal qualification for the few major patronage appointments in Suffolk and Essex counties appeared to be kinship with Thomas Hutchinson.

Only in the latter half of his administration did Bernard become identified unambiguously with Hutchinson and the "supporters of government." At first, he opposed their favorite, Agent William Bollan, with a nominee of his own, and angered the Hampshire County delegation by first approving a charter for their proposed college and then withdrawing it. Bernard's system of being all things to all people had three flaws. First, he had to make some decisions and appointments that invariably angered one side or the other. Second, as will be discussed, he loved money even more than peace and quiet, and offended the popular faction by his corruption. Third, he took office as Massachusetts underwent unprecedented domestic and imperial difficulty. Bernard tried to govern much as Newcastle and Walpole had during the stable British "Whig supremacy." He hoped to succeed by avoiding controversy and satisfying everyone's desire for patronage. Two centuries later, Sir Lewis Namier presented more formally a similar analysis of eighteenth-century Britain's achievement of political stability. But Namier realized, as Bernard did not, that such an interpretation applied only to a society without fundamental divisions over principle and policy.[44]

### ENTER THE MERCHANTS: 1758–1763

The politicization of the Boston merchant community in the late 1750s and early 1760s caused many of Bernard's problems. Before the 1750s, a sizeable number of traders had organized themselves as a pressure group only sporadically. In 1691, sixty-one merchants petitioned the crown to settle a government. In 1714, 1733, 1740, and 1748, varying numbers tried to stabilize the provincial currency. But beginning in 1758 with their threat to leave the province if taxes remained exorbitant, the merchants consistently flexed their political muscle. They organized to oppose the writs of assistance and customs house corruption in 1761; formed a Society for the Encouragement of Manufacturing in 1764, which protested the Sugar and Stamp acts and functioned as an ongoing "Merchants Club"; and, most importantly, organized the nonimportation agreements from 1768 to 1770. The merchants' regular involvement in political affairs anticipated and helped provoke a similar development among the general population.[45]

The merchants' aggressiveness can be attributed to four problems. First, as already noted, the Seven Years' War required high taxes and drove away trade. Second, in 1761 a postwar recession set in—the large number of bankruptcies during the war continued throughout the decade.[46] Other problems for which Britain could be directly blamed compounded these. Third, as Governor Bernard explained, the development of a factorage system created considerable animosity in Massachusetts, as in the southern colonies.[47]

> Formerly, the merchants of Boston were of the same nature with those of London, importers and dealers by wholesale and by no means retailers. Then merchants of London dealt for small profit that the merchants of Boston might have a reasonable profit in return. But for some years past the London merchants, for the sake of increasing their profit, have got into dealing immediately with the retailers, and thereby abolished the distribution of the merchants of Boston; so at present every merchant is a shopkeeper and every shopkeeper a merchant. Instead of dealing with respectable houses the London merchants are engaged in a great number of little shops, and for the sake of the advantages derived from trading with people who cannot dispute the terms . . . they have extended their credit beyond all bounds of prudence, and have . . . glutted this country with goods.

Finally, the customs' service renewed vigor directly threatened the merchants' West India trade. Charles Paxton, himself a Massachusetts merchant, began to seize goods obtained from illegal trade with increasing regularity. Both Thomas Hutchinson and Samuel Alleyne Otis, James Otis, Jr.,'s younger brother, agreed that Bernard "was very active in fomenting seizures for illicit trade which he made justifiable by his share in the forfeitures."[48]

Beginning in January 1761, the merchants counterattacked on several fronts. Sixty traders petitioned the General Court that Paxton and his predecessor Henry Frankland had illegally appropriated £484 in fees legitimately belonging to the province. If fines had to be paid for violating the Acts of Trade, the merchants at least hoped to eliminate the enforcement officers' profit motive. When the General Court authorized Treasurer Harrison Gray to institute lawsuits to recover the money, Bernard incurred needless grief by objecting that the attorney general should have sued since the money belonged to the king, not the province. Bernard gave in, however, after recording his protest for the benefit of his superiors.[49]

The elated merchants moved on to challenge the Superior Court's right to issue writs of assistance. These warrants permitted customs officials to search anywhere for contraband accompanied by the local justice of the peace.[50] In February 1761, the same merchants who had accused Paxton of embezzlement petitioned against the writs. James

Otis, Jr., argued the case after he had resigned his post as advocate for the admiralty for that very reason. He insisted that general search warrants were unconstitutional and violated man's natural rights to liberty and property. But Chief Justice Hutchinson and his colleagues took a more narrow view. Writs legal in England could be issued in America, and Agent Bollan duty forwarded proof that British Courts of Exchequer issued them.[51]

Constitutionality figured prominently in another case launched almost simultaneously. Merchant George Erving obtained a verdict from the Suffolk Inferior Court of Common Pleas virtually nullifying the Vice-Admiralty Court itself. Justices Samuel Watts and Samuel Welles, probably overruling either Elisha or Foster Hutchinson, if one of them sat for this case, invalidated another admiralty seizure and commented that they "must put a stop to these proceedings of the customs house officers; if they did not there would be tumult and bloodshed for the people can bear them no longer." This decision, as Bernard informed the Board of Trade, had "an immediate tendency to destroy the Court of Admiralty and with it the customs house." Upon the admiralty's appeal to the Superior Court, Thomas Hutchinson again thwarted the merchants. He ruled that "the Court of Admiralty was part of the constitution of the province, it being expressly provided for in the charter." Erving joined the Otises on the list of those swearing revenge against Hutchinson.[52]

Dissension within the ranks further plagued customs enforcement. Deputy-Collector Benjamin Barrons, suspended by Surveyor Thomas Lechmere for negligence, became "a tool of the merchants" according to Bernard, and sued his ex-superior for £10,000.[53] But John Temple, a kinsman of George Grenville and his powerful brother the Earl Temple, replaced Lechmere in 1762. Temple outdid even Barrons in undermining the customs service from within. Married to Erving's granddaughter, James Bowdoin's daughter, Temple suspended Salem's collector, Alexander Cockle, for reporting smugglers to Bernard rather than to him. He also charged that Cockle had connived with offenders to value illegal goods at far below their worth to reduce their fine. For the rest of the decade, Temple harrassed Bernard and, after 1768, his four colleagues on the newly appointed American Board of Customs. He supported the revolutionaries' charges, which may well have been true, that corrupt placemen preyed upon their trade. In return, the Bostonians let him remain in town when they forced out the other commissioners. Conversely, Temple complained to his superiors that Bernard desired only to profit from trade regulations rather than enforcing them, which *was* true. He also accused the governor of not protecting his subordinates from mobs or imprison-ment by local authorities.[54] Seventy years after William Phips had thrashed Jahleel Brenton, Britain had not yet resolved jurisdictional disputes between colonial officials, and still entrusted the most sen-sitive posts to men with widely divergent interpretations of their duties.

A half-century after the writs of assistance case, John Adams remarked of Otis's speech that "then and there the child independence was born." Adams was exaggerating. As Oliver M. Dickerson has shown, Otis's remarks did not receive wide publicity. Furthermore, his speech did not mark the provincial debut of natural rights ideology: it had been previously used to oppose naval impressment and the excise. But if the novelty of Otis's arguments and long-range effects of this case have been exaggerated, the dramatic impact of the merchants' legal offensive cannot be doubted.[55] Hutchinson's and Ber-nard's efforts on behalf of the customs house provoked unprecedented challenges to the authority of the Superior Court, supplied the political agenda for 1761 and 1762, and bolstered the country faction and its new leaders, the Otises.

Otis and his cohorts pounced first on their most powerful enemy, the Superior Court. In February 1762, the house voted to investigate the powers and behavior of the judges for the first time in provincial history. It took a leaf from a recent dispute in New York and sug-gested the possibility of judges serving as long as they executed their duties faithfully and without corruption, rather than at the governor's and council's pleasure. Two months later, the deputies defeated, fifty to forty-three, a bill to exclude the justices from sitting in the legislature. Since most of the representatives served as justices of the peace or Inferior Court judges themselves, the motion did not carry. But nearly half the house agreed with James Otis's arguments against excessive influence and plural officeholding despite such obvious in-consistency. More convincing indices of the assembly's resentment ap-pear in its refusal to vote the judges an increase in salary or vote Chief Justice Hutchinson a higher amount than the others. In March 1762, the legislature tried to outlaw general writs of assistance and replace them with special writs stipulating the premises to be searched. Ber-nard vetoed the bill as "surely repugnant to the laws of England"—on the recommendation of Hutchinson and the Superior Court.[56]

Otis and the house majority also struck at Bollan and Bernard for their complicity in Hutchinson's judicial decisions. The deputies fired Bollan for the last time in April 1762, with the approval of two-thirds of the house and even by one vote in the council. Jasper Mauduit, a seventy-year-old London draper and dissenter of whom Hutchinson, for one, had never heard, took Bollan's place by a margin of fifty-four to thirty-six. Hutchinson himself, according to his enemies, tried to replace Bollan and received most of the other votes. Bernard took the worst possible course with respect to Bollan. He refused to take sides until after the dismissal passed, prompting Hutchinson to blame him for not forestalling it. Then he gratuitously criticized the popular party for "the hasty and indeliberate manner in which this business was determined."[57]

Bernard himself came under more direct attack when a new house met in May 1762. During a month's recess, the governor and council had innocently, with public funds, outfitted a ship to drive a French privateer away from some fishing vessels. The £72 expenditure provoked an apocalyptic response from the pen of James Otis, Jr., on behalf of the representatives' right of taxation. Otis insisted that once "a people give up this privilege the government will soon become arbitrary." It would then be "of little consequence to the people whether they were subject to George or Lewis, the King of Great Britain or the French King, if both were arbitrary, as both would be if they could be taxed without Parliament." Bernard termed these "hard words" and insisted that "it has never been in my thoughts to make the least invasion" of the "privileges of the people." Popular rights, however, could be interpreted differently.[58]

Between 1758 and 1763, the Boston merchant community organized against the prerogative faction's efforts to enforce the Navigation Acts more strictly. It is crucial to emphasize that leading prerogative politicians—Charles Paxton, Bollan, Thomas Hutchinson, and the members of the Superior Court—not Britain, tried to render the writs of assistance more effective. Given the simultaneous corruption and scandal in the customs service, many merchants could interpret such behavior only as a ploy to get rich and curry favor with the home authorities. The prerogative leaders seemed to be selling out their country and further depressing its economy. Hence, after 1765, the country faction interpreted British measures to tax Massachusetts and limit its self-government as instigated by the court faction.

Still, the court faction retained some of its strength. In 1763, it elected General Timothy Ruggles to replace the elder James Otis as speaker of the house by nine votes over Boston's Royall Tyler. The same year, the General Court chose Richard Jackson, a friend and correspondent of both Bernard and Hutchinson, to serve as Jasper Mauduit's assistant. The popular party preferred Mauduit's brother Israel. The court won three of five roll calls in the house between 1762 and 1765, and selected two of the three delegates to the Stamp Act Congress in 1764 (Oliver Partridge and Timothy Ruggles, who presided over that body; James Otis, Jr., was the third).[59] Despite its unpopular stand on the writs in the early 1760s, the court faction retained enough of its wartime prestige to compete on equal terms with the country faction.

### THE SPHERE OF POLITICS BROADENS: 1761–1765

Others besides the merchants came to life politically in the early 1760s. Religion, politically uncontroversial since the days of the Mathers, again became an issue. The old problems of the currency and the settlement of frontier surfaced again. Probably as a result of economic hardship and demobilization, an unprecedented amount of disorganized rioting and crime occurred.[60] With the French defeated, the people of Massachusetts began to quarrel among themselves.

When Bernard arrived in Massachusetts, no one expected religious controversy of any sort. The Congregationalist majority's dislike of the Anglican church had abated to the point where a General Court with only four Anglican members chose King's Chapel rector, the Reverend Henry Caner, to deliver the funeral sermon for King George II.[61] However, the halcyon days soon ended. The Old Light, Bostonian religious establishment, closely linked to the dissenting interest in England, suddenly found itself confronted by two challenges: from the militant Anglicans of the Society for the Propagation of the Gospel, and from western Massachusetts' political leaders demanding a college for that section.

The Church of England menace took the form of East Apthorp, a young Massachusetts Anglican. Apthorp returned from England in 1761 to found a "mission" at Cambridge just as Massachusetts Congregationalists and British dissenters were forming their own society to spread Christianity to the western Indians. Old Lights—including future patriots Jonathan Mayhew, Andrew Eliot, Samuel Cooper, and Charles Chauncy—joined New Lights and future Tories under Andrew Oliver's presidency in this postwar effort to preserve religious unity. When the Privy Council rejected the charter because it might complicate British Indian policy, the Congregational clergy spotted a connection between Apthorp's appearance and the refusal.[62] Eliot complained that "it is strange that the gentlemen who profess Christianity will not send the gospel to the heathen themselves nor permit it to be sent by others."[63] At the same time, Jonathan Mayhew spread rumors that Governor Bernard was deeply involved in a plot to bring an Anglican bishop to New England.[64]

The episcopacy quarrel politicized the Boston clergy much as the customs house fight had the merchants. In each case, British officials insensitive to the province's tremendous sacrifices and aspirations provoked a strong reaction. They engendered suspicion of a general plot to undermine New England's political, economic, and religious institutions. In their separate causes, the commercial and the spiritual leaders of Massachusetts joined with James Otis and the popular party, and thus indirectly with each other. The popular party used the prospect of a bishop as an effective propaganda tool for the rest of the decade, although the plans had been jettisoned long since in Great Britain.

While the Boston divines nervously awaited the arrival of a bishop, Israel Williams and nearly everyone of importance in Hampshire County confronted them with a petition to the General Court. The signers demanded a new college because Harvard was:[65]

> unhappily situated so near the capital where luxury and wickedness (to our shame) prevailed, . . . the youth who were allowed too frequently to resort there, were corrupted in their morals; that, instead of pursuing their studies, they too generously spent their time in places of idleness and vanity.

Oxenbridge Thacher attributed a less elevated motive to Williams: "the monarch of the county . . . took great offence of his son being placed some years ago something lower in a class at our college than befitted the son of a king." Although Williams's plan passed the house by a small majority, the council rejected it at the instigation of the Boston ministers.[66] Hutchinson ultimately threw his influence against the college and tried to placate Williams.[67]

In addition to siding against an old friend on the question of a college for Hampshire County, Hutchinson could not muster all his customary support on a new currency debate. He fought the popular party's plan to combat the postwar recession by monetizing gold. This would have increased the money supply, but Hutchinson argued that it would also bring back the inflation which had been absent since 1749. On 3 February 1762, the house approved the measure sixty to forty-three. Despite Hutchinson's insistence that bimetallism equalled depreciation, the governor and council went along with the deputies. No inflation occurred, but the lieutenant-governor noted that "all the rest of the court and country [were] against me and a great clamor raised in all the papers."[68]

The recession also had violent consequences. David Flaherty has discovered an increase in serious crime during the sixties. Economic decline and the return of many soldiers probably produced a rise in unemployment and restlessness. The General Court had to pass harsher laws to prevent throwing rocks through windows and lighting bonfires. The streets of Boston became dangerous at night. Restlessness also surfaced in a number of riots, notably a fracas at a militia training session in 1764, and in increasingly violent battles on Pope's Day—when Boston's North End and South End mobs clashed each year in a ceremonial brawl. Although the crowd did not enter politics until the Stamp Act riots, the increase in random violence indicates that hardships of war provoked dissatisfaction among the general population. To add to postwar hard times, a drought struck Massachusetts in 1762 and 1763. Boston in particular suffered from the Great Fire in 1760 which destroyed some ten percent of the town, a smallpox epidemic in 1764, and a violent winter storm the same year that seriously damaged the waterfront area.[69]

The cessation of hostilities required painful readjustment for many. But for those whose land claims in the District of Maine were finally free from Indian attacks, peace meant opportunity. In 1761, York County had to be divided, and Cumberland added, to keep pace with the growth of new settlements. The rest of the province added thirty-seven new towns from 1759 to 1765, whereas none had been developed between 1755 and 1758. Peace renewed the possibility for factional conflict between various speculators and land companies. The principal dispute occurred between the Kennebeck Company—headed by John Hancock, James Bowdoin, and John Temple—and the heirs of Samuel Waldo, led by his son-in-law, Thomas Flucker, and including future loyalists David Phips, Richard Lechmere, Andrew Boardman, William Vassall, and Nathaniel Saltonstall. Even before the great events of 1765, quarrels in the Maine wilderness anticipated future political alignments.[70]

Nearly every issue of importance between 1760 and 1765 pitted the prerogative faction against a key social or economic group. As a result, roll calls on various issues in the General Court became much more consistent than before. For example, thirty-three representatives opposed sending Thomas Hutchinson as agent to England on the morning of 1 February 1764. Only three of them voted that afternoon to grant General Gage the seven hundred troops he requested. Conversely, of the thirty-nine members who supported Hutchinson, only four did not support Gage. Similarly, in 1762, only twenty-one of eighty deputies changed from the prerogative faction to the popular or vice versa on two such superficially unrelated votes as the monetization of gold and keeping Superior Court justices out of the legislature.

Previously, representatives' votes on military, fiscal, and personal issues had exhibited much more flexibility. But during the first years of Bernard's administration, every roll call served as a test of Thomas Hutchinson's popularity and influence. The various groups that united to lead the Revolution cemented their ties during these years. The proof lies in the diverse reasons given for the destruction of Hutchinson's house in the Stamp Act riot of 26 August 1765. Not only did his opponents spread rumors that he had written the law, but different sources blamed nearly every issue of the past five years for the riot. Hutchinson himself alternatively attributed it to his support for the customs house and a sermon by Jonathan Mayhew. He also speculated that some of the Kennebeck proprietors thought he possessed documents that disputed their title. Finally, house leader Jerathmeel Bowers of Swansea blamed Hutchinson's financial policies.[71] By 1765, issues that annoyed various powerful groups in Massachusetts—lawyers, land speculators, clergymen, merchants, soft money advocates—were linked indissolubly with Hutchinson and the court. The country faction therefore opposed British legislation not only for its obviously pernicious effects, but to overcome its rival. Governor Bernard knew this: "everything that for years past has been the cause of any discontent was revived: a private resentment against persons in office worked themselves [sic] in and enabled [the popular politicians] to excite themselves under the mask of the public weal."[72]

John Murrin has noted that "Massachusetts was never more badly divided than on the eve of the Revolution."[73] At least four of the usual preconditions of rebellion described by political theorists existed. First, warfare had produced heavy taxation, economic hardship, and widespread discontent with the government. Second, more immediate disasters occurred in the early sixties, especially in Boston. Third, a heavily factionalized elite had already begun to lose its ability to maintain law and order. Finally, overzealous imperial officials and Anglicans thwarted Massachusetts' efforts to recoup its declining trade, alleviate its domestic financial distress, and validate its wartime sufferings through increased missionary activity.[74] Britain continued to dash provincial hopes after 1763. It thereby destroyed any chance that Massachusetts' inhabitants would allow a future voice to the faction that had persuaded them to sacrifice their lives and prosperity for the past twenty years.

# The Fragmentation of Massachusetts

The court faction survived the writs of assistance. Many of its members helped retain their popularity by supporting the Congregational missionary society and bimetallism. The hopeless ineptitude of Jasper Mauduit, the country-backed agent, undoubtedly strengthened it as well. But whatever the court's chances in the postwar era, its failure to take a strong, unequivocal stand against the Stamp Act led quickly to its demise.

We can only wonder what the popular party ever saw in Mauduit. Despite a general instruction that he compromise neither "the natural rights of the colonies,"[75] nor "of British subjects," Mauduit remained inactive while Parliament debated the Sugar Act because he received no explicit instruction on that measure. He therefore judged it best, "as we could not oppose [it], to make a virtue of our submission." He also advised compliance with the Stamp Act as few people of consequence in Parliament objected to the measure. Mauduit reasoned that "of the several inland duties that of the stamps is the most equal, required the fewest officers, and was attended with the least expense to collect it." Instead of standing up for the colonists' rights as he was instructed, Mauduit gave them advice about bowing to the inevitable.[76]

Mauduit was equally remiss in seeking Massachusetts' war compensation. The province always insisted that its exertions went far beyond those of the other colonies and entitled it to special treatment. Unlike Bollan, Mauduit did little to press this point. Again he urged acquiescence. Compensation for about half their expenditures satisfied the other colonies. Massachusetts would thus appear "in a very disadvantageous light to present a petition to Parliament setting forth that we are content with nothing less than the whole of ours." Mauduit's insistence that Massachusetts was simply one more colony illustrated his ignorance of its circumstances. Bollan reported that "all the other governments laugh at this province for employing him." In the last analysis, Massachusetts' reimbursement came to under forty percent.[77]

The province soon began to doubt Mauduit's qualifications. In January 1764, the house voted forty-six to forty to replace him with an agent born in Massachusetts. The only candidate willing to serve was Thomas Hutchinson. He was promptly elected by the lopsided margin of eighty to eight in the house, although the former vote clearly indicates his less than overwhelming popularity. The court only narrowly convinced the house that the opposition had bungled the job of defending the province's rights. But James Otis had a limited revenge on Hutchinson by ensuring that he did not accept the post although he was willing to go. Otis first convinced Governor Bernard that Hutchinson wanted the agency to replace him as governor. Although Bernard concurred "immediately to discredit a report that I was afraid of him," he privately persuaded his second-in-command that their superiors in Britain would frown on a lieutenant-governor who left his post without permission. "This," the jubilant Bernard wrote to Richard Jackson, "is the best end that could have happened"; he both kept Hutchinson out of harm's way and got rid of Mauduit. The house voted thirty-nine to thirty-three to excuse Hutchinson; Bernard commented that "the friends of lieutenant-governor decreased faster than his opponents." Even as late as 1764, Bernard and Hutchinson were by no means a team. In fact, on the same day Hutchinson was excused from the agency, James Otis, Sr., received his Barnstable appointments.[78]

Although Hutchinson threw his support to Richard Jackson, Bernard's candidate for the agency, the house perversely voted to retain Mauduit, who served until February 1765. Then it finally elected Bernard's man Jackson over his predecessor by a vote of forty-five to forty-one. The council one sidedly approved Jackson, seventeen to three. Hutchinson's obvious desire for the agency, and then his sudden refusal, delayed the change. But Mauduit's continued inaction made some substitution inevitable. That he made such a good showing despite his ineptitude illustrates the precariousness of Hutchinson's and Bernard's popularity by 1764.[79]

Besides electing Jackson, the court faction persuaded the General Court to distinguish Massachusetts from the other North American colonies by protesting the Stamp Act on the grounds of expediency, traditional colonial privileges, and hardship rather than right. Once again, Hutchinson played the major role. Bernard wrote that the council was "very steady and moderate" in supporting Hutchinson; the house either had to acquiesce or face the prospect of sending a petition that came only from one house of the legislature. This success sealed the court's doom. Britain did not even notice Massachusetts' moderation, much less reward it. Speaker of the House Thomas Cushing instructed Mauduit that "the house of representatives were clearly for a declaration of the exclusive right of the people of the colonies to tax themselves . . . by birth and by charter, but they could not prevail with the council, though they made several trials." The house directed Mauduit to govern his behavior according to James Otis's *The Rights of the British Colonies* rather than by his official instructions. Mauduit instead presented Hutchinson's case.[80]

Governor Bernard, who had called the legislature into special session in October 1764, to protest the proposed Stamp Act, foolishly predicted that Hutchinson's mild "representations will be successful as they must receive great weight from the dutiful manner in which they are framed." He was deceiving himself. Six months earlier he had written that "the late parliamentary proceedings and what is still to be expected must rouse the turbulent to a higher pitch, and give a new spirit to our demagogues."[81] The earlier forecast proved more accurate. The Stamp Act ended provincial politics. The riots of August 1765 introduced the populace as an active, continuous political force and destroyed the court faction forever. Its previous success, always tenuous, had depended on convincing the population that Massachusetts and imperial interests were reconcilable.

After 1765 this proved impossible. The prerogative's strength on the eve of the Stamp Act appears in the forty-two to forty-one vote of February 1765, approving a grant of £40 to Hutchinson for his services as chief justice.[82] During the 1766 elections, the Boston newspapers named and condemned the thirty-two deputies who had favored submission to the Stamp Act. The electorate responded by removing nineteen.[83] In 1768, the assembly voted ninety-two to seventeen not to rescind their circular letter to the other colonial legislatures advocating concerted resistance. This time the Boston propagandists used a picture as well as thousands of words: they published an engraving of the seventeen, prodded by devils, marching into the jaws of Hell. The towns returned five.[84] From 1769 to the Revolution, the strength of the court faction in the house could literally be counted on the fingers of one hand.

To retain their posts and, perhaps more importantly, to prove to themselves that their policies did not fail, Bernard and Hutchinson minimized the extent of the debacle. After 1765, whenever the house was not actually drawing up a protest or a crowd was not physically rioting in the streets, they predicted a return to dutiful obedience. Similarly, they deluded themselves about a number of roll calls in the house. In 1766 and 1768, Hutchinson and some future loyalists lost their council seats by narrow margins. But instead of recognizing the vestige of a tradition that elected competent administrators with long records of public service regardless of faction, they predicted their resurgence.[85] Hutchinson similarly misinterpreted his election in 1767 and 1772 to serve on the Massachusetts–New York boundary commissions (in the former case he defeated James Otis, Jr., fifty-five to forty-four) as an endorsement of his political principles rather than his personal abilities. Only wishful thinking enabled him to say on the latter occasion that "they have shown more real confidence in me than they have ever placed in any of my predecessors."[86]

With the possible exception of New Hampshire, only

Massachusetts of all the North American provinces possessed a court faction sufficiently powerful to challenge the country's control of the General Assembly. Such a prerogative party must be distinguished from the planters of Virginia and South Carolina, who had succeeded in persuading their lieutenant-governors to cooperate with them. It also bore little resemblance to the factions in New York and Pennsylvania that alternately assumed the popular or prerogative side depending on the governor's relationship with the other.[87] Only Massachusetts had a faction dedicated on principle as well as interest to achieving a modus vivendi with imperial policy. It began to prevail after 1735, reached its peak in the forties and fifties, thanks to war, and retained considerable respect until 1765.

The prerogative's ability to withstand the crises of the early 1760s indicates it was much better entrenched after the French and Indian War than it had been after Queen Anne's War. The court faction built up by Joseph Dudley crumbled without much trouble in 1719 and 1720. But the Hutchinsonians survived even James Otis and the writs of assistance. A powerful prerogative group capable of sustaining itself in peacetime was beginning to emerge.

Similar signs had appeared in the late 1730s after Governor Belcher had compromised the major issues of the early eighteenth century. After the Land Bank crisis Shirley quickly reestablished legislative cooperation even before war with France broke out in 1744. War accelerated the trend toward political stability. In addition to the cyclical fluctuations in royal power depending on war and peace, Massachusetts between 1735 and 1765 became increasingly "Anglicized."[88]

War greatly strengthened the trend toward Anglo-American cooperation apparent between 1735 and 1744. Many representatives and townsfolk, swept up in the military and the administration of war, acquired a "calling" through the great mid-century wars. (See Table 4.) Between 1760 and 1765, the court faction could surmount its callous efforts to regulate Massachusetts' trade as its contributions to victory remained fresh in mind. But when the prerogative faction failed to protest the Stamp Act vigorously, the respect it had acquired over three decades dissipated at once. Developments after 1765 aborted the real chance that Massachusetts might develop a permanent peacetime stability similar to the mother country's own.[89]

# Notes to Chapter VII

1. *Journals of the House of Representatives of Massachusetts Bay* (Boston, 1919– ), 36: 272. (Hereafter cited as *House Journals.*)

2. Thomas Hutchinson, *The History of the Colony and Province of Massachusetts Bay,* (Cambridge, 1936), 3: 41–42.

# Notes to Chapter VII

3. John A. Schutz, *Thomas Pownall: Defender of American Liberty* (Glendale, California, 1961). Bernard Bailyn, *The Ordeal of Thomas Hutchinson* (Cambridge, 1974), presents evidence that Pownall was probably responsible for stealing the letters which Benjamin Franklin sent to Massachusetts to ruin Hutchinson's administration. In his unpublished autobiography, in "Hutchinson in America," Hutchinson spends more time attacking Pownall than all the revolutionaries put together. Egremont Manuscripts #2664, British Museum (microfilm at MHS).

4. Thomas Hutchinson to Lord Loudoun, 3 February 1757, 16 March 1757, MHS, photostats of Loudoun's letters to Hutchinson from Loudoun Papers, Huntington Library, San Marino, California; Hutchinson, "Hutchinson in America," pp. 61–63.

5. Thomas Hutchinson to William Bollan, 24 April 1762, 15 November 1762, Massachusetts Archives, 26: 22, 58–59, State House, Boston (pagination to typescript copy prepared by Catherine B. Mayo at MHS). On 4 October 1764, Hutchinson wrote to Bollan that "I should never have had any difficulties with him [Pownall] if I had complied with his repeated importunate solicitations to foresake you"; *ibid.*, p. 197.

6. Bollan predicted accurately, if verbosely, that:

> The great desire of some persons of consequence in the ministry to raise a revenue out of this trade is a matter that very nearly affects the present and future interest of the province, as the sums to be raised in it by these designs taking effect may be very considerable; and establish[ing] a practice of raising a revenue by Act of Parliament upon trade in the colonies may be attended with the greatest prejudice and unspeakable danger and disadvantage to them.

See generally the Bollan Papers, NEHGS; quotation from letter of 19 April 1754. These manuscripts afford an excellent glimpse into the efforts of some members of the ministry throughout the 1750s to implement the measures which provoked the Revolution.

7. James Otis, Jr., to Jasper Mauduit, 28 October 1762, *Mauduit Papers, MHSC*, (1918), 72: 76.

8. On Bollan's extravagance, see Francis Bernard to Richard Jackson, 26 July 1763, Bernard Papers (Sparks Manuscripts X), 3: 84, Houghton Library, Harvard University.

9. In December 1759, after a year of embarrassing efforts to find another recipient for the war bounty's latest installment, the General Court rehired Bollan for this purpose only. The governor insisted on John Pownall as a corecipient, and a dispute developed over whose name should appear first in the commission. Bollan obtained precedence by the narrow margin of forty-two to thirty-eight. Four days after Pownall left Massachusetts, the province restored him as sole agent. *House Journals*, 35: 97; 37: 34; Hutchinson, "Hutchinson in America," p. 72. Towns are judged pro- or anti-Shirley based on their composite roll calls during his administration; towns which divided equally were classed as pro-Shirley, since the seventy-one to thirteen vote against Foye (whom the governor supported) was so overwhelming.

10. Thomas Hutchinson to Israel Williams, 20 August 1759, Williams Papers, MHS.

11. Pownall delegated to Hutchinson the task of convincing his friends to change their minds. While admitting that Phelps was "a dishonor to the bench," Hutchinson prophetically chided Williams that "a man who is determined to serve his country must submit to harder things than this." Israel Williams to Thomas Hutchinson, 9 June 1759; Memorial of justices to Thomas Pownall [early 1759]; Hutchinson to Williams, 10 February, 2 June, 10 June, 11 June, 2 July, 10 August 1759; John Worthington to Williams, 1 January 1760, all in Israel Williams Papers; William H. Whitmore, *The Massachusetts Civil List, 1630–1774* (Albany, 1870), p. 140.

12. Hancock was elected to the council for the first time in 1758 and managed the governor's property—as did his nephew John—when he left the province. Francis Ber-

# Notes to Chapter VII

nard to John Pownall, 7 June 1762, Bernard Papers, 3: 193; Thomas Hancock to Governor Lawrence of Nova Scotia, 19 May 1760, Hancock Papers, Box 12, folder 2, NEHGS; Schutz, *Pownall,* p. 165.

13. Otis sought election to the council in 1757 and 1759 and failed both times, blaming the first defeat on Thomas Hutchinson and Andrew Oliver, who had "a bad opinion" of his conduct. Otis had been informed that Hutchinson told the council that "I never did carry things while in the court by any merit but only by doing little low dirty things for Governor Shirley such as persons of worth refused to meddle with." The second time, Otis was undone by his replacement in the house, Edward Bacon, who after obtaining Otis's blessing, persuaded the house that his fellow townsman was already "powerful enough." *The Diaries of Benjamin Lynde and Benjamin Lynde, Jr.,* ed. Fitch E. Oliver (Boston, 1880), p. 186; Memorandum of James Otis, Sr., [1757]; Edward Bacon to James Otis, Sr., 14 May 1759; James Otis, Sr., to James Otis, Jr., 13 June 1759, Otis Papers, Box 1, Columbia University. The house tried to make it up to Otis by unanimously choosing him speaker in 1761, *House Journals,* 37: 5.

14. John J. Waters, Jr., *The Otis Family in Provincial and Revolutionary Massachusetts* (Chapel Hill, 1968), p. 117.

15. John J. Waters, Jr., and John A. Schutz, "Patterns of Massachusetts Colonial Politics: The Writs of Assistance and the Rivalry between the Otis and Hutchinson Families," *William and Mary Quarterly,* 3rd. ser. 24 (1967): 558. Tyng had nearly been expelled from the house in 1756 for making the following remarks about Speaker Thomas Hubbard: "If the speaker puts a nonsensical question, I have a right to oppose it." "The speaker has no right to set me down, unless by order of the house." "The speaker treated me with an uncommon degree of warmth of temper." *House Journals,* 33: 127.

16. Isaac Royall—a Charlestown merchant who owned a sugar plantation on Antigua—endeavored to obtain the lieutenant-governorship. Pownall permitted Sir William Pepperrell to retain the command of Castle William, which traditionally went to the lieutenant-governor, and created the title of lieutenant-general and commander of the militia especially for Pepperrell. Sir William returned the favor by unsuccessfully challenging Hutchinson's right to preside at the council. Hutchinson, "Hutchinson in America," pp. 60–64; Thomas Hutchinson to Israel Williams, 5 June 1758, 17 July 1758, Williams Papers; Hutchinson, *History,* 3: 43. William Brattle also supported Pownall; Hutchinson to Williams, 25 August 1760, Williams Papers.

17. Hutchinson, "Hutchinson in America," pp. 66–68. For the dispute over rangers, see *House Journals,* 34: 140, 218; for the quarrel over the size of the army, *ibid.,* 35: 286, 313.

18. *House Journals,* 34: 186.

19. Quoted in Stanley Pargellis, *Lord Loudoun in America* (New Haven, 1933), pp. 351, 269; Hutchinson, "Hutchinson in America," pp. 69–70.

20. Statistics that would put the reimbursement at £328,000 can be calculated from Thomas Pownall to William Pitt, 29 September 1758, Massachusetts Archives, 56: 301; and Francis Bernard to Board of Trade, 1 August 1764, Bernard Papers, 3: 162, Houghton Library, Harvard University. See also Lawrence Henry Gipson, *The British Empire Before the American Revolution,* (New York, 1936–1972), 10: 38–52; the figure I use is from Jack P. Greene, "Social Context and the Causal Pattern of the American Revolution: A Preliminary Consideration of New York, Virginia, and Massachusetts" in *La Revolution Americaine et L'Europe* (Paris, 1979), p. 31. Leslie V. Brock, *Currency in Provincial America, 1700-1764,* p. 594; William Pencak, "The Social Structure of Revolutionary Boston: Evidence from the Great Fire of 1760, *Journal of Interdisciplinary History,* 10 (1979): 267–278.

21. *A&R,* 4: 810, 880, 910, 1024; 5: 28, 46, 104, 423; Brock, *Currency of the American Colonies,* p. 594. The "supply of the treasury" for each year was payable over the next few years.

# Notes to Chapter VII

22. War contracts for supplies seemed to confirm the popular faction's charges of corruption. See William T. Baxter, *The House of Hancock: Business in Boston, 1724–1775* (Cambridge, 1950), pp. 92–110, 118–123, 139–141, 150–156, 253–255; John J. Waters, Jr., *The Otis Family in Provincial and Revolutionary Massachusetts* (Chapel Hill, 1968); Zemsky, *Merchants, Farmers, and River Gods*, chs. 6, 8; Theodore Thayer, "The Army Contractors for the Niagara Campaign, 1755–1756," *William and Mary Quarterly*, 3rd. ser. 14 (1957): 31–46.

23. See *A&R*, 4: 107, 442, 393, for these two paragraphs. Prices rose sharply during the Seven Years' War and businessmen complained of depressed trading conditions during and after it. See William S. Sachs, "Agricultural Conditions in the Northern Colonies Before the American Revolution," *Journal of Economic History*, 13 (1953): 274–293, and "The Business Outlook in the Northern Colonies, 1750–1775" (Columbia University, Ph.D. diss., 1957).

24. Britain also disallowed the 1765 province act against absconding debtors, which had led to their names appearing in the newspapers.

25. Lord Loudoun to [The Massachusetts House of Representatives?], 29 January 1757, Williams Papers; *House Journals*, 35: 351; Thomas Hutchinson to Loudoun, 21 February 1757, Loudoun Papers; various letters in Massachusetts Archives, vol. 56. Pargellis, *Lord Loudoun*, pp. 175–176, 185–186, 214–215, 269–278; Schutz, *Pownall*, pp. 125–130.

26. Lord Loudoun to Thomas Pownall, 8 November, 15 November, 8 December 1757, Massachusetts Archives, 56: 256–266; Pownall to Loudoun, 26 December 1757, *ibid.*, pp. 278–280; *House Journals*, 34: 208, 256.

27. Jeremiah Gridley to a Mr. McAdams, 2 February 1757, Loudoun Papers; Hutchinson, *History*, 3: 46–48.

28. *House Journals*, 34: 307.

29. In addition to provoking Pownall, Livermore and his followers of course angered Hutchinson and those committed to a maximum war effort. Israel Williams, commander of the western frontier, exclaimed, somewhat cryptically "I am determined to let Livermore know my mind; if he hearkens, well: otherwise I shall take another method and perhaps ruin him." Israel Williams to [Lord Loudoun?], 16 March 1757, Loudoun Papers; *House Journals*, 34: 105; Schutz, *Pownall*, pp. 115–116; *House Journals*, 35: 313, 338, 356.

30. Francis Bernard to Lord Halifax, 18 July 1760, Bernard Papers, 1: 269; Bernard to John Pownall, 28 April 1761, *ibid.*, pp. 316–317; *House Journals*, 38: 11, 16. The house disingenuously replied: "it is with regret we observe your excellency's apprehension that a party spirit is among us . . . we are wholly ignorant of it."

31. Thomas Hutchinson to Israel Williams, 4 March 1760, Williams Papers; Francis Bernard to John Pownall, 2 March 1761, Bernard Papers, 1: 299; Bernard to Viscount Barrington, 20 April 1768, *ibid.*, 5: 106.

32. Francis Bernard to Jeffrey Amherst, 30 May 1762, 2 June 1762, 29 August 1762, 26 September 1762, Bernard Papers, 2: 155, 157, 280, 282; Bernard to Earl of Halifax, 18 February 1764, *ibid.*, 3: 144. Bernard to Richard Jackson, 9 April 1763, *ibid.*, pp. 51–53. Bernard spent £1,000 of his own money improving and settling his grant before it was rejected. Bernard to Lord Hillsborough, 15 October 1764, *ibid.*, 2: 178–179.

33. See Francis Bernard to Jeffrey Amherst, 25 April 1762, 5 May 1762, 29 August 1762, 26 September 1762, Bernard Papers, 2: 137, 143, 155, 177, 280; Bernard to Thomas Gage, 15 January 1764, *ibid.*, 3: 17. On illegal trade, see the above-mentioned letters to Amherst, and Bernard to William Pitt, 8 November 1760, *ibid.*, 1: 284. Agent Richard Jackson wrote to Hutchinson on 3 March 1766, that "Mr. Bernard's letters on

the public affairs have been read in both houses of Parliament and have not only done great credit to himself . . . but contributed much to the repeal of the Stamp Act." Massachusetts Archives, 25: 69.

34. *House Journals,* 38: 302; 37: 250; Francis Bernard to Board of Trade, 17 April 1762, Bernard Papers, 2: 180.

35. Francis Bernard to John Pownall, 30 October 1763, *ibid.,* 2: 185; Bernard to Earl of Halifax, 1 November 1764, *ibid.,* 3: 181; Bernard to Board of Trade, 26 December 1763, 1 August 1764, *ibid.,* 2: 90; 3: 162; Bernard to Richard Jackson, 24 April 1764, *ibid.,* p. 232; *House Journals,* 41: 95.

36. Governor Hugh Palliser of Newfoundland to Francis Bernard, 1 July 1766, Massachusetts Papers, MHS; Thomas Hutchinson to ?, June 1768, Massachusetts Archives, 26: 647–648; Bernard to Admiral Samuel Hood, 18 January 1769, Bernard Papers, 7: 216; Bernard to Lord Hillsborough, 11 July 1768, *ibid.,* pp. 3–7; Bernard to Lord Shelburne, 21 March 1768, *ibid.,* 6: 294.

37. Francis Bernard to Viscount Barrington, 1 May 1762, 20 February 1762, *ibid.,* 2: 190, 27; Bernard to Richard Jackson, 29 October 1762, *ibid.,* p. 214.

38. For an objective account of the chief-justice affair, see Attorney General Edmund Trowbridge to William Bollan, 15 July 1762, *Mauduit Papers,* pp. 65–67. The question of whether Hutchinson really asked for the post will always remain open. I think a letter from Andrew Oliver to Israel Williams of 1 September 1760 stating "the lieutenant-governor is so diffident of his fitness, that if he could be brought to accept the place yet I am persuaded he will never serve in it" (Williams Papers) is convincing. Of course, it is impossible to prove Hutchinson never asked for the post. See Thomas Hutchinson to William Bollan, 15 November 1762, 6 March 1762, Massachusetts Archives, 26: 58, 15.

39. *House Journals,* 40: 255; 41: 206; Whitmore, *Massachusetts Civil List,* pp. 88, 104, and Table 6.

40. Israel Williams to Francis Bernard, 19 August 1761, Williams Papers; John Cushing to Thomas Hutchinson, 15 December 1760, Massachusetts Archives, 25: 120.

41. Oxenbridge Thacher to Benjamin Prat, [1762]. Thacher Papers, MHS. Ellipses omitted.

42. The existence of plural officeholding may at first glance contradict the notion that there was a shortage of jobs. But there were so few appointive offices in Massachusetts other than justices of the peace (sheriffs, probate judges and registers, County and Superior Court justices) that the number of plural officeholders was few. Ellen Brennan, *Plural Office Holding in Massachusetts, 1760–1780* (Chapel Hill, 1945), finds little opposition to the practice before the Otises' attack on Hutchinson. Both Otises were plural officeholders themselves.

43. Peter Oliver, sometime representative for Middleborough, had no other qualification to sit on the Superior Court than the fact that his brother, Andrew Oliver, was Hutchinson's brother-in-law. Half the Suffolk County Court of Common Pleas consisted of Eliakim Hutchinson and Foster Hutchinson, who had never served as representatives, and had obtained their posts because they were Governor Shirley's son-in-law and Thomas Hutchinson's brother, respectively. Andrew Oliver, Jr., was appointed to the Essex County Court for similar reasons in 1761. Whitmore, *Massachusetts Civil List,* pp. 68, 77, 83; see John M. Murrin, "The Legal Transformation: The Bench and Bar of Eighteenth-Century Massachusetts," in Stanley N. Katz, ed., *Colonial America: Essays in Politics and Social Development* (Boston, 1971), pp. 415–449, for the rise of the bar.

44. Compare Namier's writings on British politics such as *The Structure of Politics at the Accession of George III* (London, 1929) and *England in the Age of the American*

# Notes to Chapter VII

*Revolution* (London, 1930) with *Facing East* (New York, 1948) and *Vanished Supremacies: Essays on European History, 1815–1918* (New York, 1958).

45. The scope of this study prohibits the sort of detailed analysis of individual merchants and divisions among them which will appear in John Tyler's Princeton dissertation, "The First Revolution: The Boston Mercantile Community and the Acts of Trade, 1760–1774." I thank him for sharing his fine work with me. Gary Nash, "Social Change and the Growth of Pre-Revolutionary Urban Radicalism," in Alfred Young, ed., *The American Revolution* (De Kalb, Ill., 1976), pp. 21–23, shows how in 1760 the prerogative leaders' plan to abolish the Town Meeting failed.

46. See the discussion of bankruptcy laws in the *House Journals,* 34: 29, 33, 34, 48, 56, 63; Francis Bernard to Board of Trade, 18 April 1765, Bernard Papers, 3: 203. After Wheelwright defaulted, John Rowe, a wealthy Boston merchant reported "general consternation in the town occasioned by the repeated bankruptcies." Anne Cunningham, ed., *The Diary and Letters of John Rowe* (Boston, 1903), pp. 74–75.

47. Francis Bernard to Earl of Shelburne, 21 March 1768, Bernard Papers, 6: 293. Total trade (exports and imports) for New England declined from £500,000 or £600,000 annually in the late 1750s to between £300,000 and £400,000 from 1761 to 1763 before recovery began in 1764. *Historical Statistics of the United States* (Washington, 1960), p. 757. A general interpretation linking the rise of the factorage system and the American Revolution may be found in Joseph Ernst and Marc Egnal, "An Economic Interpretation of the American Revolution, *William and Mary Quarterly,* 3rd. ser. 29 (1972): 3-32.

48. Hutchinson, "Hutchinson in America," p. 75; see also Thomas Hutchinson to Israel Williams, 17 November 1763, Williams Papers; Samuel Alleyne Otis to James Otis, Sr., 20 October 1761, described Bernard as follows: "he is poor and wants to make what money he can of us; but whether this is the case, or if it's true whether he ought to oppress the industrious merchants to fill his own pocket and gild his own chariot with another's gold; or aggrandize his family with his neighbors property, I don't pretend to say." Otis Papers, MHS. Bernard complained to Viscount Barrington on 3 March 1761, that "this government is the worst supported, considering its importance and trouble, of any in the king's gift." He received barely £300 more than he had in New Jersey! Bernard Papers, 1: 302. Paxton had been a nuisance since 1732, when as a young official he had begun taking offenders to the local court, a practice in abeyance since the days of Jahleel Brenton. Suffolk Inferior Court of Common Pleas, 1732, pp. 404–405, New Court House, Boston.

49. *House Journals,* 37: 231–246.

50. Ironically, the writs themselves were a recent reform. Before Governor Shirley, customs officials had searched at will. Shirley, as Attorney Jeremiah Gridley pointed out, required them to obtain a writ of assistance, as was customary in England:

> This is properly a writ of assistants, not assistance; not to give the officers a greater power, but as a check upon them. For by this they may not enter into any house without the presence of the sherriff or a civil officer, who will be always supposed to have an eye over and be a check upon them.

Shirley was forced to make a further reform by Thomas Hutchinson. When two customs officials were about to force open his brother's warehouse using such a writ, Hutchinson threatened legal action on the grounds that the governor had no power to issue search warrants. Henceforth, the Superior Court, assuming the powers of a British Court of Exchequer, had to consent to their issuance. Hutchinson, *History,* 3: 67; Josiah Quincy, Jr., *Reports of Cases Argued and Adjudged in the Superior Court of Judicature of the Province of Massachusetts Bay, 1761–1772* (Boston, 1865), p. 57.

51. Quincy, *Reports of Cases,* pp. 51–57 and Appendix I.

52. Frances Bernard to Board of Trade, 6 August 1761, 28 August 1761, Bernard Papers, 2: 45–52. Francis Bernard to Thomas Pownall, 28 August 1762, *ibid.,* pp. 9–11.

53. Francis Bernard to [John Pownall,?] 19 January, 28 April, 28 June, and 6 July 1761; Bernard to Viscount Barrington, 10 August 1761; Bernard to Thomas Pownall, 28 August 1761, *ibid.,* 1: 296–297, 315–323; 2: 2–6.

54. See, generally, Jordan D. Fiore, "The Temple-Bernard Affair: A Royal Custom House Scandal in Essex County." *Essex Institute Historical Collections,* 90 (1954): 58–83; and the Customs House Papers, Box 2, *passim,* MHS.

55. John Adams to William Tudor, 29 March 1817, John Adams, *Works,* ed. Charles Francis Adams (Boston, 1850–1856), 10: 248; see also, *ibid.,* pp. 183, 233, 272, 276, 292, 314, for Adams's observations on the case in his old age. Oliver M. Dickerson, "The Writs of Assistance as a Cause of the American Revolution," in Richard B. Morris, ed., *The Era of the American Revolution* (New York, 1939), pp. 40–71. Otis's assumption of the popular party's leadership undoubtedly had something to do with the sudden reduction of Boston's taxes in 1761 from one-fifth to one-eighth of the province's total. He thus united the Bostonian merchant opposition with the majority of the deputies, convincing them the prerogative faction in particular and not Boston in general was responsible for the province's ills. *House Journals,* 38: 103. By 1772, Boston paid only nine and one half percent of the total tax; tax list in Massachusetts Archives, vol. 321.

56. *House Journals,* 38: 239, 299, 319; 39: 138; Quincy, *Report of Cases,* p. 299. For Otis's newspaper assault on Hutchinson and plural officeholding, see Malcolm Freiberg, "Prelude to Purgatory: Thomas Hutchinson in Massachusetts Politics, 1760–1770," (Brown University, Ph.D. diss., 1950), esp. pp. 61–65; and James Otis, Jr., to Jasper Mauduit, 20 October 1761, *Mauduit Papers,* p. 76.

57. Thomas Hutchinson to William Bollan, 24 April 1762, 15 November 1762, Massachusetts Archives, 26: 22, 58; Hutchinson to Richard Jackson, 15 November 1767, *ibid.,* pp. 56–57; Francis Bernard to John Pownall, 25 April 1762, Bernard Papers, 2: 183; James Otis, Jr., to Jasper Mauduit, 23 April 1762, *Mauduit Papers,* p. 30; Jonathan Mayhew to Thomas Hollis, 6 April 1762, *ibid.,* p. 31. Hutchinson, in the letter to Bollan cited in this note, wrote that "two lawyers of the same name carry all before them in the house. B[ratt]le at the board heads the party there."

58. The assembly also showed symbolic support for Otis's efforts by replacing Green and Russell, the regular printers of the assembly's journals, with Edes and Gill, who published the *Boston Gazette* in which Otis voiced his hatred for Hutchinson. *House Journals,* 39: 104, 119; 41: frontispiece. Edes and Gill did a poor job typographically, and Green and Russell were reinstated the following year.

59. James Otis, Sr., to James Otis, Jr., 30 May 1762, Otis Papers, Columbia University; Thomas Cushing to Jasper Mauduit, 30 June 1763, *Mauduit Papers,* p. 124.

60. Even the Great Awakening was not mentioned in the correspondence of the leading political actors of the 1740s or the *House Journals.* The unorganized rioting and disorder in the early sixties awaits full investigation.

61. Francis Bernard to John Pownall, 6 April 1761, Bernard Papers, 1: 307.

62. See Carl Bridenbaugh, *Mitre and Sceptre: Transatlantic Faiths, Ideas, Personalities, and Politics, 1689–1775* (New York, 1962), ch. 8; *Mauduit Papers,* pp. 104–114; *A&R,* 4: 523. The bipartisan support for this endeavor illustrates the extent to which the province tried to preserve its wartime unity and crusading fervor, even if the issue was more symbolic than substantive. Other future loyalists who participated included Isaac Royall, John Erving, William Brattle, Robert Hooper, Ezekiel Goldthwait, and Thomas Sparhawk.

# Notes to Chapter VII

63. Andrew Eliot to Jasper Mauduit, 1 June 1763, *Mauduit Papers*, p. 119, Jonathan Mayhew to Thomas Hollis, 6 April 1762, *ibid.*, p. 30.

64. In April 1762, James Otis, Jr., used Agent Bollan's Anglicanism as a further argument to ensure his replacement. He wrote to Mauduit that "a dissenting agent is a bitter pill to an Oxonian, a bigot, a plantation governor whose favorite plans are filling his own pockets at all hazards, pushing the prerogative of the crown beyond all bounds, and propagating high church principles." Otis used the same arguments without success to oppose the choice of Richard Jackson. Jackson, however, was elected forty to thirty-two in the house and eleven to five in the council. James Otis to Jasper Mauduit, 28 October 1762, *ibid.*, p. 76; Francis Bernard to Richard Jackson, 23 January 1763, Bernard Papers, 2: 249–250.

65. The peitition is reprinted in Henri Lefavour, "The Proposed College in Hampshire County in 1762," *MHSP*, 66 (1936–41): 53.

66. Oxenbridge Thacher to Benjamin Prat [1762], Thacher Papers, MHS; in an anonymous letter of 1 April 1762 (Miscellaneous Bound Manuscripts, MHS), the writer claimed that many of the representatives who supported the new college did so only because they knew the council would reject the plan, and they wanted the Hampshire delegates to support the construction of a new hall at Harvard. Thacher remarked that the general population of Hampshire County, headed by sometime Northampton representative Gideon Lyman, also opposed the college. Thacher's testimony, if correct, points to underlying discontent with the "monarch" and his minions which openly appeared in riots to protest the Stamp Act.

67. Governor Bernard granted the college a charter on his own authority, transforming a religious controversy into a constitutional issue. Both houses protested that he had no such right and persuaded him to revoke it. According to Thacher, "Summa [Hutchinson] was put to his trumps" on this question because he was both "the idol of the clergy" and "in a strict alliance offensive and defensive with the monarch of H[ampshire]." Rumors floated about that Bernard planned to solicit the charter in England, but he took no further steps. Oxenbridge Thacher to Benjamin Prat [1762], Thacher Papers; Francis Bernard to Board of Trade, 12 April 1762, Jonathan Mayhew to Thomas Hollis, 6 April 1762, and Charles Chauncy to Jasper Mauduit, 12 October 1762, all in *Mauduit Papers*, pp. 70–73.

68. Hutchinson, *History*, 3: 72; *House Journals*, 38: 224; Thomas Hutchinson to ?, 14 and 16 May 1762, Massachusetts Archives, 26: 26.

69. David Flaherty, unpublished paper delivered at the Convention of the Organization of American Historians, 19 April 1975; *House Journals*, 38: 76, 84; 39: 77; Cunningham, ed., *Diary and Letters of John Rowe*, pp. 61, 67–70; Samuel Alleyne Otis to James Otis, Jr., 11 September 1764, Otis Papers, Columbia University; Dirk Hoerder, *Mobs and People: Crowd Action in Massachusetts During the Revolution, 1765–1780* (Berlin, 1971), pp. 111-113; Great Fire Manuscripts, Ms. Am. 1809, Boston Public Library.

70. For a full history of these land companies, see Gordon E. Kershaw "*Gentlemen of Large Property and Judicious Men*": *The Kennebeck Proprietors, 1749–1775* (Somersworth, N.H., 1975); also Henry Knox Papers, vols. 50–51, documents for 1763–1770, MHS; and G.B. Warden, *Boston, 1689–1776* (Boston, 1970), pp. 356–357. Kershaw notes there were loyalists like Sylvester Gardiner in the Kennebeck Company, but the majority of the company appear to have been revolutionaries whereas most of Waldo's heirs were loyalists.

71. Hutchinson, *History*, pp. 89–90; Freiberg, "Prelude to Purgatory," pp. 114–116. Thomas Hutchinson to Francis Bernard, 26 August 1769, Massachusetts Archives, 26: 783.

72. Francis Bernard to Earl of Halifax, 31 August 1765, Bernard Papers, 4: 149.

# Notes to Chapter VII

73. John M. Murrin, "Anglicizing an American Colony," (Yale University, Ph.D. diss., 1966), p. 271.

74. These factors are enumerated in Robert Foster and Jack P. Greene, eds., *Preconditions of Revolution in Early Modern Europe* (Baltimore, 1970), pp. 13–16.

75. See Mauduit's instructions in *Mauduit Papers,* pp. 39–44; if that were not enough, he had received a detailed letter from the house justifying the rights of Englishmen to make their own laws in response to Bollan's warnings that a plot was afoot to require that all colonial laws contain suspending clauses. This letter of 1762 is important because it shows objections against parliamentary taxation were preceded by a more general refusal to obey *any* Act of Parliament that denied the province's right to legislate for itself; Massachusetts Archives, 56: 386–397; for Bollan's warnings, see his letters to the assembly of 8 May 1761, and to Andrew Oliver, 12 February 1762, *Mauduit Papers,* pp. 16–17, 24.

76. Jasper Mauduit to the House of Representatives, 2 February, 7 February, and 26 May, 1764, Massachusetts Archives, 22: 350, 363, 375.

77. Same to same, 8 February 1763, *Mauduit Papers,* p. 100; Hutchinson, *History,* 3: 57; William Bollan to House of Representatives, 8 July 1762, *Mauduit Papers,* p. 58. Compensation depended as much—if not more—on careful accounting than on actual exertions. See n. 20 in this chapter.

78. *House Journals,* 41: 236, 258, 264; Francis Bernard to Richard Jackson, 2 February 1764, Bernard Papers, 3: 123; Hutchinson, *History,* 3: 76. See James Otis, Jr., to Jasper Mauduit, 14 February 1763, and Thomas Cushing to Jasper Mauduit, 28 October 1763, *Mauduit Papers,* pp. 95, 130, for Bernard's fears and Hutchinson's aspirations. Despite the widespread belief that Hutchinson sought the governorship, none of his letters indicate interest in the post until the mid-sixties, at which time he responded—with Bernard's dismissal or resignation imminent—to British feelers that he would accept the post if it were offered to him. Freiberg, "Prelude to Purgatory," pp. 154–155, shows that Hutchinson was willing to accept the chair if it were offered. Hutchinson's efforts to appoint his unqualified sons to important posts, on the other hand, are matters of record; the absence of similar letters written on his own behalf should be conclusive evidence that he did not seek posts for himself.

79. Francis Bernard to Richard Jackson, 16 February 1765, Bernard Papers, 3: 281. Even Otis was not impressed by Mauduit. On 21 February 1763, referring to one of the agent's letters, he said: "Damn the letter and damn Mr. Mauduit. I don't care a farthing for either but I hate the lieutenant-governor shoud prevail in everything." Same to same, 21 February 1763, *ibid.,* 2: 262.

80. Francis Bernard to Richard Jackson, 17 November 1764, *ibid.,* 3: 263; Thomas Cushing to Jasper Mauduit, 17 November 1764, *Mauduit Papers,* p. 170.

81. *House Journals,* vol.41, p. 134; Francis Bernard to John Pownall, 11 July 1764, Bernard Papers, vol. 3, p. 239.

82. *House Journals,* 41: 19.

83. *Ibid.,* vol. 43, preface; *Boston Gazette,* 17 February, 31 March, 14 April, 28 April, 1766.

84. *House Journals,* 45: 89; the seventeen names were also posted on the Liberty Tree; Francis Bernard to Lord Hillsborough, 28 June 1768, Bernard Papers, 6: 335.

85. Francis Bernard to John Pownall, 30 May 1766, Bernard Papers, 5: 116; Thomas Hutchinson to Thomas Hutchinson, Jr., 29 May 1766, Massachusetts Archives, 26: 447; Thomas Hutchinson to ?. [June 1768], *ibid.,* p. 637.

86. Thomas Hutchinson to Richard Jackson, 24 March 1767, ibid., p. 555; Hutchinson to Governor William Tryon of New York, 26 April 1772, *ibid.,* 27: 565.

87. For a general discussion of types of factionalism in the American colonies, see Jack P. Greene, "Changing Interpretations of Early American Politics," in Ray Allen Billington, ed., *The Reinterpretation of Early American History* (San Marino, Calif., 1966), pp. 151–184. The Delancey faction in New York and Allen group in Pennsylvania were also ousted as loyalists, but they had not consistently supported royal policy and had in fact led their provinces' opposition to the Stamp Act. I view their loyalism as less deeply rooted. New York's Livingstons and Franklin's party in Pennsylvania, which supported the Revolution, remained more passive in 1765.

88. For Anglicization, see Murrin, "Anglicizing an American Colony." Anglicization and the effects of war can be understood as complementary processes.

89. Support for the court faction in Massachusetts, unlike that in Britain, rested more on experience and involvement in war than on patronage. There simply were not enough profitable posts in the province and many of the most lucrative contracts went to men who did not serve in the legislature. Even military commissions for officers paid monthly salaries of only £6 to £10 Massachusetts money per month for men on active duty. See *A&R*, 4: 218, for a sample table of salaries.

# VIII

## THE CROWD
## ENTERS POLITICS
## 1765–1775

### THE PRE-REVOLUTIONARY CROWD

*B*OTH CONTEMPORARY observers and historians have made much of the "mobbish turn" in eighteenth-century Massachusetts. Focusing on Boston, many writers have also distinguished lower-class rioters from an upper-class establishment that feared and opposed crowd action.[1] But their evidence consists of a handful of exceptional, atypical incidents spread out over nearly eight decades. Indiscriminately labelling the province or town as turbulent obscures important changes and continuities in styles of protest.

Patterns of crowd and political violence mirrored provincial factionalism. During peacetime, individuals committed violence against each other whereas crowds restricted themselves to remedying local emergencies. During war, crowds responded to outrages, committed by Britain, while directing threats of violence (but no provable incidents) against prominent politicians. After 1765, the crowd became a constant political force. It consciously aimed to produce fundamental changes in British imperial policy and to destroy the prerogative faction. With the Revolution, the general population played an active role in political factionalism for the first time.

A catalogue of all significant instances of crowd or political violence in Boston between the Glorious Revolution and the Stamp Act riot bears out these patterns.

1. Little is known about the anti-impressment riots of the early 1690s. However, Sir Robert Robertson complained that a visit to

Boston placed naval officers in danger. One Josiah Brodbent wrote that "press masters are knocked down at noon time of day."[2]

2. In 1693, Governor Sir William Phips personally assaulted customs collector Jahleel Brenton and Captain Richard Short. (Short had also been responsible for impressing inhabitants; his press gang had assaulted two Massachusetts assemblymen.)[3]

3. Lieutenant-Governor Thomas Povey ordered the provincial garrison at Castle William in Boston Harbor to fire on H.M.S. *Swift* commanded by Robert Jackson. Jackson had impressed sailors without the required warrant from the governor, and then had attempted to leave the province.[4]

4. Three food riots occurred in Boston in April 1709, May 1713, and July 1729.[5] Andrew Belcher, the province's commissary-general, occasioned the first two by his insensitivity to local food shortages. In the first instance, a crowd cut away the rudder of one of Belcher's ships that was about to export grain to Europe. About fifty men tried to force the ship to land but "several sober men" talked them out of it. The Superior Court tried and acquitted some rioters for "unlawful assembly." The riot followed, and preceded, unsuccessful attempts by the Boston selectmen to convince Governor Dudley to proclaim an embargo on foodstuffs.

The town then began to buy grain and sell it to the impoverished at low prices. Nevertheless, four years later, on 20 May 1713, someone among two-hundred people searching for grain, shot and wounded Lieutenant-Governor William Tailer when he attempted to stop them. Belcher had again exported badly needed supplies. This time, the selectmen's petition to Dudley for an embargo succeeded. The General Court passed an emergency measure requiring any ship importing grain to sell it immediately at a fixed price. In his address to the legislature on 28 May, the governor complained that he had been unable to "come at the knowledge of any persons . . . of reputation or estate," whom he blamed for the riot, and requested assistance in discovering these ringleaders. The assembly and council did not even consider the message.

Henceforth, the selectmen regularly bought and stored grain for the benefit of the poor. A third shortage occurred in 1729 that resulted in the immediate erection of a permanent public granary. Elisha Cooke's enemies blamed Boston's final food riot before the Revolution on the Caucus, but they lacked the necessary evidence to implicate any leading figures. Five obscure men were arrested and fined from £5 to £20 for participating in the uprising.

5. On 16 August 1711, a number of British soldiers and officers,

accompanied by two merchants, began a riot in Charlestown. Lt. Dalby Thomas, Esq., commander of H.M.S. *Weymouth*, Second Lieutenant John Stanley, Henry Thornton, commander of the *Weymouth's* marines, and merchants Rowlands Dee and Lewis Loton rented some calashes to go riding. When Stanley asked for a whip for his horse, John Sprague, from whom he had rented it, said the animal did not require one. Stanley then borrowed a whip from Lt. Thomas and used it on Sprague and Ebenezer Austin of Charlestown. A riot broke out between the *Weymouth's* crew and some inhabitants in which Sprague, Captain Charles Chambers, and "many others" were wounded with gunfire or cutlasses. Over twenty sailors were involved. The following day, a special session of the Middlesex Court of General Sessions met and bound over the principal actors for trial at Cambridge on 28 August. Six participants were fined from £20 (Stanley) to £5.[6]

6. In March or April 1721, John Yeomans, Esq., struck Elisha Cooke in Richard Hall's public house and offered "many threatening speeches" against him. He pleaded guilty, was fined 20s., and bound to good behavior at £50. Not long after, Christopher Taylor, a Boston mariner, accosted at least three men on King Street (Thomas Smith, Jacob Wendell, and Jeremiah Allen) and deliberately refused to show any sign of physical respect for Governor Shute as he passed by. Taylor defended Cooke, damned Yeomans for striking "an old married man," threatened to "get his blood" and pull his and the governor's beard. He also proclaimed his allegiance to "the Old Charter and would lose ten lives if he had it on that account." The jury acquitted him of sedition, but he pleaded guilty to disturbing the peace.[7]

7. On 14 November 1721, someone threw a "bomb" into Cotton Mather's window while he sought to introduce smallpox inoculation at the height of an epidemic. Many people, including William Douglass, Boston's only professionally trained physician, believed that inoculation—which gave the patient a mild case of smallpox to produce resistance—did more harm than good. A note attached to the missile read "Cotton Mather, you dog, damn you: I'll inoculate you with this, a pox on you."[8]

8. Someone attempted to assassinate Governor Samuel Shute late in 1722. In response, he barricaded himself in his mansion and secretly left the province by night.[9]

9. In December 1723, a crowd beat and dragged through the streets two crew members of a ship seized for customs violations because they agreed to testify for the crown.[10]

10. On the afternoon of 22 October 1733, Representative William Brattle of Cambridge reported that one Giles Dulac Tidmarsh of Boston had assaulted him for a speech made that morning. That very day, after several years' resistance, the assembly finally gave the governor and council authority to spend appropriated money without supervision. Brattle had been in the forefront of the opposition since his election to the house in 1729. Most probably, Brattle changed his mind and Tidmarsh resented the decision. At any rate, the deputies issued a warrant for Tidmarsh's arrest that carried a reward of £50.[11]

11. In 1734 "under the countenance of some well-meaning magistrates," a bawdy house was destroyed, and another in 1737.[12]

12. On 3 December 1735, four persons armed with "cutlasses and clubs" attacked Customs Surveyor John Blanchard, who had seized eight hogsheads of molasses for nonpayment of duty. The General Court issued warrants against the offenders.[13]

13. On 23 December 1736, the council learned that the prisoners in the wooden prison in Boston planned to escape. They had recently displayed "irregular behavior in many instances." In particular, Henry Matthews, who refused "to submit to government," threatened "death . . . to any who shall oblige him to do it." The council and house arranged for the local militia to transport the troublemakers to the province's stone jail. A committee headed by Elisha Cooke looked into the situation, but did little until a prison riot occurred on 17 January 1737. The house and council then ordered jailer Zechariah Trescott to appear before them. The examination revealed that he had "extorted excessive fees of several of the prisoners" for room and board, "prevented the prisoners receiving victuals and drink . . . sent to them by their friends," and "cruelly kept some of the prisoners in close confinement without water to their great suffering." He was fired on the spot.[14]

14. Irate inhabitants pulled down a barn blocking construction of a street in 1737.[15]

15. A crowd destroyed several vacant buildings scheduled to be used as market houses on 24 March 1737, during the controversy over whether regulated, centralized markets ought to be substituted for indiscriminate peddling in Boston. According to Reverend Benjamin Colman, about five- or six-hundred men rioted and there was "murmuring against the government and the rich people among us." "A seditious and infamous paper," attached to the town house threatened to muster a hundred men for every one the government produced if it attempted to discover the rioters. The writer also

claimed that the mob "are all royal blood." Those who "have combined together . . . to set up a private market of their own" received similar threats.

However, the conspiracy seems to have been mythical. Governor Belcher wrote that the "detestable paper" misrepresented "His Majesty's good subjects of this province as seditious and generally disposed to cast off His Majesty's lawful government." A reward of £100 to discover the seditious writer met with no response of any sort. In 1740, after protracted controversy, Boston finally decided to accept Faneuil Hall as a marketplace, although it remained closed periodically thereafter.[16]

16. During the Land Bank crisis of 1740–1741, substantial rumors existed that if Parliament suppressed the bank, its adherents would march on Boston and force reluctant merchants to accept its notes. Although a number of men in the small towns surrounding Boston were accused of fomenting rebellion, no violence occurred.[17]

17. Captain James Scott's attempt to impress men for H.M.S. *Astraea* met with armed resistance in June 1741. Scott's behavior so angered the Massachusetts council that it threatened to attack his ship. Governor Shirley, however, obtained the release of the impressed inhabitants. Scott himself was mobbed on his next visit to town.[18]

18. An old fort was furtively demolished to make room for a bowling green in March 1743.[19]

19. A press gang from H.M.S. *Wager* killed two Bostonians who resisted in November 1745. The legislature and town meeting protested the incident, and the council refused to grant any more press warrants to British naval officers.[20]

20. The Knowles Riot occurred from 17 November to 20 November 1747. Governor Shirley, the legislature, the town, and a crowd of several thousand cooperated to obtain the release of most of the forty-odd seamen and inhabitants impressed illegally by Commodore Charles Knowles.[21]

21. In 1749, Massachusetts decided to revert to a non-inflationary currency based on silver for the first time since 1690. Inhabitants of Boston threatened Thomas Hutchinson, who masterminded the scheme, and Governor Shirley, who supported it, with violence.[22]

22. Less than a month after the Knowles Riot, the Old State House burned down in Boston. Also, when Thomas Hutchinson tried to stabilize the province currency, his house burned down to the approval of a number of onlookers. Although arson has never been proven, the timing of these fires is highly suspicious.[23]

23. Recruiting officers and press gangs met with violent resistance in Boston and Marblehead in 1758.[24]

24. Riots occurred on Coronation Day in 1762, and on several occasions in 1764, to protest the arrest of several men for trespassing, to tear down a fence on Beacon Hill, and to prevent the punishment of a popular militiaman.[25]

Several conclusions may be drawn about crowd violence in provincial Boston. First, no one was killed in any of these disturbances except for the impressment riot of 1745, and then the members of a press gang caused the deaths, not the "rioters." Second, even if members of the ruling orders did not countenance the riots, town and provincial officials frequently went to great lengths to remove the grievances that provoked the disturbances. They did not—or, due to the complicity of the militia, could not—resort to counterviolence. Third, riots did not get out of hand and were almost completely restricted to the minimum disturbance needed to accomplish a specific end. Finally, none of the incidents appear to have reflected class conflict. They represented last resort responses to situations that a sizeable part of the town believed could not be handled otherwise. Ships exporting grain during shortages had to be stopped before they left the harbor, as did ships impressing men. Respectable members of the community joined the "lower orders," inflicting limited violence on those who threatened it.[26]

Before 1765, individuals rather than mobs usually undertook action against politically controversial figures. Personal violence subsided quickly. With the exception of Shute, who left the province shortly after he was shot at, the intended victims soon appeared in public with perfect safety. None were seriously injured, although Shute and Mather barely escaped death.

This catalogue does not exhaust all instances of violence that occurred in the town, but only significant cases of purposeful, collective, and political violence. Contemporaries complained periodically of the inhabitants' riotous behavior, and the legislature passed riot acts in 1721, 1751, and annually thereafter. However, this does not necessarily mean intermittent, large-scale, confusion marred Boston. It rather implies that Massachusetts was extremely sensitive to the sort of thefts and assaults that occur in any society.[27] More serious crime was rare: barely an average of 6.2 persons per year were convicted of murder, riot, burglary, counterfeiting, and grand larceny before the superior court from 1700 to 1760. Twelve night watchmen sufficed to keep order in Boston, and foreign observers called attention to the extraordinarily well behaved inhabitants.[28]

## The Crowd Enters Politics

The town and the province took pains to ensure that those groups that were potential sources of trouble (blacks, indentured servants, seamen, and the poor) obtained redress of grievances. Both legislation and custom protected them from the sort of exploitation they endured elsewhere in colonial America. They had access to the courts that generally gave them a fair and sympathetic hearing.[29] Boston had an elaborate system of poor relief in which town, church, and individual benevolence combined to combat hunger and beggary.[30] By assuring almost everyone some stake in society, Massachusetts preempted class conflict and created a willingness on the part of the lower and upper classes to riot shoulder-to-shoulder in defense of provincial rights. Social conflict did occur during the Revolution. But it united all classes against the wealthy minority that led the prerogative faction and had profited from Massachusetts' distresses.

### REVOLUTIONARY VIOLENCE

Beginning on 14 August 1765, crowd and political violence merged. For the first time since the Glorious Revolution, the mob had a greater task than merely eliminating an obvious nuisance or grievance. Massachusetts' leading political figures favored submission to the Stamp Act. The Boston crowd no longer had to oppose isolated or atypical instances of oppression. It had to persuade British imperial administration to reverse its entire colonial policy and to destroy a well-entrenched and respected faction. To accomplish these ambitious goals, Massachusetts had to become politicized both intensively and extensively: the country faction had to persuade the people to regard politics as a personal matter of liberty or slavery, and also to increase the number of inhabitants who held such attitudes. The tactics by which the revolutionary leadership accomplished these purposes drastically transformed the nature of Massachusetts' politics in several ways.

First, the Boston Caucus, Loyal Nine, and prominent individuals transformed the crowd from a sporadic nonpolitical force into a quasi-institutionalized instrument of the popular party. "Gentlemen of the first fortune," recognized the crowd's leader, a shoemaker named Ebenezer Mackintosh, as a "general" and gave him a uniform. The altered festivities of Pope's Day, 1765, symbolized the new mob. Instead of heading the South Enders' battle with the North Enders, Mackintosh led a united parade of two-thousand inhabitants. He walked "arm in arm" with Colonel William Brattle, the commander of the province's militia, who "complimented him on the order he kept and told him his post was one of the highest in the government." Brattle (a future loyalist, ironically) thereby indicated that leading political opponents of Bernard and Hutchinson supported the crowd.[31]

To complement the crowd, the Bostonians created other institutions: the Sons of Liberty, the nonimportation enforcement machinery, and the Committees of Correspondence. All required sustained participation in politics by unprecedented numbers of people. An informal system of government was constructed to sidestep the prerogative faction.[32]

In addition to creating new organizations, the revolutionary movement altered existing ones. In 1766, the representatives led by James Otis, Jr., systematically purged the council of "Tories." Political allegiance had never before completely supplanted administrative competence and public service as criteria for election.[33] Turnovers in the upper house and the number of newly elected councillors vetoed by the governor reached new heights. And no supporter of the prerogative polled more than a literal handful of votes out of several hundred in the elections for Boston representatives after 1765.[34]

Similarly, the house of representatives changed its role to reflect increased popular involvement in politics. In 1766, it ordered a gallery built. Hitherto, the assembly had kept its debates secret to enable the delegates to speak their minds without fear of political repercussions. Once the people entered the chamber, however, the galleries subjected unpopular deputies to verbal abuse and threats of physical violence if they did not adopt radical views. Even Samuel Alleyne Otis admitted that the spectators intimidated moderate representatives.[35]

New modes of communication accompanied novel institutions. Before 1765, political pamphlets had been issued only on rare occasions. Groups of them had appeared in response to specific issues (the Land Bank, Hutchinson's redemption scheme, the Excise, the Otis–Hutchinson feud of 1761). Then none surfaced for several years. Newspapers, too, had rarely published political news and contented themselves most of the time with reprinting laws and governors' speeches. The revolutionary crisis changed that. Several new journals emerged, notably the patriot *Massachusetts Spy*, John Mein's loyalist *Chronicle*, and Andrew Oliver's loyalist *Censor*. All the Boston papers carried articles discussing the imperial crisis. In addition to the printed word, the revolutionaries introduced poetry, songs, and engravings as weapons in the political struggle. As early as the first Stamp Act riot of 1765, the following immortal verse appeared on an effigy of Stamp Master Andrew Oliver:[36]

# The Crowd Enters Politics

The Virtuous Patriot at the Hour of Death, from the cover of Low's *Astronomical Diary* for 1775.

It's a glorious sight to see
A Stamp Man hanging on a tree.
He that takes this down is an enemy to his country.
Fair freedom's glorious cause I've meanly quitted
Betrayed my country for the sake of a little pelf
But at last the devil has me outwitted
Instead of stamping others I hang myself.

The revolutionary movement made media wizards of composer William Billings, engraver Paul Revere, and printer Isaiah Thomas. It became an avenue for their social mobility and made them important political figures in their own right. James Otis's and Samuel Adams's disquisitions on natural rights may have provided the intellectual self-justification the leadership required. But to obtain rank and file support they had to appeal to the senses as well as the mind. Not only contemporary Bostonians, but future generations of Americans, have visualized the Boston Massacre through Paul Revere's engraving. Only historians seem to care that it erred in depicting the soldiers firing in unison at the command of Captain Preston, supported by the Customs Commissioners from an upper story of the house. One need only examine a print of Governor Thomas Hutchinson roasting in Hell and tormented by devils to realize the quantum change in the intensity and importance of politics in a few years. A complementary engraving depicted "The Virtuous Patriot at the Hour of Death" being welcomed into heaven by angels.[37] Such imagery was absent from political debates before 1765.

The language of political discourse changed along with its content. Thomas Hutchinson studied this problem seriously. For example, he noted that the word "subjection" had previously never meant anything more than "subject to the supreme legislative authority of Britain, in common with their fellow subjects in the island." But the word had "been improved to alienate the subject in colonies" and had become synonymous with oppression. Revolutionary writers sought out "big sounding words" without regard for their true meaning to captivate the populace:

> That which used to be called the "court house," or the "town house," had acquired the name of the "state house"; "the House of Representatives of Massachusetts Bay" had assumed the name of "His Majesty's Commons"; the debates of the assembly are styled "parliamentary debates"; "the acts of Parliament," "acts of the British Parliament"; "the province laws," "the laws of the land"; "the charter," a grant from royal grace or favor, is styled the "compact."

On the other hand, terms such as "riots, routs, and unlawful assemblies" ceased to excite "great horror" because of frequent usage. Although historians have not generally followed up Hutchinson's insight, Richard Merritt has discovered increasing use of the word "American" and other "Symbols of American Community" beginning in the mid-1760s.[38]

Massachusetts' entire popular culture, as well as its language, became more political after 1765. Holidays, iconography, and heroes

Traitor (Thomas Hutchinson) at the Hour of Death, from the cover of Gleason's
*Massachusetts Calendar*, 1774.

changed. Celebrations of the Stamp Act's repeal, the Stamp Act riots, and the Boston Massacre replaced Pope's Day, the Harvard Graduation, and Coronation Day as Massachusetts' principal patriotic holidays.[39] The new celebrations, unlike the old, referred to immediate events in which much of the population had participated rather than to remote deeds and people.

Hand in hand with a new set of holidays came a new set of icons. Instead of burning Popes and Pretenders in effigy, the crowd substituted Stamp Master Andrew Oliver, Governors Hutchinson and Bernard, and the local customs establishment.[40] Contemporary popular heroes supplemented veneration of the Puritan founders. Leading patriots nicknamed themselves after European incendiaries: William Molineux became Pasquale Paoli, the Corsican rebel. (Mackintosh named his son Pasquale Paoli Mackintosh.) His fellow conspirators dubbed Josiah Quincy "Wilkes" after England's leading troublemaker of the mid-1760s. One anonymous pamphleteer took the pseudonym "Joyce, Jr.," after a leading radical of the English Civil War.[41] To be sure, the revolutionaries also modelled themselves on the ancient Romans and their Puritan ancestors. But they found more recent exemplars too.

Finally, the entire province began to take the active interest in politics that had always characterized Boston. Printers set up political newspapers in Salem, Cambridge, Newburyport, and Worcester. Instructions from towns to their representatives on matters of provincial concern had rarely been seen outside of Boston. But beginning in 1765, when over fifty towns ordered their deputies to oppose the Stamp Act, such communications became frequent. Finally, according to Hutchinson, "tumults, riots, and other marks of discontent, [which] were hardly known, except in an instance, now and then, in some of the maritime towns," spread throughout the province. Riots occurred in, among other places, Salem, Marblehead, Newbury, Scituate, Plymouth, Hampshire County, and Maine.[42] Throughout Massachusetts, the popular party successfully enlisted public support for its efforts to combat new imperial policies. The prerogative party, committed to maintaining the traditional framework of government, found itself clamoring for order within the inoperable court system it dominated.

### WHO MADE THE REVOLUTION?

The American Revolution definitely involved more people in Massachusetts politics than ever before. But which people were they?

# The Crowd Enters Politics

Some historians have maintained that the Massachusetts revolutionary movement was homogeneous and dominated by respectable citizens. Others insist that it embodied class conflict between the reformist, wealthy merchants and the truly revolutionary artisans, seamen, mechanics, and lower-class elements who comprised the Sons of Liberty. I find the latter case less than persuasive. Class antagonism undoubtedly existed in Boston. Revolutionary pamphleteers played upon it effectively to provoke hatred for the loyalists. Even more frequently, the loyalists, upper-class revolutionaries, and even the Town Meeting blamed the "rabble" for social ills and disturbances almost as a reflex action. But evidence that these tensions may have translated themselves into political alignments is scanty. Similarly, the country faction directed its rhetoric, and crowds focused their resentment against wealthy *loyalists*, not against the rich in general. The "consensus" interpretation is better supported with respect to revolutionary Boston.[43]

Serious problems exist with the notion that a radical lower class forced elite merchants to assume more extreme stances than they would have preferred, and then went on to initiate crowd actions far exceeding the wishes of their putative superiors. First, much of the impressionistic evidence that "levelling principles have had such spread" comes from the pens of loyalists such as Thomas Hutchinson and Francis Bernard, or neutrals like John Rowe. No revolutionary ever wrote that "it [the second Stamp Act riot] was now become a war of plunder, of general levelling, and taking away the distinction of rich and poor so that the gentlemen who had promoted and approved" the proceedings "became now as fearful for themselves," as did Governor Bernard. Hutchinson and Bernard had a vested interest in persuading British colonial administration that the respectable citizenry opposed the most extreme protests. They frequently overestimated their strength in letters home to convince themselves that their administrations had not been total disasters. More importantly, they might well have been removed (Bernard ultimately was) had they proven incapable of maintaining their authority. Furthermore, as during the Land Bank, upper-class politicians blanketly labelled their foes "lower-class" as a means of discrediting them. At any rate, it is somewhat paradoxical that historians writing "from bottom up" must base their case so heavily on the remarks of obviously biased, wealthy, and powerful individuals.[44]

The Boston Town Meeting also disavowed responsibility for revolutionary excesses. As in the great 1747 impressment riot, it blamed the disorders on "foreign seamen, servants, negroes, and other persons of mean and vile condition." The Town Meeting attributed the Stamp Act riots to "persons unknown." It even denied that the 1768 riot that drove the Customs Commissioners from Boston had occurred at all. Such reticence is understandable. Rebellion did not escape severe punishment in the eighteenth-century British Empire, as the fate of the Highland Scots after Culloden proves. The community had to defend itself for British consumption after each crowd action. In hiding the true source of mob behavior, it shared a common interest with the very loyalist officials it opposed. As merchant Henry Bass wrote to Samuel Phillips Savage following the two Stamp Act riots: "We do everything in order to keep this and the first affair private, and are not a little pleased to hear that Mackintosh has the credit of the whole affair." Tory General Timothy Ruggles sarcastically observed "it has always been their practice, soon after the exertions of a mob, to call a town meeting and vote themselves innocent."[45]

To be sure, crowds had a strong lower-class component. Most of the population, after all, belonged to the lower and middle classes. But the point is whether their "betters" in general, not the small Tory group Hutchinson and Bernard sometimes considered synonymous with the upper class, approved of and led their actions. The statistical evidence to be presented in this chapter suggests strongly that they did. Crowds undoubtedly also acted on a different ideology than the legalistic natural rights doctrines that motivated lawyers such as John Adams and James Otis: the introduction of eschatalogical imagery into songs, prints, and tracts proves this. And perhaps at times, the lower orders indeed threatened to get out of control or take independent action. But the fact remains that they did not. On the desirability of ridding America of the damnable Tories, people of all classes united.[46]

Finally, disguises must be mentioned. Upper-class men who joined a crowd would not want to be identified, since they might be labelled as ringleaders and singled out for severe punishment. They would be more easily recognized by the upper-class targets of their action. Rioting can be dirty work. It is hard to imagine people dressing up for it. Governor Bernard noted over fifty disguised gentlemen in the first Stamp Act riot, and of course only "Indians" were invited to the Tea Party.[47] In sum, the evidence historians have used to argue class division within the Boston revolutionary movement is suspect.

Statistical correlation of the Boston 1771 tax register—listing approximately eighty percent of adult male taxpayers—with membership records of the town's revolutionary organizations and catalogues of loyalists suggests class unity rather than division.[48] Several precautions must be taken before using the 1771 tax list. It only recorded certain forms of wealth: rental value of real estate occupied per dwelling (if several families inhabited one building, they were bracketed), merchants' inventories, money lent at interest, factorage, and various forms of property that were simply enumerated but assigned no monetary value. Nevertheless, two points can be demonstrated. First, the wealthier a household, the more likely it was that it occupied a more highly valued dwelling: good correlation exists between housing rents and probate inventories for 1771–1774. Second, those assessed for some form of mercantile wealth were generally richer than non-merchants. This held for Boston in 1790, when the town recorded actual wealth. Then, merchants possessed on average more than twice as much as lawyers, the second wealthiest group.[49] The wealth of various prominent groups in Boston during the revolutionary crisis relative to the entire population may therefore be ascertained.

Membership lists survive for four important revolutionary organizations not ostensibly limited to members of one class: the 350 Sons of Liberty who on 14 August 1769, attended a celebration to commemorate the fourth anniversary of the Stamp Act riots;[50] 49 members of the North End Caucus in 1772;[51] 97 participants in the Boston Tea Party;[52] and the committee of 53 selected by the town in April 1775, to carry out the dictates of the Continental Congress.[53] In addition, three lists exist of organizations limited exclusively to merchants: the 61 protestors against the Writs of Assistance (1761),[54] the 146 members of a society to encourage manufacturing (1764),[55] and 242 supporters of the nonimportation agreements (1769).[56] Finally, using the catalogues compiled by James Stark,[57] E. Alfred Jones,[58] and Lorenzo Sabine,[59] the name of any loyalist sufficiently obnoxious to attract attention has survived.

Given this data, three questions may be posed and answered. First, was any class disproportionately represented among the revolutionary organizations or the loyalists? Second, did change occur over time—did the respectable inhabitants desert the movement as it became more radical? Finally, if attrition occurred, did the loyalists benefit or did the disgruntled merely pronounce a plague on both houses?

All the relevant lists indicate that with the exception of the Tea Party members, who composed a crowd rather than a formal organization, the revolutionary societies and the loyalists were overwhelmingly upper-class. Table 11 records the number of male inhabitants in each rental category and translates these figures into percentages. Table 12 summarizes the proportion of merchants in the Sons of Liberty and among the loyalists. Twice as many loyalists, in proportion to the population, and nearly three times as many Sons of Liberty had mercantile wealth.[60]

# The Crowd Enters Politics

The Sons of Liberty and the Caucus do not emerge as lower-class complements to the merchants' organizations. Rather, membership in the groups overlapped considerably. Of the 242 merchants participating in the nonimportation movement, 94 belonged to the Sons of Liberty. Twenty-eight of the 35 members of the North End Caucus who could be traced on the tax lists possessed mercantile wealth; 22 had belonged to the Sons of Liberty three years earlier. Interestingly, only 24 of the 35 men actually came from the North End (Wards 1 to 5), the poorest area of town.[61]

In its organized capacity, the resistance movement in Boston was primarily, although by no means exclusively, upper-class. The presence of some men with lower assessments indicates that influential poorer men were not thereby excluded. The Tea Party statistics reveal that an economically representative sample of the population participated in the revolutionary crowd. The real division in Boston was within the upper class itself, whose members became progressively disenchanted with opposition tactics as the 1760s and 1770s progressed. Of 61 merchants who protested the writs in 1761, 22 became loyalists, as did 43 of the 146 members of the 1764 manufacturing society. Most of the attrition occurred after 1768, since support for the nonimportation movement was nearly universal. Of the 260 merchants listed by Samuel Phillips Savage and William Palfrey, 180 joined with no recorded reluctance, 54 agreed to sign if the agreement was general, 8 promised to abide by it even though they refused to sign, and only 18 refused to cease importation. Nevertheless, 50 of the 242 supporters became loyalists, as did 52 of the 350 Sons of Liberty. The proportion of Boston's merchants or inhabitants who became loyalists cannot be definitively known, but it was nowhere near a majority. Thirty-six percent of the 1761 protestors, thirty percent of the 1764 society, and twenty-one percent of the nonimportation subscribers opposed the Revolution. (Of course, it is false to assume that everyone who was not a loyalist was an active revolutionary.)

That few merchants became open loyalists before 1774 and 1775, when many of them signed addresses commending Governors Hutchinson and Gage, does not confirm the theory that the merchants who remained in the revolutionary movement lost any of their zeal or influence. The committee of fifty-three entrusted in 1775 with executing the Continental Congress's mandates illustrates the continuity of leadership during the 1760s: thirty-two of the thirty-eight members who could be traced on the tax list possessed mercantile wealth. Forty-eight percent came from the eleven percent of householders renting dwellings assessed at £31 or more. Forty-five had belonged either to the Sons of Liberty or were involved in nonimportation in 1768. A strictly economic analysis of the American Revolution in Boston reveals continuous upper-class domination. Men of all classes united against the visible, upper-class loyalists. Class conflict only broke out, if at all, once the loyalists were eliminated.

Age accounts for differences between Massachusetts' revolutionaries and loyalists more than class. Most prominent Tories were old enough to be the revolutionaries' fathers. Although a handful of important patriots were in their sixties and seventies, the number of elderly loyalists is astonishing. In addition to those leaders cited in the next chapter, who averaged sixty years of age in 1775, the following loyalists all belonged to an earlier generation than their adversaries: Robert Hooper (b. 1709); Judges John Cushing (b. 1695), Chambers Russell (b. 1713), and Eliakim Hutchinson (b. 1711); George Erving (b. 1693); James Murray (b. 1713); Isaac Winslow (b. 1709); Charles Paxton (b. 1707); the Rev. Henry Caner (b. 1707); Christopher Minot (b. 1706); Edward Lloyd (b. 1710); William Vassall (b. 1715); Sheriff Stephen Greenleaf (b. 1704); Ralph Inman (b. 1713); Sylvester Gardiner (b. 1707); Ezekiel (b. 1715) and Thomas (b. 1717) Goldthwait; Benjamin Faneuil (b. 1704); and Byfield Lyde (b. 1704). The members of the Boston Tea Party averaged twenty-eight or twenty-nine years of age. The typical member of the North End Caucus was born in 1735; the typical committeeman to enforce Congress's edicts in 1775 was a year older. Many of these men had been active in the resistance movement since the Stamp Act crisis of 1765. (See Tables 13–14.)[62]

Recently, perhaps inspired by events of the 1960s, historians have begun to link political and social upheaval with generational conflict. Philip Greven, Robert Gross, and Kenneth Lockridge have hypothesized that overpopulation in eastern Massachusetts, caused by a high birthrate and low death rate over four generations of settlement, had two important consequences. On the one hand, small inheritance prospects forced many men to leave their homes and start life afresh without the benefit of traditional family support. On the other hand, those who remained were subject to their fathers' authority until they died or received their inheritances. The older generation's longevity ensured that many did not acquire property until they were well into adulthood.[63]

Higher ages at marriage is usually a sign of increasing economic difficulty for young people. This pattern held in Boston among the revolutionaries. (See Table 16.) Before 1760, it had been customary for men to marry before the age of twenty-five, usually between twenty-one and twenty-three. After 1760, marriages of men in their late twenties became more common. When the Revolution broke out, weddings by men over thirty became the rule rather than the exception.[64] Two prominent examples of this trend are John Adams, who had to struggle for nine years after his graduation from Harvard until he could begin a family at age twenty-nine, and John Hancock who emerged from his uncle Thomas's shadow at twenty-seven. He did not marry until 1775 at age thirty-eight. John Waters, Jr., and Winthrop D. Jordan have respectively shown that James Otis, Jr., and Thomas Paine (to take a case outside Massachusetts) endured similar difficult transitions to responsible adulthood.[65]

Much evidence supports the notion of an economic crisis for young men in Boston and its environs. As Table 17 shows, migration into Boston, indicated by Warning Out Lists, changed radically in the mid-1760s.[66] These records do not indicate who was forced to leave town. They recorded who entered so these people would not be eligible for relief if they could not support themselves. During nearly two decades of war, migration had been primarily female and predominantly local. Beginning in 1765, migration not only increased astronomically but became primarily male. The newcomers now came not only from Massachusetts, but from other colonies and overseas. The end of warfare, the disbanding of the army, and a postwar depression reinforced in Massachusetts by the catastrophic drought of 1763 to 1764 accounted for the presence of so many additional single men in Boston.[67] They undoubtedly swelled the size and added to the vigor of the "Boston mob." All in all, revolutionary Boston provides the ideal proof for an idea recently advanced by Mary K. Matossian and William D. Schaffer that a surplus of discontented and single young men accompanies political revolution.[68]

To go one step further, can it be hypothesized that young men in revolutionary Boston psychologically transferred their family experiences to the loyalists? They would thereby have legitimately released suppressed emotions that would have cost them their inheritances or have violated cultural norms requiring respect for parents. Evidence exists for such an interpretation, one which meshes nicely with Philip Greven's argument in *The Protestant Temperament*. For revolutionaries raised in highly authoritarian "New Light" "evangelical" families, "the mother country and the father-king became symbolic representations of the dangerous, seductive, and powerful tyrants of their childhood." Similarly, those raised "moderately" whose parents sought a "voluntary but necessary" obedience knew "that power, in the persons of parents, actually had the upper hand" while "liberty, therefore, always had to be defended." Tories, on the other hand, were usually raised "genteely" in "benign and indulgent" families that considered "struggle with authority unimagineable." To be sure, psycho-historical interpretations are highly speculative, but this one aids in understanding the appeal of revolutionary rhetoric.[69]

A good starting point in exploring the revolutionaries' resentment is to consider the intriguing similarities between accusations against witches in the 1690s and Tories in the 1760s. As John Demos has shown, witches tended to be elderly women (or their daughters) who lived on the outskirts of Salem and had ceased to play an active role in its social and religious life; frequently they expressed contempt for community values. Similarly, many Tories were elderly men (or their sons) who had retired from Boston to suburban country houses and disdained the Town Meeting, Pope's Day parades, and other Bostonian institutions; many had become Anglicans. The accusers of the witches were mostly young girls, whom Demos hypothesizes led extremely repressed lives under the direction of their mothers. The charges made against the witches, that they indulged in violent, physical rather than sexual excesses, indicated such was the nature of girls' hostility.[70]

Do the sort of charges the younger revolutionaries made against the Tories maintain the analogy with witchcraft? They do. Just as the young girls felt physically repressed, the young revolutionaries felt economically stifled. Attacks on loyalists mention the vices that David Hackett Fischer, in *Growing Old in America*, describes as the characteristic faults attributed to the elderly by colonials. As Cotton Mather put it: "Old age is often too covetous, too sparing, too hoarding and ready to lay up. . . . Old folks often seem to grasp the hardest for the world, when they are just going out of it."[71] Covetousness, both of wealth and power, was the very sin with which the patriots repeatedly charged Thomas Hutchinson and his cohorts. For example, John Adams's diary reveals attacks against Hutchinson's "ambitious and avaricious disposition" accompanied by an exhaustive catalogue of the political offices he and his family held. Adams also listed the special grants Hutchinson had cajoled the legislature into awarding him for his various services to the province. He compared Hutchinson's quest for "wealth and power" with the "corruption" and "tyranny" of Julius Caesar, and described graphically how Hutchinson had turned the Superior Court into a family fief. Adams's denunciations are typical; that he confided them to his diary indicates sincere belief rather than propagandistic intent.[72]

More than once, Adams wished the leading loyalists were dead. When Lieutenant-Governor Andrew Oliver died in 1774, Adams commented on the remarkable longevity of his enemies. He noted that "this is but the second death which had happened among the conspirators, the original conspirators against the public liberty, since the conspiracy was first regularly formed, and begun to be executed, in 1763 or 4." The following day, Adams observed that an "exhibition" displayed effigies of Oliver's brother-in-law Thomas Hutchinson and brother Peter to remind them "of the fate of Empson and Dudley, two British traitors, whose trunks were exposed with their heads off, and the blood fresh streaming after the ax."[73]

While wishing for the loyalists' deaths, Adams also depicted them as obstacles to, or murderers of, the younger generation. When Hutchinson refused to open the Superior Court without the required stamps in 1765, Adams regarded it as a plot against his efforts to become an established lawyer: "I was but just getting into my gears, just getting under sail, and an embargo is laid upon my ship. . . . I have groped in dark obscurity, till of late, and had just become known and gained a small degree of reputation, when this execrable project was set on foot for my ruin as well as that of America in general, and of Great Britain." Later he charged that "Governor Hutchinson and his political creators and creatures on both sides of the Atlantic . . . destroyed a Thacher, a Mayhew, and Otis [the first two died, the last went insane]." In an unsent letter to Hutchinson written under the pseudonym Chrispus Attucks, Adams called Hutchinson a "murderer" who was "chargeable before God and man with our blood."[74]

The loyalists' plural officeholding and solicitude for their own families undoubtedly exacerbated the revolutionaries' resentment. The long-lived loyalists engrossed political offices and refused to surrender them; when vacancies occurred, the appointment of their unqualified sons and relatives heightened the revolutionaries' own sense of deprivation. Political reality recapitulated and exaggerated the most unfavorable characteristics of family life in revolutionary Massachusetts.[75]

In yet another application of familial rhetoric, the revolutionaries condemned the loyalists as unworthy sons of America. By withdrawing to the pleasures of private life or self-aggrandizement at public expense, they had clearly renounced their patrimony. These "first born sons of Hell," as the *Boston Gazette* called them, "for a little filthy lucre" "betray[ed] and murder[ed] their country" and would have succeeded were they not "confounded at the light of the sun, and tremble[d] at the countenance of the sons of honor and virtue."

Proudly noting that former Governor Shirley had never heard of the "brace of Adamses," John Adams remarked, "is it not a pity, that a brace of so obscure a breed, should be the only ones to defend the household, when the generous mastiffs and best blooded hounds are all hushed to silence by the bones and crumbs that are thrown to them." The Massachusetts revolutionaries regarded themselves as the legitimate heirs to liberty and property that had been unjustly stolen.[76]

The age pressures that heightened revolutionary fervor in Boston also appear in recruitment records for the continental army. True, young, single, and poor men have made up the rank and file of many armies. But scholars seeking to discredit economic distress as a motive for the American Revolution must deal with the issue that most of those who fought against "taxation without representation," from Boston at any rate, were too poor or too young to be taxed and to vote. As one of the most distressed areas in North America—especially after the siege of 1775–1776—Boston supplied a tremendous number of soldiers for the revolutionary cause: 2,471 men enlisted, which nearly equalled the town's 2,588 polls as of 1771. Of these, 666 gave their ages; seventy-two percent were under thirty. Only 215 soldiers' names could be found on the 1771 tax list, of whom 196 were not duplicated. Their wealth profile resembles that of the Tea Party participants. (See Table 11.) With only 135 exceptions, the Bostonians served over three months, unlike the militia of surrounding towns that turned out for Lexington, Concord, and Bunker Hill and then went home. The devastation wreaked by British soldiers on Boston returned to haunt them. Boston not only led the pre-revolutionary agitation, but provided much of the manpower to sustain the war.[77]

It would be wise not to take this interpretation too far. The blatant hatred of the aged, which John Gillis has found during the French Revolution, did not exist in Massachusetts. Nevertheless, revolutionary rhetoric suggests the appearance of social and psychological preconditions that paved the way for drastic changes in attitudes toward the old. In *Growing Old in America*, David Hackett Fischer has described a revolution in American age relationships that began around 1770. During the colonial period, younger inhabitants respected the elderly to such an extent that Fischer terms colonial society a "gerontocracy." In part, the scarcity of old people accounted for their "veneration." However, as the number of elderly increased, they blocked young men's desires for land, families, and careers. Reverence for the elderly consequently declined.[78] This process took an extraordinarily acute form in revolutionary Boston. The end of

warfare with the French, economic crisis, and the migration of unattached men to Boston made it especially difficult for young men to
become functioning adults with families and independent incomes.
The loyalists, as revolutionary ideology revealed, appeared as greedy,
power-hungry father figures who conspired to suppress the younger
generation. The political crisis of Massachusetts in the mid-eighteenth
century reflected the personal crises of many young men. A government monopolized by elderly men insisted on deference but proved
unwilling to fulfill its obligations to a worthy, long-suffering
populace. Extremely sensitive when deprived of liberty and property
they considered rightfully theirs, the revolutionaries capped their
triumph by banishing the loyalists, trying them for treason in absentia,
confiscating their estates, and disinheriting their legal heirs who had
done no wrong.

People of certain ages and socioeconomic circumstances were more
likely to take different roles in the Massachusetts Revolution.
However, these psychological and material differences should not be
elevated into causes of the Revolution. The cause obviously was that
British legislation after 1763 provoked the province. However, as
with Massachusetts' special relationship to the mother country in wartime and the peculiar political system that resulted, the revolutionary
movement's social profile helps to explain Massachusetts' leading role
and the form the Revolution took.

# *Notes to Chapter VIII*

1. See especially G.B. Warden, *Boston: 1689–1776* (Boston, 1970); Dirk Hoerder,
*Mobs and People: Crowd Action in Massachusetts During the American Revolution*,
(Berlin, 1971); Jesse Lemisch, "Jack Tar in the Street: Merchant Seamen in the Politics
of the American Revolution," *William and Mary Quarterly*, 3rd. ser. 25 (1961):
371–407; for contemporary complaints see William Shirley to Board of Trade,
1 December 1747 in *Correspondence of William Shirley*, ed. C.H. Lincoln (New York,
1912), pp. 414–416; Thomas Barrow, *Trade and Empire: The British Customs Service
in Colonial America, 1660–1675* (Cambridge, 1967), p. 90; and Carl Bridenbaugh,
*Cities in the Wilderness: The First Century of Urban Life in America* (New York, 1938;
2nd edition, 1955), pp. 382–383; and Carl Bridenbaugh, *Cities in Revolt* (New York,
1955), p. 117.

2. Deposition of Sir Robert Robertson, 15 January 1694, Phips Papers, 2: 153,
Frederick Lewis Gay Transcripts, MHS; Josiah Brodbent to Francis Nicholson, 21 June
1692, *ibid.*, p. 12.

3. Discussed above, ch. 2.

4. *CSP*, 20: #768; deposition of Josiah Gee, 21 September 1702, Boston Public
Library.

5. Bridenbaugh, *Cities in the Wilderness*, pp. 196, 282–282, 353–354; Legislative
Records of the Massachusetts Council, 9: 274, Massachusetts Archives, State House,

Boston; Samuel Gardner Drake, "Notes on the History of Boston," 1: 30, Boston Public Library.

6. Middlesex County Court of General Sessions, volume for 1686–1688, 1692–1723, pp. 269–270, Middlesex Files Folio 49X, Middlesex County Court House, Cambridge.

7. Suffolk Court of General Sessions 1719–1725, pp. 76, 80–82; New Court House, Boston. I am indebted to John Murrin for references 6 and 7.

8. Cotton Mather, *Diary*, (Boston, 1911), 2: 657; Kenneth Silvermen, ed., *Selected Letters of Cotton Mather* (Baton Rouge, 1971), p. 134.

9. Peter Oliver, *Origin and Progress of the American Rebellion*, ed. Douglass Adair and John A. Schutz (Stanford, 1961), p. 27; Thomas Hutchinson, *The History of the Colony and Province of Massachusetts Bay*, (Cambridge, 1936), 2: 217.

10. Barrow, *Trade and Empire*, pp. 89–90.

11. *Journals of the House of Representatives of Massachusetts* (Boston, 1919–     ), 11: 309, 313. (Hereafter cited as *House Journals*.)

12. William Douglass, *A Summary, Historical and Political of . . . North America*, (London, 1755), 1: 238; Bridenbaugh, *Cities in the Wilderness*, pp. 388–389.

13. *House Journals*, 13: 135.

14. *Ibid.*, 14: 176, 226, 238, 242.

15. Boston Record Commissioners' *Reports* (Boston, 1880–1902), 14: 5.

16. Benjamin Colman to Jonathan Coram, 8 May 1737, Colman Papers, MHS. The other relevant documents were sent by Governor Jonathan Belcher to the Duke of Newcastle, 1 June 1737, State Papers, 11: 4–10, Frederick Lewis Gay Transcripts, MHS. See also Warden, *Boston*, p. 122; Bridenbaugh, *Cities in the Wilderness*, pp. 352–353. The evidence for class antagonism in this incident is questionable. Colman does not say whether specific rich people or the rich as a class were a subject of resentment; the only member of the crowd who partially revealed his identity, the author of the anonymous letters, wrote elegant and forceful prose. The division of the lower and middle classes over markets is unknown, but support of voters from one or both would have been necessary to carry the final vote in favor of the market in 1740.

17. See especially Andrew M. Davis, "Provincial Banks, Land and Silver," *PCSM*, 3 (1905–1907): 2–41, esp. 24.

18. Deposition of Thomas Paine, 9 June 1741, Robert Treat Paine Papers, vol. 1, MHS; *House Journals*, 19: 195–199, 205; Massachusetts Archives, 53: 83–85, 115–116.

19. Warden, *Boston*, p. 114.

20. *House Journals*, 22: 204–205.

21. John Lax and William Pencak, "The Knowles Riot and the Crisis of the 1740s in Massachusetts," *Perspectives in American History*, 10 (1976): 163–214.

22. John A. Schutz, *William Shirley: King's Governor of Massachusetts* (Chapel Hill, 1961), p. 146.

23. Warden, *Boston*, p. 138; Thomas Hutchinson, "Hutchinson in America," 50, Egremont Manuscript, #2664, British Museum, (microfilm at MHS).

24. John A. Schutz, *Thomas Pownall: Defender of American Liberty* (Glendale, California, 1951), pp. 125–130.

25. Hoerder, *Mobs and People*, pp. 111–113.

26. The situation in Massachusetts supports the arguments of Pauline Maier, *From Resistance to Revolution: Colonial Radicals and the Development of American Opposi-*

*tion to Britain, 1765–1776* (New York, 1972), for violence as a tool of the community rather than a vehicle for lower-class discontent.

27. These offenses, which troubled contemporaries a great deal, could be tried before justices of the peace. Few of their records, however, survive.

28. Bridenbaugh, *Cities in the Wilderness*, pp. 382–383; Bridenbaugh, *Cities in Revolt*, p. 117. David Flaherty, paper delivered at the Organization of American Historians, 19 April 1975, found 493 prosecutions for crimes greater than petty theft in the Superior Court records over 30 years (1700–1709, 1720–1730, 1740–1749); 50.7 percent of the offenders were guilty. Many riots and less than capital crimes were tried before justices of the peace and courts of quarter sessions. Joseph Bennett, "History of New England," *MHSP*, 5 (1860–1862): 121.

29. Robert Twombly and George Moore, "Black Puritan: The Negro in Seventeenth Century Massachusetts," *William and Mary Quarterly*, 3rd. ser. 24 (1967): 224–242; Lawrence Towner, "Fondness for Freedom: Servant Protest in Puritan Society," *ibid.*, 19 (1962): 201–220; Richard B. Morris, *Government and Labor in Early America* (New York, 1946), pp. 225–278; L. Kinvin Wroth, "The Massachusetts Vice-Admiralty Courts," in *Law and Authority in Colonial America*, George A. Billias, ed. (Barre, MA, 1965), pp. 32–73, esp. pp. 40–42. William E. Nelson, *The Americanization of the Common Law* (Cambridge, 1975), pp. 47, 63, after a thorough examination of court records, writes: "The rules of law promoting economic and hence social stability also served as a precondition, of which contemporaries seemed unaware, to community morality and religiosity. . . . The pursuit of those ends and the hindering of competition finally helped to facilitate the government of the province. Since pre-revolutionary Massachusetts could not be governed by means of coercion, rules could be made into efficient law only when they were a compromise among all groups in a community." Also, "the law . . . created a society in which . . . all men were assured of the bare necessities of life . . . and every man was secure in this enjoyment of those necessities and luxuries to which he had been accustomed."

30. Bennett, "History of New England," p. 112; Douglass, *Summary*, 1: 541–542; Marcus W. Jernegan, *The Laboring and Dependent Classes in Early America* (New York, 1931), pp. 208–209; Robert E. Brown, *Middle-Class Democracy and the Revolution in Massachusetts, 1691–1780* (Ithaca, 1955), p. 17.

31. Francis Bernard to John Pownall, 5 November 1765, Bernard Papers, 5: 21, Sparks Manuscripts 10, Houghton Library, Harvard University; Bernard to Richard Jackson, 19 November 1765, *ibid.*, p. 43.

32. See among other sources, Charles M. Andrews, "The Boston Merchants and the Non-Importation Movement," *PCSM*, 19 (1916–1917): 159–259; Richard D. Brown, *Revolutionary Politics in Massachusetts: The Boston Committee of Correspondence and the Towns, 1772–1774* (Cambridge, 1970).

33. Francis G. Walett, "The Massachusetts Council, 1766–1774: The Transformation of a Conservative Institution," *William and Mary Quarterly*, 3rd. ser. 6 (1949): 605–627. See Table 7.

34. Boston *Records*, vols. 16 and 18, election returns at annual May meetings. See Table 10.

35. Samuel Alleyne Otis to ?, 17 June 1766, Otis Papers, vol. 2, Columbia University.

36. George Baldwin to Loammi Baldwin, 15 August 1765, Miscellaneous Bound Manuscripts, MHS. More generally, see the appropriate sections of Philip Davidson, *Propaganda and the American Revolution* (Chapel Hill, 1941).

37. The soldiers at the Boston Massacre fired sporadically and no customs commis-

# Notes to Chapter VIII

sioners aided them. See Hiller Zobel, *The Boston Massacre* (New York, 1970), esp. pp. 198, 296–298.

38. Hutchinson, *History,* 3: 60, 108, 296; Josiah Quincy, ed., *Reports of Cases Argued and Adjudged in the Superior Court of Judicature of the Province of Massachusetts Bay Between 1761 and 1772* (Boston, 1865), p. 261; Richard L. Merritt, *Symbols of American Community, 1735–1775* (New Haven, 1966).

39. Francis Bernard to Lord Shelburne, 24 August 1767, Bernard Papers, 6: 224; *Boston Gazette,* 21 April 1769; Davidson, *Propaganda and the American Revolution,* pp. 196–198.

40. Francis Bernard to Admiral Collborn, 1 November 1765, Bernard Papers, 4: 85; Bernard to Lord Shelburne, 19 March 1768, *ibid.,* 6: 282.

41. Thomas Hutchinson to ?, n.d., Massachusetts Archives, 26: 968, pagination to typescript prepared by Catherine B. Mayo at MHS; Hutchinson to Francis Bernard, 22 May 1770, *ibid.,* p. 1,070; see also George Anderson's two articles on Ebenezer Mackintosh, *PCSM,* 26 (1924–1926): 15–64, 348–361; and Albert C. Matthews' two articles on "Joyce, Jr.," *ibid.,* 8 (1906): 90–104; *MHSP,* 44 (1910): 280–294.

42. For literature, see bibliography in Davidson, *Propaganda and the American Revolution;* for instructions, Robert Dinkin, "Massachusetts: A Deferential or a Democratic Society," (Columbia University, Ph.D. diss., 1968), ch. 5. Instances of random violence appear in Hutchinson, *History,* 3: 135, 208; Israel Williams' charge to a grand jury, n.d., first folder, Israel Williams Papers, MHS; Francis Bernard to Thomas Gage, 16 September 1768, Bernard Papers, 7: 198; John Cushing to Thomas Hutchinson, 2 and 6 February 1766, Massachusetts Archives, 25: 40, 117; Thomas Goldthwait to Hutchinson, 16 February 1772, *ibid.,* p. 498.

43. For the former view, see Brown, *Middle-Class Democracy;* Warden, *Boston;* Maier, *From Resistance to Revolution;* for the latter, Dirk Hoerder, *Mobs and People;* Andrews, "The Colonial Merchants and Non-Importation"; Davidson, *Propaganda and the American Revolution,* pp. 63–82; Arthur M. Schlesinger, *The Colonial Merchants and the American Revolution* (New York, 1917), p. 92.

44. Thomas Hutchinson to Thomas Whately, 3 October 1771, Massachusetts Archives, 27: 19; Francis Bernard to Lord Halifax, 31 August 1765, Bernard Papers, 4: 149, Sparks Manuscripts 10, Houghton Library, Harvard University; George A. Billias, *Massachusetts Land Bankers of 1740* (Orono, ME, 1959).

45. *Boston Records,* 16: 187, 303–310; Henry Bass to Samuel Phillips Savage, 19 December 1765, *MHSP,* 44 (1910–1911): 609; Ruggles reference cited in Scott McIntosh, "Liberty and Property, Arms and God: The Political Culture of the Crowds in Boston, 1765–1775" (Princeton University, A.B. thesis, 1979), p. 23.

46. See McIntosh, "Liberty and Property," for an excellent balanced discussion of differences and similarities in class mentalities among crowd participants. Gary Nash, *The Urban Crucible* (Cambridge, 1979), pp. 351–362, indicates Whig leaders had a bit of difficulty controlling the crowd, but nevertheless continued to dominate the movement. There was far less internal struggle in Boston than in New York or Philadelphia.

47. Francis Bernard to Earl Halifax, 16 August 1765, Bernard Papers, 4: 142.

48. Massachusetts Archives, 132: 92–147, State House, Boston.

49. See footnote to Table 11 for my argument for using the tax list. For 1790, see Allan Kulikoff, "The Progress of Inequality in Revolutionary Boston," *William and Mary Quarterly,* 3rd. ser. 28 (1971): 385.

50. *Massachusetts Historical Society, Proceedings,* 5 (1869–1870): 140–142.

# Notes to Chapter VIII

51. "Records of the North End Caucus," in E.H. Goss, *The Life of Colonel Paul Revere*, (Boston, 1902), 2: 635–644.

52. Francis S. Drake, ed., *Tea Leaves: Being a Collection of Letters and Documents Relating to the Shipment of Tea to the American Colonies in the Year 1773 by the East India Company* (Boston, 1854), pp. xii-cxiv.

53. *Massachusetts Historical Society, Proceedings,* 12 (1898): 139–141.

54. Josiah Quincy, Jr., ed., *Reports of Cases Argued and Adjudged in the Superior Court of Judicature of the Province of Massachusetts Bay* (Boston, 1865), pp. 411–412.

55. "Members of the Society for the Encouragement of Trade and Commerce," (1764?), Ezekiel Price Papers, MHS.

56. Somewhat overlapping lists are in the William Palfrey Papers, vol. 2, Houghton Library, Harvard University, and the Samuel Phillips Savage Papers, MHS, 2: 147–148.

57. *Loyalists of Massachusetts* (Boston, 1902).

58. *Loyalists of Massachusetts* (London, 1930).

59. *Biographical Sketches of the Loyalists of the American Revolution,* 2 vols. (Boston, 1864). Among them, Stark, Jones, and Sabine have gleaned compensation requests, those who signed various Tory manifestoes in 1774 and 1775, Canadian records, and Massachusetts' government records of loyalists who did not flee the country.

60. The argument that those who cannot be traced were probably transients and poor people does not hold in this case; Drake located nearly every Tea Party member although nearly three-quarters did not appear on the tax register. Many had the same surnames as those found on the tax lists but did not head households. Others came from the surrounding towns. It should also be noted that the missing fifth of the tax records are mostly from the Eleventh Ward, which was wealthy (Massachusetts Archives, 132: 147). If patterns found elsewhere held in this ward, well over twenty percent, possibly as high as forty percent, or most of the untraceable names are thereby accounted for.

61. Dirk Hoerder, *Mobs and People,* p. 47, asserts that 'the North End Caucus consisted of small merchants and independent artisans, averaging £22 14s. 8d. real estate in the valuation list for 1771." He describes the caucuses as "organizations to counterbalance the influence of the merchants from the top of the economic scale." Hoerder is equating the annual rental value of property occupied (not necessarily owned) that was taxed, with the total amount of real estate owned. A house listed at £22 would rank in the top fifteen percent of the town. Hoerder's tracing of Tea Party members (ibid., p. 421), although based on the same method, nevertheless arrives at similar results as mine: a few wealthy members were found in this predominately poorer group, although I attribute "poverty" to age rather than class structure.

62. The occupational patterns of the Tea Party members do not suggest permanent poverty, but young men having trouble getting started. Twelve were merchants, two shopkeepers, eight apprentices, one sailor, a "mechanic," a soldier, and an usher at a school. Thirty-one were artisans (housewrights, coopers, shipwrights, etc.). Many of the rest were probably apprentices. These occupations would have generally carried more wealth, as Kulikoff in "The Progress of Inequality," p. 385, notes. But in colonial America, what superficially appear to be class distinctions could be age differences, as men acquired more property as they grew older. See John J. Waters, Jr., "Patrimony, Succession, and Social Stability: Guilford, Connecticut in the Eighteenth Century," *Perspectives in American History,* 10 (1976); 131–160; James A. Henretta, "Families and Farms: Mentalite in Pre-Industrial America," *William and Mary Quarterly,* 3rd. ser. 35 (1978): 6–9; and Christopher M. Jedrey, *The World of John Cleaveland* (New York, 1979).

# Notes to Chapter VIII

63. Philip Greven, *Four Generations: Population, Land and Family in Colonial Andover* (Ithaca, 1970); Kenneth A. Lockridge, "Land, Population, and the Evolution of New England Society, 1630–1790; and an Afterthought," Stanley Katz, ed. *Colonial America: Essays in Politics and Social Development*, (Boston, 1971), pp. 466–491; Robert Gross, *The Minutemen and Their World* (New York, 1976), pp. 68–109.

64. Boston Marriage and Birth Records, vols. 24, 30, and 31 in *Town Records* (Boston, 1894, 1898, 1903).

65. Winthrop D. Jordan, "Familial Politics: Thomas Paine and the Killing of the King, 1776," *Journal of American History*, 60 (1973): 294–308; John Waters, Jr., "James Otis, Jr., An Ambivalent Revolutionary," *History of Childhood Quarterly*, 1 (1973): 142–150.

66. Overseers of the Poor Manuscripts, MHS. All sorts of people were warned out including such well-to-do figures as William Taylor, son of the former acting governor of Massachusetts, and the commander of H.M.S. *Rose*, a British warship stationed in the harbor. Some of the names that are not duplicated in the Boston Records can be traced to the 1771 tax list, indicating warning out did not require the individual to leave. See Table 17 for statistics.

67. For postwar economic difficulties, see especially Anne Cunningham, ed., *Diary and Letters of John Rowe* (Boston, 1903), pp. 61, 67–70; G.B. Warden, *Boston, 1689–1776*, ch. 8; Nash, *The Urban Crucible*, ch. 12.

68. Mary K. Matossian and William D. Schaffer, "Family Fertility and Political Violence, 1700–1900," *Journal of Social History*, 11 (1977): 137–178.

69. Philip Greven, *The Protestant Temperament: Patterns of Child-Rearing, Religious Experience, and the Self in Early America* (New York, 1977), esp. pp. 335–364, quotations at 339–340. Many examples in which the colonists claimed to be dutiful children abused by an ungrateful parent, with converse arguments by loyalists and Britons, can be found in Edwin G. Burrows and Michael Wallace, "The Ideology and Psychology of National Liberation," *Perspectives in American History*, 6 (1972): 167–306. Kenneth S. Lynn, *A Divided People* (Westport, CT, 1977), pp. 105–111, is also highly suggestive. He shows patriot leaders generally had considerable autonomy within a normal family structure while growing up, whereas loyalists either had no effective father or an overly domineering one, both situations which would lead to a heightened need for dependency and security and reinforce conservative traits. Lynn differs from Greven in that he looks primarily at revolutionary leaders, who conform to the "moderate" form of childrearing. See also sources cited in n. 65 in this chapter.

70. John Demos, "Underlying Themes in the Witchcraft of Seventeenth Century New England," *American Historical Review*, 75 (1970): 1,311–1,326.

71. David Hackett Fischer, *Growing Old in America* (New York, 1977), ch. 1.

72. Lyman Butterfield, ed., *The Diary and Autobiography of John Adams* (Cambridge, 1960), 1: 260, 332; 2: 34, 39.

73. *Ibid.*, 1: 324; 2: 90, 91.

74. *Ibid.*, 1: 265; 2: 55, 84.

75. For the attack on plural officeholding (and its reinstitution on a larger scale by the very men who condemned it once the Revolution began), see Ellen Brennan, *Plural Officeholding in Massachusetts, 1760–1780* (Chapel Hill, 1945).

76. Quoted in Philip G. Davidson, *Propaganda and the American Revolution* (Chapel Hill, 1941), pp. 130, 141; *Adams Diary*, 2: 55; Greven, *The Protestant Temperament*, pp. 348–354, has some very interesting observations on the revolutionaries' need to prove their manhood.

77. Many Bostonians served several years. Philip Swain of Tufts University has computed this data from *Massachusetts Soldiers and Sailors of the American Revolution* for

a forthcoming article on Boston's soldiers. He has also shown that in Dedham's south precinct, eighteen of thirty-two enlistees—a lower percentage than Boston—were under thirty but only four served longer than three months. They were twenty-one, twenty-five, twenty-seven, and thirty-two. In Roxbury, only sixteen of seventy-five men served more than three months, only twenty-two more than one, and just eight of these had paid taxes in 1771. If these towns are typical, most of the militia turned out for Lexington, Concord, and Bunker Hill, while young men who did not pay taxes provided more permanent service. I thank David Ader, Arthur Landry, and David Peete of Tufts University for this information.

78. I thank Dr. James Smith Allen of *The Journal of Family History* for calling my attention to John Gillis's *Youth in History: Tradition and Change in European Age Relations, 1770 to the Present* (New York, 1974). Fischer, *Growing Old in America,* chs. 1–2.

# IX

## LOYALIST AND PATRIOT LEADERSHIP

### The Two Cultures of Revolutionary Massachusetts

*T*HE MASSACHUSETTS loyalists did not comprise an economic class. However, by defining a class as people who share a distinctive experience and ideology, then they can be so identified. Comparing loyalist and revolutionary leadership reveals that prominent loyalists tended to be relatively elderly men who had shaped Massachusetts' politics since the 1740s. They had guided the war effort as soldiers and committee leaders in the house and council. As members of the prerogative faction, they owed their prominence to provincial administrative services. They had little use for popular or local politics. Also, they abhorred Whig rhetoric criticizing government for corruption and usurpation of popular rights. On the other hand, the loyalists greatly admired the British Empire, as its officials consulted with them and treated them with respect. Their careers hinged on their ability to convince Massachusetts and Britain that their interests were compatible.

Revolutionary leadership, however, consisted for the most part of younger men who entered politics for the first time in the 1760s. The old stalwarts of the popular faction such as Tyng, Prat, the Allen brothers, Livermore, Waldo, and Kilby had died, retired, or become less active in the late fifties or early sixties. Their places could not be taken by other assembly leaders as most of these belonged to the prerogative faction. Instead, members of the various groups aggrieved by British policy and the prerogative faction—lawyers, Boston merchants, others associated with the town meeting, and clergymen—created the more broadly based revolutionary movement. Unlike the loyalists, who in general came from families with long traditions of provincial service, the revolutionaries for the most part hailed from families new to provincial politics. As such, they did not hesitate to criticize uninhibitedly the prerogative faction and its administrative and elitist mentality. After the Stamp Act, they went on to pioneer new methods of organizing and expressing the general population's discontent with British colonial policy.

Lists of those eighteen loyalist and eighteen patriot leaders prominent enough to be mentioned in *The Dictionary of American Biography* illustrate these patterns.[1] In Tables 18 and 19, column 1 tells whether an individual achieved prominence in public service before 1760. Column 2 indicates which leaders came from politically important families, defined here as fathers, grandfathers, or uncles who served as either house leaders or councillors. Column 3 reveals whether political success followed from personal socioeconomic success (yes) or participation in revolutionary politics (no). Column 4 gives residences.

To be sure, some similarities exist between loyalist and patriot leaders. Most were of English ancestry although Bowdoin, Revere, and Flucker came from French Huguenot stock. This disproportion of English names conformed to the ethnic composition of the province. With the exceptions mentioned above, to whom Thomas Young, Harrison Gray, and Richard Draper must be added, all of the leaders traced their ancestry from settlers who arrived during the "Great Migration" of 1630–1640. Twenty-eight of thirty-six leaders on both sides went to Harvard College. Hawley and Worthington attended Yale. Edes, Gill, Young, Draper, Flucker, and Gray did not go to college.

But the differences between loyalist and revolutionary leaders are more significant than the similarities. The average loyalist was sixty years old in 1775; the typical revolutionary, forty-six. Only three of eighteen revolutionaries had made political names for themselves before 1760, as opposed to twelve of the eighteen loyalists. Four of the patriots and fourteen of the Tories came from politically prominent families: sixteen of the loyalists, but only four of their adversaries, followed the traditional road to political importance. The former assumed positions of importance after they had shown their mettle in the private sector and performed lower-level administrative work. The latter, on the other hand (for the most part because of their ages), became known through the Revolution itself. Finally, the revolutionaries loved Boston and its exciting if undignified Town Meeting politics, whereas the metropolis's lack of deference, high taxes, and unhealthy climate repelled the loyalists. With three exceptions the patriot leaders were Bostonians: six had moved to the metropolis from other towns or even New York (Dr. Thomas Young). The loyalists showed a distinct tendency to move away from the city: eight of the thirteen Tories who lived in the Boston metropolitan area were either full-time or part-time suburbanites. Only Thomas Flucker moved from Charlestown to Boston. Patriots loaned money to Bostonians at interest and invested in the town's economy whereas loyalists did not; loyalists had also retired from town politics, which they found too democratic and raucous.[2]

The loyalists' and revolutionaries' different life experiences translated themselves into ideology. Three general characteristics linked behavior and thought. Loyalists tended to be inductive thinkers, materialists, and individualists. Because of their long experience with provincial institutions, they governed their actions by traditional norms. They envisioned solutions to problems in terms of the social order that had treated them well. Their political and economic success also led them to stress the material benefits of the British connection. And their personalized pursuit of power and wealth caused them to arrive at highly individualized political decisions. Loyalists had difficulty making up their minds, cooperating with each other, organizing a counterrevolution, or even participating in "politics" as opposed to administration. Their age and retirement from Boston town politics to scattered country seats undoubtedly played a role here too.

Unlike the well-established loyalists, the revolutionaries, who stood outside the political establishment, thought deductively and acted idealistically and communally. First, their lack of practical experience stood them in good stead. They did more than detect faults in the existing pattern of Anglo-American relations (many loyalists did also). They also challenged it more radically than through innocuous protests. Second, the patriots judged British policy by deductive appeals to abstract generalities rather than by existing institutions. They spurned the economic benefits of membership in the Empire as corrupting, having experienced few themselves.[3] Finally, since they emerged as heroes through a collective movement designed to free one community from restrictions imposed by another, they theoretically oriented their thought and action toward communal well-being and scorned self-seeking. These three general differences in loyalist and revolutionary ideology can be observed by considering their ideas on six topics: liberty, economy, politics, psychology, logic, and history.

Liberty meant something different for each side. The revolutionaries almost always spoke of the community's liberty, in its collective capacity, to govern itself without interference. John Adams's writings as "Novanglus" in 1774 epitomized this idea of liberty: "none were indicted for pulling down the Stamp Office, because this was thought an honorable and glorious action, not a riot."[4] The patriots did not fight for Andrew Oliver's "liberty" to enjoy the peaceful possession of his property unless a jury convicted him of a crime, even though they simultaneously protested that Vice-Admiralty Courts without juries would similarly dispossess those who violated the Stamp and Navigation acts. Liberty meant collective self-determination, as it has to so many colonies seeking to become nations.

Numerous examples exist of how communal necessity rendered individual liberty irrelevant. Chief Justice Peter Oliver had no right to accept a salary in 1774 from Parliament in defiance of the popular will. The General Court argued that Oliver had received the money "out of the revenue unjustly and unconstitutionally levied and extorted from the inhabitants of the North American colonies," and "perversely and corruptly done as aforesaid against the known sense of the body of the people." Oliver not only had no right to exercise his own political opinion; he could be impeached by the house of representatives as "an enemy to the constitution," even though, as Governor Hutchinson commented wryly, he would "have just cause to complain of being deprived of a trial by jury."[5]

No legitimate self-defense existed against the community. The press condemned Hutchinson for pardoning one Ebenezer Richardson, who had been convicted of murdering a member of a crowd that was attacking his house. In a related incident, the town of Boston sponsored the publication of A Short Narrative of the Horrid Massacre in Boston (1770) and jeopardized the possibility of an unprejudiced trial for the indicted British soldiers. But it saw no inconsistency in censuring Andrew Oliver's attempt to produce countervailing depositions for the defense as "garbled extracts" designed to aid "persons of wicked intentions to abuse the nation and injure the colonies."[6] Given such a communal definition of liberty, Massachusetts could deny Britain's power to levy stamp or rum taxes while having imposed precisely the same taxes under provincial auspices. Tories could be denied the right to free speech, a fair trial, or an unmolested existence by a society that insisted, as did John Adams, that "a democratical despotism is a contradiction in terms."[7]

Popular consent to laws, especially those involving revenue, was the primary focus of revolutionary liberty. In two of the most influential pamphlets of the revolutionary crisis—*The Rights of the British Colonies Asserted and Proved* (1764) and *A State of the Rights of the Colonies* (1772)—James Otis and Samuel Adams, respectively, insisted that "the supreme power cannot take from any man any part of his property, without his consent in person, or by representative," and conversely, that "each man enjoyed the right to keep his own earnings in his own hands until he shall in person, or by his representative, think fit to part with the whole or any portion of it."[8] Yet neither Otis nor Adams objected to the Massachusetts franchise requirement of £40 sterling in property or a 40 shilling freehold. Their basic justification of the Revolution only escapes contradiction if "no taxation without representation" means that each *community* must be taxed only through representative institutions. Communal liberty ensured that a man who cannot vote is represented by virtue of living within a real, living community with a common interest.

For the Tories, excluded from the communal consensus within which revolutionary liberty operated, it simply meant despotism. "Freeman" (Andrew Oliver), writing in the *Censor*, criticized this idea of freedom: "some of the untenable doctrines of our popular leaders, together with the absurd, arbitrary, and tyrannical measures they have taken in support of what they call liberty . . . are subversive of what we call our civil rights." "Liberty" could not mean self-determination of the community as a whole for the Tories, for they had no desire to redefine the Anglo-American political system. Rather, it approximated the right of the individual to enjoy due process under existing laws. Daniel Leonard's "Massachusettensis" explained "that each member of the community is entitled to protection: for this he pays taxes, for this he relinquishes his right of revenging injuries and redressing wrongs." Once the "Whigs had usurped the power of the province," real liberty vanished because of "mobs and riots, the invasions of and demolitions of dwelling-houses and other property, [and] personal abuse." The "sufferers were loyal subjects, violaters of no law."[9]

Thomas Hutchinson carried this argument one step further and developed the notion that no community could justly violate the tenets of traditional moral law. He charged that "it has been publicly asserted by some of the heads of the [revolutionary] party, who call themselves sober men, that the good of the public is above all con siderations, and that morality may be dispensed with and immorality is excusable, when this great good [independence] can be obtained by such measures." Communal necessity could never justify destruction of individual freedom. Peter Oliver, in his apocalyptic *History . . . of the American Rebellion*, described "absolute liberty" as "absolute tyranny in disguise." The revolutionaries enforced a "political orthodoxy," which Oliver labelled "uncontrolled either by the laws of God or man." In the loyalists' view, the Massachusetts Revolution parallelled the "totalitarian democracy" J.L. Talmon claims the French Revolution instituted.[10]

The loyalists did not merely develop their conception of liberty in response to persecution; they deeply believed in it. When Governor Hutchinson ruled a Boston occupied by British troops, he did not silence town meetings, stifle the press, or harrass prominent Whigs. The loyalists refused to combat their opponents by illegal means, for this would have ended the very system of government for which they contended. Their definition of liberty rather grew logically out of their personal experience, in addition to their status as a beleaguered minority. Successful in their private careers, they naturally considered individual freedom the foundation of social well-being. Their adversaries, on the contrary, first attained success through revolutionary activity. With equal logic they insisted that the individual and his rights be subsumed by society as a whole.

Second, the financial success of the loyalists promoted a positive attitude toward commerce, individual aggrandizement, and the role of the mother country in safeguarding the larger Anglo-American world within which they made their fortunes. Peter Oliver praised Britain for the "millions in bounties" spent "to encourage the growth and produce of her plantations." Massachusetts in particular "had been nursed in its infancy with every gratification that the most forward child could wish for." Daniel Leonard found mercantilism a laudable policy that prevented "one part of the Empire from being enriched at the expense of and to the impoverishing of another." Admiralty Advocate Robert Auchmuty explained his loyalty from "the duty which he justly owed his sovereign, the government to which he . . . and [his] fellow subjects were indebted for their material care and the blessings of earthly plenty."[11]

The loyalists praised Britain's military protection as well as its economic policies. Even Thomas Hutchinson, who thought that the Acts of Trade injured American commerce, believed them a reasonable imposition because "we certainly cannot enjoy and subsist without the protection of our mother country over our trade at sea, as well as our personal estate." Peter Oliver and Daniel Leonard maintained that British assistance in the French and Indian War was both absolutely necessary for victory and undertaken at the colonies' request. They felt what held in the past would hold in the future. "Destitute of British protection . . . behind which we have increased to a degree almost exceeding the bound of probability," Leonard wrote, "would not our trade, navigation and fishery, which no nation dares violate or invade, when distinguished by British colors, become the sport and prey of the maritime nations of Europe?"[12]

For the revolutionaries, however, such arguments rang hollow indeed. Men who had never been successfully acquisitive considered wealth and commerce morally corrupting and incompatible with patriotism. Samuel Adams did not only "converse with poverty," but he claimed to have espoused her: "however disagreeable a companion she may be thought to be by the affluent and luxurious who were never acquainted with her," he insisted that "I could live happily with her for the remainder of my days, if I can thereby contribute to the redemption of my country." Adams generalized his own experience to conclude that in America "we have yet some share of public virtue remaining: we are not afraid of poverty, but disdain slavery." Charles Chauncy also condemned "sordid avarice" as the "accursed thing" that "must be taken away from a people, if they would reasonably hope to stand before their enemies." And John Adams believed "the spirit of commerce corrupts the morals of families," and castigated those "passions, prejudices, and attachments" that led to the pursuit of private interest.[13] Here the revolutionaries echoed the Bostonians' own deprivations.

If America's liberty and morals were on the brink of destruction, England's had passed the point of no return. James Otis described in graphic, if not accurate, detail the corrupting effect of wealth on the British ruling classes. In a speech to the assembly, he asked rhetorically: "the unthinking multitude are taught to revere [them] . . . as little Deities—for what? Not their virtues sure." No one could find a "set of people under the canopy of His Majesty more venal, more corrupt and debauched in their principles." Oxford and Cambridge only taught them "smoking, whoring, and drinking." "Button-makers, pin-makers [industrialists], horse-jockeys [nobles], courtiers, pensioners, pimps, and whoremasters" comprised the House of Commons.[14]

The revolutionaries found it logically necessary to deny that Britain protected or aided the colonies' prosperity or protection in any shape, manner, or form. Otherwise taxation could be justified as payment for services rendered. In fact, they argued that Britain owed its prosperity to America, which gave generously of its resources in fighting the mother country's wars. Such statements carried considerable weight in Massachusetts. John Adams wrote that Britain only protected North America "for her own interest, because all the profits of our trade centered in her lap. But it ought to be remembered that her name, not her purse, nor her fleet, ever protected us until the last war." Even then, "the annual millions from America enabled her to do it." An anonymous writer was moved to put the same argument in verse:[15]

> Spurn the Relation—She's no more a mother,
> Than Lewis to George, a most Christian Brother,
> In French wars and Scotch, grown generous and rich,
> She gives her dear children pox, slavery, and itch.

In place of the commercial self-interest the loyalists used to justify British rule, the revolutionaries stipulated that only virtue—disinterested public-spirited behavior—cemented a good society. Samuel Adams hoped that the Revolution would transform America into a "Christian Sparta." John Adams found in America "so much rascality, so much venality and corruption, so much avarice and ambition, such a rage for profit and commerce among all ranks and degrees of men," that he feared for the future of the country. But he hoped the very experience of revolution would have a purgative effect, and "inspire us with many virtues, which we have not, and correct many errors, follies and vices, which threaten to disturb, dishonor, and destroy us."[16]

A virtuous society rewarded itself by choosing equally pure rulers. As the Massachusetts Sons of Liberty wrote to John Wilkes in 1768, his constituents had "lately manifested an incontestable proof of virtue" by electing him to Parliament, since he was "one of those incomparably honest men reserved to them by Heaven to bless." Two years later Samuel Adams told Wilkes that "no character appears with a stronger luster in my mind, than that of a man who nobly perservered in the cause of public liberty and virtue through the rage of persecution . . . but I dare say you are indeed better by it. The sharpest persecution for the sake of one's country can never prove a real injury to an honest man." Suffering in a glorious cause purified the soul. One of the most *personally* immoral men in England, Wilkes cleansed himself through *public* virtue.[17]

The notion that all considerations of personal interest must be laid aside for the common good obsessed at least two leading revolutionaries. James Otis, in his Writs of Assistance Speech (1761), felt obliged to insist that "this wanton exercise of . . . power by the customs officers is not a chimerical suggestion of a heated brain." And John Adams concluded his *Dissertation on the Canon and Feudal Law* (1765) by disclaiming that his remarks "did not stem from the vapor of a melancholy mind, nor the effusions of envy, disappointed ambition, nor of a spirit of opposition to government, but from the emanations of a heart that burns for its country's welfare."[18] Otis suffered periodic insanity and Adams confided his chronic career worries to his diary. Both men longed to make public figures. By denying their sins in two of their earliest public actions perhaps they hoped somehow to exorcise them.

Even the revolutionaries' defense of smuggling need not contradict their communalism and idealism. To survive, Massachusetts had to make good an unfavorable balance of trade of five or ten to one against it. A largely illegal West India commerce paid for the flood of imports with which predominantly loyalist or British merchants had inundated the country. It also supplied the specie that paid the taxes redeeming treasury notes. Smuggling provided virtually the only source of wealth left to Massachusetts, a fact amply demonstrated by the revolutionaries' method of retaliating economically against Great Britain. The non-importation agreement of 1768–1770 did not ban trade with the West Indies, but only with the mother country and Europe. The overwhelming support for these pacts among both the population and merchants (the merchants favored it two-hundred and fifty to eighteen, and only sixty-two expressed any reluctance whatsoever) indicated that the importation of English manufactures had become concentrated in a few—largely loyalist—hands.[19] Non-importation enabled the community to recover its economic health at the expense of the same group that had profited from its distresses. The West India trade was so essential to the northern colonies that they willingly and inconsistently paid the three penny reduced to one penny in 1766) per gallon duty on molasses, which netted the British treasury some £30,000 annually until the Revolution. Perhaps Benjamin Franklin's remark that the colonists could pay external but not internal taxes was right after all. No matter what they *said*, the colonists in fact submit to duties on their trade.

Third, the loyalists and revolutionaries differed over the importance, desirability, and optimal degree of political activity. Perhaps because of their advanced age, many loyalists participated in politics with reluctance. Some even tried to convince themselves that they were not interested at all. (The revolutionaries later displayed similar proclivities when they reached their fifties and sixties.) James Murray wrote about the Revolution as though it were presumptuous even to do so. His letter describing the Stamp Act ended abruptly with the phrase: "Enough of politics, let us leave them to abler heads." Later he concluded another note: "Enough of politics, let us return to the fireside." The loyalists frequently yearned to foresake the public world and return to their families and estates. Many of them had already retired from business.[20] Peter Oliver's ambivalence about politics appears in a letter of 1766 to Thomas Hutchinson: "I have some thoughts of studying politics though I have done with them. The road is dirty, but it is healthy to dabble in gutters." John Worthington declined becoming an involved counterrevolutionary when he refused Hutchinson's offer of a seat on the Superior Court. His excuses were personal: "the little fondness I have for the place of my birth, the respect I have for the people with whom I have always lived, and the particular connections I have among them, would make me very averse to take that absence of my family."[21]

Many leading loyalists dreaded entering the political arena. Israel Williams admitted that "I seldom read the public papers." Samuel Quincy retired from politics altogether and went to England to avoid taking a stand on the Revolution. Robert Auchmuty found his admiralty post "extremely arduous and unpleasant," not so much because of harrassment, but because it required "too much of his time, of which both his health and interest compelled him to be very frugal, his common law practice, on which his bread depended, demanding by far the greatest part of it." In the late 1750s even Thomas Hutchinson wrote repeatedly to Israel Williams that he had no more interest in politics and toyed with retirement. He asked leave to resign the governorship almost immediately after taking the post, and did resign in 1774.[22]

The collective ineffectiveness of the Massachusetts loyalists may be attributed to this apathy. These elderly men had been conditioned all their lives to consider public service as an administrative rather than a political activity. It took place within the limits of legislature. Unlike the revolutionaries they saw no conflict between public and private interest.

If the loyalists found personal participation in politics distasteful, they considered popular involvement disastrous. Having moved beyond the town meeting and assembly and to the council or appointive office, they expressed their dislike of the "popular" elements of the constitution whenever the people repudiated their leadership. Daniel Leonard argued that only a small ruling group could participate intelligently in politics since "the bulk of the people are generally but little versed in matters of state; want of inclination or opportunity to figure in public life makes them content to rest the affairs of government in the hands where accident or merit has placed them." But "there is a latent spark . . . in their breasts, capable of being kindled into a flame; to do this has always been the employment of the disaffected . . . the generality of the people are thus made the dupes of artifice and the mere stilts of ambition." Peter Oliver described the multitude as "wound up by any hand who might first take the winch." During the Revolution, "government was in the hands of a mob, both in form and substance, and it was in vain to combat a whirlwind or hurricane." And Thomas Hutchinson, though quite happy with the provincial constitution, never had any kind words for the Town Meeting. Like many loyalists, he hoped to convert Boston into a self-selecting corporation.[23]

The loyalists identified provincial well-being with the nonpopular element of the constitution they themselves monopolized. The revolutionaries believed all legitimate political power came from the people. They owed their careers to "the people" in various guises—crowds, town meetings, Sons of Liberty, and the assembly. Men who rose to power through revolutionary politics lauded active political participation as a glorious, heroic endeavor that ought to be undertaken by everyone (unless one was Tory, of course). John Adams articulated this ideal explicitly. In contrast to Leonard, he considered government "a plain, simple, intelligible thing, founded in nature and reason and quite comprehensible by common sense." Self-rule suited America especially because it possessed "more knowledge and civility among the common people [than] in any part of the world." Furthermore, "wherever a general knowledge and sensibility have prevailed among the people, arbitrary government and every kind of oppression have lessened and disappeared in proportion."[24]

Preferred loyalist and revolutionary personality traits followed from their political theory. "Prudence" and "temperance" commended themselves highly to the loyalists, whereas the revolutionaries cherished a great "zeal" for liberty. This, too, followed from their personal biographies. The loyalists advanced their careers during war, when conflicting political interests had to strike a balance. Andrew Oliver wrote in the *Censor* that while "it does great honor for any member of the country to . . . interest himself in its welfare and maintain with a well-tempered zeal those forms and institutions by which the public good is secured," it was nevertheless "a great mistake" when men "suffer their passions to be engaged." Peter Oliver thought that "it would have been imprudent" for the loyalists to have countered their opponents by organizing in a similar fashion. Thomas Hutchinson also considered "prudence a part of morality" and practiced this doctrine by rewriting many of his letters several times, allowing some of his finest thoughts to go unpublished, and carefully choosing when and how he articulated his convictions.[25]

The revolutionaries, in contrast to the loyalists, achieved importance by expressing their principles as strongly as possible. They would have heartily agreed with Barry Goldwater that extremism in the defense of liberty was no vice. Samuel Adams praised "that generous ardor for civil and religious liberty, which in the face of every danger, and even death itself, induced our fathers to forsake the bosom of their native country and begin a settlement on bare creation." Conversely, those who lacked such an unconditional commitment deserved whatever tyranny might be inflicted upon them. John Adams blamed the province for allowing itself to have been "soothed, flattered and intimidated" by Hutchinson and his connections into an "infamous tameness and submission." He urged his countrymen not to be "wheedled out of your liberty by any pretenses of politeness, delicacy, or decency," which were but euphemisms for "hypocrisy, chicanery, and cowardice."[26]

Fifth, the loyalists and revolutionaries used different modes of reasoning to formulate their political ideas. As men who had been involved in practical politics for decades, the loyalists came to their ultimate positions by induction. They observed prerevolutionary Massachusetts and liked what they saw. Timothy Ruggles promised "to contribute everything in my power to convince those rebellious wretches of their folly and wickedness in despising the best government both in theory and administration that ever yet blest the earth we inhabit." Israel Williams pleaded with a jury to indict rioters against the government under which it was "our happy lot and privilege to live." He argued that the Massachusetts "constitution, considered in all its circumstances" was preferable "to what any state or commonwealth in the world enjoyed at the present day." The loyalists agreed with Peter Oliver that "perfection in any thing human is not to be expected," but also that the colonies rose "by easy gradations, to such a state of prosperity and happiness as was almost enviable."[27] They justified the continuance of the present regime on the pragmatic ground that, comparatively speaking, it was as good as possible. They did not probe the theoretical principles to which a good government ought to conform. To a large extent, Massachusetts' material prosperity, despite a quarter-century of war, closed most loyalist political discussions.

The revolutionaries, outsiders to the system that did so much for the loyalists, did not induce their ideas from observation of existing circumstances. They deduced them from ideal principles concerning the legitimate, original purpose of society in general and the British constitution in particular. They scorned the "present" glorified by their opponents because it failed to match an ideal "past." Both Adamses and James Otis believed that liberty had existed purely in the Anglo-Saxon past, only to be corrupted by "the canon and feudal law," which John Adams described as "the two greatest systems of tyranny" in Christian times. Otis blamed William the Conqueror for this change: "Liberty was better understood and more fully enjoyed by our ancestors before the coming of the first Norman tyrants than ever after, 'till was found necessary for the foundation of the kingdom to combat the arbitrary and wicked proceedings of the Stuarts."[28] Unlike the loyalists, who appealed to a history embodied in the present set of institutions, the patriots stressed a mythical past. If current trends continued the future would be even worse, but by reversing them a glorious new page in human history would be written.

The revolutionaries did not derive the rights of men from a given political situation, but postulated, with James Otis, "first principles" from which "to *deduce* the civil rights of the British colonies." Samuel Adams deduced the rights of colonists as men, Christians, and subjects. All men deserved "life, liberty, and property" and "if men should through fear, fraud or mistake . . . give up any essential natural right, the eternal law of reason and the great end of society would absolutely vacate such renunciation."[29]

The revolutionaries' use of deductive logic also appeared in their criticisms of post-1763 British policy. They not only attacked its tangible effects, but also the consequences that had to follow if Britain pursued these principles to their absolute limits. Otis wrote that with one tax as a precedent, "why may not the Parliament lay stamps, land taxes, establish tithes to the Church of England and so indefinitely. I know of no bounds." Losing one right meant losing all on principle: "the very act of taxing . . . if continued, seems to be in effect an entire disfranchisement of every civil right." Samuel Adams spelled out the consequences of taxation in detail: "if the breath of a British House of Commons can originate an act for taking away all our money, our lands will go next or be subject to rack rents from haughty and relentless landlords who will ride at ease, while we are trodden in the dirt." Josiah Quincy saw "pensioners, stipendiaries, and salary-men (unknown before) hourly multiplying on us, to riot in the spoils of miserable America. . . . Are not our estates given to corrupt sycophants, without a design, or even a pretence, of soliciting our assent, and our lives put into the hands of those whose tender mercies are cruelties?" And John Adams concluded that "no one of any feeling, born and educated in this once happy country, can consider the numerous distresses, the gross indignities, the barbarous ignorance, the haughty usurpations, *that we have reason to fear* are meditating for ourselves, our children, our neighbors, in short, for all our countrymen and posterity, without the utmost agonies of heart and many tears." The revolutionaries looked upon parliamentary taxation, though less fiscally onerous than the province's own, to a tyranny "as was never before borne by any people under Heaven."[30]

But if America reversed this development, it would once again fulfill the millennial hopes of the Puritan founders and prophecies of divines such as Cotton Mather and Jonathan Edwards. Joseph Warren's Boston Massacre Oration for 1775 praised the victims for "having redeemed your country, and secured the blessing to future generations, who, fired by your example, shall emulate your virtues and learn from you the heavenly art of making millions happy." He urged his listeners upon their own deaths to "drop the mantle to some young Elisha, and take your seats with kindred spirits in your native skies." The next year, Peter Thatcher's oration stated that "driven from other regions of the globe" freedom "wishes to find an asylum in the wilds of America." The Reverend Charles Chauncy raged that "our cause is so just that if human efforts should fail, a host of angels would be sent to support it." His colleague Samuel Cooper viewed America as a beacon for the entire human race: "we seem called by Heaven to make a large portion of this globe a seat of knowledge and liberty, of agriculture, commerce and arts, and, what is more important than all, of Christian piety and virtue. . . . Thus will our country resemble the new city which St. John saw 'coming down from God out of Heaven.' "[31] America became God's chosen nation even before it secured independence.

The revolutionaries' propensity to consider their cause the incarnation of absolute good almost assured their identification of the Tories with Satan and the Antichrist. Nathan Truman of Sandwich wrote to the elder James Otis describing the "formal hypocrite"—probably Thomas Hutchinson—in such terms: "while the *Son of God* (in whom this abandoned wretch professes to believe) has sacrificed his own life to promote the *happiness* and secure the *freedom* of mankind, *He* can deliberately sacrifice the *Truth* and thereby his *Savior* to procure *misery, chains, bloodshed, and death* for the same species." One pamphlet, which paraphrased the Book of Revelation, compared Lords Bute and Manfield and Governors Bernard and Hutchinson with the four horsemen of the Apocalypse. An oration delivered to the Sons of Liberty in 1766 depicted Lord Bute as the seven-headed beast who would appear at the end of the time, and beseeched the Sons not to buy stamps "as good Christians and lovers of your country, lest by touching any paper with this impression, you receive the mark of the *beast*," which meant instant damnation.[32] Even if the patriots did not take this language literally, it testified to their belief that America played the key role in the eternal cosmic struggle between good and evil.

The loyalists, on the contrary, undertook no world-historical mission. These long-term officeholders considered politics merely one of life's aspects; it did not serve as a means of personal and societal redemption. They were practical politicians confronted in old age by an unprecedented mass movement that left them intellectually divided and bewildered.

Whereas the revolutionaries for the most part maintained a united ideological front until war broke out, different loyalists had their own interpretations. On the extreme right stood Peter Oliver. He not only approved of the Stamp Act but only quarrelled with the Intolerable Acts because they were not intolerable enough. Thomas Hutchinson and Andrew Oliver occupied the center. As Oliver put it, they hoped for some good effect from "moderation" and sought to compromise the crisis "without giving up the rights of the crown or violating the constitution" of the province. Finally, some loyalists shared their opponents' conviction that Britain was indeed plotting to extinguish American liberty. Israel Williams considered the Declaratory Act, which asserted Parliament's right to tax the colonies at will, an "unprecedented stretch of power" that "teem[ed] with injustice."[33]

Many loyalists did not know what to think. John Singleton Copley told his wife that he blamed the Revolution on Britain's "attempt to tax the colonies." But he criticized the "violent Sons of Liberty" as well. Samuel Quincy could do little but cry and trust in the Lord. He considered it "my duty patiently to submit to the event." He only hoped that "in the midst of the confusions that darken our native land we may still, by a rectitude of conduct, entertain a rational hope that the Almighty Governor of the Universe will in his own time remember mercy." Israel Williams may have been a great Indian fighter, but the Revolution rendered him intellectually helpless. On the one hand, he thought that "the restrictions the colonies are already under by Act of Parliament effect our civil rights," and "who can tell to what length things may be carried." But he nevertheless considered the resistance movement a product of "intemperance, injustice, fraud and deceit, lying, perjury, theft . . . contempt of religion [and] want of due submission to family and government."[34]

## Loyalist and Patriot Leadership

Finding British policy too weak to punish the incendiaries and yet provocative of the population as a whole, the loyalists considered themselves the last bastions of virtue on either side of the Atlantic. In this respect they resembled their opponents. But whereas revolutionary "virtue" was political and social, the loyalists' version provided them with an excuse to turn inward, wring their hands, and do little except lament their fate.

In sum, the dissimilarities between loyalist and revolutionary leadership in Massachusetts form an interrelated configuration. The loyalists acquired through personal experience a view of the world that differed radically from that of the general population. Their very success in managing the mid-century wars had estranged them from popular values.

No claim is made here for the wider applicability of this theory. In fact, the special nature of loyalism in Massachusetts helps explain the peculiarities of its revolutionary movement. Loyalists in Massachusetts were numerically minuscule;[35] nevertheless, before 1775, the patriots viewed them with greater suspicion and directed more violence against them than in any other colony. This paradox can be resolved if it is realized that only in Massachusetts (and New Hampshire) did a successful competitor with the popular party exist that consistently and unambiguously identified itself with the royal prerogative.[36] To contest this court faction a new popular leadership emerged in the sixties. Headed by ministers, lawyers, and writers in addition to merchants, it developed a general following and increased the scope and intensity of the politics. The loyalists, powerful in legislative, traditional politics, found themselves impotent before revolution.

The Massachusetts Revolution can be understood analogously with the causes of the French Revolution as viewed by Alfred Cobban.[37] Before 1789, as before 1776, class conflict proved less important than the unreasonable burdens placed on members of all classes by the governing elite. As Martin Göhring has also written of the French Revolution, "there was a parting of the ways between the state and the nation."[38] In both cases a population tired of sacrifices rose almost unanimously against an administrative elite. Cobban has shown that political newcomers who used rebellion to gain fame and fortune guided the French Revolution.[39] They soon eclipsed the few officeholders from the old regime, such as Mirabeau and Lafayette. In Massachusetts, too, men politically active before 1760 left the resistance movement and became loyalists (including some members of the Erving family, William Brattle, and Harrison Gray). Others such as the Otises and Joseph Hawley faded from leadership as tactics grew more radical. Intellectuals—printers, pamphleteers, ministers, lawyers, clergymen—replaced many of them. In both societies, new career possibilities for intellectuals opened in the mid-eighteenth century. Ambitious young men in Massachusetts could advance through law, publishing, and the political use of the pulpit. In France, a "community of letters" created jobs for young writers who aspired to emulate the great Voltaire. In both cases, the inability of the new professions to increase sufficiently their practitioners' status, income, and political influence paved the way for revolution.[40]

The Massachusetts Revolution was anomalous. Whereas most loyalists in other colonies remained outside of the politically dominant classes—Anglicans, backcountry dwellers, royal officeholders—in Massachusetts a disproportionate number came from the most entrenched and powerful families in the province. A new group of leaders, more representative of society, appeared not only to oppose British postwar policy, but to overthrow its local defenders as well. The Massachusetts revolutionaries had to eliminate such a well-entrenched faction dedicated to preserving imperial authority before resistance could be organized.[41]

# *Notes to Chapter IX*

1. I have added three loyalists: William Brattle, Thomas Flucker, and Harrison Gray, respectively the commander of Massachusetts' militia, the province secretary, and the province treasurer. Otherwise, I have avoided any subjective criteria of importance. Biographical information from the *Dictionary of American Biography* (New York, 1928–1961); Clifford K. Shipton, *Biographical Sketches of Those Who Attended Harvard College* (Boston, 1873–      ); James Stark, *Loyalists of Massachusetts* (Boston, 1902); information for Hawley and Worthington from Frank B. Dexter, *Yale Biographies and Annals, 1701–1745* (New York, 1885); for Revere, Esther Forbes, *Paul Revere and the World He Lived In* (Cambridge, 1942), esp. ch. 4; for Otis, John Waters, Jr., *The Otis Family in Provincial and Revolutionary Massachusetts* (Chapel Hill, 1960), esp. pp. 64–72.

2. See William Pencak and Ralph J. Crandall, "Metropolitan Boston Before the American Revolution: An Urban Interpretation of the Imperial Crisis," forthcoming, and William Pencak, "The Revolt Against Gerontocracy: Genealogy and the Massachusetts Revolution," *National Genealogical Society Quarterly*, 66 (1978): 291–294.

3. I do not wish to imply that loyalists were greedy and corrupt while the patriots were unsullied by a desire for power and wealth. I am rather pointing out certain patterns of thought to which their experiences inclined them. Andrew Oliver, for example, gave away much of his money to charitable causes. Almost all loyalists considered themselves to be standing up for justice against anarchy and tyranny. On the other hand, James Otis, Jr., was (by 1770 literally) insanely ambitious, and many leading patriots felt pinched by Britain's campaign against the lucrative, illegal West India trade. But the loyalists argued their case in terms of the material benefits of empire, whereas

their adversaries, while of course criticizing the cramping of American trade, stressed the injustices of *Britain's* profiting at their expense rather than their own desire for prosperity. Hancock and Bowdoin, the wealthiest leaders, did not reap the fruits of empire at first hand. They had inherited their wealth from an uncle and father, respectively, who had profited from the war and generally supported the prerogative faction.

4. Bernard Mason, ed., *The American Colonial Crisis: The Daniel Leonard–John Adams Letters to the Press, 1774–1775* (New York, 1972), p. 120.

5. Massachusetts Papers, 20 February 1774, vol. 2, MHS.

6. *Boston Gazette,* 27 September 1773; Massachusetts Papers, 13 July 1770, vol. 2.

7. Mason, ed., *Colonial Crisis,* p. 174.

8. These two pamphlets are conveniently reprinted in Merrill Jensen, ed., *Tracts of the American Revolution: 1763–1776* (New York, 1967), quotations at pp. 26 and 242.

9. The *Censor,* 4 January 1772; Mason, ed., *Colonial Crisis,* p. 60.

10. Thomas Hutchinson to Israel Williams, 23 February 1774, Williams Papers, MHS; Oliver, *Origin,* pp. 34, 159–160; J.L. Talmon, *The Origins of Totalitarian Democracy* (New York, 1960). Philip Greven, *The Protestant Temperament* (New York, 1977), pp. 341–347, has an interesting discussion of the psychological basis of the contrasting definitions of liberty.

11. Oliver, *Origin,* p. 146; Mason, ed., *Colonial Crisis,* p. 23; E. Alfred Jones, *Loyalists of Massachusetts* (London, 1930), p. 12. Note the paternal analogies here as well. The loyalists supported British authority with the same sort of arguments parents use to justify governing children. The Sons of Liberty spoke the language of familial rebellion against the mother country. This dichotomy can also be linked to the revolutionaries' relative youth and family problems, and to the Tories' own solicitude to provide their children with government offices.

12. Thomas Hutchinson, *The History of the Colony and Province of Massachusetts Bay,* (Cambridge, 1936), 2: 338–340; Oliver, *Origin,* p. 146; Mason, ed., *Colonial Crisis,* p. 81.

13. Henry Cushing, ed., *Works,* (New York, 1904–1908), 3: 28; Jensen, ed., *Tracts,* p. 252; John Adams to Mercy Otis Warren in Worthington Chauncy Ford, ed., *The Warren-Adams Letters,* (Boston, 1917), 1: 222–223. The examples from the Adamses in this note were found in Stephen Patterson, *Political Parties in Revolutionary Massachusetts* (Madison, 1973), p. 64, who presents a good discussion of revolutionary economic ideology.

14. New England Papers, 2: 91, 96–98, Sparks Manuscripts, 43, Houghton Library, Harvard University.

15. Mason, ed. *Colonial Crisis,* p. 129; *Boston Gazette,* 2 December 1765.

16. Cushing, ed., *Works,* 4: 238; John Adams to Abigail Adams, 3 July 1776, in Lyman H. Butterfield, ed., *Adams Family Correspondence,*(Cambridge, 1963), 2: 28; same to same, 28 April 1776, *ibid.,* 1: 401.

17. Miscellaneous Manuscripts, (6 June 1768), 2: 14, MHS; *ibid.,* 28 December 1770. It is a moot point whether the Sons of Liberty were acquainted with Wilkes's private character; they do not appear to have been interested.

18. Richard B. Morris, ed., *The American Revolution; 1763–1783* (New York, 1970), p. 4; George A. Peek, ed., *The Political Writings of John Adams* (New York, 1954), p. 21.

19. The eighteen included Hutchinson's sons and the Clarke brothers of Tea Party fame who dealt mostly in English goods. See lists of importers and nonimporters in

# Notes to Chapter IX

William Palfrey Papers, vol. 2, Houghton Library, Harvard University, and Samuel Phillips Savage Papers, 2: 147–148, MHS.

20. John Tyler informs me that many wealthy loyalists had given up active trade. See his forthcoming Princeton dissertation "The First Revolution: The Boston Mercantile Community and the Acts of Trade, 1760–1774."

21. James Murray to John Murray, 13 November 1765 and 12 June 1766, in *Letters of James Murray, Loyalist* (Boston, 1901), pp. 154, 155. Murray was a Scottish immigrant via North Carolina, the younger son of a British nobleman. Peter Oliver to Thomas Hutchinson, 18 January 1766, Massachusetts Archives, 25: 111. State House, Boston. Pagination for this collection to the typescript copy prepared by Catherine B. Mayo at the MHS; John Worthington to Hutchinson, 3 April 1769, Massachusetts Archives, 25: 304.

22. Israel Williams to Thomas Hutchinson, 20 July 1769, Massachusetts Archives, 25: 347; Stark, *Loyalists*, pp. 368–369; Jones, *Loyalists*, p. 12; Thomas Hutchinson to Israel Williams, 17 July and 25 September 1758, 14 June 1759, Williams Papers, MHS.

23. Mason, ed., *Colonial Crisis*, p. 14; Oliver, *Origin*, pp. 25, 26; Hutchinson, *History*, 3: 63; 2: 148.

24. Peek, ed., *Political Writings of John Adams*, pp. 4, 10, 12.

25. The *Censor*, 14 December 1771; Oliver, *Origin*, p. 65; Thomas Hutchinson to ?, 12 November 1771, Massachusetts Archives, 26: 440.

26. Jensen, ed., *Tracts*, p. 254; Peek, ed., *Political Writings of John Adams*, pp. 10, 14, 16. See also Greven, *The Protestant Temperament*, pp. 354–358, for different attitudes toward "enthusiasm" and "gentility" of loyalists and revolutionaries.

27. Stark, *Loyalists*, p. 252; Israel Williams to a Grand Jury, undated [mid-1760?], Williams Papers; Oliver, *Origin*, pp. 9, 145.

28. Peek, ed., *Political Writings of John Adams*, p. 5; Jensen, ed., *Tracts*, p. 21.

29. Jensen, ed., *Tracts*, pp. 22, 235, 238.

30. *Ibid.*, pp. 28, 32, 241, 243; *Boston Gazette*, 3 October 1768; Peek, ed., *Political Writings of John Adams*, p. 21; Mason, ed., *Colonial Crisis*, p. 120. My emphasis.

31. Quoted by Philip Davidson, *Propaganda and the American Revolution* (Chapel Hill, 1941), p. 198; William Tudor, *Life of James Otis* (Boston, 1823), p. 148; Samuel Cooper, *A Sermon on the Commencement of the Constitution and the Inauguration of the New Government* (Boston, 1780).

32. Nathan Truman to James Otis, Sr., 10 July 1773, Otis Papers, vol. 3, MHS; *The First Book of the American Chronicle of the Times* (Boston, 1768); *A Discourse Addressed to the Sons of Liberty Near the Liberty Tree in Boston* (Boston, 1766).

33. Andrew Oliver to John Pownall, 11 December 1773, Andrew Oliver Letter Book, 2: 152, Frederick Lewis Gay Transcripts, MHS; Israel Williams to Thomas Hutchinson, 5 January 1767, Massachusetts Archives, 25: 127.

34. Oliver, *Origin*, p. 113; Stark, *Loyalists*, pp. 294, 368–369; Williams's speech to a grand jury, Williams Papers.

35. Wallace Brown, *The King's Friends* (Providence, 1965), pp. 19–44, 294–298.

36. New York's and Pennsylvania's powerful loyalists had sometimes taken the "popular" side. See Patricia U. Bonomi, *A Factious People* (New York, 1971), ch. 7; James H. Hutson, *Pennsylvania Politics, 1746–1770* (Princeton, 1972) ch. 4.

37. See particularly *The Social Interpretation of the French Revolution* (Cambridge, 1964) and *Aspects of the French Revolution* (New York, 1968). I am indebted to Professor Darline Levy of Barnard College for discussing the French Revolution with me.

38. Quotation from Martin Gohring, "The Advent of the French Revolution in Retrospect," trans. Melvin Cherno and Peter Amann, in Peter Amann, ed., *The Eighteenth Century Revolution: French or Western?* (Boston, 1963), p. 93.

39. Cobban, *Aspects of the French Revolution*, pp. 90–112.

40. Robert Darnton, "The High Enlightenment and the Low Life of Literature in Pre-Revolutionary France," *Past and Present*, 51 (1971): 81–115.

41. In this chapter, I am greatly indebted to the questions raised by George A. Billias, "The First Un-Americans: The Loyalists in Revolutionary Historiography," in George A. Billias and Alden T. Vaughan, eds., *Perspectives on Early American History: Essays in Honor of Richard B. Morris* (New York, 1973), pp. 282–324.

# X

---

## POSTSCRIPT

## MASSACHUSETTS
## AND THE MID-CENTURY
## COLONIAL CRISIS

$\mathcal{S}$HORTLY after the French and Indian War began in 1754, Benjamin Franklin warned his fellow Americans to "Join or Die." Beneath the diagram of a snake divided into several pieces depicting the fragmented British provinces, he lamented the "extreme difficulty of bringing so many different governments and assemblies to agree in any speedy and effectual measures for our common defense and security, while our enemies have the very great advantage of being under one direction, with one council and one purse."[1] Franklin's argument applied not only to the need for combination at this juncture among the mainland provinces. It articulated a general truth: states hampered by internal bickering fail to mobilize their military resources effectively and rapidly find their domestic weaknesses compounded by impotence in foreign affairs.

Franklin need only have turned to eighteenth-century Europe for proof of his statement.[2] Successful states developed efficient means of collecting taxes, conscripting soldiers, and eliminating resistance to political centralization. Such techniques forged the principal tool of national survival—a competitive military establishment. The sorry decline of Poland, Sweden, and the Ottoman Empire from their seventeenth-century glory stemmed from the monarch's inability to check the nobility's autonomy. On the other hand, Prussia and England overcame relatively small populations by developing brutal but effective means of recruiting Europe's most powerful army and navy. They successfully integrated the landowning class into the civil and military administration. France, Austria, and Russia represented the intermediate case of large nations that eliminated local privileges and opposition intermittently and imperfectly, but maintained major power status through sheer size and periodically strong rulers. Nations able to neutralize the institution that eighteenth-century America associated most with liberty—the legislative assembly—survived and increased in strength. States that preserved these traditional privileges for their subjects deteriorated or expired.

But British North America neither united nor died. Throughout the early decades of the eighteenth century, untroubled by massive expansion or major social problems, the provincial legislatures had the luxury to devote themselves to the sort of "quest of power" against royal government that would have been suicidal in Europe. Gaining power to initiate and pass laws, control finances, and judge their own elections and privileges, the assemblies used their control over the governor's salary to turn him into a compliant instrument of their will or a pitiable figure of impotent rage. To justify their activities, the lower houses used the rhetoric of anti-Stuart English Parliamentarians, bolstered by the more recent Whig ideology. Both considered the great problem of government to be the preservation of popular virtue and liberty against administrative corruption and tyranny.[3]

However, governments that existed primarily as "negatives"—as observers sometimes called the three branches of colonial legislatures—found themselves poorly equipped to deal with the great changes in American society that began roughly around 1740. From this time until the American Revolution, despite their great formal powers and efforts to preserve them, social problems burst the narrow boundaries within which the local legislatures were able to deal with them. The "quest for power" could not continue once society impinged on politics. The deputies either had to become less obstructionist or be supplanted, as they ultimately were, first by British authority, then by a national government.

Most of the colonies' problems stemmed from extraordinary population growth that led to economic and territorial expansion. The population of British North America grew from about nine-hundred-thousand in 1740 to over two million by 1770, prompting Benjamin Franklin and Parson Malthus, among others, to deduce that nations untroubled by famine or debilitating warfare naturally doubled in numbers every generation. Immigration, sporadic since the end of the seventeenth century, came in waves from Germany, Scotland, and Ireland as well as England, adding ethnic tensions to the problem of how to absorb the newcomers. The Great Awakening challenged the religious establishment in most colonies. Simultaneously, in many places, the economy boomed: colonies exporting £718,000 of goods in 1740 sent over £1,100,000 overseas in 1763; imports, £813,000 in 1740, reached £1,631,000 the year Britain drove France from the continent. By 1750, as Jack P. Greene, speaking for many historians, has noted, "the colonies possessed virtually all of the conditions necessary for self-governing states," and "had achieved a high degree of competency."[4]

Yet the activities of the provincial governments did not match the competency of the colonists. In colony after colony, law and order broke down as the legislatures proved incapable of managing defense or frontier expansion. Georgia failed as a proprietary experiment and became a royal colony in 1754. South Carolina needed British troops to put down the Cherokees in 1760. A decade later, when it refused to grant local courts to the violence-ridden backcountry, the legislature confronted the "Regulators," a frontier movement where vigilantes took justice into their own hands. In North Carolina, the problem was too much rather than too little government: the extortions of eastern officials provoked the full-scale Regulator rebellion on the western frontier. Virginia set off the French and Indian War by its territorial expansion into the Ohio Valley in 1754, and fought Lord Dunmore's War on the eve of the American Revolution for the same purpose. (Maryland possessed the dubious honor of being the only province to contribute virtually nothing to the French and Indian War.) Pennsylvania's Quaker ruling class, after trying to keep the province out of the war, had to resign en masse in 1756 when it realized the irrelevance of such pacifist principles. Eight years later the "Paxton Boys," enraged at the eastern majority's lack of concern in the face of Pontiac's Conspiracy (which also had to be put down by British soldiers), marched on Philadelphia and had to be talked out of rebelling by Benjamin Franklin. Both New Jersey and New York suffered from land riots—those in New York on Livingston Manor in 1765 again requiring British intervention—provoked by increasing numbers of tenant farmers subject to what they considered exorbitant rents. New York also engaged in violent boundary disputes with New Hampshire over the future state of Vermont. Except for Maryland and Delaware, every province in North America outside New England faced a serious crisis of legitimacy or had to call in the British army to preserve law and order in the decades after 1750.

Britain thus became obliged to protect the colonists from each other while it launched an unprecedented effort to save them from the

French. In the war, also, the colonists' record did them little credit. Efforts to determine voluntary quotas of men and money failed, as at the Albany Congress of 1754. Throughout the war, British officers had to negotiate with the colonies for troops and funds. Even when the Americans made a sizeable contribution, the manner of raising soldiers and supplies practically undid it. Men agreed to serve only for a specific year, campaign, or territory close to their home, making their use on extended campaigns difficult. A new complement had to be enlisted every year, and everywhere British officers complained about the soldiers' poor quality, the exorbitant prices charged by local farmers and merchants for supplies, and the recalcitrance of colonial legislatures in voting requisitions promptly.[5] Furthermore, trade with the enemy was so extensive, requiring periodic embargoes, that at least one historian has argued it kept the French West Indies from starvation and surrender.[6] And when Britain won, it had to erect a chain of forts from the Gulf of Mexico to the St. Lawrence to prevent Indian uprisings against land-engrossing settlers and speculators.[7] To help fund the £400,000 annual cost, Parliament imposed the Stamp and Townsend Acts and tried to obtain greater revenues from the customs service.

Yet at least one province in British North America proved an exception to the rule. Whatever its internal difficulties, Massachusetts never suffered a breakdown of authority comparable to its fellow colonies. Instead, between the outbreak of King George's War and the Peace of Paris, Massachusetts accomplished a great transformation remarkably similar to the state-building process of the European powers. Rousing itself from a quarter-century's lethargy, it achieved feats of taxation and mobilization that Frederick the Great himself might have envied. Under the tutelage of Governor William Shirley, the Bay Colony changed from one of the most truculent provinces in the empire to the most cooperative. To be sure, this very helpfulness led to intense contact with the British military, who complained that Massachusetts still insisted on fighting its own war in its own way. But unlike the other colonies, Massachusetts was not in danger and could well have defended itself had it been invaded—Lexington and Concord proved that. As local authority broke down elsewhere, it grew in Massachusetts.

To effect this about-face, the very nature of Massachusetts' political system had to change. A legislature concerned primarily with obstructing plans to strengthen royal authority and resolving disputes presented by towns and individuals became an active body that designed and implemented vast military campaigns. A potent faction devoted to the royal prerogative developed virtually *ex nihilo*, supplanting the influence of the previously dominant country party. For a quarter of a century, Massachusetts waged total war.

In so doing, the Bay Colony nearly bankrupted itself. Unlike the southern and middle colonies, possessed of vast tracts of fertile farmland suitable for feeding the West Indies and supplying the tobacco and rice markets of Europe, Massachusetts had only enjoyed primary access to these lucrative trades before New York and Philadelphia emerged as major ports in their own right. It could barely feed itself, and had to export its fish to buy grain. The Bay Colony survived in the mid-eighteenth century on a negative balance of trade with Britain of approximately five to one. Few new immigrants came to Massachusetts. The population rose only from about 150,000 in 1740 to 210,000 by 1770, and much of this came from natural increases in already overcrowded towns. Per capita net worth for white males, £131 sterling in the southern colonies, £51 in the middle, averaged only £32 in New England.[8] Much of this relative poverty can be traced to war taxation, the neglect of agriculture and trade with so many men in the army, and additional blows to the Boston economy from impressment and the extremely heavy taxes laid by the province on the capital.

When Britain, understandably, began to seek a more rational mode of imperial administration at the end of the "Great War for the Empire," it mistakenly concentrated on the colony that had invested the most, both financially and psychologically, in the war. As Kerry Trask has shown, beset by military fiascos, droughts, and economic decline, Massachusetts turned its exertions into a "war for paradise," which would not only herald Christ's victory over the Antichrist, but restore a lost earthly prosperity.[9] Instead, postwar depression and imperial regulation interacted with each other to provoke the fiercest revolutionary movement on the continent.

In protests against British regulation, Massachusetts frequently stressed its tremendous war contributions even though it had not been attacked in over a half-century. On 13 June 1764 the house of representatives criticized parliamentary taxation, arguing that "in the last war, we exerted ourselves much beyond our natural strength, and thereby we have incurred a heavy load of debt, which all the resources in our power will hardly clear from us for many years. Can it be possible that the duties to be imposed, and the taxes to be levied, shall be assessed without the voice of one American in Parliament?" Similarly, one of Oxenbridge Thacher's principal *Sentiments of a British American* was that "the colonies contributed their full proportion to those conquests which adorn and dignify the present reign. One of them in particular raised in one year seven thousand men to be commanded by His Majesty's general, besides maintaining many guards and garrisons on their own frontiers." James Otis took up the cry in his *Rights of the British Colonists Asserted and Proved*, where he appealed not only to natural rights but also to past experience:[10]

> We have spent all we could raise, and more; for notwithstanding the parliamentary reimbursements of part, we still remain much in debt. The province of the Massachusetts, I believe, has expended more men and money in war since the year 1620, when a few families first landed at Plymouth, in proportion to their abilities than the three kingdoms together. The same, I believe, may be truly affirmed of many of the other colonies, though the Massachusetts has undoubtedly had the heaviest burden.

Even the Massachusetts loyalists, whatever they may have argued publicly, knew in their heart of hearts that Otis was right. Thomas Hutchinson may have written in his *History of Massachusetts* that without British help the colonies "would have been extirpated by the French" and that Britain had "expended a far greater sum" rescuing the colonies during the "Great War for the Empire" "than the whole property, real and personal, in all the colonies would amount to." But in private he argued differently against the Stamp Act. The colonists had contributed more men to the common cause in proportion to their population than England itself. They had defended themselves for the century before 1754 without much help, and had increased Britain's own strength and prosperity, not vice versa. And whatever the colonies' contribution as a whole, "no other government has been at any expense to set against" Massachusetts.[11]

On the eve of the Revolution, Massachusetts loyalist Isaac Royall begged Lord Dartmouth not to punish the province for the Boston Tea Party. "This province, Sir, has always been foremost even beyond its ability, and notwithstanding the present unhappy disputes would perhaps be so again if there should be the like occasion for it in promoting the honor of their king and nation. Witness their twice saving Nova Scotia from falling into French hands, the reduction of Louisbourg . . . and many other expensive and heroic expeditions against the common enemy."[12] When Royall's plea fell on deaf ears, the province somehow pulled together the resources and manpower to mount one final "expensive and heroic expedition," but this time on its own behalf. Massachusetts thereby led British North America and humanity out of an age where people were "subjects" of kings and into an "Age of the Democratic Revolution," which proclaimed that rulers possessed responsibilities rather than prerogatives, and that peoples enjoyed rights rather than privileges.

## Notes to Postscript

1. *Boston Gazette*, 21 May 1754.

2. See generally Charles Tilly, ed., *The Formation of the Nation State in Western Europe* (Princeton, 1975), esp. pp. 5–83.

3. See generally Jack P. Greene, *The Quest for Power: The Lower Houses of Assembly in the Southern Royal Colonies* (Chapel Hill, 1963), and "Political Mimesis: A Consideration of the Historical Origins of Legislative Behavior in the British Colonies in the Eighteenth Century," *American Historical Review*, 75 (1969): 337–360; Bernard Bailyn, *The Origins of American Politics* (New York, 1969).

4. *Historical Statistics of the United States* (Washington, 1970), p. 1,176; Jack P. Greene, "An Uneasy Connection: An Analysis of the Pre-conditions of the American Revolution," in Stephen G. Kurtz and James H. Hutson, eds. *Essays on the American Revolution* (Chapel Hill, 1973), p. 35.

5. Alan Rogers, *Empire and Liberty: American Resistance to British Authority 1755-1763* (Berkeley, 1974).

6. W.J. Eccles, *France in America* (New York, 1972), p. 174.

7. See especially Jack Sosin, *Whitehall and the Wilderness* (Lincoln, NE, 1963), and John Shy, *Toward Lexington: The Role of the British Army in the Coming of the American Revolution* (Princeton, 1965).

8. *Historical Statistics of the United States* (Washington, 1970), p. 1,175.

9. Kerry Trask, "In Pursuit of Shadows: A Study of Collective Hope and Despair in Provincial Massachusetts During the Era of the Seven Years' War, 1740 to 1765" (University of Minnesota, Ph.D. diss., 1971).

10. Joseph Felt, *A Historical Account of Massachusetts Currency* (Boston, 1839), p. 151; Bernard Bailyn, ed. *Pamphlets of the American Revolution, 1750-1765* (Cambridge, 1965), pp. 481, 492.

11. Thomas Hutchinson, *The History of the Colony and Province of Massachusetts Bay*, (Cambridge, 1936), 3: 59, 253; Edmund S. Morgan, ed., "Thomas Hutchinson and the Stamp Act," *New England Quarterly*, 21 (1948): 488–489; Thomas Hutchinson to William Bollan, 14 July 1760, Massachusetts Archives, 25: 14–17. Pagination to typescript prepared by Catherine Barton Mayo at the MHS.

12. Isaac Royall to Lord Dartmouth, 18 January 1774, Large Manuscripts, MHS. I thank David Ader for this reference.

# TABLES

## Tables

I have sought to make these statistics as accurate as possible. However, given a small number of multiple names in Boston and the human error factor in dealing with thousands of people, some inaccuracy is probably inevitable. On the other hand, as I discovered from correcting my own statistics at various stages of writing, I can assert confidently that none of the problems would be sufficiently large enough to alter the general conclusions I have drawn from this data.

**TABLE 1**    Cumulative Voting Records of Massachusetts Towns on All Roll Calls, 1726–1765

| | | | | | | Totals | |
| --- | --- | --- | --- | --- | --- | --- | --- |
| Suffolk | Total | 1726 | 1739–1740 | 1751–1756 | 1757–1765 | Fiscal issues | Political issues |
| Boston | 36–46 | 0–4 | 7–4 | 17–16 | 12–22 | 19–26 | 17–20 |
| Roxbury | 9–13 | 1–0 | 0–1 | 4–8 | 4–4 | 3–8 | 6–5 |
| Dorchester | 8–9 | 1–0 | 0–2 | 2–6 | 5–1 | 2–6 | 6–3 |
| Milton | 6–13 | 0–1 | 0–3 | 4–6 | 2–3 | 1–8 | 5–5 |
| Braintree | 7–15 | 0–1 | 0–0 | 5–9 | 2–5 | 4–7 | 3–8 |
| Weymouth | 4–16 | 0–1 | 0–3 | 1–9 | 3–3 | 0–12 | 4–4 |
| Hingham | 4–21 | 0–1 | 0–3 | 4–9 | 0–8 | 0–4 | 4–17 |
| Dedham | 11–8 | 1–0 | 2–1 | 2–6 | 6–1 | 4–7 | 7–1 |
| Medfield | 1–18 | 0–0 | 1–0 | 0–10 | 0–8 | 1–7 | 0–11 |
| Stoughton | 3–12 | 0–0 | 1–2 | 2–4 | 0–6 | 2–3 | 1–9 |
| Needham | 9–7 | 0–0 | 0–3 | 9–2 | 0–2 | 5–6 | 4–1 |
| Brookline | 1–2 | 0–1 | 0–1 | 1–0 | 0–0 | 1–1 | 0–1 |
| Wrentham | 3–13 | 1–0 | 0–3 | 1–3 | 1–7 | 1–7 | 2–6 |
| Medway | 1–8 | 0–0 | 0–0 | 0–5 | 1–3 | 0–7 | 1–1 |
| Chelsea | 8–3 | 0–0 | 1–1 | 0–1 | 7–1 | 1–2 | 7–1 |
| *Essex* | | | | | | | |
| Salem | 24–9 | 2–0 | 4–2 | 12–7 | 6–0 | 13–8 | 11–1 |
| Ipswich | 8–14 | 1–0 | 1–5 | 1–8 | 5–1 | 1–11 | 7–3 |
| Newbury | 4–24 | 1–0 | 2–0 | 0–12 | 1–12 | 2–9 | 2–15 |
| Marblehead | 13–4 | 0–0 | 1–2 | 8–2 | 4–0 | 7–4 | 6–0 |
| Lynn | 2–17 | 0–0 | 0–2 | 2–9 | 0–6 | 0–10 | 2–7 |
| Andover | 10–8 | 0–0 | 0–2 | 5–3 | 5–3 | 4–5 | 6–3 |
| Beverly | 7–13 | 1–0 | 0–3 | 5–3 | 1–7 | 4–6 | 3–7 |
| Rowley | 4–17 | 0–1 | 1–2 | 2–7 | 1–7 | 3–7 | 1–10 |

Source: *Journals of the House of Representatives of Massachusetts Bay* (Boston, 1919– ).

Note: The first number in each column represents the number of times the town agreed with the court's position; the second number represents agreement with the country's position.

**TABLE 1**

*-continued-*

| Essex *(cont.)* | Total | 1726 | 1739-1740 | 1751-1756 | 1757-1765 | Totals Fiscal issues | Political issues |
|---|---|---|---|---|---|---|---|
| Salsbury | 3-15 | 1-0 | 0-1 | 2-7 | 1-7 | 0-6 | 4-9 |
| Haverhill | 6-13 | 0-1 | 0-3 | 2-6 | 4-3 | 3-8 | 3-5 |
| Gloucester | 6-7 | 1-0 | 0-1 | 3-3 | 2-3 | 2-4 | 4-3 |
| Danvers | 0-6 | 0-0 | 0-0 | 0-0 | 0-6 | 0-1 | 0-5 |
| Bradford | 3-17 | 0-1 | 0-3 | 2-8 | 1-5 | 2-8 | 1-9 |
| Almsbury | 6-11 | 0-1 | 0-2 | 2-7 | 4-1 | 2-7 | 4-4 |
| Topsfield | 1-16 | 1-0 | 0-3 | 0-7 | 0-6 | 0-9 | 1-7 |
| Wenham | 0-6 | 0-1 | 0-3 | 0-2 | 0-0 | 0-3 | 0-3 |
| Middleton | 0-2 | 0-0 | 0-2 | 0-0 | 0-0 | 0-2 | 0-0 |
| Rumford | 1-0 | 0-0 | 1-0 | 0-0 | 0-0 | 1-0 | 0-0 |
| *Middlesex* | | | | | | | |
| Cambridge | 18-7 | 0-1 | 1-0 | 10-6 | 7-0 | 6-3 | 12-4 |
| Charlestown | 13-5 | 2-0 | 2-0 | 6-4 | 3-1 | 7-3 | 6-2 |
| Watertown | 11-9 | 1-0 | 1-1 | 7-4 | 2-4 | 5-5 | 6-4 |
| Woburn | 8-8 | 0-1 | 0-1 | 4-4 | 4-2 | 4-4 | 4-4 |
| Reading | 9-15 | 1-0 | 0-2 | 4-9 | 4-4 | 3-9 | 6-6 |
| Concord | 15-4 | 1-0 | 1-1 | 7-2 | 6-1 | 6-1 | 9-3 |
| Newton | 17-5 | 0-1 | 3-0 | 8-3 | 6-1 | 11-2 | 6-3 |
| Sudbury | 8-11 | 0-1 | 1-2 | 3-6 | 4-2 | 4-7 | 4-4 |
| Groton | 11-3 | 1-0 | 1-0 | 5-3 | 4-0 | 4-3 | 7-0 |
| Marlborough | 3-17 | 1-0 | 1-2 | 1-8 | 0-7 | 2-8 | 1-9 |
| Billerica | 7-15 | 0-1 | 0-3 | 6-5 | 1-6 | 4-8 | 3-7 |
| Framingham | 7-14 | 0-1 | 1-1 | 4-6 | 2-6 | 3-7 | 4-7 |
| Chelmsford | 9-8 | 0-1 | 0-2 | 2-4 | 7-1 | 2-6 | 7-2 |
| Lexington | 10-8 | 1-0 | 0-3 | 4-3 | 5-2 | 4-6 | 6-2 |

TABLE 1

*–continued–*

| Middlesex (cont.) | Total | 1726 | 1739–1740 | 1751–1756 | 1757–1765 | Totals Fiscal issues | Totals Political issues |
|---|---|---|---|---|---|---|---|
| Malden | 6–13 | 0–1 | 0–2 | 3–7 | 3–3 | 3–7 | 3–6 |
| Weston | 17–5 | 1–0 | 3–0 | 7–4 | 6–1 | 7–4 | 10–1 |
| Medford | 7–5 | 0–0 | 1–1 | 4–3 | 2–1 | 2–3 | 5–2 |
| Westford | 4–5 | 0–0 | 0–3 | 0–2 | 4–0 | 2–2 | 2–3 |
| Waltham | 8–9 | 0–0 | 2–1 | 4–3 | 2–5 | 5–4 | 3–5 |
| Lincoln | 9–1 | 0–0 | 0–0 | 3–1 | 6–0 | 2–1 | 7–0 |
| Dunstable | 2–1 | 1–0 | 1–1 | 0–0 | 0–0 | 1–1 | 1–0 |
| Sherburne | 3–6 | 0–1 | 2–1 | 0–2 | 1–2 | 2–4 | 1–2 |
| Littleton | 6–3 | 1–0 | 0–0 | 4–2 | 1–1 | 2–3 | 4–0 |
| Stow | 2–4 | 0–0 | 0–0 | 0–1 | 2–3 | 0–2 | 2–2 |
| Hopkinton | 3–5 | 0–0 | 1–1 | 0–4 | 2–0 | 1–4 | 2–1 |
| Holliston | 0–1 | 0–0 | 0–0 | 0–1 | 0–0 | 0–1 | 0–0 |
| Townsend | 1–0 | 0–0 | 0–0 | 0–0 | 1–0 | 0–0 | 1–0 |
| *Hampshire* | | | | | | | |
| Springfield | 17–0 | 1–0 | 3–0 | 6–0 | 7–0 | 6–0 | 11–0 |
| Northampton | 11–5 | 1–0 | 3–0 | 4–4 | 3–1 | 6–4 | 5–1 |
| Hadley | 9–4 | 1–0 | 2–0 | 4–2 | 2–2 | 6–2 | 3–2 |
| Hatfield | 12–3 | 1–0 | 2–0 | 4–3 | 5–0 | 5–3 | 7–0 |
| Deerfield | 11–3 | 1–0 | 1–0 | 4–2 | 5–1 | 5–3 | 6–0 |
| Sheffield | 4–1 | 0–0 | 0–0 | 2–1 | 2–0 | 3–1 | 1–0 |
| Westfield | 10–4 | 1–0 | 2–0 | 6–2 | 1–2 | 6–1 | 4–3 |
| Sunderland | 3–4 | 0–0 | 0–0 | 1–2 | 2–2 | 0–2 | 3–2 |
| Brimfield | 4–9 | 0–0 | 0–1 | 0–5 | 4–3 | 1–4 | 3–5 |
| Enfield | 0–2 | 0–0 | 0–2 | 0–0 | 0–0 | 0–2 | 0–0 |
| Suffield | 1–2 | 1–0 | 0–2 | 0–0 | 0–0 | 0–2 | 1–0 |

**TABLE 1**

*–continued–*

| Worcester | Total | 1726 | 1739–1740 | 1751–1756 | 1757–1765 | Totals Fiscal issues | Totals Political issues |
|---|---|---|---|---|---|---|---|
| Worcester | 8–2 | 0–0 | 0–2 | 3–0 | 5–0 | 2–2 | 6–0 |
| Lancaster | 10–12 | 0–1 | 1–2 | 5–6 | 4–3 | 5–7 | 5–5 |
| Leicester | 4–11 | 0–0 | 0–2 | 3–5 | 1–4 | 1–8 | 3–3 |
| Brookfield | 8–6 | 0–0 | 1–1 | 5–3 | 2–2 | 4–3 | 4–3 |
| Lunenburg | 5–9 | 0–0 | 0–1 | 3–5 | 2–3 | 1–5 | 4–4 |
| Oxford | 3–3 | 0–0 | 0–0 | 0–2 | 3–1 | 0–2 | 3–1 |
| Mendon | 4–14 | 0–1 | 0–2 | 3–7 | 1–4 | 2–8 | 2–6 |
| Rutland | 8–4 | 0–0 | 0–0 | 5–4 | 3–0 | 3–4 | 5–0 |
| Sutton | 5–12 | 0–0 | 0–1 | 4–5 | 1–6 | 2–6 | 3–6 |
| Southborough | 3–4 | 0–0 | 0–0 | 0–4 | 3–0 | 0–3 | 3–1 |
| Westborough | 3–4 | 0–0 | 0–0 | 2–0 | 1–4 | 1–0 | 2–4 |
| Shrewsbury | 2–10 | 0–0 | 1–0 | 0–4 | 1–6 | 1–3 | 1–7 |
| Bolton | 3–7 | 0–0 | 0–0 | 1–4 | 2–3 | 2–3 | 1–4 |
| Sturbridge | 2–7 | 0–0 | 1–1 | 1–3 | 0–3 | 1–6 | 1–1 |
| Harvard | 0–5 | 0–0 | 0–1 | 0–3 | 0–1 | 0–4 | 0–1 |
| Woodstock | 1–2 | 1–0 | 0–2 | 0–0 | 0–0 | 0–2 | 1–0 |
| Oxbridge | 6–6 | 0–0 | 0–2 | 5–3 | 1–1 | 3–6 | 3–0 |
| Upton | 0–2 | 0–0 | 0–2 | 0–0 | 0–0 | 0–2 | 0–0 |
| Hardwick | 6–1 | 0–0 | 0–0 | 3–1 | 3–0 | 2–1 | 4–0 |
| Petersham | 2–1 | 0–0 | 0–0 | 0–0 | 2–1 | 1–0 | 1–1 |
| Dudley | 0–1 | 0–0 | 0–0 | 0–0 | 0–1 | 0–0 | 0–1 |

**TABLE 1** *—continued—*

| | | | | | | Totals | |
|---|---|---|---|---|---|---|---|
| *Plymouth* | Total | 1726 | 1739–1740 | 1751–1756 | 1757–1765 | Fiscal issues | Political issues |
| Plymouth | 15–4 | 1–0 | 1–1 | 6–2 | 7–1 | 6–3 | 9–1 |
| Scituate | 8–12 | 0–1 | 0–2 | 3–6 | 5–3 | 1–9 | 7–3 |
| Marshfield | 14–2 | 0–0 | 2–1 | 5–1 | 7–0 | 5–2 | 9–0 |
| Duxbury | 11–4 | 1–0 | 0–0 | 6–2 | 4–2 | 3–3 | 8–1 |
| Bridgewater | 9–13 | 0–0 | 0–3 | 3–8 | 6–2 | 2–8 | 7–5 |
| Middleborough | 7–8 | 0–1 | 0–1 | 4–4 | 3–2 | 3–4 | 4–4 |
| Rochester | 9–5 | 1–0 | 0–1 | 5–3 | 3–1 | 4–3 | 5–2 |
| Pembroke | 4–14 | 0–1 | 0–2 | 1–8 | 3–3 | 2–8 | 2–6 |
| Plympton | 2–16 | 0–1 | 0–1 | 2–8 | 0–6 | 2–8 | 0–9 |
| Kingston | 2–8 | 0–0 | 0–2 | 2–3 | 0–3 | 1–6 | 1–2 |
| Hanover | 3–10 | 0–0 | 0–0 | 3–5 | 0–5 | 1–6 | 2–4 |
| Abington | 1–8 | 0–0 | 0–0 | 0–6 | 1–2 | 0–5 | 1–3 |
| *Barnstable* | | | | | | | |
| Barnstable | 12–5 | 0–0 | 0–1 | 8–4 | 4–0 | 5–5 | 7–0 |
| Sandwich | 7–8 | 1–0 | 0–1 | 3–3 | 3–4 | 2–5 | 5–3 |
| Eastham | 7–4 | 0–0 | 2–0 | 3–1 | 2–3 | 4–1 | 3–3 |
| Yarmouth | 2–3 | 0–0 | 1–1 | 0–0 | 1–2 | 1–1 | 1–2 |
| Harwich | 7–4 | 0–0 | 0–1 | 2–3 | 5–0 | 1–4 | 6–0 |
| Falmouth | 3–4 | 0–0 | 1–0 | 0–0 | 2–4 | 1–1 | 2–3 |
| Truro | 1–0 | 1–0 | 0–0 | 0–0 | 0–0 | 0–0 | 1–0 |

## Tables

**TABLE 1**

*—continued—*

| Bristol | Total | 1726 | 1739–1740 | 1751–1756 | 1757–1765 | Totals | |
| | | | | | | Fiscal issues | Political issues |
|---|---|---|---|---|---|---|---|
| Bristol | 3–1 | 1–0 | 2–1 | * | * | 2–1 | 1–0 |
| Taunton | 5–13 | 1–0 | 0–2 | 4–9 | 0–2 | 1–12 | 4–1 |
| Rehobto | 4–14 | 1–0 | 0–2 | 3–5 | 0–7 | 2–7 | 2–7 |
| Swanzey | 6–12 | 1–0 | 1–2 | 3–4 | 1–6 | 3–7 | 3–5 |
| Dartmouth | 5–10 | 0–0 | 0–0 | 5–5 | 0–5 | 4–3 | 1–7 |
| Norton | 4–15 | 0–1 | 0–3 | 3–5 | 1–6 | 1–8 | 3–7 |
| Attleborough | 3–11 | 1–0 | 0–2 | 2–4 | 0–5 | 1–5 | 2–6 |
| Dighton | 2–4 | 0–1 | 0–1 | 2–1 | 0–1 | 1–2 | 1–2 |
| Freetown | 3–3 | 1–0 | 0–0 | 0–1 | 2–2 | 0–1 | 3–2 |
| Little Compton | 2–0 | 1–0 | 1–0 | 0–0 | 0–0 | 1–0 | 1–0 |
| Tiverton | 1–1 | 0–0 | 1–1 | 0–0 | 0–0 | 1–1 | 0–0 |
| *York* | | | | | | | |
| York | 3–19 | 0–0 | 1–2 | 1–12 | 1–5 | 1–11 | 2–8 |
| Kittery | 5–11 | 1–0 | 0–1 | 3–7 | 1–3 | 3–5 | 2–6 |
| Wells | 11–8 | 1–0 | 1–1 | 5–6 | 4–1 | 6–5 | 5–3 |
| Berwick | 1–9 | 1–0 | 0–1 | 0–4 | 0–4 | 0–4 | 1–5 |
| Falmouth | 10–8 | 1–0 | 1–2 | 3–6 | 5–0 | 3–8 | 7–0 |
| Biddeford | 2–4 | 0–0 | 0–1 | 0–3 | 2–0 | 0–4 | 2–0 |
| North Yarmouth | 6–2 | 0–0 | 0–0 | 3–1 | 3–1 | 2–1 | 4–1 |
| Scarborough | 2–7 | 0–0 | 0–0 | 1–5 | 1–2 | 1–4 | 1–3 |
| Brunswick | 1–0 | 0–0 | 0–0 | 1–0 | 0–0 | 1–0 | 0–0 |

*Become part of Rhode Island.

**TABLE 1**

*—continued—*

| | Total | 1726 | 1739–1740 | 1751–1756 | 1757–1765 | Totals | |
| | | | | | | Fiscal issues | Political issues |
|---|---|---|---|---|---|---|---|
| *Dukes* | | | | | | | |
| Edgartown | 4–2 | 0–0 | 1–0 | 1–2 | 2–0 | 1–2 | 3–0 |
| Chilmark | 0–1 | 0–0 | 0–0 | 0–0 | 0–1 | 0–1 | 0–0 |
| Tisbury | 0–1 | 0–0 | 0–0 | 0–0 | 0–1 | 0–1 | 0–0 |
| *Nantucket* | | | | | | | |
| Sherburne | 8–2 | 0–0 | 1–0 | 4–2 | 3–0 | 3–2 | 5–0 |
| *Berkshire* | | | | | | | |
| Stockbridge | 2–0 | 0–0 | 0–0 | 0–0 | 2–0 | 0–0 | 2–0 |
| Tyringham | 2–0 | 0–0 | 0–0 | 0–0 | 2–0 | 0–0 | 2–0 |

# Tables

**TABLE 2**   Roll Calls in the Massachusetts House of Representatives, 1726–1765

| Date | Subject | Court | Country |
|------|---------|-------|---------|
| 1726 | Explanatory Charter | 48(30)Y | 32 (6)N |
| 1739 | Redeem paper before 1742 | 19(14)Y | 53(24)N |
| 1740 | Stop Land Bank | 37(18)Y | 59(28)N |
| 1741 | Stop Land Bank | 28(15)Y | 42(22)N |
| 1749* | Abolish Paper Money | 40(32)Y | 37 (?)N |
| 1751 | Restore Paper Money | 33(19)N | 46(27)Y |
| 1751 | Restore Paper Money | 31(17)N | 28(15)Y |
| 1751 | Inflationary Tax Bill | 26(13)N | 36(12)Y |
| 1753 | Treasurer to give bond | 13 (8)N | 71(37)Y |
| 1753 | Monetize gold, keep paper | 25(11)N | 53(22)Y |
| 1754 | Increase Shirley's salary | 41(24)Y | 44(20)N |
| 1754 | Increase Treasurer Foye's salary | 23(14)Y | 42(21)N |
| 1754 | Excise Bill | 17 (9)N | 52(26)Y |
| 1754 | Plan of Union | 41(28)Y | 37(19)N |
| 1754 | Postpone Plan of Union | 31(21)Y | 48(30)N |
| 1755 | Pay for Hubbard's defense vs. Fowle | 57(36)Y | 28(18)N |
| 1755 | Reinforce Crown Point forces | 39(19)Y | 12 (1)N |
| 1756 | Excise collectors may sit in court | 11 (5)Y | 42(23)N |
| 1757 | Use militia for defense | 32(26)Y | 48(20)N |
| 1758 | Agent Bollan to be retained | 34(29)Y | 38(16)N |
| 1759 | Bollan's precedence over John Pownall | 42(35)Y | 38(18)N |
| 1762 | Monetize gold | 43(41)N | 60(47)Y |
| 1762 | Superior Court judges' exclusion from house | 50(48)N | 43(29)Y |
| 1764 | Excuse Hutchinson as agent | 39(30)N | 33(30)Y |
| 1764 | Vote troops for Gage | 37(34)Y | 40(30)N |
| 1765 | Pay Hutchinson as chief justice | 42(38)Y | 41(24)N |

Source: *Journals of the House of Representatives of Massachusetts Bay* (Boston, 1919–   ).

Notes: A significant number of militia officers and justices of the peace voted against the court party, indicating the promise of patronage or threat of its withdrawal did not determine the General Court's behavior.

Parentheses indicate the number of military and civil appointees. Y = Yea; N = Nay.

*From James Allen's list of those in favor and Hutchinson's tally. Not recorded in *House Journals*.

# Tables

TABLE 3 Leaders of the House of Representatives, 1715–1768

| Name | Town | Inclusive Dates of Leadership | Number of Years a Leader |
|------|------|------|------|
| John Burrill* | Lynn | 1715–1718 | 4 |
| John White | Haverhill | 1715–1717 | 3 |
| William Payne | Boston | 1715 | 1 |
| Oliver Noyes | Boston | 1715–1720 | 4 |
| Elisha Cooke* | Boston | 1715–1737 | 18 |
| Adam Winthrop* | Boston | 1715 | 1 |
| Samuel Thaxter* | Hingham | 1715–1718 | 2 |
| Anthony Stoddard* | Boston | 1716 | 1 |
| Daniel Parker | Hingham | 1716 | 1 |
| John Stoddard* | Northampton | 1716–1746 | 13 |
| Charles Chambers* | Charlestown | 1716–1723 | 6 |
| Edward Hutchinson* | Boston | 1717–1718 | 2 |
| Jonathan Remington* | Cambridge | 1717–1728 | 7 |
| Joseph Wadsworth* | Boston | 1717–1726 | 2 |
| Habijah Savage | Boston | 1717–1732 | 2 |
| William Dudley* | Roxbury | 1718–1728 | 11 |
| Timothy Lindall | Salem | 1718–1721 | 4 |
| Thomas Turner | Scituate | 1718 | 1 |
| William Clarke* | Boston | 1719–1722 | 4 |
| John Gardner | Salem | 1719–1721 | 3 |
| Francis Fullam | Weston | 1719–1722 | 4 |
| John Clarke* | Boston | 1720–1723 | 4 |
| John Chandler* | Woodstock | 1725–1731 | 7 |
| William Throop | Bristol | 1720–1723 | 3 |
| Henry Somersby | Newbury | 1720 | 1 |
| Edmund Goffe | Cambridge | 1721 | 1 |
| John Wainwright | Ipswich | 1721–1738 | 15 |
| William Heath | Roxbury | 1721 | 1 |
| Ebenezer Pomroy* | Northhampton | 1721–1740 | 4 |
| Nathaniel Knowlton | Ipswich | 1721 | 1 |
| William Hutchinson | Boston | 1721 | 1 |
| Robert Spurr | Dorchester | 1721 | 1 |
| Ebenezer Stone* | Newton | 1721 | 1 |
| Daniel Epes | Salem | 1721–1743 | 4 |
| John Dyer | Plymouth | 1722 | 1 |
| John Quincy* | Braintree | 1722–1745 | 18 |
| Ezekiel Lewis* | Boston | 1723–1730 | 8 |
| Peter Osgood | Salem | 1723 | 1 |
| James Cawley | Marblehead | 1723 | 1 |
| Thomas Cushing* | Boston | 1724–1730 | 4 |
| John Ballantine | Boston | 1726–1727 | 2 |
| Samuel Welles* | Boston | 1727–1760 | 13 |

Source: *Journals of the House of Representatives of Massachusetts Bay* (Boston, 1919–    ).

Note: Leaders are defined as those who served on fifteen committees per year or more.

*Members subsequently elected to Council.

| Name | Town | Inclusive Dates of Leadership | Number of Years a Leader |
|------|------|------|------|
| Edward Howe | Dighton | 1727–1734 | 7 |
| Ebenezer Wright | Northampton | 1727 | 1 |
| Edward Goddard* | Framingham | 1727–1731 | 3 |
| Amos Turner | Scituate | 1727 | 1 |
| Thomas Tilestone | Dorchester | 1727 | 1 |
| Elisha Bisby | Pembroke | 1728–1734 | 4 |
| Stephen Eastwick | Kittery | 1728 | 1 |
| William Brattle* | Cambridge | 1729–1755 | 9 |
| Benjamin Lynde, Jr.* | Salem | 1729–1731 | 3 |
| Thomas Berry* | Ipswich | 1730 | 1 |
| John Wolcott | Salem | 1730 | 1 |
| Joseph Gerrish | Newbury | 1730–1747 | 6 |
| Charles Church | Bristol | 1730–1733 | 2 |
| Stephen Hall | Charlestown | 1730 | 1 |
| Thomas Cushing, Jr. | Boston | 1731–1745 | 15 |
| Joseph Lemon | Charlestown | 1731 | 1 |
| John Choate* | Ipswich | 1732–1760 | 15 |
| John Chandler, Jr.* | Worcester | 1732–1742 | 10 |
| Robert Hale | Beverly | 1734–1757 | 15 |
| Benjamin Prescott | Groton | 1734–1738 | 5 |
| Samuel Danforth* | Cambridge | 1734–1738 | 4 |
| Job Almy | Tiverton | 1734–1740 | 2 |
| William Pynchon | Springfield | 1734–1739 | 2 |
| John Alden | Duxbury | 1735 | 1 |
| Joseph Dwight* | Brookfield | 1735–1751 | 5 |
| Joseph Warren | Plymouth | 1735–1743 | 4 |
| Richard Saltonstall* | Haverhill | 1736–1738 | 2 |
| Thomas Hutchinson* | Boston | 1737–1748 | 10 |
| Ezekiel Cheever* | Charlestown | 1737–1742 | 3 |
| John Wheelwright* | Boston | 1737 | 1 |
| Timothy Prout | Boston | 1737–1743 | 4 |
| Samuel Sewall | Boston | 1738 | 1 |
| Daniel Lewis | Pembroke | 1744–1745 | 2 |
| Timothy Dwight | Northampton | 1744–1765 | 8 |
| Benjamin Pickman | Salem | 1744–1746 | 2 |
| Joseph Buckminister | Framingham | 1744–1760 | 10 |
| John Hobson | Rowley | 1744–1746 | 3 |
| Isaac Royall* | Charlestown | 1746–1751 | 5 |
| Thomas Wisewall | Dorchester | 1745 | 1 |
| Thomas Foster* | Plymouth | 1745–1767 | 15 |
| James Otis, Sr.* | Barnstable | 1745–1768 | 17 |
| Jabez Fox* | Falmouth | 1745–1750 | 3 |

*Members subsequently elected to Council.

TABLE 3      *–continued–*

| Name | Town | Inclusive Dates of Leadership | Number of Years a Leader |
|------|------|------------------------------|--------------------------|
| William Richardson | Lancaster | 1745–1761 | 8 |
| Samuel Tupper | Sandwich, Medford | 1745–1750 | 2 |
| Richard Reed | Marblehead | 1756 | 1 |
| Benjamin Prat | Boston | 1757–1759 | 3 |
| Ebenezer Nichols | Reading | 1757–1764 | 4 |
| Thomas Morey | Norton | 1757–1763 | 7 |
| Timothy Paine* | Worcester | 1757–1762 | 5 |
| Edward Bacon | Barnstable | 1757–1759 | 3 |
| Caleb Cushing* | Salisbury | 1757–1759 | 3 |
| Michael Dalton | Newbury | 1757 | 1 |
| Thomas Lancaster | Rowley | 1757–1760 | 2 |
| John Osgood | Andover | 1757 | 1 |
| Nathaniel Stone | Harwich | 1757 | 1 |
| John Turner | Salem | 1757–1758 | 2 |
| Samuel Waldo, Jr. | Falmouth | 1757–1759 | 2 |
| Artemus Ward* | Shrewsbury | 1757–1768 | 7 |
| Oliver Fletcher | Chelmsford | 1758–1761 | 4 |
| Thomas Goldthwait | Chelsea | 1758–1763 | 6 |
| Edward Hartwell | Lunenburg | 1758–1760 | 3 |
| Nathaniel Hatch | Dorchester | 1758–1761 | 4 |
| Josiah Johnson | Woburn | 1758 | 1 |
| Samuel Niles | Braintree | 1758–1759 | 2 |
| Joseph Sayer | Welles | 1758–1761 | 3 |
| William Bourne | Marblehead | 1759–1765 | 4 |
| Jerathmeel Bowers | Swanzey | 1759–1768 | 10 |
| Stephen Higginson | Salem | 1759 | 1 |
| John Temple | Reading | 1759 | 1 |
| Israel Turner | Pembroke | 1759 | 1 |
| Royall Tyler* | Boston | 1759–1763 | 5 |
| George Watson | Plymouth | 1759 | 1 |
| James Fowle | Marblehead | 1760 | 1 |
| John Phillips | Boston | 1760–1762 | 3 |
| Jeremiah Powell* | North Yarmouth | 1760–1764 | 4 |
| Charles Preston | Concord | 1760–1761 | 2 |
| Nathaniel Ropes* | Salem | 1760 | 1 |
| Ezra Taylor | Southborough | 1760–1764 | 3 |
| Thomas Cushing | Boston | 1761–1768 | 8 |
| James Otis, Jr. | Boston | 1761–1768 | 8 |
| Eliphalet Pond | Dedham | 1761 | 1 |
| Ebenezer Thayer | Braintree | 1762–1767 | 3 |
| Oxenbridge Thacher | Boston | 1762–1764 | 3 |

| Name | Town | Inclusive Dates of Leadership | Number of Years a Leader |
|---|---|---|---|
| Francis Waldo | Falmouth | 1762 | 1 |
| Thomas Hubbard* | Boston | 1746–1758 | 13 |
| Andrew Hall | Medford | 1746–1750 | 5 |
| Samuel Adams, Sr. | Boston | 1746–1747 | 2 |
| Thomas Read | Westford | 1746 | 1 |
| Josiah Brewer | Weston | 1746–1747 | 2 |
| Benjamin Lincoln* | Hingham | 1746–1747 | 2 |
| Andrew Boardman | Cambridge | 1746 | 1 |
| Timothy Ruggles* | Sandwich, Hardwick | 1746–1767 | 12 |
| James Russell* | Charlestown | 1746–1760 | 9 |
| John Jones | Hopkinton | 1746–1760 | 2 |
| William Collins | Lynn | 1746–1748 | 2 |
| Ephraim Curtiss | Sudbury | 1746–1747 | 2 |
| Joseph Wilder | Lancaster | 1746 | 1 |
| Eleazar Porter* | Hadley | 1746–1752 | 4 |
| Samuel Lyscom | Southborough | 1746 | 1 |
| James Williams | Taunton | 1746 | 1 |
| Edward White | Brookline | 1747 | 1 |
| William Read | Lexington | 1747 | 1 |
| John Worthington* | Springfield | 1747–1764 | 10 |
| Daniel Pierce | Harvard | 1747 | 1 |
| Simon Frost | Kittery | 1747–1749 | 2 |
| John Gardner | Salem | 1747 | 1 |
| Samuel Witt | Marlborough | 1747–1764 | 10 |
| Josiah Edson | Bridgewater | 1747–1766 | 2 |
| Phineas Lyman | Suffield | 1747 | 1 |
| John Tyng | Boston | 1748–1759 | 11 |
| Isaac Little* | Marshfield | 1748–1749 | 2 |
| Israel Williams* | Hatfield | 1748–1758 | 5 |
| Josiah White | Norton | 1749 | 1 |
| John Storer | Wells | 1749–1754 | 3 |
| Peter Oliver* | Middleborough | 1749–1751 | 2 |
| Samuel Waldo* | Boston | 1749 | 1 |
| Samuel Livermore | Waltham | 1749–1764 | 13 |
| Daniel Howard | Bridgewater | 1749–1762 | 6 |
| Harrison Gray | Boston | 1750–1752 | 3 |
| Samuel White | Brookline Taunton | 1750–1759 | 8 |
| Edmund Trowbridge | Cambridge | 1750–1763 | 5 |
| John Brown | Leicester | 1750–1768 | 8 |

*Members subsequently elected to Council.

TABLE 3                    –continued–

| Name | Town | Inclusive Dates of Leadership | Number of Years a Leader |
|------|------|------------------------------|--------------------------|
| Joseph Williams | Roxbury | 1750–1768 | 12 |
| Benjamin Newhall | Lynn | 1750–1761 | 5 |
| John Bailey | Marblehead | 1750 | 1 |
| Noah Sprague | Rochester | 1750–1767 | 3 |
| David Stockbridge | Hanover | 1750–1760 | 5 |
| Thomas Pratt | Weymouth | 1750 | 1 |
| Joseph Hawley | Northampton | 1751–1768 | 5 |
| John Winslow | Marshfield | 1752–1765 | 6 |
| Elijah Williams | Deerfield | 1752 | 1 |
| Gamaiel Bradford* | Duxbury | 1752–1757 | 4 |
| Edward Sheaffe | Charlestown | 1752–1768 | 6 |
| Ezra Richmond | Dighton | 1753 | 1 |
| William Fletcher | Cambridge | 1753 | 1 |
| James Bowdoin* | Boston | 1753–1755 | 3 |
| Henry Gibbs | Newton | 1754–1756 | 4 |
| Jedidiah Prebble | Falmouth | 1753 | 1 |
| John Tasker | Marblehead | 1754–1756 | 2 |
| Josiah Quincy | Braintree | 1754–1757 | 4 |
| Richard Saltonstall | Haverhill | 1754 | 1 |
| Moses Marcy | Sturbridge | 1754 | 1 |
| William Bowdoin | Needham | 1754–1755 | 2 |
| Josiah Dwight | Springfield | 1754–1755 | 2 |
| William Stevens | Gloucester | 1754–1758 | 3 |
| John Hunt | Watertown | 1754–1755 | 2 |
| William Cooper | Boston | 1755 | 1 |
| Jeremiah Gridley | Brookline | 1755–1757 | 3 |
| Robert Hooper | Marblehead | 1755 | 1 |
| Nathaniel Sparhawk* | Kittery | 1755–1759 | 3 |
| John Leach | Beverly | 1755 | 1 |
| John Bradbury* | York | 1755–1761 | 7 |
| Benjamin Read | Lexington | 1755–1757 | 2 |
| Nathaniel Russell | Littleton | 1755 | 1 |
| James Humphrey* | Weymouth | 1755–1768 | 14 |
| Daniel Epes | Salem | 1755 | 1 |
| Stephen Hall* | Medford | 1755–1768 | 6 |
| Estes Hatch | Dorchester | 1755 | 1 |
| Samuel Health | Roxbury | 1755–1756 | 2 |
| Henry Vassall | Cambridge | 1755 | 1 |
| Benjamin Hills | Malden | 1755 | 1 |
| Thomas Steele | Leicester | 1755 | 1 |
| Thomas Flucker* | Boston | 1756–1760 | 5 |

| Name | Town | Inclusive Dates of Leadership | Number of Years a Leader |
|---|---|---|---|
| Joseph Gerrish* | Newbury | 1756–1766 | 9 |
| Gideon Lyman | Northampton | 1756 | 1 |
| Elisha Jones | Weston | 1756–1763 | 7 |
| John Murray | Rutland | 1756–1768 | 5 |
| John Chandler | Worcester | 1764 | 1 |
| Samuel Dexter* | Dedham | 1764–1768 | 5 |
| Thomas Gray | Boston | 1764 | 1 |
| Joseph Lee | Cambridge | 1764–1765 | 2 |
| George Leonard* | Norton | 1764–1765 | 2 |
| Samuel Adams | Boston | 1765–1768 | 4 |
| Dudley Atkins | Newburyport | 1765 | 1 |
| Walter Spooner | Dartmouth | 1765–1767 | 3 |
| William Williams | Pittsfield | 1765 | 1 |
| Jonathan Bagley | Almsbury | 1766–1767 | 2 |
| William Browne | Salem | 1766 | 1 |
| Joseph Dorr | Mendon | 1766 | 1 |
| Jedidiah Foster | Brookfield | 1766 | 1 |
| Abijah Fuller | Newton | 1766–1768 | 3 |
| Henry Gardner | Stow | 1766 | 1 |
| John Hancock* | Boston | 1766–1768 | 3 |
| Josiah Johnson | Woburn | 1766 | 1 |
| Jedidiah Prebble* | Falmouth | 1766–1768 | 3 |
| Daniel Epes | Danvers | 1767 | 1 |
| Aaron Wood | Boxford | 1767 | 1 |
| James Weaver | Plymouth | 1768 | 1 |

*Members subsequently elected to Council.

# Tables

**TABLE 4**   Towns With More Than Three Percent of House Leaders

| | I. 1715–1739, Composite | |
| Town | Number of Leaders | Percentage |
| --- | --- | --- |
| Boston | 89 | 32 |
| Charlestown | 20 | 7 |
| Braintree | 18 | 6 |
| Ipswich | 16 | 5 |
| Salem | 15 | 5 |
| Northampton | 15 | 5 |
| Roxbury | 11 | 4 |
| 27 towns* | 109 | 39 |

| | II. 1740–1768, Composite | |
| Town | Number of Leaders | Percentage |
| --- | --- | --- |
| Boston | 114 | 15 |
| Charlestown | 25 | 3 |
| Roxbury | 21 | 3 |
| Barnstable | 21 | 3 |
| Weymouth | 21 | 3 |
| 86 towns† | 570 | 75 |

Source: *Journals of the House of Representatives of Massachusetts Bay* (Boston, 1919–    ).

Notes: House leaders include those who served on fifteen or more committees. Men who were leaders more than once are counted for each year of service.

Administrative work required by warfare after 1740 involved a far greater number of representatives in committees than previously. War made the house an administrative as well as deliberative body. This process undoubtedly strengthened the court faction.

*26 percent of all represented towns that sent members to the General Court.

†70 percent of all represented towns that sent members to the General Court.

# Tables

**TABLE 5** Committee Activity of Members of the House of Representatives

| Year | On Over 15 Committees | On 5 to 15 Committees | On 0 to 5 Committees | Total Members in the House |
|------|------|------|------|------|
| | | Number of House Members | | |
| 1715 | 6 (4) | 7 (4) | 73 (23) | 86 (31) |
| 1716 | 10 (10) | 8 (4) | 71 (24) | 89 (38) |
| 1717 | 8 (7) | 10 (7) | 74 (25) | 92 (39) |
| 1718 | 10 (8) | 12 (10) | 73 (31) | 95 (49) |
| 1719 | 11 (9) | 5 (2) | 80 (29) | 96 (40) |
| 1720 | 12 (9) | 10 (6) | 75 (25) | 97 (40) |
| 1721 (1) | 6 (5) | 17 (9) | 75 (19) | 98 (33) |
| 1721 (2) | 9 (6) | 16 (8) | 68 (20) | 93 (34) |
| 1722 | 12 (11) | 14 (7) | 63 (15) | 89 (33) |
| 1723 | 12 (11) | 19 (12) | 64 (15) | 95 (38) |
| 1724 | 7 (5) | 17 (9) | 74 (22) | 98 (36) |
| 1725 | 6 (5) | 14 (8) | 75 (24) | 95 (37) |
| 1726 | 7 (6) | 20 (14) | 72 (23) | 99 (43) |
| 1727 (1) | 6 (4) | 21 (15) | 65 (23) | 92 (42) |
| 1727 (2) | 7 (4) | 19 (12) | 66 (22) | 92 (38) |
| 1728 | 12 (7) | 15 (10) | 67 (29) | 94 (46) |
| 1729 | 9 (6) | 13 (7) | 67 (27) | 89 (40) |
| 1730 (1) | 10 (6) | 14 (8) | 67 (22) | 91 (36) |
| 1730 (2) | 10 (5) | 11 (5) | 79 (21) | 100 (31) |
| 1731 | 12 (7) | 13 (6) | 69 (21) | 94 (34) |
| 1732 | 11 (8) | 10 (5) | 71 (27) | 92 (40) |
| 1733 | 9 (6) | 18 (10) | 66 (24) | 93 (40) |
| 1734 | 15 (11) | 16 (11) | 68 (36) | 99 (58) |
| 1735 | 15 (14) | 17 (12) | 70 (40) | 102 (66) |
| 1736 | 9 (8) | 20 (14) | 78 (41) | 107 (63) |
| 1737 | 12 (8) | 19 (12) | 75 (37) | 106 (57) |
| 1738 | 11 (9) | 19 (13) | 78 (39) | 108 (61) |
| 1739 | 18 (9) | 16 (14) | 70 (27) | 104 (50) |
| 1740 | 17 (11) | 13 (10) | 78 (36) | 108 (57) |
| 1741 | 24 (15) | 21 (12) | 70 (28) | 115 (55) |
| 1742 | 18 (14) | 17 (10) | 74 (36) | 109 (60) |
| 1743 | 22 (19) | 23 (12) | 60 (31) | 105 (62) |
| 1744 | 26 (25) | 20 (13) | 58 (22) | 104 (60) |
| 1745 | 26 (19) | 27 (9) | 48 (39) | 101 (67) |
| 1746 | 40 (29) | 24 (18) | 45 (20) | 109 (67) |
| 1747 | 31 (27) | 34 (18) | 51 (21) | 116 (66) |

Source: *Journals of the House of Representatives of Massachusetts Bay* (Boston, 1919–    ).

Notes: Before the 1730s, when Governor Belcher distributed appointments to conciliate the country faction, a significant increase or decrease in appointees coincided with the prerogative's strength or weakness. This indicates a general popular awareness of the issues and suggests the representatives truly embodied public opinion among the voters. I do not wish to engage in the democracy versus deference debate, but it seems clear that many towns in Massachusetts elected their deputies based on their politics in addition to general respect for their abilities or social prominence.

Militia officers and justices of the peace are in parentheses.

# Tables

TABLE 5

## –continued–

| | Number of House Members | | | |
|---|---|---|---|---|
| Year | On over 15 Committees | On 5 to 15 Committees | On 0 to 5 Committees | Total Members in the House |
| 1748 | 19 (17) | 27 (21) | 55 (21) | 101 (59) |
| 1749 | 26 (24) | 19 (10) | 57 (28) | 102 (62) |
| 1750 | 26 (21) | 18 (16) | 47 (17) | 91 (54) |
| 1751 | 18 (16) | 14 (11) | 55 (21) | 87 (48) |
| 1752 | 19 (15) | 19 (14) | 50 (29) | 88 (58) |
| 1753 | 22 (16) | 30 (10) | 52 (30) | 104 (56) |
| 1754 | 38 (25) | 32 (23) | 40 (16) | 110 (64) |
| 1755 | 38 (27) | 24  (9) | 38 (19) | 100 (55) |
| 1756 | 40 (28) | 19 (12) | 53 (20) | 112 (60) |
| 1757 | 40 (35) | 23 (18) | 43 (19) | 106 (72) |
| 1758 | 31 (27) | 21 (16) | 50 (17) | 102 (60) |
| 1759 | 38 (34) | 23 (18) | 47 (19) | 108 (71) |
| 1760 | 37 (31) | 22 (18) | 48 (40) | 117 (89) |
| 1761 | 32 (31) | 38 (31) | 54 (29) | 124 (91) |
| 1762 | 24 (23) | 35 (33) | 47 (39) | 106 (95) |
| 1763 | 22 (22) | 43 (38) | 48 (36) | 113 (96) |
| 1764 | 26 (24) | 26 (24) | 62 (40) | 114 (88) |
| 1765 | 25 (22) | 30 (29) | 60 (46) | 115 (97) |
| 1766 | 35 (31) | 24 (20) | 66 (40) | 125 (91) |
| 1767 | 30 (29) | 28 (24) | 60 (48) | 118 (101) |
| 1768 | 21 (20) | 26 (22) | 80 (55) | 127 (97) |

# Tables

TABLE 6     Justices of the Peace in Massachusetts

| County | 1692 | 1702 | 1715 | 1733 | 1761 |
|---|---|---|---|---|---|
| Suffolk | 13 | 19 | 26 | 54 | 133 |
| Essex | 10 | 14 | 20 | 43 | 72 |
| Middlesex | 1 | 12 | 14 | 28 | 53 |
| Hampshire | 5 | 5 | 4 | 10 | 17 |
| Plymouth | 5 | 5 | 5 | 17 | 36 |
| Bristol | 6 | 5 | 15 | 19 | 22 |
| Barnstable | 6 | 4 | 10 | 22 | 22 |
| York | 6 | c. 6* | c. 6 | 17 | 25 |
| Nantucket | 4 | c. 2 | 2 | 4 | 8 |
| Dukes | 3 | c. 3 | 3 | 6 | 8 |
| Worcester | — | — | — | 13 | 40 |
| Lincoln | — | — | — | — | 10 |
| Cumberland | — | — | — | — | 11 |
| Berkshire | — | — | — | — | 5 |
| Total | 59 | c. 75 | c. 105 | 233 | 462 |

| *Population of Massachusetts Divided by Number of J.P.'s†* | 800 | 800 | 800 | 500 | 500 |
|---|---|---|---|---|---|

Sources: Compiled from William H. Whitmore, *The Massachusetts Civil List* (Albany, 1870). Population figures taken from *Historical Statistics of the United States* (Washington, D.C., 1960), p. 756.

*Estimated figures indicated by "c."

†Ratios are to the nearest hundred.

# Tables

## TABLE 7  New Councillors Elected Each Year, 1692–1776

| Year | | Year | | Year | | Year | | Year | |
|---|---|---|---|---|---|---|---|---|---|
| 1693 | 11 [1] | 1709 | 1 | 1725 | 3 [1] | 1741 | 3 [13] | 1758 | 2 |
| 1694 | 4 | 1710 | 0 | 1726 | 3 | 1742 | 15 | 1759 | 4 |
| 1695 | 2 | 1711 | 1 | 1727 | 7 | 1743 | 7 | 1760 | 2 |
| 1696 | 1 | 1712 | 1 | 1728 | 4 | 1744 | 5 | 1761 | 4 |
| 1697 | 0 | 1713 | 2 | 1729 | 2 [2] | 1745 | 1 | 1762 | 2 |
| 1698 | 3 | 1714 | 4 [1] | 1730 | 8 | 1746 | 4 | 1763 | 2 |
| 1699 | 1 | 1715 | 6 [1] | 1731 | 7 | 1747 | 5 | 1764 | 3 |
| 1700 | 3 | 1716 | 3 | 1732 | 2 [1] | 1748 | 0 | 1765 | 2 |
| 1701 | 1 | 1717 | 1 | 1733 | 3 [1] | 1749 | 1 | 1766 | 4 [6] |
| 1702 | 1 | 1718 | 5 [1] | 1734 | 5 | 1750 | 0 | 1767 | 1 [5] |
| 1703 | 7 [5] | 1719 | 2 | 1735 | 4 | 1751 | 0 [1] | 1768 | 1 [5] |
| 1704 | 2 [2] | 1720 | 1 [2] | 1736 | 2 | 1752 | 3 | 1769 | 1 [10] |
| 1705 | 1 | 1721 | 3 [1] | 1737 | 5 [1] | 1753 | 2 | 1770 | 12 [2] |
| 1706 | 4 [2] | 1722 | 4 [2] | 1738 | 4 | 1754 | 1 | 1771 | 2 [2] |
| 1707 | 4 | 1723 | 0 [1] | 1739 | 2 [1] | 1755 | 2 | 1772 | 2 [1] |
| 1708 | 5 [2] | 1724 | 8 | 1740 | 2 [2] | 1756 | 1 | 1773 | 4 [3] |
| | | | | | | 1757 | 3 | 1774 | 2 [13] |

Sources: Compiled from William H. Whitmore, *The Massachusetts Civil List* (Albany, 1870).

Notes: When the country faction was at its strongest, more councillors were voted out each year. In war, generally, few were placed. (The major exception is early in Governor Dudley's administration.) This indicates that the legislature, like the voters, acted on political as well as administrative or deferential criteria in voting for candidates.

The numbers in brackets represent councillors vetoed by the governor.

# Tables

**TABLE 8** Unpublished Surviving Votes Received by Candidates for Election to the Massachusetts Council

| 1726* | Total Voters: 25 Council plus 89 Representatives = 114 | | |
|---|---|---|---|

*Massachusetts Bay*

| | | | |
|---|---|---|---|
| Penn Townsend | 110 | John Turner | 105 |
| William Tailer | 111 | Daniel Oliver | 109 |
| Nathaniel Byfield | 77 | Thomas Palmer | 54: 51: |
| Benjamin Lynde | 112 | | 52: 53† |
| Addington Davenport | 109 | Stephen Sewall | 50: 41: |
| Thomas Hutchinson | 111 | | 18‡ |
| John Clark | 54: 76† | Johnathan Belcher | 49: 38: |
| William Brown | 112 | | 33‡ |
| Thomas Fitch | 107 | John Stoddard | 44: 40: |
| Edmund Quincy | 110 | | 43: 45‡ |
| Adam Winthrop | 70 | Daniel Hubbard | 35‡ |
| Jonathan Dowse | 76 | Anthony Stoddard | 35‡ |
| Paul Dudley | 106 | Daniel Epes | 30‡ |
| Samuel Thaxter | 78 | | |

*Plymouth*

| | | | |
|---|---|---|---|
| John Cushing, Jr. | 102 | Sylvanus Bourne | 90 |
| John Otis | 89 | Edward Winslow | 97 |

*Maine*

| | | | |
|---|---|---|---|
| John Wheelwright | 87 | Eliakim Hutchinson | 52 |
| John Hammond | 84 | | |

*Sagadahoc*

| | | |
|---|---|---|
| Spencer Phips | 86 | |

| 1740§ | Total Voters: 24 Council plus 104 Representatives = 128 | | |
|---|---|---|---|

*Massachusetts*

| | | | |
|---|---|---|---|
| William Dummer | 62‡ | Edward Hutchinson | 122 |
| John Turner | 112 | William Dudley | 92 |

Notes: Published returns appear sporadically in Samuel Sewall's *Diary* and in a fragment of *MHSP* 2nd. ser., 6: 388–389. Most of the returns listed omit one or two names; eighteen councillors came from the old Massachusetts Bay colony, four had to own land in the old Plymouth colony, three in Maine, one in Sagadahoc, and two were elected at large.

Politically controversial or unpopular councillors generally received lower totals than most, who tried to avoid controversial stands. I discuss these at appropriate points in the text.

*Boston Public Library, Manuscript Collection.

†Subsequent ballots, which required fewer voters to obtain a majority.

‡Not elected.

§Lowell Papers 1657–1830, MHS.

TABLE 8      *–continued–*

### 1740§ (cont.)

| | | | |
|---|---|---|---|
| Jonathan Remington | 65 | Anthony Stoddard | 110 |
| John Osborne | 110 | Thomas Berry | 120 |
| Ebenezer Burrill | 120 | Samuel Welles | [?] |
| Francis Foxcroft | 118 | Spencer Phips | 41‡ |
| Ezekiel Lewis | 72 | Nathaniel Hubbard | 117 |
| Josiah Willard | 84 | John Cushing | 121 |
| Benjamin Lynde | 117 | Shubael Gorham | 81 |
| Richard Bill | 121 | William Pepperrell | 111 |
| Samuel Danforth | 122 | Jeremiah Moulton | 100 |
| Paul Dudley | 75 | Samuel Crane | 84 |
| Jacob Wendell | 125 | John Jeffries | 87 |
| Joseph Wilder | 88 | William Brown | 62 |

1741§     Total Voters: 26 Council plus 104 Representatives = 130

*First Ballot*

| | | | |
|---|---|---|---|
| John Turner | 47‡ | Anthony Stoddard | 58‡ |
| Edward Hutchinson | 37‡ | Samuel Welles | 38‡ |
| William Dudley | 52‡ | Thomas Berry | 52‡ |
| Jonathan Remington | 36‡ | Joseph Waldo | 45‡ |
| John Osborne | 55‡ | Benjamin Lynde | 52‡ |
| Ebenezer Burrill | 54‡ | Richard Bill | 57‡ |
| Ezekiel Lewis | 48‡ | [?] Russell | 46‡ |
| Francis Foxcroft | 112 | Samuel Danforth | 125 |
| Josiah Willard | 54‡ | John Jeffries | 31‡ |
| Jacob Wendell | 50‡ | | |

*Second Ballot (120 voters)*

| | | | |
|---|---|---|---|
| James Minot | 73 | Estes Hatch | 71 |
| Henry Burstead | 69 | John Read | 76 |
| John Clark | 70 | Ephraim Wilder | 70 |
| William Foye | 74 | John Greenleaf | 72 |
| Samuel White | 68 | Nathaniel Estes | 71 |
| Edward Goddard | 71 | Edward Hutchinson | 23‡ |
| Robert Auchmuty | 59‡ | John Osborn | 30‡ |
| Samuel Adams | 68 | John Turner | 23‡ |
| Thomas Norton | 75 | Anthony Stoddard | 52‡ |
| William Stoddard | 68 | Richard Bill | 20‡ |
| Peter Chardon | 62‡ | | |

*Third Ballot (123 voters)*

| | | | |
|---|---|---|---|
| Anthony Stoddard | 63 | Robert Auchmuty | 40‡ |
| John Osborne | 49‡ | | |

*Fourth Ballot (126 voters)*

| Richard Bill | 102 | George Leonard | 74 |
|---|---|---|---|
| Nathaniel Hubbard | 102 | Shubael Gorham | 119 |
| John Cushing | 122 | John Otis | 70 |

*Fifth Ballot*

| William Pepperrell | 75 | Dominim Jordan | 74 |
|---|---|---|---|
| Jeremiah Moulton | 110 | John Jeffries | 77 |
| Samuel Came | 68 | | |

*At Large*

| Josiah Willard | 67 | Jacob Wendell | 63 |
|---|---|---|---|

| 1745§ | | (Incomplete) | |
|---|---|---|---|
| John Osborne | 81 | Ebenezer Burrill | 70 |
| John Jeffries | 61 | Samuel Danforth | 103 |
| Francis Foxcroft | 110 | Jonathan Greenleaf | 72 |
| Jacob Wendell | 119 | Paul Dudley | 61 |
| Anthony Stoddard | 72 | Samuel Waldo | 61 |
| Joseph Wilder | 85 | Samuel Watts | 68 |
| William Foye | 115 | Thomas Hubbard | 69 |
| John Read | 103 | Shubael Gorham | 69 |
| Daniel Russell | 94 | George Leonard | 69 |
| Thomas Berry | 74 | John Cushing | 69 |
| Ezekiel Lewis | 66 | | |

1751‖     Total Voters: 25 Council plus 91 Representatives = 116

*Massachusetts*

| John Osborne | 108 | Joseph Wilder | 103 |
|---|---|---|---|
| Ezekiel Lewis | 82 | Benjamin Lynde | 115 |
| Francis Foxcroft | 115 | Daniel Russell | 110 |
| Josiah Willard | 103 | Samuel Danforth | 103 |
| Jacob Wendell | 110 | William Foye | 75 |

§Lowell Papers 1657–1830, MHS.

‖ Curwen Papers vol. 4, American Antiquarian Society.

#Disallowed by Lieutenant-Governor Phips because Royall had schemed to replace John Wentworth, a close ally of Governor Shirley, as Governor of New Hampshire.

**Otis Papers, Box 2, MHS.

TABLE 8                      *–continued–*

*Massachusetts (cont.)*

| | | | |
|---|---|---|---|
| Samuel Watts | 112 | Ezekiel Cheever | 93 |
| Jonathan Greenleaf | 109 | John Pynchon | 97 |
| John Chandler | 111 | Thomas Hutchinson | 70 |
| John Quincy | 115 | Andrew Oliver | 65 |

*Plymouth (108 voters)*

| | | | |
|---|---|---|---|
| John Cushing | 103 | Sylvanus Bourne | 97 |
| George Leonard | 103 | John Otis | 95 |

*Maine (99 voters)*

| | | | |
|---|---|---|---|
| William Pepperrell | 99 | Jeremiah Moulton | 84 |
| John Hill | 91 | | |

*Sagadahoc (108 voters)*

| | |
|---|---|
| John Wheelwright | 63 |

*At Large (113 voters)*

| | | | |
|---|---|---|---|
| James Minot | 98 | Isaac Royall | 57 ‡ |

1764**      125 Voters

*Massachusetts*

| | | | |
|---|---|---|---|
| Thomas Hutchinson | 116 | John Chandler | 98 |
| Benjamin Lynde | 116 | Harrison Gray | 123 |
| Samuel Danforth | 114 | John Russell | 121 |
| Thomas Hubbard | 122 | Thomas Flucker | 120 |
| Isaac Royall | 119 | Israel Williams | 95 |
| John Erving | 122 | Nathaniel Ropes | 120 |
| Andrew Oliver | 123 | Thomas Paine | 113 |
| James Bowdoin | 124 | Timothy Ruggles | 88 |
| Thomas Hancock | 121 | Royall Tyler | 61† |

*Plymouth*

| | | | |
|---|---|---|---|
| George Leonard | 109 | James Otis [Sr.] | 110 |
| Gamaliel Bradford | 116 | Peter Oliver | 58† |

*Maine*

| | | | |
|---|---|---|---|
| John Hill | 113 | John Bradbury | 113 |
| Nathaniel Sparhawk | 113 | | |

*Sagadahoc*

| | |
|---|---|
| William Brattle | 71† |

# Tables

TABLE 9   Towns Formed in Massachusetts, Excluding Maine
1630–1776

| Year | Number of Years | Year | Number of Years | Year | Number of Years | Year | Number of Years |
|------|------|------|------|------|------|------|------|
| 1630 | 5 | 1667 | 2 | 1704 | 0 | 1741 | 2 |
| 1631 | 5 | 1668 | 4 | 1705 | 0 | 1742 | 1 |
| 1632 | 0 | 1669 | 2 | 1706 | 0 | 1743 | 1 |
| 1633 | 2 | 1670 | 1 | 1707 | 0 | 1744 | 0 |
| 1634 | 1 | 1671 | 1 | 1708 | 1 | 1745 | 0 |
| 1635 | 5 | 1672 | 0 | 1709 | 1 | 1746 | 1 |
| 1636 | 2 | 1673 | 3 | 1710 | 1 | 1747 | 0 |
| 1637 | 2 | 1674 | 1 | 1711 | 1 | 1748 | 0 |
| 1638 | 2 | 1675 | 1 | 1712 | 4 | 1749 | 0 |
| 1639 | 4 | 1676 | 0 | 1713 | 3 | 1750 | 0 |
| 1640 | 3 | 1677 | 1 | 1714 | 5 | 1751 | 2 |
| 1641 | 2 | 1678 | 0 | 1715 | 2 | 1752 | 2 |
| 1642 | 2 | 1679 | 0 | 1716 | 0 | 1753 | 7 |
| 1643 | 1 | 1680 | 0 | 1717 | 1 | 1754 | 5 |
| 1644 | 2 | 1681 | 1 | 1718 | 1 | 1755 | 0 |
| 1645 | 2 | 1682 | 1 | 1719 | 1 | 1756 | 0 |
| 1646 | 1 | 1683 | 2 | 1720 | 1 | 1757 | 0 |
| 1647 | 0 | 1684 | 1 | 1721 | 0 | 1758 | 0 |
| 1648 | 1 | 1685 | 1 | 1722 | 0 | 1759 | 4 |
| 1649 | 1 | 1686 | 1 | 1723 | 0 | 1760 | 2 |
| 1650 | 2 | 1687 | 0 | 1724 | 2 | 1761 | 5 |
| 1651 | 1 | 1688 | 0 | 1725 | 3 | 1762 | 9 |
| 1652 | 2 | 1689 | 0 | 1726 | 2 | 1763 | 4 |
| 1653 | 0 | 1690 | 0 | 1727 | 4 | 1764 | 3 |
| 1654 | 0 | 1691 | 1 | 1728 | 2 | 1765 | 10 |
| 1655 | 3 | 1692 | 1 | 1729 | 3 | 1766 | 1 |
| 1656 | 2 | 1693 | 0 | 1730 | 1 | 1767 | 4 |
| 1657 | 0 | 1694 | 6 | 1731 | 1 | 1768 | 3 |
| 1658 | 0 | 1695 | 1 | 1732 | 4 | 1769 | 0 |
| 1659 | 0 | 1696 | 0 | 1733 | 1 | 1770 | 3 |
| 1660 | 1 | 1697 | 1 | 1734 | 3 | 1771 | 3 |
| 1661 | 1 | 1698 | 0 | 1735 | 4 | 1772 | 1 |
| 1662 | 1 | 1699 | 0 | 1736 | 0 | 1773 | 3 |
| 1663 | 0 | 1700 | 0 | 1737 | 0 | 1774 | 4 |
| 1664 | 0 | 1701 | 0 | 1738 | 2 | 1775 | 1 |
| 1665 | 0 | 1702 | 1 | 1739 | 4 | 1776 | 0 |
| 1666 | 0 | 1703 | 0 | 1740 | 1 | | |

Source: Paul Guzzi, *Historical Data Relating to Counties, Cities and Towns in Massachusetts* (Boston, 1975).

Note: Towns were formed either by subdivision of existing communities or as frontier settlements. That few of the former emerged in war years indicates that not only did expansion come to a halt, but quarrels within established towns diminished considerably.

# Tables

TABLE 10  Votes Received by and Factional Affiliation of Successful Candidates for Boston Representatives, 1692–1774

CT = Court, CY = Country, ? = Factional Unknown

### 1692

| | |
|---|---|
| Penn Townsend | CT |
| John Clark | CT |
| Adam Winthrop | CT |
| Theophilius Frary | ? |

### 1693

| | |
|---|---|
| Penn Townsend | CT |
| Edward Bromfield | CT |
| Timothy Thornton | CY |
| Theophilius Frary | ? |

### 1694 and 1695

| | |
|---|---|
| Penn Townsend | CT |
| Edward Bromfield | CT |
| Theophilius Frary | ? |
| Timothy Thornton | CY |

### 1696 (134 voters)

| | | |
|---|---|---|
| John Eyre | 88 | CY |
| Penn Townsend | 85 | CT |
| Nathaniel Byfield | 82 | CT |
| Nathaniel Oliver | 74 | CT |
| Thomas Brattle | 67 | CT* |

### 1697

| | |
|---|---|
| Samuel Legg | CT |
| Penn Townsend | CT |
| Nathaniel Byfield | CT |
| Joseph Bridgham | ? |

### 1698 (340 voters)

| | | |
|---|---|---|
| John Eyre | 218 | CY |
| Samuel Legg | 200 | CT |
| Nathaniel Byfield | 196 | CT |
| Penn Townsend | 172 | CT |
| Francis Foxcroft | 156 | ?* |
| Timothy Thornton | 124 | CY* |
| Edward Bromfield | 119 | CT* |
| Theophilius Frary | 113 | ?* |

### 1699 (323 voters)

| | | |
|---|---|---|
| Andrew Belcher | 239 | CY |
| John Eyre | 178 | CY |
| John White | 175 | CT |
| Theophilius Frary | 165 | ? |

### 1699 (cont.)

| | | |
|---|---|---|
| Edward Bromfield | 156 | CT* |
| Samuel Legg | 146 | CT* |
| Nathaniel Byfield | 122 | CT* |
| Francis Foxcroft | 86 | ?* |

### 1700

| | |
|---|---|
| Timothy Clark | CY |
| Isaiah Tay | CY |
| James Barnes | CY |
| Bozoun Allen | CY |

### 1701

| | |
|---|---|
| John White | CT |
| Andrew Belcher | CY |
| Nathaniel Oliver | CT |
| Samuel Legg | CT |

### 1702

| | |
|---|---|
| John White | CT |
| Samuel Checkley | CT |
| Nathaniel Oliver | CT |
| Samuel Legg | CT |

### 1703-I (244 voters)

| | | |
|---|---|---|
| Samuel Legg | 242 | CT |
| Samuel Checkley | 240 | CT |
| Elisha Cooke, Sr. | 238 | CY |
| Ephraim Savage | 232 | ? |

### 1703-II (459 voters)

| | | |
|---|---|---|
| Samuel Legg | 451 | CT |
| Samuel Checkley | 446 | CT |
| Thomas Oakes | 440 | CY |
| Ephraim Savage | 435 | ? |

### 1704

| | |
|---|---|
| Elisha Cooke | CY |
| Thomas Oakes | CY |
| Ephraim Savage | ? |
| Samuel Checkley | CT |

### 1705–1707

| | |
|---|---|
| Elisha Cooke | CY |
| Elizur Holyoke | CY |
| Ephraim Savage | CY |
| Samuel Checkley | CT |

Source: Boston Records Commissioners' *Reports* (Boston, 1880–1902), vols. 8, 12, 14, 16, 18. Election returns for 1696, 1698, 1699, and 1703 from Samuel Sewall's *Diary*.

*Not elected.

CT = Court, CY = Country, ? = Factional Unknown

| 1708 | | | 1719 (454 voters) | | |
|---|---|---|---|---|---|
| John Clark | CY | | Isaiah Tay | 431 | ? |
| James Barnes | CY | | Elisha Cooke | 293 | CY |
| Thomas Hutchinson | CT | | William Clark | 253 | CY |
| Ephraim Savage | ? | | Oliver Noyes | 238 | CY |

| 1709 | | | 1720 | | |
|---|---|---|---|---|---|
| John Clark | CY | | Isaiah Tay | | ? |
| James Barnes | CY | | Elisha Cooke | | CY |
| Thomas Hutchinson | CT | | William Clark | | CY |
| Thomas Fitch | CT | | Oliver Noyes | | CY |

| 1710 | | | 1721 (247 voters) | | |
|---|---|---|---|---|---|
| John Clark | CY | | John Clark | 235 | CY |
| James Barnes | CY | | Elisha Cooke | 233 | CY |
| Thomas Hutchinson | CT | | William Clark | 233 | CY |
| Ephraim Savage | ? | | William Hutchinson | 223 | CY |

| 1711–1713 | | | 1722 (205 voters) | | |
|---|---|---|---|---|---|
| John Clark | CY | | John Clark | 188 | CY |
| Thomas Hutchinson | CT | | Elisha Cooke | 177 | CY |
| Thomas Fitch | CT | | Isaiah Tay | 158 | ? |
| Addington Davenport | CT | | William Clark | 158 | CY |

| 1714 | | | 1723 (275 voters) | | |
|---|---|---|---|---|---|
| John Clark | CY | | John Clark | 258 | CY |
| Thomas Hutchinson | CT | | Elisha Cooke | 248 | CY |
| Oliver Noyes | CY | | Isaiah Tay | 232 | ? |
| Adam Winthrop | CT | | Ezekiel Lewis | 272 | CY |

| 1715 | | | 1724 (209 voters) | | |
|---|---|---|---|---|---|
| Oliver Noyes | CY | | John Clark | 193 | CY |
| Elisha Cooke, Jr. | CY | | Isaiah Tay | 134 | ? |
| William Payne | CY | | Ezekiel Lewis | 176 | CY |
| Anthony Stoddard | CY | | Thomas Cushing | 132 | CY |

| 1716 | | | 1725 (332 voters) | | |
|---|---|---|---|---|---|
| Oliver Noyes | CY | | Isaiah Tay | 256 | ? |
| Elisha Cooke | CY | | Thomas Cushing | 310 | CY |
| William Payne | CY | | Ezekiel Lewis | 301 | CY |
| Anthony Stoddard | CY | | William Clark | 194 | CY |

| 1717–1718 (votes for 1717) | | | 1726 (203 voters) | | |
|---|---|---|---|---|---|
| Isaiah Tay | 226 | ? | Joseph Wadsworth | 112 | CT |
| Joseph Wadsworth | 185 | CT | Thomas Cushing | 110 | CY |
| Edward Hutchinson | 182 | CT | Ezekiel Lewis | 107 | CY |
| Habijah Savage | 181 | CT | *Second Ballot (181 voters)* | | |
| | | | John Ballantine | 91 | CT |

CT = Court, CY = Country, ? = Factional Unknown

| 1727 | | |
|---|---|---|
| Joseph Wadsworth | 178 | CT |
| Thomas Cushing | 175 | CY |
| Ezekiel Lewis | 164 | CY |
| Nathaniel Greene | 121 | CT |

*1728 (248 voters)*

| | | |
|---|---|---|
| Elisha Cooke | 218 | CY |
| Thomas Cushing | 189 | CY |
| Ezekiel Lewis | 220 | CY |
| Samuel Welles | 159 | CY |

*1729 (192 voters)*

| | | |
|---|---|---|
| Elisha Cooke | 188 | CY |
| Thomas Cushing | 190 | CY |
| Ezekiel Lewis | 190 | CY |
| Samuel Welles | 184 | CY |

*1730 (474 voters)*

| | | |
|---|---|---|
| Elisha Cooke | 465 | CY |
| Thomas Cushing | 471 | CY |
| Ezekiel Lewis | 470 | CY |
| Samuel Welles | 468 | CY |

*1731 (450 voters)*

| | | |
|---|---|---|
| Elisha Cooke | 391 | CY |
| Thomas Cushing | 442 | CY |
| Ezekiel Lewis | 402 | CY |
| Samuel Welles | 366 | CY |

*1732 (655 voters)*

| | | |
|---|---|---|
| Samuel Welles | 537 | CY |
| Thomas Cushing, Jr. | 554 | CY |
| Habijah Savage | 332 | CT |

*Second Ballot (649 voters)*

| | | |
|---|---|---|
| Elisha Cooke | 346 | CY |

*1733 (600 voters)*

| | | |
|---|---|---|
| Elisha Cooke | 541 | CY |
| Samuel Welles | 396 | CY |
| Thomas Cushing, Jr. | 541 | CY |

*Second Ballot (554 voters)*

| | | |
|---|---|---|
| Oxenbridge Thacher | 296 | CY |

*1734 (604 voters)*

| | | |
|---|---|---|
| Elisha Cooke | 346 | CY |
| Thomas Cushing, Jr. | 547 | CY |
| Oxenbridge Thacher | 317 | CY |

*Second Ballot (603 voters)*

| | | |
|---|---|---|
| Samuel Welles | 302 | CY? |

*1735 (517 voters)*

| | | |
|---|---|---|
| Elisha Cooke | 373 | CY |
| Oxenbridge Thacher | 303 | CY |
| Thomas Cushing, Jr. | 464 | CY |
| Timothy Prout | 378 | CY |

*1736 (266 voters)*

| | | |
|---|---|---|
| Elisha Cooke | 250 | CY |
| Oxenbridge Thacher | 200 | CY |
| Thomas Cushing, Jr. | 248 | CY |
| Timothy Prout | 249 | CY |

*1737 (240 voters)*

| | | |
|---|---|---|
| Elisha Cooke | 216 | CY |
| Thomas Cushing, Jr. | 219 | CY |
| Timothy Prout | 127 | CY |

*Second Ballot (221 voters)*

(no choice)

*Third Ballot (179 voters)*

| | | |
|---|---|---|
| Thomas Hutchinson | 134 | CT |

*1738 (481 voters)*

| | | |
|---|---|---|
| Thomas Cushing | 468 | CY |
| Thomas Hutchinson | 359 | CT |
| John Read | 289 | CT |
| Samuel Sewall | 295 | CT |

*1739 (624 to 672 voters)*

| | | |
|---|---|---|
| Thomas Cushing | 624 | CY |
| Edward Bromfield | 430 | CY |
| James Allen | 336 | CY |
| Christopher Kilby | 411 | CY |

*1740 (408 to 426 voters)*

| | | |
|---|---|---|
| Thomas Cushing | 408 | CY† |
| Edward Bromfield | 371 | CY |
| James Allen | 213 | CT |

†Cushing is identified as an important friend of Shirley in a letter from Thomas Hancock to Christopher Kilby, 5 May 1746, Hancock Letter-Book, MHS.

# Tables

TABLE 10 *–continued–*

CT = Court, CY = Country, ? = Factional Unknown

*Second Ballot (507 voters)*

| | | |
|---|---|---|
| Thomas Hutchinson | 273 | CT |

*1741 (495 voters)*

| | | |
|---|---|---|
| Thomas Cushing | 446 | CY |
| Timothy Prout | 414 | CY‡ |
| Edward Bromfield | 431 | CY |
| James Allen | 323 | CT |

*Second Election 1741 (? voters)*

| | | |
|---|---|---|
| Thomas Cushing | 280 | CY |
| Timothy Prout | 267 | CY |
| Edward Bromfield | 200 | CY |
| James Allen | 262 | CT |

*1742 (525 voters)*

| | | |
|---|---|---|
| Thomas Cushing | 510 | CT |
| Timothy Prout | 439 | CY |
| Edward Bromfield | 322 | CT |
| James Allen | 372 | CY |

*1743 (451 voters)*

| | | |
|---|---|---|
| Thomas Cushing | 438 | CT |
| Timothy Prout | 287 | CY |
| Thomas Hutchinson | 422 | CY |
| Andrew Oliver | 309 | CY |

*1744 (532 voters)*

| | | |
|---|---|---|
| Thomas Cushing | 500 | CT |
| Timothy Prout | 434 | CY |
| Thomas Hutchinson | 302 | CY |
| Andrew Oliver | 309 | CY |

*1745 (342 voters)*

| | | |
|---|---|---|
| Samuel Welles | 175 | CT |
| Thomas Cushing | 326 | CT |
| Thomas Hutchinson | 186 | CT |
| Andrew Oliver | 218 | CT |

*1746 (443 voters)*

| | | |
|---|---|---|
| Samuel Welles | 403 | CT |
| Thomas Hutchinson | 249 | CT |
| Andrew Oliver | 413 | CT |
| Thomas Hubbard | 267 | CT |

*1747 (451 voters)*

| | | |
|---|---|---|
| Thomas Hutchinson | 292 | CT |
| Thomas Hubbard | 416 | CT |
| James Allen | 270 | CY |
| Samuel Adams | 281 | CY |

*1748 (723 voters)*

| | | |
|---|---|---|
| Thomas Hubbard | 704 | CT |
| Thomas Hutchinson | 406 | CT |
| James Allen | 389 | CY |
| John Tyng | 369 | CY |

*1749 (684 voters)*

| | | |
|---|---|---|
| Thomas Hubbard | 678 | CT |
| Samuel Waldo | 539 | CY |
| John Tyng | 513 | CY |
| James Allen | 543 | CY |

*1750 (541 voters)*

| | | |
|---|---|---|
| Thomas Hubbard | 520 | CT |
| John Tyng | 348 | CY |
| James Allen | 365 | CY |
| Harrison Gray | 296 | CY |

*1751 (463 voters)*

| | | |
|---|---|---|
| Harrison Gray | 300 | CY |
| James Allen | 253 | CY |
| John Tyng | 263 | CY |

*Second Ballot*

| | | |
|---|---|---|
| Thomas Hubbard "great majority" | | CT |

*1752 (327 voters)*

| | | |
|---|---|---|
| Thomas Hubbard | 270 | CT |
| Harrison Gray | 204 | CY |
| James Allen | 202 | CY |
| John Tyng | 175 | CY |

*1753 (445 voters)*

| | | |
|---|---|---|
| Thomas Hubbard | 411 | CT |
| James Allen | 282 | CY |
| Samuel Welles | 266 | CT |
| James Bowdoin | 249 | CT |

*1754 (603 voters)*

| | | |
|---|---|---|
| Samuel Welles | 392 | CT |
| James Allen | 549 | CY |
| Thomas Hubbard | 586 | CT |
| James Bowdoin | 430 | CT |

*1755 (492 voters)*

| | | |
|---|---|---|
| Thomas Hubbard | 373 | CT |
| John Tyng | 367 | CY |
| James Bowdoin | 411 | CT |
| William Cooper | 259 | CY |

‡Prout criticized the Louisbourg campaign in a letter to William Pepperrell of 3 July 1745, Belknap Papers, vol. 2, MHS.

## Tables

TABLE 10 *—continued—*

CT = Court, CY = Country, ? = Factional Unknown

*1756 (533 voters)*

| Samuel Welles | 301 | CT |
| Thomas Hubbard | 362 | CT |
| John Tyng | 347 | CY |
| Thomas Flucker | 459 | CT |

*1757 (528 voters)*

| Thomas Hubbard | 444 | CT |
| Thomas Flucker | 500 | CT |
| Benjamin Prat | 447 | CY |

*Second Ballot*

| John Tyng | 401 | CY |
| Samuel Welles | 349 | CT* |

*1758 (369 voters)*

| Thomas Hubbard | 300 | CT |
| John Tyng | 234 | CY |
| Thomas Flucker | 291 | CT |
| Benjamin Prat | 309 | CY |

*1759 (469 voters)*

| Thomas Hubbard | 380 | CT |
| John Tyng | 291 | CY |
| Benjamin Prat | 302 | CY |

*Second Ballot*

| Thomas Flucker | | CT |

*1760 (997 voters)*

| Royall Tyler | 863 | CY |
| Thomas Flucker | 629 | CT |
| Samuel Welles | 604 | CT |
| John Philips | 928 | CT |

*1761 (334 voters)*

| John Philips | | CT |
| Royall Tyler | | CY |
| James Otis | | CY |
| Thomas Gray | | CT |

*1762 (629 voters)*

| Royall Tyler | 609 | CY |
| John Philips | 613 | CT |
| James Otis | 619 | CY |
| Thomas Cushing | 400 | CY |

*1763 (1089 voters)*

| Royall Tyler | 809 | CY |
| Thomas Cushing | 908 | CY |
| James Otis | 989 | CY |
| Oxenbridge Thacher | 716 | CY |

*1764 (449 voters)*

| ‖ Royall Tyler | 420 | CY# |
| Thomas Cushing | 373 | CY |
| James Otis | 423 | CY |
| Oxenbridge Thacher | 430 | CY |

*1765*

| Thomas Cushing | NA | CY# |
| Samuel Adams | NA | CY |
| James Otis | NA | CY |
| John Hancock | NA | CY |

*1766 (746 voters)*

| James Otis | 642 |
| Thomas Cushing | 676 |
| Samuel Adams | 671 |
| John Hancock | 437 |

*1767 (618 voters)*

| James Otis | 575 |
| Thomas Cushing | 557 |
| Samuel Adams | 574 |
| John Hancock | 618 |

*1768 (448 voters)*

| James Otis | 410 |
| Thomas Cushing | 433 |
| Samuel Adams | 432 |
| John Hancock | 414 |

*1769 (508 voters)*

| James Otis | 502 |
| Thomas Cushing | 502 |
| Samuel Adams | 503 |
| John Hancock | 505 |

*1770 (513 voters)*

| James Bowdoin | 439 |
| Thomas Cushing | 510 |
| Samuel Adams | 510 |
| John Hancock | 511 |

*Not elected

§After 1764, all candidates represented the country faction.

‖ Elected to council: Thomas Gray . . . . . .352 out of 527 CT replaced Tyler.

#The Town Meeting minutes for the election of these representatives are missing.

CT = Court, CY = Country, ? = Factional Unknown

| *1771 (410 voters)* | | *1773 (419 voters)* | |
|---|---|---|---|
| James Otis | 399 | Thomas Cushing | 418 |
| Thomas Cushing | 410 | John Hancock | 417 |
| John Hancock | 410 | Samuel Adams | 413 |
| Samuel Adams | 403 | William Phillips | 416 |
| *1772 (723 voters)* | | *1774 (536 voters)* | |
| Thomas Cushing | 699 | Thomas Cushing | 524 |
| John Hancock | 690 | Samuel Adams | 535 |
| Samuel Adams | 505 | John Hancock | 536 |
| William Phillips | 668 | William Phillips | 534 |

TABLE 11   Annual Rental Value of Real Estate Assessed Per Household in Boston for All Male Inhabitants, Members of Revolutionary Organizations, and Loyalists Traceable on the 1771 Tax Lists (in Pounds, Massachusetts Money)

| Rental Value (in pounds) | Inhabitants | Sons of Liberty | North End Caucus | Tea Party | Committee of 1775 | Loyalists | Soldiers |
|---|---|---|---|---|---|---|---|
| 0– 5 | 549(26) | 6 (3) | 0 (0) | 8(28) | 0 (0) | 11 (7) | 48(24) |
| 6–10 | 582(28) | 17 (9) | 7(20) | 7(24) | 5(13) | 19(12) | 65(33) |
| 11–15 | 309(15) | 20(11) | 2 (6) | 4(14) | 5(13) | 30(19) | 18 (9) |
| 16–20 | 300(15) | 45(24) | 12(34) | 5(18) | 5(13) | 30(19) | 32(16) |
| 21–30 | 129 (6) | 21(11) | 5(14) | 3(10) | 4(10) | 16(10) | 16 (8) |
| 31–40 | 146 (6) | 37(20) | 4(11) | 1 (4) | 12(30) | 30(19) | 11 (6) |
| over 40 | 91 (4) | 41(21) | 5(14) | 1 (4) | 7(18) | 19(12) | 6 (3) |
| Total | 2106 | 187 | 35 | 29 | 38 | 155 | 196 |

Sources: Inhabitants from 1771 Tax List, Massachusetts Archives 132: 92–147; Sons of Liberty from list in the *Massachusetts Historical Society Proceedings* 5 (1869–1870), 140–142; North End Caucus from list in E. H. Goss, *The Life of Colonel Paul Revere* (Boston, 1902), vol. 2, 635–644; Tea Party participants from Francis G. Drake, *Tea Leaves: Being a Collection of Letters and Documents Relating to the Shipment of Tea to the American Colonies in the Year 1773 By the East India Company* (Boston, 1854), xii–cxiv; Committee of 1775 from list in *Massachusetts Historical Society Proceedings* 12 (1898), 139–141; loyalists from lists in James Stark, *Loyalists of Massachusetts* (Boston, 1902); E. Alfred Jones, *Loyalists of Massachusetts* (London, 1930); Lorenzo Sabine, *Biographical Sketches of the Loyalists of the American Revolution*, 2 vols. (Boston, 1864); Soldiers from data compiled by Philip Swain, Jr. from *Massachusetts Soldiers and Sailors of the American Revolution.*

# TABLE 11 — continued —

| Number of Estates | House Rental | Average Probated Worth |
|---|---|---|
| 3 | £ 0– 5 | £ 33 |
| 14 | £ 6–10 | £ 316 |
| 5 | £11–15 | £ 545 |
| 12 | £16–20 | £1211 |
| 22 | over £20 | £1824 |

Notes: Is the Tax List of 1771 usable? G.B. Warden, in "The Distribution of Property in Boston, 1692–1775," *Perspectives in American History*, 10 (1976): 81–129, and "Inequality and Instability in Eighteenth-Century Boston: A Reappraisal," *Journal of Interdisciplinary History*, 6 (1976): 585–614, has argued that the assessments were so subject to favoritism and political manipulation, and correlated so badly with the actual value of real estate transactions, that the lists cannot be used. However, there is no reason such a correlation should exist because occupancy and not ownership was taxed. As I show in "The Social Structure of Revolutionary Boston: Evidence from the Great Fire of 1760," *ibid.* 10: (1979) 267–278, only about a quarter of all Bostonians owned real property. In fact, comparing probate inventories (volumes 71–74, Old County Court House, Boston) of people who died shortly after the tax lists were drawn up (1771–1774) reveals that, in general, wealthier people lived in more expensive dwellings.

Three cautionary notes: One, some individuals with little wealth occupied expensive dwellings and vice versa, but a clear statistical trend appears that justifies using the tax list for the limited purpose of arguing that, in general, wealthier people lived in more expensive houses. I agree with Warden that the tax list cannot be used to ascertain the structure of inequality, but it does not appear to have distorted the rental value of occupied real estate. Two, when more than one household occupied the same dwelling, they were "bracketed" with one figure assigned for the building. I have divided the value of the house equally in those cases; tax lists from Newburyport and Charlestown in the same series in the Massachusetts Archives indicate that in urban areas equally divided occupancy was almost invariably the rule. (Hitherto, historians have assumed "bracketed" inhabitants were poor and held no wealth at all.) Three, the fact that wealthy people had a much better chance of being entered in probate records casts grave doubts on their use as indices of wealth distribution. On the other hand, those few relatively poorer inhabitants who did get into probate records also appear in the lower reaches of the 1771 tax list, which validates careful use of the latter.

Percentages are in parentheses.

# TABLE 12   Percentages of Loyalists and Sons of Liberty with Mercantile Wealth on the 1771 Boston Tax Register

| | Total | Number with Mercantile Wealth | Percent with Mercantile Wealth |
|---|---|---|---|
| Surviving Assessments | 2106 | 531 | 25 |
| Loyalists | 155 | 77 | 50 |
| Sons of Liberty | 187 | 133 | 71 |

Source: Boston Tax List, Massachusetts Archives 132: 92–147; Sons of Liberty from list in the *Massachusetts Historical Society Proceedings*, 5 (1869–1870), 140–142; loyalists from lists in James Stark, *Loyalists of Massachusetts* (Boston, 1902); E. Alfred Jones, *Loyalists of Massachusetts* (London, 1930); Lorenzo Sabine, *Biographical Sketches of the Loyalists of the American Revolution*, 2 vols. (Boston, 1864).

## TABLE 13    Profile of Tea Party Participants

| Name | Born | Married | Tax Rental (1771) |
|---|---|---|---|
| Joseph Bassett | 1738 | — | |
| Nathaniel Barber | 1738 | 1776 | £37 |
| Henry Bass | 1739 | 1767 | £16 |
| Thomas Bolter | 1735 | 1757 | |
| David Bradlee | 1742 | 1764 | |
| Thomas Bradlee | 1744 | 1765 | £ 3 |
| Nathaniel Bradlee | 1746 | 1769 | |
| Josiah Bradlee | 1754 | 1777 | |
| James Brewer | 1739 | — | |
| Seth Ingersoll Brown | 1750 | 1777 | |
| Stephen Bruce | — | 1776 | £20 (2) |
| Benjamin Burt | 1749 | — | |
| Nicholas Campbell | 1732 | — | |
| Thomas Chase | 1746 | 1771 | |
| Benjamin Clarke | 1748 | 1773 | |
| John Cochran | 1750 | — | |
| Gilbert Colesworthy | 1744 | 1769 | £10 |
| Greshom Collier | — | — | |
| Adam Collson | 1738 | 1764 | £20 (2) |
| John Foster Condy | — | 1777 | £33 (2) |
| Samuel Cooper | 1755 | 1785 | |
| John Crane | 1744 | 1766 | |
| Robert Davis | 1747 | 1768 | |
| Edmund Dolbear | 1757 | 1778 | |
| Joseph Eaton | — | — | |
| Joseph Eayres | 1726 | 1755 | £11 |
| Joseph Eckley | — | 1771 | £ 4  (2) |
| William Ethridge | — | 1764 | |
| Samuel Fenno | 1745 | 1767 | |
| Samuel Foster | 1751 | — | |
| Nathaniel Frothingham | 1746 | — | |
| Nathaniel Greene | 1745 | 1769 | £13 |
| Samuel Hammond | 1748 | — | |
| William Hendley | 1742 | — | |
| Samuel Hobbes | 1750 | — | |
| John Gammell | 1749 | 1773 | |
| Samuel Gore | 1751 | 1774 | |
| Moses Grant | 1743 | 1768 | £47 (2) |
| John Hooton | 1754 | 1785 | £23 |
| Samuel Howard | 1752 | 1777 | £20 |
| Edmund C. Howe | 1742 | 1776 | £ 4 |

Sources: The Boston Birth and Marriage Records, Boston Records Commissioners' *Reports*, vols. 24, 30, 31 (Boston, 1880–1902); Boston Tax List, Massachusetts Archives 132: 92–147; Francis G. Drake, *Tea Leaves: Being a Collection of Letters and Documents Relating to the Shipment of Tea to the American Colonies in the Year 1773 By the East India Company* (Boston, 1854), xii–cxiv.

Note: Taxation is explained in Table 11. Numbers in parentheses indicate the number of households in a dwelling. The value of an individual's dwelling was almost certainly an equal share, or the first figure divided by the second.

| Name | Born | Married | Tax Rental (1771) |
|---|---|---|---|
| Richard Hunnewell | 1736 | 1754 | £11 |
| Richard Hunnewell, Jr. | 1756 | — | |
| Jonathan Hunnewell | 1759 | 1787 | |
| Thomas Hunstable | 1741 | 1766 | £ 5 (3) |
| Abraham Hunt | 1748 | 1771 | £26 (3) |
| Daniel Ingersoll | 1750 | 1774 | |
| David Kinnison | 1736 | — | |
| Joseph Lee | 1735 | 1755 | |
| Amos Lincoln | 1753 | 1781 | |
| Matthew Loring | 1750 | 1786 | |
| Thomas Machin | 1744 | — | |
| Archibald MacNeil | 1750 | — | |
| Ebenezer Mackintosh | 1742 | 1766 | |
| John May | 1748 | 1772 | |
| Thomas Melville | 1751 | 1774 | £ 6 (2) |
| William Molineux | 1726 | 1747 | £47 |
| Thomas Moore | 1753 | 1774 | £13 (2) |
| Anthony Moore | 1752 | — | |
| Joseph Mountford | 1750 | 1777 | £16 (5) |
| Eliphalet Newell | 1735 | 1757 | |
| Joseph Palmer | 1750 | — | |
| Jonathan Parker | 1728 | 1752 | |
| Jonathan Payson | 1743 | 1763 | £27 |
| Samuel Peck | 1734 | 1756 | |
| John Peters | 1727 | 1751 | |
| William Pierce | 1744 | 1765 | |
| Lendall Pitts | 1747 | 1778 | |
| Samuel Pitts | 1745 | — | £27 (3) |
| Thomas Porter | — | — | |
| Henry Prentiss | 1749 | 1775 | £13 |
| Edward Proctor | 1733 | 1754 | £27 (3) |
| Henry Purkett | 1755 | — | |
| John Randall | 1750 | 1778 | |
| Paul Revere | 1735 | 1757 | £20 |
| Joseph Roby | 1724 | 1752 | £37 (2) |
| John Russell | — | — | |
| William Russell | 1748 | 1771 | £16 (4) |
| Robert Sessions | 1752 | — | |
| Joseph Shed | 1732 | 1753 | £ 7 |
| Peter Slater | 1760 | 1784 | |
| Samuel Sloper | 1747 | 1770 | |
| Thomas Spear | — | — | |
| Samuel Sprague | 1753 | 1771 | |
| John Spurr | 1748 | 1783 | |
| James Starr | 1741 | 1767 | |
| Phineas Stearns | 1736 | — | |

TABLE 13        *–continued–*

| Name | Born | Married | Tax Rental (1771) |
|------|------|---------|-------------------|
| Ebenezer Stevens | 1751 | 1774 | |
| Dr. Elisha Story | 1743 | 1767 | |
| James Swan | 1744 | 1776 | |
| Benjamin Tucker | 1733 | — | |
| Thomas Urann | 1750 | 1781 | |
| Josiah Wheeler | 1743 | — | |
| Jeremiah Williams | — | — | |
| Thomas Williams | 1754 | — | |
| Nathaniel Wills | 1755 | — | |
| Joshua Wyeth | 1758 | — | |
| Dr. Thomas Young | 1732 | — | |

## TABLE 14     Profile of the North End Caucus

| Name | Born | Married | Tax Rental (1771) |
|------|------|---------|-------------------|
| John Adams | 1735 | 1764 | |
| Samuel Adams | 1722 | 1744 | |
| Nathaniel Appleton | 1731 | 1754 | £40 |
| Henry Bass | 1739 | 1767 | £16 |
| Nathaniel Barber | 1738 | 1768 | £37 |
| Benjamin Burt | 1729 | 1754 | £16 |
| John Ballard | — | 1751 | £30 (2) |
| John Boit | 1731 | 1769 | £18 |
| Adam Collson | 1738 | 1764 | £20 (2) |
| Thomas Christie | 1736 | 1760 | |
| Dr. Benjamin Church | 1734 | 1758 | |
| John Foster Condy | — | — | £33 (2) |
| Ezekiel Cheever | 1720 | 1743 | £27 |
| Caleb Champney | 1740 | 1773 | £16 (2) |
| Samuel Emmes | — | — | £41 |
| Benjamin Edes | 1732 | 1755 | £20 |
| Joseph Greenleaf | 1720 | 1749 | £20 (2) |
| Moses Grant | 1743 | 1768 | £47 |
| Thomas Hichburn | — | 1758 | £28 |
| Nathaniel Holmes | 1728 | 1747 | £60 |
| William Haskins | — | 1764 | £20 |
| William Hickling | 1742 | — | £27 |
| Gabriel Johonnot | 1748 | 1766 | |
| Benjamin Kent | 1707 | 1740 | £33 (2) |
| Thomas Kendall | 1745 | — | |

Sources: The Boston Birth and Marriage Records, Boston Records Commissioners' *Reports*, vols. 24, 30, 31 (Boston, 1880–1902); Boston Tax List, Massachusetts Archives 132: 92–147; E. H. Goss, *The Life of Colonel Paul Revere* (Boston, 1902), vol. 2, 635–644.

## TABLE 14     *–continued–*

| Name | Born | Married | Tax Rental (1771) |
|------|------|---------|-------------------|
| John Lambert | — | — | £ 8 |
| John Lowell | 1743 | 1768 | £13 |
| William Molineux | 1726 | 1747 | £47 |
| John Merritt | 1738 | 1762 | |
| John Matchett | — | — | £27 |
| Thomas H. Peck | — | — | £53 |
| Isaac Pearse | — | — | £20 |
| Isaac Pearse, Jr. | 1738 | 1786 | £16 (2) |
| Elias Parkman | 1718 | 1746 | £20 (2) |
| Edward Proctor | 1733 | 1754 | £27 (3) |
| John Pulling | 1737 | 1771 | £30 |
| Paul Revere | 1735 | 1757 | £20 |
| Abiel Ruddock | 1742 | — | £33 (2) |
| James Swan | — | — | |
| Jonathan Stoddard | 1739 | — | £20 |
| Elisha Story | 1743 | 1767 | |
| John R. Sigourney | 1740 | 1764 | £40 |
| Asa Stoddard | — | 1765 | £16 |
| Ebenezer Symmes | 1737 | 1763 | |
| John Symmes | 1741 | 1766 | |
| Thomas Urann | 1723 | 1750 | |
| Joseph Warren | 1741 | 1764 | £40 |
| John Winthrop | 1747 | 1778 | |
| Thomas Young | 1732 | — | |

## TABLE 15     Profile of Committee, 1775

| Name | Born | Married | Tax Rental (1771) |
|------|------|---------|-------------------|
| Samuel Barrett | 1738 | 1761 | £47 |
| John Bradford | — | — | |
| Richard Boynton | 1721 | 1745 | |
| Herman Brimmer | 1739 | — | |
| Martin Brimmer | 1737 | 1777 | |
| Samuel Adams | 1722 | 1744 | |
| Benjamin Austin | 1717 | 1742 | £49 |
| Samuel Austin | 1721 | 1746 | £33 |
| John Avery Jr. | 1739 | 1769 | |

Sources: The Boston Birth and Marriage Records, Boston Records Commissioners' *Reports*, vols. 24, 30, 31 (Boston, 1880–1902); Boston Tax List, Massachusetts Archives 132: 92–147; *Massachusetts Historical Society Proceedings* 12 (1898), 139–141.

| Name | Born | Married | Tax Rental (1771) |
|---|---|---|---|
| Peter Boyer | 1726 | 1757 | £36 |
| Nathaniel Barber | 1738 | 1776 | £37 |
| Thomas Boylston | 1721 | 1744 | £27 |
| Henry Bromfield | 1727 | 1749 | |
| Enoch Brown | — | — | |
| Cyrus Baldwin | — | — | £13 |
| Henry Bass | 1739 | 1767 | £16 |
| Joshua Brackett | — | 1763 | £40 |
| Thomas Cushing | 1725 | 1747 | |
| Ezekiel Cheever | 1720 | 1743 | £27 |
| Benjamin Church | 1734 | 1758 | |
| Thomas Chase | 1746 | 1771 | |
| John Foster Condy | — | — | £33 (2) |
| Edward Davis | 1739 | 1766 | £47 |
| Caleb Davis | — | 1760 | |
| William Davis | 1738 | — | £20 |
| Joseph Eayres | 1726 | 1755 | £11 |
| Bossenger Foster | 1743 | 1766 | £27 (2) |
| William Greenleaf | 1738 | — | £47 |
| Joseph Greenleaf | 1720 | 1749 | £20 (2) |
| Moses Gill | 1734 | 1759 | £80 |
| Moses Grant | 1743 | 1768 | £47 (2) |
| Ebenezer Hancock | 1741 | 1767 | £27 |
| James Ivers | — | 1753 | |
| Charles Jarvis | 1748 | 1773 | |
| Thomas Marshall | 1719 | 1746 | £33 |
| John Marston | 1720 | 1749 | £40 |
| Nathaniel Noyes | 1743 | 1771 | £33 (2) |
| William Phillips | 1722 | 1744 | £93 |
| John Pitts | 1737 | 1779 | £27 (3) |
| Samuel Pitts | 1745 | — | £27 (3) |
| William Powell | — | 1759 | |
| Elias Parkman | 1718 | 1746 | £20 (2) |
| Edward Proctor | 1733 | 1754 | £27 (3) |
| Job Prince | — | — | £40 |
| Isaac Pierce | — | — | £20 |
| Samuel Partridge | 1741 | 1768 | £27 |
| Paul Revere | 1735 | 1757 | £20 |
| Abiel Ruddock | 1742 | — | £33 |
| Fortesque Vernon | — | 1738 | £47 |
| Oliver Wendell | 1733 | 1762 | £40 |
| William Whitwell | 1737 | 1762 | £40 |
| Joseph Warren | 1741 | 1764 | £40 |
| Benjamin Waldo | — | 1777 | |
| Jonathan Williams | — | — | £40 |

# Tables

## TABLE 16  Revolutionaries' Ages of Marriage

| Tea Party | Under 25 | 25 to 29 | 30 or over |
|---|---|---|---|
| Before 1760 | 11 | 2 | 0 |
| 1760–1764 | 2 | 1 | 0 |
| 1765–1769 | 9 | 5 | 1 |
| 1770–1774 | 10 | 3 | 0 |
| After 1774 | 4 | 7 | 8 |

| Caucus | Under 25 | 25 to 29 | 30 or over |
|---|---|---|---|
| 1740s | 4 | 2 | 1 |
| 1750s | 5 | 2 | 0 |
| 1760–1764 | 4 | 3 | 0 |
| 1765–1769 | 1 | 5 | 1 |
| 1770–1774 | 0 | 1 | 2 |
| After 1774 | 0 | 0 | 2 |

| Committee | Under 25 | 25 to 29 | 30 or over |
|---|---|---|---|
| 1740s | 6 | 7 | 0 |
| 1750s | 3 | 3 | 0 |
| 1760–1764 | 2 | 2 | 0 |
| 1765–1769 | 1 | 5 | 1 |
| 1770–1774 | 0 | 3 | 0 |
| After 1774 | 0 | 0 | 3 |

| Composite | Under 25 | 25 to 29 | 30 or over |
|---|---|---|---|
| 1740s | 8 | 9 | 1 |
| 1750s | 16 | 6 | 0 |
| 1760–1764 | 7 | 5 | 0 |
| 1765–1769 | 11 | 12 | 1 |
| 1770–1774 | 10 | 6 | 2 |
| After 1774 | 4 | 7 | 11 |

Sources: Boston Records Commissioners' *Reports*, vols. 24, 30, 31; Francis G. Drake, *Tea Leaves: Being a Collection of Letters and Documents Relating to the Shipment of Tea to the American Colonies in the Year 1773 By the East India Company* (Boston, 1854), xii-cxiv; E. H. Goss, *The Life of Colonel Paul Revere* (Boston, 1902), vol. 2, 635–644; *Massachusetts Historical Society Proceedings* 12 (1898), 139–141.

Note: Composite not equal to other three groups added together because of overlapping membership.

# Tables

TABLE 17  Migration into Boston by Household, 1745–1773

| | From Elsewhere in Massachusetts | | | |
|---|---|---|---|---|
| | M | F | M + F | Total |
| 1745 | 2 | 10 (1) | 10 (7) | 22 (8) |
| 1746 | 1 | 1 | 4 (1) | 6 (1) |
| 1747 | 1 | 6 (2) | 11 (8) | 18 (10) |
| 1748 | 3 | 15 (3) | 5 (4) | 23 (7) |
| 1749 | 2 | 15 (2) | 6 (1) | 23 (3) |
| 1750 | 3 | 8 (3) | 5 (4) | 16 (7) |
| 1751 | 3 | 3 (1) | 1 (1) | 7 (2) |
| 1752 | 7 | 15 (3) | 5 (2) | 27 (5) |
| 1753 | 8 (1) | 22 (4) | 22 (18) | 52 (23) |
| 1754 | 10 (4) | 15 (2) | 10 (7) | 35 (13) |
| 1755 | 12 | 21 (2) | 18 (14) | 51 (16) |
| 1756 | 8 (1) | 17 (2) | 18 (8) | 43 (11) |
| 1757 | 18 | 32 (4) | 15 (10) | 65 (14) |
| 1758 | 4 (1) | 38 (14) | 12 (12) | 54 (27) |
| 1759 | 7 | 27 (8) | 13 (8) | 47 (16) |
| 1760 | 12 | 34 (2) | 6 (5) | 52 (7) |
| 1761 | 4 | 18 (4) | 12 (8) | 34 (12) |
| 1762 | 4 | 42 (2) | 20 (14) | 66 (16) |
| 1763 | 2 | 30 (3) | 16 (11) | 48 (14) |
| 1764 | 10 | 30 (5) | 10 (6) | 50 (11) |
| 1765 | 68 (1) | 109 (8) | 29 (19) | 206 (28) |
| 1766 | 64 (2) | 74 (4) | 19 (14) | 157 (20) |
| 1767 | 68 (2) | 72 (4) | 18 (13) | 158 (19) |
| 1768 | 55 (2) | 44 (3) | 31 (11) | 130 (26) |
| 1769 | 69 (3) | 80 (8) | 29 (15) | 178 (26) |
| 1770 | 47 | 39 (4) | 16 (13) | 102 (17) |
| 1771 | 51 (1) | 69 (8) | 19 (16) | 139 (25) |
| 1772 | 52 | 33 | 25 (22) | 110 (22) |
| 1773 | 37 (1) | 16 (2) | 19 (13) | 72 (16) |

Source: Overseers of the Poor Records, Warning Out lists, Massachusetts Historical Society.

Note: M = Male; F = Female; M + F = Husband and Wife. The numbers in parentheses indicate those with dependents.

TABLE 17      *–continued–*

| | M | F | | M + F | | Total | |
|---|---|---|---|---|---|---|---|
| | | | | | From Outside of Massachusetts | | |
| 1745 | 3 | 15 | (6) | 9 | (5) | 27 | (11) |
| 1746 | 3 | 12 | (5) | 5 | (4) | 20 | (9) |
| 1747 | 1 | 6 | (4) | 6 | (2) | 13 | (6) |
| 1748 | 5 | 6 | | 1 | | 12 | (0) |
| 1749 | 6 | 10 | (2) | 3 | (1) | 19 | (3) |
| 1750 | 1 | 3 | | 6 | (1) | 10 | (1) |
| 1751 | 5 | 1 | | 2 | | 8 | (0) |
| 1752 | 11 | 14 | (3) | 6 | (2) | 31 | (5) |
| 1753 | 15 | 13 | (2) | 6 | (4) | 34 | (6) |
| 1754 | 28 (1) | 9 | (2) | 18 | (13) | 55 | (16) |
| 1755 | 15 (2) | 7 | (2) | 21 | (15) | 43 | (19) |
| 1756 | 14 (1) | 17 | (3) | 11 | (8) | 42 | (12) |
| 1757 | 20 | 24 | (5) | 17 | (12) | 61 | (17) |
| 1758 | 11 (1) | 75 | (44) | 15 | (11) | 101 | (56) |
| 1759 | 4 | 21 | (5) | 13 | (7) | 38 | (12) |
| 1760 | 10 | 11 | (2) | 4 | | 25 | (2) |
| 1761 | 5 | 14 | (1) | 2 | (1) | 21 | (2) |
| 1762 | 4 | 10 | (2) | 5 | (4) | 19 | (6) |
| 1763 | 3 (1) | 10 | | 19 | (11) | 32 | (12) |
| 1764 | 10 | 13 | (2) | 10 | (4) | 33 | (6) |
| 1765 | 101 | 29 | (6) | 26 | (12) | 156 | (18) |
| 1766 | 66 (2) | 45 | (6) | 35 | (22) | 146 | (30) |
| 1767 | 119 (6) | 43 | (10) | 37 | (14) | 199 | (30) |
| 1768 | 62 (2) | 23 | (2) | 23 | (16) | 108 | (20) |
| 1769 | 88 | 58 | (15) | 37 | (21) | 183 | (36) |
| 1770 | 91 (1) | 24 | | 27 | (17) | 142 | (18) |
| 1771 | 44 (2) | 30 | (6) | 31 | (18) | 105 | (26) |
| 1772 | 65 (2) | 25 | (4) | 53 | (38) | 143 | (44) |
| 1773 | 40 (1) | 11 | (1) | 12 | (7) | 63 | (9) |

TABLE 17

–continued–

| | M | F | Total | M + F | Total |
|---|---|---|---|---|---|
| 1745 | 5 | 25 (7) | | 19 (12) | 49 (19) |
| 1746 | 4 | 13 (5) | | 9 (5) | 26 (10) |
| 1747 | 2 | 12 (6) | | 17 (10) | 31 (16) |
| 1748 | 8 | 21 (3) | | 6 (4) | 35 (7) |
| 1749 | 8 | 25 (4) | | 9 (2) | 42 (6) |
| 1750 | 4 | 11 (3) | | 11 (5) | 26 (8) |
| 1751 | 8 | 4 (1) | | 3 (1) | 15 (2) |
| 1752 | 18 | 29 (6) | | 11 (4) | 58 (10) |
| 1753 | 23 (1) | 35 (6) | | 28 (22) | 86 (29) |
| 1754 | 38 (5) | 24 (4) | | 28 (20) | 90 (29) |
| 1755 | 27 (2) | 28 (4) | | 39 (29) | 94 (35) |
| 1756 | 22 (2) | 34 (5) | | 29 (16) | 85 (23) |
| 1757 | 38 | 56 (9) | | 32 (22) | 126 (31) |
| 1758 | 15 (2) | 113 (58) | | 27 (23) | 155 (93) |
| 1759 | 11 | 48 (13) | | 26 (15) | 85 (28) |
| 1760 | 22 | 45 (4) | | 10 (5) | 77 (9) |
| 1761 | 9 | 32 (5) | | 14 (9) | 55 (14) |
| 1762 | 8 | 52 (4) | | 25 (18) | 85 (22) |
| 1763 | 5 (1) | 40 (3) | | 35 (22) | 80 (26) |
| 1764 | 20 | 43 (7) | | 20 (10) | 83 (17) |
| 1765 | 169 (1) | 138 (14) | | 55 (31) | 362 (46) |
| 1766 | 130 (4) | 119 (10) | | 54 (36) | 303 (50) |
| 1767 | 187 (8) | 115 (14) | | 55 (27) | 357 (49) |
| 1768 | 117 (4) | 67 (5) | | 54 (37) | 238 (46) |
| 1769 | 157 (3) | 138 (23) | | 66 (36) | 361 (62) |
| 1770 | 138 (1) | 63 (4) | | 43 (30) | 244 (35) |
| 1771 | 95 (3) | 99 (14) | | 50 (34) | 244 (51) |
| 1772 | 117 (2) | 58 (4) | | 78 (60) | 253 (66) |
| 1773 | 77 (2) | 27 (3) | | 31 (20) | 135 (25) |

TABLE 18  Profile of Loyalist Leaders

| Name | Born | Prominence | Family | Success | Residence |
|---|---|---|---|---|---|
| Robert Auchmuty | ? | No | Yes | Yes | Boston–Roxbury |
| William Brattle | 1706 | Yes | Yes | Yes | Cambridge |
| Mather Byles* | 1707 | | | | Boston |
| Richard Clarke | 1711 | No | Yes | Yes | Boston |
| Samuel Curwen | 1715 | No | Yes | Yes | Salem |
| Richard Draper | 1727 | No | No | No | Boston |
| Thomas Flucker | 1719 | Yes | No | Yes | Charlestown–Boston |
| Harrison Gray | 1711 | Yes | No | Yes | Boston |
| Thomas Hutchinson | 1711 | Yes | Yes | Yes | Boston–Milton |
| Daniel Leonard | 1742 | No | Yes | Yes | Taunton |
| Joshua Loring | 1716 | Yes | Yes | Yes | Boston–Roxbury |
| Benjamin Lynde | 1700 | Yes | Yes | Yes | Salem |
| Andrew Oliver | 1706 | Yes | Yes | Yes | Boston–Dorchester |
| Peter Oliver | 1713 | Yes | Yes | Yes | Boston–Middleborough |
| Timothy Ruggles | 1711 | Yes | Yes | Yes | Harwich–Worcester |
| Jonathan Sewall | 1728 | Yes | Yes | Yes | Cambridge |
| Israel Williams | 1709 | Yes | Yes | Yes | Northampton |
| John Worthington | 1719 | Yes | Yes | Yes | Springfield |

Sources: *Dictionary of American Biography*. Biographical information indicated in footnotes to Chapter 1.

*Clergyman

TABLE 19   Profile of Revolutionary Leaders

| Name | Born | Prominence | Family | Success | Residence |
|------|------|------------|--------|---------|-----------|
| John Adams | 1735 | No | No | No | Braintree–Boston |
| Samuel Adams | 1722 | No | No | No | Boston |
| James Bowdoin | 1726 | Yes | No | No | Boston |
| Charles Chauncy* | 1702 | | | | Boston |
| Samuel Cooper* | 1725 | | | | Boston |
| Thomas Cushing | 1725 | No | Yes | No | Boston |
| Benjamin Edes | 1732 | No | No | No | Boston |
| John Gill | 1732 | No | No | No | Boston |
| John Hancock | 1736 | No | Yes | No | Boston |
| Joseph Hawley | 1723 | Yes | No | Yes | Northampton |
| Jonathan Mayhew* | 1720 | | | | Martha's Vineyard–Boston |
| James Otis | 1725 | Yes | Yes | Yes | Barnstable–Boston |
| Josiah Quincy | 1744 | No | Yes | No | Braintree–Boston |
| Paul Revere | 1735 | No | No | No | Boston |
| Isaiah Thomas | 1749 | No | No | No | Boston–Worcester |
| James Warren | 1726 | No | No | Yes | Plymouth |
| Joseph Warren | 1741 | No | No | Yes | Roxbury–Boston |
| Thomas Young | 1732 | No | No | No | New York–Boston |

Sources: *Dictionary of American Biography.* Biographical information indicated in footnote 1 to Chapter 9.

*Clergyman

# BIBLIOGRAPHY

## MANUSCRIPTS

Boston. *Boston Public Library.*

Drake, Samuel Gardner. "Notes on the History of Boston."
Great Fire Manuscripts.
"Illegal Trade." Letters of William Shirley, William Bollan, and
   Robert Auchmuty.

Boston. *Massachusetts Archives.*

Thomas Hutchinson Letter Books, vols. 25–27. (Typescript prepared by
   Catherine Barton Mayo and Malcolm Freiberg at the Massachusetts
   Historical Society.)
Legislative Records of the Massachusetts Council, vols. 6–10.
Massachusetts Archives, vols. 8, 20, 35, 53 (Samuel Waldo Papers), 56,
   102, 106, 107, 108, 130, 132–134 (Tax Register of 1771).

Boston. *Massachusetts Historical Society.*

Jonathan Belcher Letter Book, vol. 5.
Belknap Papers.
Benjamin Colman Papers.
Cooke Family Papers, in Saltonstall Papers.
Customs House Papers.
Joseph Dudley–William Blathwayt Papers.
Diary of Sir Henry Frankland.
Frederick Lewis Gay Transcripts.
Thomas Hancock Letter Book.
Thomas Hutchinson–Lord Loudoun Letters. (Photostat of originals at the
   Huntington Library, San Marino, California).
Hutchinson, Thomas. 'Hutchinson in America.' (Microfilm of Egremont
   Manuscript #2664, British Museum, London).
Henry Knox Papers, vols. 50–51.
Large Manuscripts.

Lowell Family Papers, 1657–1830.
Massachusetts Papers.
Miscellaneous Bound Manuscripts.
Miscellaneous Manuscripts.
Andrew Oliver Letter Book, vols. 1–2.
Otis Papers.
Overseers of the Poor Manuscripts, Warning Out Book, 1745–1793.
Robert Treat Paine Papers.
Pepperrell Papers.
Phips Papers, vols. 1–6.
Ezekiel Price Papers.
Josiah Quincy, Jr. Papers.
Samuel Phillips Savage Papers.
William Shirley–John Thomlinson Letters.
State Papers, vols. 8–12.
William Tailer Letter Book.
Oxenbridge Thacher Papers.
Israel Williams Papers.

Boston. *New England Historic Genealogical Society.*

William Bollan Papers.
Hancock Papers.
Letter of Benjamin Prescott to John Chandler.

Boston. *Suffolk County Courthouse.*

Extended Record Books. Suffolk County Court of Common Pleas,
   Social Law Library.
Suffolk County Probate Records.

*Cambridge, Massachusetts. Houghton Library, Harvard University.*

Francis Bernard Papers, Sparks Manuscripts.
New England Papers, Sparks Manuscripts.
William Palfrey Papers.

*New York, New York. Butler Library, Columbia University.*

Otis Papers.

*Worcester, Massachusetts. American Antiquarian Society.*

Curwen Papers.

## NEWSPAPERS

The *Boston Gazette.*
The *Censor.*
The *Independent Advertiser.*
The *New England Courant.*

## PUBLISHED PRIMARY SOURCES

The eighteenth century works listed below can be found in *Early American
   Imprints, 1639–1800* (Worcester, MA, The American Antiquarian Society,
   1962–   ).
*The First Book of the American Chronicle of the Times.* Boston: 1768.
*A Discourse Addressed to the Sons of Liberty Near the Liberty Tree in Boston.*
   Boston: 1776.
*A Letter to the Freeholders and other Inhabitants of the Province.* Boston: 1742.
*A Letter to the Freeholders and other Qualified Voters.* Boston: 1749.

# Bibliography

*A Letter to the Freeholders and other Inhabitants of the Town of Boston.* Boston: 1750.

*News From Robinson Crusoe's Island.* Boston: 1720.

*A Plea for the Poor and Distressed Town of Boston.* Boston: 1754.

*The Review.* Boston: 1754.

*The Voice of the People.* Boston: 1754.

*Adams Family Correspondence.* Edited by Lyman H. Butterfield. 2 vols. Cambridge: Harvard University Press, 1963.

Adams, John. *A Defence of the Constitutions of the United States.* London: J. Stockdale, 1794.

———. *Diary and Letters.* Edited by Lyman H. Butterfield. 4 vols. Cambridge: Harvard University Press, 1961.

———. *Political Writings.* Edited by George A. Peek. New York: Liberal Arts Press, 1954.

———. *Works.* Edited by Charles Francis Adams. 10 vols. Boston: Little, Brown, 1850–1856.

Adams, Samuel. *Works.* Edited by Harry A. Cushing. 4 vols. New York: G.P. Putnam's Sons, 1904–1908.

Allen, James. *A Letter to the Freeholders and other Inhabitants of Boston.* Boston: 1749.

Andrews, Charles M., ed. *Narratives of the Insurrections.* New York: Charles Scribner's Sons, 1915.

[Ashurst, Sir Henry.] "A Memorial of the Present Deplorable State of New England." *Massachusetts Historical Society Collections* 5th ser. 7 (with a reply by Paul Dudley).

Bailyn, Bernard, ed. *Pamphlets of the American Revolution, 1750–1765.* Cambridge: Harvard University Press, 1965.

Belcher, Jonathan. *Letter Books. Massachusetts Historical Society Collections* 6th ser. 6,7.

Bennett, Joseph. "History of New England." *Massachusetts Historical Society Proceedings* 1st ser. 5(1860–1862):111–121.

*Boston Records Commissioners' Reports.* vols. 8, 10, 12, 14, 16, 18, 24, 30, 31. (Boston Town Records). Boston: 1880–1902.

"Committee of Fifty-Three" (1775). *Massachusetts Historical Society Proceedings* 12(1898):179–181.

Cooke, Elisha. *Mr. Cooke's Just and Seasonable Vindications. . . .*Boston: 1720.

Cooper, Samuel. *The Crisis.* Boston: 1754.

———. *A Sermon on the Commencement of the Constitution and the Inauguration of the New Government.* Boston: 1780.

*Danforth Papers. Massachusetts Historical Society Collections* 2nd ser. 8.

Davis, Andrew M., ed. *Colonial Currency Reprints.* 4 vols. Boston: Prince Society, 1910–1911.

Douglass, William. *A Summary, Historical and Political . . . of North America.* 2 vols. London: 1755.

Drake, Francis S., ed. *Tea Leaves: Being a Collection of Letters and Documents Relating to the Shipment of Tea to the American Colonies. . . .*Boston: A.O. Crane, 1884.

Dudley Papers in Appendix to *Winthrop Papers. Massachusetts Historical Society Collections* 6th ser. 3.

Dudley-Mather Letters. *Massachusetts Historical Society Collections* 1st ser. 4.

Fletcher, William. *The Good of the Country Impartially Considered.* Boston: 1754.

Ford, Worthington C., et. al., eds. *Journals of the House of Representatives of Massachusetts Bay.* Boston: Massachusetts Historical Society, 1919– .

# Bibliography

Goodell, Abner C., and Ames, Ellis, eds. *The Acts and Resolves of the Province of Massachusetts Bay.* 21 vols. Boston: Wright and Potter, 1869–1922.

Greene, Evarts B., and Harrington, Virginia. *American Population Before the Federal Census of 1790.* New York: Columbia University Press, 1932.

Hall, Michael G., et. al., eds. *The Glorious Revolution in America.* Chapel Hill: University of North Carolina Press, 1964.

Thomas Hinckley Papers. *Massachusetts Historical Society Collections* 4th ser. 2.

Hutchinson, Thomas. *The History of the Colony and Province of Massachusetts Bay.* Edited by Lawrence Shaw Mayo. 3 vols. Cambridge: Harvard University Press, 1936.

————. "Strictures Upon the Declaration of the Congress at Philadelphia . . ." Reprinted in *The Remembrancer* 4(1776):26–42.

Jensen, Merrill, ed. *Tracts of the American Revolution.* Indianapolis: Bobbs-Merrill, 1967.

*Diaries of Benjamin Lynde and Benjamin Lynde, Jr.* Edited by Fitch E. Oliver. Boston: Private Printing, 1880.

*Maine Historical Society Collections* 2nd ser. 4,6.

Mason, Bernard, ed. *The American Colonial Crisis: The Daniel Leonard-John Adams Letters to the Press, 1774–1775.* New York: Harper and Row, 1972.

Mather, Cotton. "Account of His Father's Agency."*Massachusetts Historical Society Collections* 1st. ser. 8.

————. *The Deplorable State of New England. Massachusetts Historical Society Collections* 5th. ser. 7.

————. *Diary.* 2 vols. Boston: The Prince Society, 1911–1912.

————. *Selected Letters.* Edited by Kenneth Silverman. Baton Rouge: Louisiana State University Press, 1971.

Mather, Increase. "Autobiography." Edited by Michael G. Hall. *American Antiquarian Society Proceedings* 71(1961).

*Mather Papers. Massachusetts Historical Society Collections* 4th ser. 1.

*Jasper Mauduit Papers. Massachusetts Historical Society Collections* 74(1918).

Morgan, Edmund S., ed. "Thomas Hutchinson and the Stamp Act." *New England Quarterly* 21(1948):468–489.

Morris, Richard B., ed. *The American Revolution: 1763–1783.* New York: Harper and Row, 1970.

Murray, James. *Letters of James Murray, Loyalist.* Boston: Printed but not published, 1901.

Samuel Nowell paper. *Massachusetts Historical Society Collections* 5th ser. 1.

North End Caucus Records. In *The Life of Colonel Paul Revere* by E.H. Goss. Vol. 2, pp. 635–644. Boston: J.G. Cupples, 1902.

Oliver, Peter. *Origin and Progress of the American Rebellion.* Edited by Douglass Adair and John A. Schutz. Stanford: Stanford University Press, 1961.

Quincy, Josiah, Jr., ed. *Reports of Cases Argued and Adjudged in the Superior Court of Judicature of the Province of Massachusetts Bay, 1761–1772.* Boston: Little, Brown, 1865.

Randolph, Edward. *Edward Randolph: Including His Letters and Official Papers.* Edited by Robert Noxon Toppan. 7 vols. Boston: The Prince Society, 1898–1909.

Rowe, John. *Diary and Letters of John Rowe.* Edited by Anne Cunningham. Boston: W.B. Clarke, 1903.

Sainsbury, W. Noel, et. al., eds. *Calendar of State Papers, Colonial Series.* 45 vols. London: The Public Record Office, 1869–

*Saltonstall Papers.* Edited by Robert L. Moody. *Massachusetts Historical Society Collections* 80(1975).

# Bibliography

Sewall, Samuel. *The Diary of Samuel Sewall.* Edited by M. Halsey Thomas. 2 vols. New York: Farrar, Straus and Giroux, 1973.

———. Fragment from Samuel Sewall's Diary. *Massachusetts Historical Society Publications* 2nd ser. 6(1895):388.

———. *Letter Book.* 2 vols. *Massachusetts Historical Society Collections* 6th ser. 1,2.

Shirley, William. *Correspondence of William Shirley.* Edited by C.H. Lincoln. 2 vols. New York: Macmillan, 1912.

Shurtleff, Nathaniel B., ed. *Records of the Governor and Company of the Massachusetts Bay.* 6 vols. Boston: W. White, 1853–1854.

Slotkin, Richard, and Folsom, James K., eds. *So Dreadfull a Judgement: Puritan Responses to King Philip's War.* Middletown, Connecticut: Wesleyan University Press, 1978.

Sons of Liberty List. *Massachusetts Historical Society Proceedings* 1st ser. 6(1869–1870):140–142.

Stachiw, Myron, ed. *Massachusetts Soldiers and Sailors During the French and Indian Wars 1722–1870.* Boston: New England Historic Genealogical Society, 1979.

*The Warren-Adams Letters.* 2 vols. Boston: Massachusetts Historical Society, 1917.

Walker, Williston, ed. *Creeds and Platforms of Congregationalism.* New York: Charles Scribner's Sons, 1893.

Welsteed, William. *The Dignity and Duty of Civil Magistrates.* Boston: 1751.

Whitmore, William H., ed. *Andros Tracts.* 3 vols. Boston: The Prince Society, 1868–1874.

———. *The Massachusetts Civil List, 1630–1774.* Albany: J. Munsell, 1870.

Winthrop, John. *The History of New England.* Edited by James K. Hosmer. 2 vols. New York: Charles Scribner's Sons, 1908.

*Winthrop Papers. Massachusetts Historical Society Collections* 5th ser. 6,8; 6th ser. 5.

*Year Book of the Society of Colonial Wars in the Commonwealth of Massachusetts.* Boston: The Society of Colonial Wars, 1899.


## PUBLISHED SECONDARY WORKS

Adams, James Truslow. *The Founding of New England.* Boston: Atlantic Monthly, 1921.

Akagi, Roy H. *The Town Proprietors of the New England Colonies: A Study of Their Development, Origins, Activities, and Controversies, 1620–1770.* Philadelphia: University of Pennsylvania Press, 1924.

Allen, David Grayson. "The Zuckerman Thesis and the Process of Legal Rationalization in Provincial Massachusetts." *William and Mary Quarterly* 3rd. ser. 29(1972):443–460.

Amann, Peter, ed. *The Eighteenth Century Revolution: French or Western?.* Boston: D.C. Heath and Co., 1963..

Anderson, George. "Ebenezer Mackintosh."*Publications of the Colonial Society of Massachusetts* 16(1924–26):15–64, 348–361.

Andrews, Charles M. "The Boston Merchants and the Non-Importation Movement." *Publications of the Colonial Society of Massachusetts* 19(1916–1917):119–129.

———. *The Colonial Period of American History.* Vol. 4. New Haven: Yale University Press, 1938.

Aston, Trevor, ed. *Crisis in Europe.* London: Routledge and Kegan, 1965.

Bailyn, Bernard. *The New England Merchants in the Seventeenth Century.* Cambridge: Harvard University Press, 1957.

# Bibliography

———. *The Ordeal of Thomas Hutchinson.* Cambridge: Harvard University Press, 1974.

———. *The Origins of American Politics.* New York: Random House, 1969.

———. "Religion and Revolution: Three Biographical Studies." *Perspectives in American History.* 4(1970):85–122.

Baldwin, Alice M. *The New England Clergy and the American Revolution.* New Haven: Yale University Press, 1936.

Banks, Charles E. "Religious 'Persecution' as a Factor in Emigration to New England, 1630–1640," with a rebuttal from Samuel Eliot Morison. *Massachusetts Historical Society Proceedings* 63 (1929–1930): 136–144.

Barnes, Viola F. *The Dominion of New England.* New Haven: Yale University Press, 1923.

———. "The Rise of William Phips." *New England Quarterly* 1(1928):271–299.

Barrow, Thomas. *Trade and Empire: The British Customs Service in Colonial America, 1660–1775.* Cambridge: Harvard University Press, 1967.

Battis, Emory. *Saints and Sectaries: Anne Hutchinson and the Antinomian Controversy in the Massachusetts Bay Colony.* Chapel Hill: University of North Carolina Press, 1962.

Baxter, William T. *The House of Hancock: Business in Boston, 1724–1775.* Cambridge: Harvard University Press, 1950.

Berthoff, Rowland. *An Unsettled People: Social Order and Disorder in American History.* New York: Harper and Row, 1971.

Billias, George A. "The First Un-Americans: The Loyalists in Revolutionary Historiography." In *Perspectives on Early American History,* edited by Alden T. Vaughan and George A. Billias. New York: Harper and Row, 1973.

———. *Massachusetts Land Bankers of 1740.* Orono: University of Maine Studies, 1954.

Bonomi, Patricia U. *A Factious People.* New York: Columbia University Press, 1971.

———. "The Middle Colonies: Embryo of the New Political Order." In *Perspectives on Early American History,* edited by Alden T. Vaughan and George A. Billias, pp. 63–92. New York: Harper and Row, 1973.

Bowes, Francis T. "The Loyalty of Barnstable in the Revolution." *Publications of the Colonial Society of Massachusetts* 25(1974):325–348.

Boyer, Paul. "Borrowed Rhetoric: The Massachusetts Excise Controversy of 1754." *William and Mary Quarterly* 3rd. ser. 21(1964):328–351.

Boyer, Paul, and Nissenbaum, Stephen. *Salem Possessed: The Social Origins of Witchcraft.* Cambridge: Harvard University Press, 1974.

Breen, Timothy. *The Character of a Good Ruler: A History of Puritan Political Ideas 1630–1730.* New Haven: Yale University Press, 1970.

———. "Who Governs?: The Town Franchise in Seventeenth Century Massachusetts." *William and Mary Quarterly* 3rd. ser. 27(1970):460–474.

Breen, Timothy, and Foster, Stephen. "Moving to the New World: The Character of Early Massachusetts Immigration." *William and Mary Quarterly* 3rd. ser. 30(1973):189–222.

———. "The Puritans' Greatest Achievement: A Study of Social Cohesion in the Seventeenth Century." *Journal of American History* 60(1973):5–22.

Brennan, Ellen. *Plural Office-Holding in Massachusetts, 1760–1780.* Chapel Hill: University of North Carolina Press, 1945.

Bridenbaugh, Carl. *Cities in the Wilderness: The First Century of Urban Life in America, 1625–1742.* 2nd. ed. New York: Knopf, 1955.

# Bibliography

——. *Mitre and Sceptre: Transatlantic Faiths, Ideas, Perspectives, and Politics, 1689-1775*. New York: Oxford University Press, 1962.

——. *Vexed and Troubled Englishmen*. New York: Oxford University Press, 1968.

Brock, Leslie V. *The Currency of the American Colonies, 1700-1764*. New York: Arno, 1975.

Brown, B. Katherine. "The Controversy over the Franchise in Puritan Massachusetts." *William and Mary Quarterly* 3rd ser. 33(1976):212-241.

——. "Freemanship in Puritan Massachusetts." *American Historical Review* 59(1954):865-883.

Brown, B. Katherine, et. al. Exchange of letters on the Massachusetts franchise. *William and Mary Quarterly* 3rd ser. 25(1968):330-339.

Brown, Richard D. *Revolutionary Politics in Massachusetts: The Boston Committee of Correspondence and the Towns, 1772-1774*. Cambridge: Harvard University Press, 1970.

Brown, Wallace. *The Good Americans*. New York: Morrow, 1969.

——. *The King's Friends*. Providence: Brown University Press, 1965.

Buel, Richard. "Democracy and the American Revolution: A Frame of Reference." *William and Mary Quarterly* 3rd. ser. 21(1964):165-190.

Burrows, Edwin G., and Wallace, Michael. "The American Revolution: The Ideology and Psychology of National Liberation." *Perspectives in American History* 6(1972):167-306.

Bushman, Richard. "Corruption and Power in Provincial America." In *The Development of a Revolutionary Mentality: Library of Congress Symposium on the American Revolution*. Washington: Library of Congress, 1972.

——. *From Puritan to Yankee: Character and Social Order in Connecticut, 1690-1765*. Cambridge: Harvard University Press, 1967.

Calhoon, Robert M. *The Loyalists in Revolutionary America*. New York: Harcourt, Brace, and Jovanovich, 1973.

Clark, Charles E. *The Eastern Frontier: The Settlement of New England, 1610-1763*. New York: Knopf, 1970.

Cobban, Alfred. *Reinterpretation of the French Revolution*. New York: Norton, 1968.

——. *The Social Interpretation of the French Revolution*. Cambridge, England: Cambridge University Press, 1969.

Colegrove, Kenneth. "New England Town Mandates." *Publications of the Colonial Society of Massachusetts* 21(1920):411-449.

Cook, Edward M., Jr. *The Fathers of the Towns: Leadership and Community Structure in Eighteenth Century New England*. Baltimore: Johns Hopkins University Press, 1976.

Craven, Wesley F. *White, Red, and Black*. Charlottesville: University of Virginia Press, 1971.

Darnton, Robert. "The High Enlightenment and the Low Life of Literature in Pre-Revolutionary France." *Past and Present* 51(1971):81-115.

Davidson, Philip. *Propaganda and the American Revolution*. Chapel Hill: University of North Carolina Press, 1941.

Davis, Andrew M. "Boston Banks and Those Who Were Interested in Them." *New England Historical and Genealogical Register* 57(1903):279-281.

——. *Currency and Banking . . . in Massachusetts Bay*. 2 vols. New York: Macmillan, 1901.

——. "Provincial Banks, Land and Silver." *Publications of the Colonial Society of Massachusetts* 3(1905-1907):2-41.

Demos, John. "Underlying Themes in the Witchcraft of Seventeenth Century New England." *American Historical Review* 85(1970):1311-1326.

# Bibliography

Dexter, Frank B. Yale Biographies and Annals, 1701–1745. New York: H. Holt, 1885.

Dickerson, Oliver M. "The Writs of Assistance as a Cause of the American Revolution." In The Era of the American Revolution, edited by Richard B. Morris, pp. 40–71. New York: Columbia University Press, 1939.

Dictionary of American Biography. New York: Charles Scribner's Sons, 1928–1961.

Dorfman, Joseph. The Economic Mind in American Civilization, 1606–1865. New York: Viking, 1946.

Dow, George F. "Shipping and Trade in Early New England." Massachusetts Historical Society Proceedings 64(1932):185–201.

Drake, Samuel Adams. The Border Wars of New England. New York: Charles Scribner's Sons, 1897.

Dudley, Dean. The History of the Dudley Family. Wakefield, MA: Private Printing, 1886.

Dunn, Richard S. Puritans and Yankees: The Winthrop Dynasty of New England, 1630–1717. Princeton: Princeton University Press, 1967.

———. Sugar and Slaves: The Rise of the Planter Class in the British West Indies. Chapel Hill: University of North Carolina Press, 1973.

Eccles, W.J. France in America. New York: Harper and Row, 1972.

Eliot, John. Biographical Dictionary. Salem: Cushing and Appleton, 1809.

Elkins, Stanley, and McKitrick, Eric. "The Founding Fathers: Young Men of the Revolution." Political Science Quarterly 76(1961):81–116.

Ernst, Joseph, and Egnal, Marc. "An Economic Interpretation of the American Revolution." William and Mary Quarterly 3rd. ser. 29(1972):3–32.

Felt, Joseph. A Historical Account of Massachusetts Currency. Boston: Perkins and Marvin, 1839.

Fiore, Jordan D. "The Temple-Bernard Affair: A Royal Customs House Scandal in Essex County." Essex Institute Historical Collections 90(1954):58–83.

Fischer, David H. Growing Old in America. New York: Oxford University Press, 1977.

Forbes, Esther. Paul Revere and the World He Lived In. Cambridge: Houghton Mifflin, 1942.

Ford, Worthington C. "The Governor and Council of Massachusetts Bay, 1714 to 1715." Massachusetts Historical Society Proceedings 15(1901):327–361.

Foster, Robert, and Greene, Jack P., eds. Preconditions of Revolution in Early Modern Europe. Baltimore: Johns Hopkins University Press, 1970.

Foster, Stephen. "The Massachusetts Franchise in the Seventeenth Century." William and Mary Quarterly 3rd. ser. 24(1967):613–623.

———. Their Solitary Way: The Puritan Social Ethic in the First Century of Settlement. New Haven: Yale University Press, 1971.

Freiberg, Malcolm. "How to Become a Royal Governor: Thomas Hutchinson of Massachusetts." Review of Politics 21(1959):646–656.

Fuess, Claude M. "Witches at Andover." Massachusetts Historical Society Proceedings 70(1913):5–20.

Gillis, John. Youth in History: Tradition and Change in European Age Relations, 1770 to the Present. New York: Academic Press, 1974.

Gipson, Lawrence H. The British Empire Before the American Revolution. 15 vols. New York: Knopf, 1936–1972.

———. The Coming of the Revolution. New York: Harper and Row, 1954.

———. "Thomas Hutchinson and the Albany Plan of Union." Pennsylvania Magazine of History and Biography 84(1950):5–35.

Greene, Jack P. "An Uneasy Connection: An Analysis of the Preconditions of the American Revolution." In Essays on the American Revolution, edited by Stephen G. Kurtz and James H. Hutson. Chapel Hill: University of North Carolina Press, 1973.

# Bibliography

————. "Changing Interpretations of Early American Politics." In *The Reinterpretation of Early American History*, edited by Ray Allen Billington. San Marino: The Huntington Library, 1966.

————. "The Growth of Political Stability: An Interpretation of Political Development in the Anglo-American Colonies, 1660–1760." In *The American Revolution: A Heritage of Change*, edited by John Parker and Carol Urness. Minneapolis: University of Minnesota Press, 1975.

————. "Political Mimesis: A Consideration of the Historical Origins of Legislative Behavior in the British Colonies in the Eighteenth Century." *American Historical Review* 75(1969):337–360.

————. *The Quest for Power: The Lower Houses of Assembly in the Southern Royal Colonies.* Chapel Hill: University of North Carolina Press, 1963.

————. "Search for Identity: An Interpretation of Selected Patterns of Social Response in Eighteenth Century America." *Journal of Social History* 4(1972):189–220.

————. "Social Context and the Causal Pattern of the American Revolution: A Preliminary Consideration of New York, Virginia, and Massachusetts." In *La Révolution Américaine et L'Europe*, pp. 25–63. Paris: Editions du Centre National de la Recherche Scientifique, 1979.

Greven, Philip. *Four Generations: Population, Land, and Family in Colonial Andover.* Ithaca: Cornell University Press, 1970.

————. *The Protestant Temperament: Patterns of Child-Rearing, Religious Experience, and the Self in Early America.* New York: Knopf, 1977.

Gross, Robert. *The Minutemen and Their World.* New York: Hill and Wang, 1976.

Haffenden, Philip S. *New England in the English Nation.* Oxford, England: Clarendon Press, 1974.

Hall, David. *The Faithful Shepherd: The New England Ministry in the Seventeenth Century.* Chapel Hill: University of North Carolina Press, 1972.

Hall, Michael G. *Edward Randolph and the American Colonies, 1676–1703.* Chapel Hill: University of North Carolina Press, 1960.

Hall, Van Beck. *Politics Without Parties: Massachusetts, 1780–1791.* Pittsburgh: University of Pittsburgh Press, 1972.

Haller, William, Jr. *The Puritan Frontier: Town Planning and New England Colonial Development, 1630–1660.* New York: Columbia University Press, 1951.

Hatch, Nathan O. "The Origins of Civil Millennialism in America: New England Clergymen, War with France, and the Revolution." *William and Mary Quarterly* 3rd. ser. 31(1974):407–430.

————. *The Sacred Cause of Liberty.* New Haven: Yale University Press, 1977.

Heimert, Alan. *Religion and the American Mind from the Great Awakening to the American Revolution.* Cambridge: Harvard University Press, 1966.

Henretta, James. "Economic Development and Social Structure in Colonial Boston." *William and Mary Quarterly* 3rd. ser. 22(1965):75–92.

————. "Families and Farms: Mentalité in Pre-Industrial America." *William and Mary Quarterly* 3rd. ser. 35(1978):6–29.

————. "Salutary Neglect": *Colonial Administration Under the Duke of Newcastle.* Princeton: Princeton University Press, 1972.

*Historical Statistics of the United States.* Washington: United States Government Printing Office, 1960. 2d. ed., 1970.

Hoerder, Dirk. *Mobs and People: Crowd Action in Massachusetts During the Revolution 1765–1780.* Berlin: Free University of Berlin, 1971.

Holifield, E. Brooks. "On Toleration in Massachusetts." *Church History* 38(1969):1–13.

Hutson, James, H. *Pennsylvania Politics, 1746–1770.* Princeton: Princeton University Press, 1972.

# Bibliography

Isaac, Rhys. "Order and Growth, Authority and Meaning in Colonial New England." *American Historical Review* 76(1971):728–737.

Jacobson, David L. *The English Liberation Heritage*. Indianapolis: Bobbs-Merrill, 1965.

Jedrey, Christopher M. *The World of John Cleaveland*. New York: Norton, 1979.

Jernegan, Marcus W. *The Labouring and Dependent Classes in Early America*. New York: Ungar, 1960, original ed., 1931.

Jones, E. Alfred. *Loyalists of Massachusetts*. London: The St. Catherine's Press, 1930.

Jordan, Winthrop D. "Familial Politics: Thomas Paine and the Killing of the King, 1776." *Journal of American History* 60(1973):294–308.

Kershaw, Gordon E. *"Gentlemen of Large Property and Judicious Men": The Kennebeck Proprietors, 1749—1775.* Somersworth, NH: New Hampshire Publishing Company, 1975.

Kimball, Everett. *The Public Life of Joseph Dudley*. New York: Longmans, Green, 1911.

Koehler, Lyle. "The Case of the American Jezebels: Anne Hutchinson and the Female Agitation During the Years of Antinomian Turmoil, 1636–1640." *William and Mary Quarterly* 3rd. ser. 31(1974):55–78.

Kulikoff, Allan. "The Progress of Inequality in Revolutionary Boston." *William and Mary Quarterly* 3rd. ser. 28(1971):375–412.

Labaree, Benjamin W. *Patriots and Partisans: The Merchants of Newburyport, 1764–1815.* Cambridge: Harvard University Press, 1962.

Laslett, Peter. *The World We Have Lost*. New York: Charles Scribner's Sons, 1965.

Lax, John, and Pencak, William. "The Knowles Riot and the Crisis of the 1740s in Massachusetts." *Perspectives in American History* 10(1976):163–214.

Leach, Douglas. "Brothers in Arms? — Anglo-American Friction at Louisbourg, 1745–1746." *Massachusetts Historical Society Proceedings* 89(1977):36–54.

Lefavour, Henri. "The Proposed College in Hampshire County in 1762." *Massachusetts Historical Society Proceedings* 66(1930):53–80.

Lemisch, Jesse. "Jack Tar in the Streets: Merchant Seamen in the Politics of the American Revolution." *William and Mary Quarterly* 3rd. ser. 25(1967):371–407.

Levy, Leonard W. *Legacy of Suppression: Freedom of Speech and Press in Early American History*. Cambridge: Harvard University Press, 1960.

Lewis, Theodore B., and Webb, Linda M. "Voting for the Massachusetts Council of Assistants, 1674–1686: A Statistical Note." *William and Mary Quarterly* 3rd. ser. 30(1973):625–634.

Lokken, Roy. "The Concept of Democracy in Colonial Political Thought." *William and Mary Quarterly* 3rd. ser. 16(1959):568–580.

Lockridge, Kenneth. "Land Population, and the Evolution of New England Society, 1630–1790, and an Afterthought." In *Colonial America: Essays in Political and Social Development*, edited by Stanley N. Katz. Boston: Little, Brown, 1971.

———. *A New England Town: The First Hundred Years: Dedham, 1636–1736.* New York: Norton, 1970.

Lovejoy, David S. *The Glorious Revolution in America*. New York: Harper and Row, 1972.

Lounsberry, Alice. *Sir William Phips*. New York: Charles Scribner's Sons, 1941.

Lucas, Paul R. "Colony or Commonwealth: Massachusetts Bay, 1661–1666." *William and Mary Quarterly* 3rd. ser. 24(1967):88–107.

———. "An Appeal to the Learned: The Mind of Solomon Stoddard." *William and Mary Quarterly* 3rd ser. 30(1973):257–292.

Lynn, Kenneth S. *A Divided People*. Westport, CT: The Greenwood Press, 1977.

# Bibliography

Maier, Pauline. *From Resistance to Revolution: Colonial Radicals and the Development of an Opposition to Britain, 1765–1776.* New York: Knopf, 1972.

Main, Jackson T. *The Social Structure of Revolutionary America.* Princeton: Princeton University Press, 1965.

Malone, Joseph J. *Pine Trees and Politics.* Seattle: University of Washington Press, 1964.

Martin, James K. *Men in Rebellion.* New Brunswick, NJ: Rutgers University Press, 1973.

Matossian, Mary K., and Schaeffer, William D. "Family Fertility and Political Violence 1700–1900." *Journal of Social History* 11(1977):137–178.

Matthews, Albert C. "Colonel Elizeus Burgess." *Publications of the Colonial Society of Massachusetts* 19(1916–1917):360–372.

———. "Joyce, Jr."*Publications of the Colonial Society of Massachusetts* 8(1906):90–104.

Merritt, Bruce G. "Anglicanism and Social Conflict in Revolutionary Deerfield." *Journal of American History* 57(1970):277–289.

Merritt, Richard L. *Symbols of American Community, 1735–1775.* New Haven: Yale University Press, 1966.

Miller, John C. "Religion, Finance, and Democracy in Massachusetts." *New England Quarterly* 6(1932):29–54.

Miller, Perry. "The Half-Way Covenant." *New England Quarterly* 6(1933):676–715.

———. *The New England Mind: From Colony to Province.* Cambridge: Harvard University Press, 1953.

———. *Orthodoxy in Massachusetts, 1630-1650.* Cambridge: Harvard University Press, 1933.

Morgan, Edmund S. *American Slavery, American Freedom.* New York: Norton, 1975.

———. "The Labor Problem at Jamestown, 1607-1618." *American Historical Review* 76(1971):595–611.

———. *Puritan Dilemma: The Story of John Winthrop.* Boston: Little, Brown, 1958.

———. *The Puritan Family: Religion and Domestic Relations in Seventeenth Century England.* New York: Harper and Row, 1966.

———. *Roger Williams: Church and State.* New York: Harcourt, Brace, and World, 1967.

———. *Visible Saints: The History of a Puritan Idea.* New York: New York University Press, 1963.

Morison, Samuel Eliot. *Builders of the Bay Colony.* Boston: Houghton Mifflin, 1930.

———. "A Quarter-Century of Expansion and Inflation in New England, 1713-1745." *Publications of the Colonial Society of Massachusetts* 19(1916–1917):271–272.

———. *Three Centuries of Harvard.* Cambridge: Harvard University Press, 1936.

Morris, Richard B. *Government and Labor in Early America.* New York: Columbia University Press, 1946.

Murdock, Kenneth. *Increase Mather: The Foremost American Puritan.* Cambridge: Harvard University Press, 1921.

Murrin, John M. "The Legal Transformation: Bench and Bar of Eighteenth Century Massachusetts." In *Colonial America: Essays in Political and Social Development,* edited by Stanley N. Katz, pp. 417–449. Boston: Little, Brown, 1971.

———. "Review Essay." *History and Theory* 11(1972):226–275.

Namier, Sir Lewis. *England in the Age of the American Revolution.* London: Macmillan, 1930.

# Bibilography

——. *The Structure of Politics at the Accession of George III.* London: Macmillan, 1929.

Nash, Gary B. "Social Change and the Growth of Pre-Revolutionary Urban Radicalism." In *The American Revolution,* edited by Alfred F. Young. De Kalb, Illinois: University of Northern Illinois Press, 1976.

——. *The Urban Crucible: Social Change, Political Consciousness, and the Origins of the American Revolution.* Cambridge: Harvard University Press, 1979.

——. "Urban Wealth and Poverty in Pre-Revolutionary America."*Journal of Interdisciplinary History* 6(1975–1976):545–584.

Nelson, William E. *The Americanization of the Common Law.* Cambridge: Harvard University Press, 1975.

Nelson, William H. *The American Tory.* Oxford, England: Clarendon Press, 1961.

Nettels, Curtis P. *The Money Supply of the American Colonies Before 1720.* Madison: University of Wisconsin Press, 1943.

Newcomer, Lee N. *The Embattled Farmers: A Massachusetts Countryside in the American Revolution.* New York: King's Crown Press, 1953.

Noble, John. "The Libel Suit of *Knowles* v. *Douglass,* 1748, 1749." *Publications of the Colonial Society of Massachusetts* 1(1895–1897):213–240.

Oberholzer, Emil. *Delinquent Saints: Disciplinary Action in the Early Congregational Churches of Massachusetts.* New York: Columbia University Press, 1956.

Olson, Alison G. *Anglo-American Politics: 1660–1775.* New York: Oxford University Press, 1973.

——. "The British Government and Colonial Union, 1754." *William and Mary Quarterly* 3rd. ser. 17(1960):22–34.

Osgood, Herbert L. *The American Colonies in the Eighteenth Century.* 4 vols. New York: Columbia University Press, 1924–1925.

——. "The American Revolution."In *Causes and Consequences of the American Revolution,* edited by Esmond Wright. New York: Quadrangle, 1966.

Paige, Lucius R. *History of Cambridge, Massachusetts.* Boston: H.O. Houghton, 1877.

Palfrey, John G. *A Compendious History of New England.* 5 vols. Boston: Little, Brown, 1856–1890.

Patterson, Stephen. *Political Parties in Revolutionary Massachusetts.* Madison: University of Wisconsin Press, 1973.

Pargellis, Stanley. *Lord Loudoun in North America.* New Haven: Yale University Press, 1933.

Paynton, Clifford T., and Blackey, Robert, eds. *Why Revolution: Theories and Analyses.* Cambridge: Schenckman and Company, 1976.

Pencak, William. "The Revolt Against Gerontocracy: Genealogy and the Massachusetts Revolution." *National Genealogical Society Quarterly* 66(1978):291–304.

——. "The Social Structure of Revolutionary Boston: Evidence From the Great Fire of 1760 Manuscripts." *Journal of Interdisciplinary History* 10(1979):267–278.

——. "Thomas Hutchinson's Fight Against Naval Impressment." *New England Historical and Genealogical Register* 132(1978):25–36.

——. "Warfare and Political Change in Mid-Eighteenth Century Massachusetts." *Journal of Commonwealth and Imperial History* 8(1980):51–73.

# Bibliography

Plumb, J.H. *The Growth of Political Stability: England, 1675–1725.* Baltimore: Penguin, 1967.

Pole, J.R. "Historians and the Problem of Early American Democracy." *American Historical Review* 67(1962):626–646.

Pope, Robert G. *The Halfway Covenant: Church Membership in Puritan New England.* Princeton: Princeton University Press, 1969.

Rakove, Jack N. *The Beginnings of National Politics.* New York: Knopf, 1979.

Roberts, Oliver A. *The History of the Ancient and Honorable Artillery Company.* 4 vols. Boston: A. Mudge and Son, 1895–1901.

Rogers, Alan. *Empire and Liberty: American Resistance to British Authority, 1755–1763.* Berkeley: University of California Press, 1974.

Rutman, Darrett B. *American Puritanism.* Philadelphia: Lippincott, 1970.

———. *Winthrop's Boston: Portrait of a Puritan Town.* Chapel Hill: University of North Carolina Press, 1965.

Sabine, Lorenzo. *Biographical Sketches of the Loyalists of the American Revolution.* 2 vols. Boston: Little, Brown, 1864.

Sachs, William S. "Agricultural Conditions in the Northern Colonies Before the American Revolution." *Journal of Economic History* 12(1953):274–293.

Schutz, John A. "Imperialism in Massachusetts During the Governorship of William Shirley, 1741–1746." *Huntington Library Quarterly* 22(1960):217–236.

———. "Succession Politics in Massachusetts, 1730–1741." *William and Mary Quarterly* 3rd. ser. 15(1958):508–520.

———. *Thomas Pownall: British Defender of American Liberty.* Glendale, CA: A.H. Clark Company, 1951.

———. *William Shirley: King's Governor of Massachusetts.* Chapel Hill: University of North Carolina Press, 1961.

Shy, John. *Toward Lexington: The Role of the British Army in the Coming of the American Revolution.* Princeton: Princeton University Press, 1965.

Sibley, John L., and Shipton, Clifford K. *Biographical Sketches of Those Who Attended Harvard College.* Boston: Massachusetts Historical Society, 1873–

Simmons, Richard C. "The Founding of the Third Church in Boston." *William and Mary Quarterly* 3rd. ser. 26(1969):241–252.

———. "Freemanship in Early Massachusetts: Some Suggestions and a Case Study." *William and Mary Quarterly* 3rd. ser. 24(1967):422–428.

Simpson, Alan. "How Democratic Was Roger Williams?" *William and Mary Quarterly* 3rd. ser. 13(1956):53–57.

Smith, James Morton, ed. *Seventeenth Century America: Essays in Colonial History.* Chapel Hill: University of North Carolina Press, 1959.

Smith, Jonathan. "Toryism in Worcester County During the War for Independence." *Massachusetts Historical Society Proceedings* 48(1915):15–25.

Snell, Ronald K. "Freemanship, Officeholding, and the Town Franchise in Seventeenth Century Springfield, Massachusetts." *New England Historical and Genealogical Register* 133(1979):163–179.

Sosin, Jack. *Whitehall and the Wilderness.* Lincoln, Nebraska: University of Nebraska Press, 1961.

Stark, James. *The Loyalists of Massachusetts.* Boston: J.H. Stark, 1902.

Stearns, Raymond P., and Brawner, David W. "New England Church 'Relations' and Continuity in Early Congregational History." *American Antiquarian Society Proceedings* 75(1965):13–45.

Steele, I.K. *Politics of Colonial Policy: The Board of Trade in Colonial Administration 1696–1720.* Oxford, England: The Clarendon Press, 1968.

Syrett, David. "Town Meeting Politics in Massachusetts: 1776–1786." *William and Mary Quarterly* 3rd. ser. 21(1964):352–366.

# Bibliography

Talmon, J.L. *The Origins of Totalitarian Democracy*. London: Secker and Warburg, 1955.

Taylor, Robert J. *Western Massachusetts in the Revolution*. Providence: Brown University Press, 1954.

Thayer, Theodore. "The Army Contractors for the Niagara Campaign, 1755–1756." *William and Mary Quarterly* 3rd. ser. 14(1957):31–46.

Tully, Charles, ed. *The Formation of the Nation State in Western Europe*. Princeton: Princeton University Press, 1975.

Towner, Lawrence. "Fondness for Freedom: Servant Protest in Puritan Society." *William and Mary Quarterly* 3rd. ser. 19(1962):201–220.

Tudor, William. *The Life of James Otis*. Boston: Wells and Lilly, 1823.

Twombly, Robert, and Moore, George. "Black Puritan: The Negro in Seventeenth Century Massachusetts." *William and Mary Quarterly* 3rd. ser. 24(1967):224–242.

Ubbelohde, Carl. *The Vice-Admiralty Courts and the American Revolution*. Chapel Hill: University of North Carolina Press, 1960.

Wall, Robert E., Jr. *Massachusetts Bay: The Crucial Decade, 1640–1650*. New Haven: Yale University Press, 1972.

———. "The Massachusetts Bay Colony Franchise in 1647." *William and Mary Quarterly* 3rd. ser. 27(1970) 136–144.

Waller, George M. *Samuel Vetch: Colonial Enterpriser*. Chapel Hill: University of North Carolina Press, 1960.

Wallett, Francis G. "The Massachusetts Council, 1766–1774: The Transformation of a Conservative Institution." *William and Mary Quarterly* 3rd. ser. 6(1949):605–627.

Warden, G.B. *Boston: 1689–1776*. Boston: Little, Brown, 1970.

———. "Inequality and Instability in Eighteenth Century Boston: A Reappraisal." *Journal of Interdisciplinary History* 6(1975–1976): 585–620.

Washburn, Wilcomb. *The Governor and the Rebel: A History of Bacon's Rebellion in Virginia*. Chapel Hill: University of North Carolina Press, 1957.

Waters, John J., Jr. "Hingham, Massachusetts, 1631–1661: An East Anglican Oligarchy in the New World." *Journal of Social History* 1(1968):351–370.

———. "James Otis, Jr., An Ambivalent Revolutionary." *History of Childhood Quarterly* 1(1973):142–150.

———. "Patrimony, Succession, and Social Stability: Guilford, Connecticut in the Eighteenth Century." *Perspectives in American History* 10(1976):131–160.

Waters, John J., Jr., and Schutz, John A. "Patterns of Massachusetts Colonial Politics: The Writs of Assistance and the Rivalry Between the Otis and Hutchinson Families." *William and Mary Quarterly* 3rd. ser. 24(1967):543–567.

Webb, Stephen Saunders. "William Blathwayt, Imperial Fixer: From Popish Plot to Glorious Revolution." *William and Mary Quarterly* 3rd. ser. 25(1968):3–21.

Williamson, Chilton. *American Suffrage: From Property to Democracy, 1760–1860*. Princeton: Princeton University Press, 1960.

Wood, George. *William Shirley, Governor of Massachusetts, 1741–1748*. New York: Columbia University Studies, 1920.

Wroth, L. Kinvin. "The Massachusetts Vice-Admiralty Courts." In *Law and Authority in Colonial America*, edited by George A. Billias, pp. 32–73. Barre, MA: Barre Publishers, 1965.

Zemsky, Robert. *Merchants, Farmers, and River Gods*. Boston: Gambit, 1971.

# Bibliography

A NOTE ON UNPUBLISHED SECONDARY WORKS
AND WORK IN PROGRESS

Despite the large amount of published material, much of the best work remains in unpublished papers and dissertations. Several exciting studies now in progress employ prosopographical and quantitative techniques to provide a precise picture of both leaders and followers in revolutionary and provincial politics. This book is richer because colonial Americanists share their own sense of community; I am grateful to all who have communicated their work and ideas to me.

Of work already completed, John M. Murrin's "Anglicizing an American Colony: The Transformation of Provincial Massachusetts" (Ph.D. thesis, Yale University, 1966) and Robert Dinkin's "Massachusetts: A Deferential or a Democratic Society?" (Ph.D. thesis, Columbia University, 1968) valuably supplement Schutz's biography of Shirley by pointing out trends that ensured a measure of cooperation at mid-century between Massachusetts and Britain. Kerry Trask's "In the Pursuit of Shadows: A Study of Collective Hope and Despair in Provincial Massachusetts During the Era of the Seven Year War, 1748 to 1765" (Ph.D. thesis, University of Minnesota, 1971) successfully combines political and intellectual history. Two of the best works on society and politics from 1660 to 1692 remain unpublished: Theodore B. Lewis's "Massachusetts and the Glorious Revolution, 1660–1692" (Ph.D. thesis, University of Wisconsin-Madison, 1967) and Timothy H. Breen's "Crisis of Authority: Local Factions and the Collapse of the Massachusetts Government, 1686–1692" (Paper presented at the Convention of the Organization of American Historians, Atlanta, Georgia, 8 April 1977). Charles Sanford's "The Days of Jeremy Dummer" (Ph.D. thesis, Harvard University, 1952) has a great deal of information on 1689–1730, and Malcolm Freiberg's "Prelude to Purgatory: Thomas Hutchinson in Massachusetts Politics" (Ph.D. thesis, Brown University, 1950) contains material on Hutchinson's early career not found in Bailyn's fine biography. Robert E. Wall, Jr.'s "Members of the Massachusetts General Court, 1634–1686," (Ph.D. thesis, Yale University, 1965) provided information on the seventeenth century deputies. William S. Sachs's "The Business Outlook in the Northern Colonies, 1750–1775," (Ph.D. thesis, Columbia University, 1957), provides evidence of almost continuous economic difficulty in Boston. A paper I was privileged to hear, David Flaherty's "Crime in Provincial Massachusetts," read at the convention of the Organization of American Historians, 19 April 1975, served as an important reference point for this study's material on violence. I am indebted to John M. Murrin for giving me a copy of a paper I trust will not remain unpublished much longer: "The Shaping of Provincial America, 1675–1725," presented at the Newberry Library Conference, May 1978. This work provides a context for dividing colonial history into periods, which influenced my own setting off of post-1740 America.

Work still in progress includes two dissertations that will do much to further the understanding of Massachusetts between 1750 to 1775. First, Fred Anderson's forthcoming Harvard thesis will discuss soldiers and military experience during the French and Indian War. I have used a superb unpublished paper, "The Experience of Provincial Military Service in Eighteenth Century North America: The Crown Point Expedition of 1756 as a Test Case." Similarly, John Tyler at Princeton University is writing an in-depth study of the Boston merchant community in the 1760s to provide information on many individuals. This forthcoming thesis is tentatively entitled "The First Revolution: The Boston Mercantile Community and the Acts of Trade, 1760–1774." An M.A. and B.A. thesis have done much to further my understanding of two crucial episodes: Cathy Mitten's "The New England Paper Money Tradition and the Massachusetts Land Bank of 1740" (Master's thesis, Columbia University, 1979) supercedes all other accounts, and Scott McIntosh's, "Liberty and Property, Arms and God: The Political Culture of the Crowds in Boston, 1765–1775" (Bachelor's thesis, Princeton University, 1979) is, with the previously cited *Urban Crucible* (1979) by Gary B. Nash, the most convincing synthesis of the conflict and consensus views of this subject for Boston that I've seen. Ralph J. Crandall's "New England's Haven Port" (Ph. D.

# Bibliography

thesis, University of Southern California, 1975) demonstrates how Charlestown underwent similar urban difficulties as Boston in the mid-eighteenth century. The information on Bostonians who moved to or from the surrounding towns comes from a paper by Ralph J. Crandall and William Pencak "Metropolitan Boston Before the American Revolution: An Urban Interpretation of the Imperial Crisis,"read at the Colonial Society of Massachusetts, Boston, MA, February 1979. Finally, several undergraduates at Tufts University, where I was a visiting assistant professor for 1978–1979, undertook documentary research which has greatly aided my own: Frank Granato on the split during the Great Awakening in the Second Church of Boston, and David Ader, Arthur Landry, David Peete, and Philip Swain on the socio-economic status and age of soldiers in revolutionary Medford, Roxbury, and Dedham. I thank Philip Swain, most especially, for sharing his promising work on the Boston soldiers during the American Revolution.

The proportion of this bibliography devoted to unpublished work illustrates the fascination eighteenth century Massachusetts politics still possesses, as well as the enormous amount of data yet to be mined and the numerous subjects not as yet adequately investigated. Massachusetts had over two hundred towns by 1780 and had fought six major wars in a century. Much about the effects of these wars on towns, families, regions, individuals, migration, economic life, and inter-colonial relations remains unknown. Now that we possess the techniques for using vital records and genealogical data to trace the movement and behavior of ordinary people, the social history of war in provincial Massachusetts can at last be written. I hope this work, which is primarily political history, can help provide a framework within which much of this detailed local research can be conducted. And may I remind researchers that there are also twelve other colonies whose wartime experiences need attention.

# INDEX

Abenaki Indians, 16, 36. *See also* Indians
Abercromby, Gen. James, 149, 154
Abolitionist movement, 1
Acadia. *See* Nova Scotia
Acts of Trade, 15, 20, 44, 93, 100, 119, 159, 164
Adams, John, 1, 124–125, 166, 202, 205, 221; and natural rights doctrine, 198, 223–226 passim; on Hutchinson, 202, 203, 204; desires loyalists' deaths, 204; on liberty, 216, 217; on commerce, 219; on England's interest in the colonies, 219
Adams, Samuel, Jr., 1; revolutionary philosophy of, 116, 125–127, 194, 217, 219, 220, 224, 225; on poverty, 219
Adams, Samuel, Sr., 107
Addington, Isaac, 40
Ages, of revolutionaries and loyalists, 201–206, 214
Agriculture, 10
Albany Congress, 135
Allen family, 100
Allen, James, 95, 127, 128–129, 133, 135, 153, 213
American Board of Customs, 165
American Revolution: Massachusetts' role in, 1, 7; causes of, 115, 122; preconditions, in Massachusetts, 121, 171, 233–239; and revolutionary ideology, 125–129, 137, 166; social conflict during, 191, 197, 201; crowd violence and, 191–196; Massachusetts' makers of, 196–206; and class, as factor, 197–201; and ages of revolutionaries and loyalists, as factor, 201–206, 213–214; psychological interpretations of, 202–205; disproportionate participation of Boston in, 205; leaders of, compared with Tories, 213–228; and meaning of "liberty" to revolutionaries and loyalists, 216–218; and rational processes of revolutionaries and loyalists, 224–226; sense of historical mission in, 226–227; compared with French Revolution, 228–229
Amherst, Gen. Jeffrey, 149, 154, 159
Andover, 12, 24
Andros, Sir Edmund, 13–18 passim, 27, 38
Anglicans. *See* Church of England
Annapolis (Nova Scotia), 123
Anne, Queen, 65
Apthorp, Charles, 130
Apthrop, East, 168
Ashurst, Sir Henry, 39–40, 43–44, 49, 50, 72
Ashurst, William, 53, 65

# Index

Assistants, House of. *See* General Court
Astraea, H.M.S., 189
Attucks, Crispus, 204
Auchmuty, Robert, 107, 117, 218, 222
Austin, Ebenezer, 187

Bacon's Rebellion, 9
Ballantine, John, 70
Bankers and banking, 5, 63–66, 67, 68, 72, 73–75, 103; and Silver Bank, 103–105. *See also* Land Bank controversy; Merchants; Money
Bank of England, 130
Bankruptcies, individual, 155–156, 163
Baptists, 11, 12, 100
Barnstable County, 3, 161
Barrington family, 158
Barrons, Benjamin, 165
Bass, Henry, 198
Bedford, John Russell, Duke of, 115, 129
Belcher, Andrew, 45, 51, 64, 186
Belcher, Gov. Jonathan, 3, 53, 62, 78, 81–83, 117, 137, 158, 189; and currency crises, 64, 65, 73, 74; administration of, 91–107, 115, 161, 175
Belcher, Jonathan, Jr., 101
Bellomont, Gov. Richard Coote, Earl of, 4, 36; administration of, 39–43, 45, 64; death of, 43
Berkshire County, 3
Bernard, Gov. Francis, 4, 150, 153, 154, 171, 197, 198, 226; administration of, 158–163; and merchants, 163–167; and religious strife, 169; and Hutchinson, 172–173 and Stamp Act issue, 173–174
Billings, William, 193
Bimetallism, 133, 150, 169, 172. *See also* Money
Blacks, 121, 123, 191, 197
Blanchard, John, 188
Blathwayt, William, 44
Boardman, Andrew, 170
Board of Trade, 18, 38; recalls Phips, 27; attitude toward Massachusetts, 37, 44–45; and Harvard College Charter, 39; rebuked by Bellomont, 42; and Dudley, 44–50 passim; attempts to reform colonial government, 61, 78; and salary debate, 62, 80, 92, 95, 96; and currency crisis, 102, 118; rebukes Bernard, 159

Bollan, William, 119, 122, 129, 130, 132, 137, 152, 153, 163, 165, 166–167
Boston, 11, 12, 40, 52–53, 64, 74, 79; founding of, 1; families of, 3; town meeting in, 66, 70, 75, 80, 81, 93, 95, 124, 197–198, 214, 223; politics in, 68–70, 81–82, 94 (*see also* Boston Caucus); illegal lumber trade in, 119; economic distress in, and military enlistments, 121–122, 205; impressment resistance in, 124, 156, 185–186, 189, 190; opposition to excise tax in, 133–134; bankruptcies in, after French and Indian War, 155–156; recession-caused violent crime in, 170; Great Fire of 1760, 170 (*see also* Crowds); burning of Old State House, 189; migration into, 202; disproportionate participation of, in American Revolution, 205
Boston Caucus, 62, 68–70, 81, 82, 93–95, 97, 98, 186, 191, 200
*Boston Gazette,* 127, 204
Boston Massacre, 1, 194, 196, 216, 226
Boston Tea Party, 1, 198, 199, 200, 201, 205, 238
Bourne, Sylvanus, 161
Bowdoin, James, 107, 165, 170, 214
Bowers, Jerathmeel, 171
Braddock, Gen. James, 115, 133, 136
Bradford, Gov. William, 45
Bradstreet, Gov. Simon, 13, 14, 15, 17, 25, 26
Brattle Street Church, 44
Brattle, William, 93, 97, 161, 188, 191–192, 228
Brenton, Jahleel, 22, 27, 37, 166, 186
Bribery, election, 69
Bridger, John, 42, 66–68, 70, 72, 73, 98
Brinley, Francis, 17
Bristol County, 3, 161
British Quartering Act of 1694, 156–157
Brodbent, Josiah, 186
Brown, Benjamin, 106
Browne, William, 15, 118
Bullivant, Benjamin, 16, 17
Bunker Hill, 205
Burgess, Elizeus, 65
Burnet, Gov. William, 78, 80–83, 91, 92, 94, 95
Bute, John Stuart, Earl of, 226–227

Byfield, Nathaniel, 22, 26, 27, 40, 46, 47, 64, 65, 67, 79, 93, 98

Cambridge, 66, 72, 168, 196. *See also* Harvard College
Canada, 9, 51–52, 77–78, 121, 133, 158; and Indians in Maine, 16; Crown Point expedition, 119, 122–123, 128, 136, 137, 154; end of French rule in, 149
Caner, Rev. Henry, 168, 201
Cape Breton, 152; expedition, 120, 122, 123, 124–125
Cartagena expedition, 121
Castle William, 40, 47, 52, 186
*Censor* (journal), 192, 217
Chambers, Capt. Charles, 187
Chandler, John, 97, 106, 118
Charles II, colonial rule, 11–12, 13
Charlestown, 52, 124, 187
Charter of 1629, and moderate/old-charter factions, 13–16, 18, 38; plea for restoration of, 43
Charter of 1691, 18
Chauncy, Rev. Charles, 120, 168, 219, 226
Choate, John, 97, 129
*Chronicle,* 192
Church of England, 12, 13, 15, 17, 44, 45, 100, 127, 150, 168–169
Church membership, 10–13
Clark, John, 79
Clarke, William, 69, 93
Class, socioeconomic, and participation in American Revolution, 197–201
Clergy: as revolutionaries, 7, 214, 228, 229; oppose accommodation with England, 11; censure General Court for religious tolerance, 12, 13; and moderate/old-charter division, 13–14; form interim government in 1689, 16; and Harvard College, 20, 39; and King George's War, 120; and religious dissent in 1760s, 168–169
Cockle, Alexander, 165
Colman and Sparhawk, 156
Colman, Benjamin, 92, 102, 188–189
Colman, John, 64, 74, 75, 78, 103, 107
Colonies: factionalism in, 1–2; British policies in, 61–62; and Franklin's Plan of Union, 135–136; inability to govern selves, 234–236. *See also names of specific colonies*
Committee of War, 76

Committees of Correspondence, 192
Concord, 1, 205, 236
Congregationalists, 39, 168–169, 172
Connecticut, 99, 101
Connecticut River Valley, 121. *See also names of specific counties, towns*
Constitutional law, 164–165
Continental Congress, 199, 200
Converse, John, 48
Cooke, Elisha, Jr., 3, 20–21, 38, 66, 187, 188; first charter mission in England, 15, 18; and Phips, 25–27; and Bellomont, 40; and Dudley, 43, 45, 53; and Boston Caucus, 62, 68–74 passim; and private bank issue, 64; and Bridger, 67–68; second charter mission, 77–83 passim; and Belcher, 93–100 passim
Cooke family, 3
Cooper, Rev. Samuel, 134, 153, 168, 226
Cooper, William, 153
Copley, John Singleton, 227
Coronation Day Riots, 190, 196
Council of Safety, 16
Counterfeiting, 64
Country faction: makeup of, 3, 228; and British policy, 5; effects of war and peace on relative strength, 5–6, 7, 62–76; pursuit of power deterred, 36; alienated by Bellomont, 40; unpopularity of, 43; and Dudley, 45, 46, 48–49; renewed vigor of, 68–70, 73–75, 77 (*see also* Boston Caucus); pamphleteering, 72, 192, 197; opposition to, in Boston, 79; as inflationists, 129; and Pownall, 149–150; bolstered, 166; and episcopacy quarrel, 169; plans to combat postwar recession, 169–170; and Mauduit, 172; and political violence, 191
Court faction: makeup of, 3; and British policy, 5; effects of war and peace on relative strength, 5–6, 7, 236–237; and Massachusetts' role in American Revolution, 7; pursuit of power deterred, 36; won over by Bellomont, 40; declines, 70; elects two of four representatives in Boston, 79; fails to win reelections, 92–94; revival until American Revolution, 94–95; dominates under Shirley, 116; as hard money faction, 129–133; advocates immigration of foreign

# Index

Protestants, 131; advocates bounties to promote growing food, 131; alienated by Pownall over patronage, 152; and bankruptcy law reform, 155; and writs of assistance, 167, 172; pitted against key social or economic groups, 170–171; and Stamp Act, 172–176; in Massachusetts, compared with other colonies, 174–176, 228, 229; sidestepped by informal system of government, 192; loyalists, as members of, 213

Court system, 20, 45, 47, 66, 93; attacked by Otis, 166–167

Craddock, George, 81–82

Crime: recession and, 170; relative lack of, 190

Crowds, 3, 81, 170; and Stamp Act riots, 1, 160, 171, 174, 192–193, 198; war protests, 6, 52–53, 116, 119, 124; and fixed-salary debate, 95; and Scotch–Irish settlers, 98; and Riot Acts, 122, 190; and Whig ideology and legitimate mob violence, 126–127, 198; and land riots, 151; as political force, 174, 191–196; as mirror of factionalism, 185; and food riots, 186; and nature of their violence, 190; and revolutionary violence, 191–196; makeup of, 197–206; and disguises, 198

Crown Point expeditions, 119, 122–123, 128, 136, 137, 154

Cumberland County, 170

Currency. See Money

Currency Act of 1751, 132

Cushing, John, 82, 161, 201

Cushing, Thomas, Jr., 173

Cushing, Thomas, Sr., 82, 93, 97

Customs service and regulations, 37, 39, 160, 163–166, 167, 187

Danforth, Samuel, 97

Danforth, Thomas, 14, 17, 25, 26, 43

Dartmouth, William Legge, Earl of, 238

Davenport, Addington, 68, 73, 93

Davenport, John, 10

Declaratory Act, 227

Dedham, 12

Deerfield, 48

Dee, Rowlands, 187

Delancey family (New York), 5

Delaware, 235

Deputies, House of, See General Court

Desertion, 40, 41, 156, 159

Disguises, in riots, 198

Douglass, Dr. William, 104, 106, 107, 116–117, 127–128, 187

Draper, Richard, 214

Drought, 131, 170, 202

Dudley family, 3

Dudley, Gov. Joseph, 13, 14, 15, 21, 22, 27, 36, 38, 39, 186; administration of, 41, 43–53, 63, 64–65, 67, 125, 175

Dudley, Paul, 53, 64–65, 66, 68–69, 72, 92, 104

Dudley, William, 66, 93

Dummer, Gov. William, 76–80

Dummer, Jeremiah, Jr., 53, 65, 66, 71, 77, 78, 82

Dummer, Jeremiah, Sr., 66

Dunbar, David, 92, 93, 94, 95, 98–100

East India Company, 150

Economics: factionalism based on, 1–2, 12; poverty and militant enthusiasm, 121–122, 237; and crime, 170; contrasting philosophies of revolutionaries and loyalists, 218–221. See also Money

Edwards, Rev. Jonathan, 120, 226

Eliot, Andrew, 168

England: defense policy of, 4–5, 156, 218–219; Massachusetts' relationship with, 4–5; patronage practices in, 3–4, 61; and France, 35; domestic crises in, 35–36; economic policies of, 91–92, 218–221; pursues colonial expansion and war, 115; moral decline of, 219. See also Board of Trade

Engravings, as political weapons, 192–194, 198

Erving family, 228

Erving, George, 165, 201

Essex County, 3, 162

Excise controversy, 133–135, 136, 192

Exeter (New Hampshire), 100

Explanatory Charter, 5, 70, 77, 79, 80, 81, 133

Factionalism: in other colonies, 1–2; in Massachusetts, 2–7, 12; effects of war and peace on, 5–7, 12, 35. See also Country faction; Court faction; General Court

# Index

Factorage system, 164
Faneuil, Benjamin, 201
Faneuil family, 100
Faneuil Hall, 189
Fishing, 137
Fitch, Thomas, 92
Fletcher, Benjamin, 23
Flucker, Thomas, 170, 214, 215
Food riots, 186
Fort Frederick, 98
Fort Ticonderoga, 149
Fowle, Daniel, 125, 126, 127, 134, 135
Foye, William, 132, 136
France and French colonies, 77, 127; and strategic importance of Massachusetts, 4. *See also names of specific colonies;* Maine
Franklin, Benjamin, 135, 221, 223, 234, 235
"Freeman," 217
French and Indian War, 6–7, 61, 120, 121, 235; Massachusetts' role in, 135, 137, 154; politics in Massachusetts during, 149; effect of, on commerce and merchants, 163; necessity of British assistance in, 219
French Huguenots, 214
French Revolution, 228–229
Frontenac, Count Louis de B., 16, 35
Frontier, 37, 48, 53, 67; settlers prevented from fleeing, 37, 41; expansion of, eases socioeconomic distress, 121. *See also names of specific counties, towns*
Frost, Charles, 100

Gage, Gen. Thomas, 159, 161, 170–171
Gardiner, Sylvester, 201
Gedney, Bartholomew, 14, 15, 38
General Court: and local affairs, 2; and patronage practices, 3–4; nonpartisan nature of representatives, 4–5; alignments in, 11; and Half-Way Covenant,11–13; and decline of factionalism in response to Randolph, 13; abolition of deputies, 14; under new charter, 18, 19; and Phips, 24–27; and Stoughton, 36–37; requests aid from England, 37; and Bellomont, 40; acting as governor, 43; and Dudley,

46–51; money issued by, 75–76; and Dummer, 79–80; moved to Salem, 81; and Belcher, 91, 93, 95–96; response to royal authority, 97; uses bills of credit to solve currency problems, 101; and debate over Land and Silver Banks, 105–108; and Shirley, 116–119, 123–124, 137; and King George's War, 123–126, 137; quarrels with British generals, 150; and Pownall, 151; and quartering issue, 157; both factions offended by Bernard's neutrality, 160–161; authorizes Gray to sue to recover fines, 164–165; and roll calls as tests of Hutchinson, 170–171; and popular involvement in politics, 192
Georgia, 235
German settlers, 2
Glorious Revolution, 13, 15–16, 35, 124
Gold, as money, 133, 169
Goldthwait, Ezekiel, 201
Goldthwait, Thomas, 201
Gordon, John, 125, 126
Gordon, William, 69
Gorges, Sir Fernando, 68
Government, local. *See* Local government
Grand Banks, 137
Gray, Harrison, 132–133, 153, 164, 214, 228
Great Awakening, 116, 121, 235
Great Migration, 214
Greene, Nathaniel, 70
Greenleaf, Stephen, 201
Grenville, George, 165
Gridley, Jeremiah, 157
Gulston, Ralph, 100

Hale, Robert, 97, 107, 128, 129
Half-Way Covenant, 11, 12, 13
Halifax, George Montague Dunk, Earl of, 115
Hall, Richard, 187
Hamilton, Alexander, 130
Hammond, Lawrence, 22
Hampshire, County, 3, 152–153, 163, 168, 169, 196
Hancock, John, 170, 202
Hancock, Thomas, 117, 153, 202
Hartford Convention, 1

307

# Index

Harvard College, 15, 20, 36, 37, 39–40, 42, 43, 46, 51, 169, 196, 214
Haverhill, 36, 48
Hawley, Joseph, 214, 229
Higginson, Nathaniel, 42–43, 50
Higginson, Rev. John, 19
Hill, Sir James, 52
Hinckley, Gov. Thomas, 26
Hingham, 66
Holidays, politicization of, 194–196
Hooper, Robert, 201
House of Commons, 94, 97
Houses of Legislature. *See* General Court
Hovering Act, 160
Hubbard, Thomas, 129, 134
Huguenots, 214
Hutchinson, Anne, 10
Hutchinson, Edward, 66, 67, 93, 103, 108
Hutchinson, Eliakim, 25, 38, 201
Hutchinson, Elisha, 25, 38, 165
Hutchinson family, 64, 150
Hutchinson, Foster, 165
Hutchinson, Thomas, 3, 70, 73, 94, 95, 101, 102
Hutchinson, Gov. Thomas, 121, 124, 226, 227, 238; and currency debate, 101, 102, 104, 107, 116, 118, 128–131, 169–170; defeats Waldo, 128; rewrite of Plan of Union, 135; argues against impressment, 137; and Pownall, 151–153, 154; and Loudoun's quartering policy, 157; and Bernard, 161–163, 164; appointed Chief Justice, 161, 162; and writs of assistance issue, 165–168, 175; and Williams, 169; test of popularity and influence of, 170–171, 174, 197; burning of his house, 171, 189; elected agent, 172–173; engravings of, 194; on changes in political rhetoric, 194; denunciations of, 203, 204, 216; loyalist philosophy of, 217–219, 222–224; wearies of politics, 222
Hutchinson, William, 72

Immigrants, 2, 81, 93, 98–99, 100, 131, 150–151, 234–235
Impressment, 41, 52, 116, 119, 120, 124, 137, 156, 185–186, 189, 190
*Independent Advertiser,* 122, 125–127, 130

Indians, 12, 16, 23, 24, 36, 37, 40, 41, 48, 71, 77, 100, 123, 127, 150, 151, 168, 170. *See also names of specific tribes;* French and Indian War
Inflation, 62–63, 73, 117, 125, 169–170. *See also* Money
Inman, Ralph, 201
Intolerable Acts, 227
Ipswich, 11
Irish settlers, 2, 81, 93, 98–99, 100
Iroquois Indians, 123

Jackson, Andrew, 45
Jackson, Benjamin, 22
Jackson, Richard, 167, 173
Jackson, Robert, 186
Jacobite Rebellion, 61, 65
James II, colonial rule of, 13, 15
Jenkins' Ear, War of, 101
Jesuits, 16, 49, 71
Johnson, Sir William, 137
Jowett, Nehemiah, 50
"Joyce, Jr.," 196
Judiciary, 4

Kennebeck Company, 170, 171
Kidd, Capt. William, 41
Kilby, Christopher, 100, 116, 127, 129, 130, 213
King George's War, 115, 118, 119–125, 137
King Philip's War, 12
King's Chapel, 18, 127, 168
King's Woods, 66–67, 98, 119
King William's War, 16, 36, 52
Knowles, Cdr. Charles, 124, 126, 127–128, 189
Knowles Riot, 124, 126, 189

Land Bank controversy, 5, 63–66, 68, 72, 73–76; reemerges under Belcher, 101, 103–105, 128, 189; abolished by Parliament, 116–118; and pamphleteering, 192
Land speculation, in Maine, 98
Language, changes in reflecting political changes, 194
Lawyers, 7, 162, 198, 213–214, 228, 229
Lechmere, Richard, 170
Lechmere, Thomas, 68, 165
Lee, Thomas, 106
Leeward, Islands, 133
Legislature. *See* General Court

# Index

Leighton, Charles, 100
Leisler, Jacob, 9, 35–36, 42
Leonard, Daniel, 218, 219, 222–223
Leonard, George, 105, 107
Leverett, John, 43, 46, 51
Lewis, Ezekiel, 79, 82, 93
Lexington, 205, 236
Liberty, meaning of, to revolutionaries and loyalists, 216–218
Lindall, Timothy, 71
Liquor, 69, 133–134
Little, Otis, 117–118
Livermore, Samuel, 130, 157, 158, 213
Livingston family (New York), 5
Lloyd, Edward, 201
Local government: and Puritans, 10; concentration of power in, 11. *See also* Boston
Locke, John, 103, 104, 125, 126
Logging, 66–67, 119. *See also* King's Woods
Lord Dunmore's War, 235
Loring, Joshua, 156
Loton, Lewis, 187
Loudoun, John Campbell, Earl of, 133, 137, 149, 151, 152; quarrel with Pownall, 153–154; quartering policy of, 156–157
Louis XIV, 35
Louisbourg expedition, 52, 119, 122, 123, 126, 127, 128, 149, 152, 238; reimbursement for, 129–130
Loyal Nine, 191
Loyalists. *See* Tories
Lyde, Byfield, 155, 201
Lyde, Edward, 66
Lynde, Benjamin, Jr., 97
Lynde, Benjamin, Sr., 116

McGovern, George, 1
Mackintosh, Ebenezer, 191–192, 196
Magistrates, House of. *See* General Court
Maine, 25, 37, 43, 53, 135, 159, 196; Indian problems in, 16, 36, 71, 77; Massachusetts' title to questioned, 17; protection of timberland in, 66–68, 98, 100, 119; Irish immigrants in, 81, 98–99, 100; Belcher and, 91, 93, 98–99, 100; peacetime controversy in, 170
Malone, Joseph J., 67

Malthus, Thomas, 234
Mansfield, William Murray, Earl of, 226
Manufacturing, 95
Marblehead, 135, 156, 196
Marcy, William, 45
Markets, 188–189
Marriage, age at, of revolutionaries, 201–202
Maryland, 235
Mason, Stephen, 44
Massachusetts: factionalism in, 1–7; lack of sectional conflict in, 3; patronage practices in, 3–4; strategic importance of, 4; political and social stability in, 9–11; boundary disputes with New Hampshire, 93, 99, 101; other states' currency circulating in, 101; enthusiasm for war in, 120–122; economic stress in, caused by hard money requirement, 131; role of, in French and Indian War, 135; illegal trade in, 136; difficulties in, after French and Indian war, 150; and compensation issue, 172; court faction in, compared with other colonies, 174–175; "Anglicization" of, 176; language and popular culture in, politicization of, 194–196; smuggling in, 221; as exception among colonies, in internal stability, 236–239; and balance of trade with England, 237
*Massachusetts Spy,* 192
Mather, Rev. Cotton, 3, 25, 69, 72, 104, 226; and charter issue, 21; and Harvard College, 39; and Dudley, 44, 46, 49–50, 53; writings of, 72, 73, 203; violence toward, during smallpox epidemic, 187, 190
Mather, Rev. Increase, 3, 25; and Half-Way Covenant, 14; and Harvard College, 15, 37, 39, 43; and Andros, 16; and charter issue, 17, 18–21, 26, 27; and Dudley, 44, 46, 50, 53
Matthews, Henry, 188
Mauduit, Israel, 167
Mauduit, Jasper, 166–167, 172, 173
Mayhew, Jonathan, 168–169, 171, 204
Mein, John, 192
Menzies, John, 67
Mercantilism, 218

# Index

Merchants, 7, 12, 13, 14, 19, 20, 24,
37–38, 41, 45, 49–50, 52, 53,
130, 213–214, 228; support for
private banks, 64–65, 73; support
for Waldo, 100; and Silver Bank,
103–105; and Shirley, 119; tax-
avoidance schemes of, 133;
bankruptcies, after French and
Indian War, 155–156; politicization
of, 163–168; wealth of, and
participation in American Revolution,
199–200; and nonimportation
agreements, 221
Merchants' Notes of 1734, 102–103,
107
Mexican War, 1
Middlesex County, 3, 161
Migration, as indicator of economic
crisis, 202
Military: officers, in local government,
4, 15; and desertion, 40, 41, 156,
159; and impressment, 41, 52, 116,
119, 120, 124, 137, 156, 185–186,
189, 190; as alternative for young,
poor, and unemployed, 121–122,
205
Milton, 93
Minot, Christopher, 201
Mobs. *See* Crowds
Molasses Acts, 152, 160
Molineux, William, 196
Money: issuance of paper, 5, 17,
62–65, 73–76, 92, 93, 96, 98,
101, 103–107, 127, 129, 132;
silver, Hutchinson and, 5, 129–130,
189; counterfeiting, 64;
Britain's attempt to reduce
supply of, 77; "new' and
"middle" tenor, 102, 136;
and Merchants' Notes, 102–103,
107; supply debate, 103–104;
maintaining valuation of, 118;
attempts to stabilize after King
George's War, 125; "old" tenor, 130,
132, 133; and British Currency
Act of 1751, 132; and bimetallism,
133, 150, 169–170, 172; and
excise controversy, 133–135, 136,
192; specie, inadequacy of, 154,
160. *See also* Land Bank
controversy; Taxes
Montreal, 149
Mount Desert Island, 159
Murray, James, 201, 221–222
Music, as political weapon, 192–193,
198
Mutiny, 40

Navigation Acts: enforcement of, 4, 13,
14, 24, 38, 40, 47, 50, 167, 216;
resistance to, 12; and Bellomont,
41; and prerogative faction, 167
Naval Office Act, 20, 39
Negroes, 122, 123, 191, 197
New Brick Church, 121
*New England Weekly Journal,* 68
New Hampshire, 20, 23, 40, 66, 120,
174, 228, 235; boundary dispute
with Massachusetts, 93, 99, 101
New Jersey, 158, 235
New Lights, 120, 168, 202
New tenor, 102, 136. *See also* Money
New York, 9, 23, 35, 37, 40, 42, 62,
99, 120, 122–123, 159, 235, 237;
political factionalism in, 2, 4, 5,
35–36, 175
Newbury, 11, 196
Newburyport, 196
Newcastle, Thomas Pelham-Holles,
Duke of, 61, 78–79, 82, 91, 92,
96, 100, 101, 115, 163
Newman, Henry, 78
Newspapers, 192, 196, 216
Niagara expedition, 136, 137
Nicholson, Francis, 23
Nixon, Richard M., 1
*Nonsuch,* H.M.S., 22
Norridgewock Indians, 16, 36, 71. *See
also* Indians
North Carolina, 2, 235
Northampton, 12
North End, Boston's, 170, 191–192
North End Caucus, 199, 200, 201
"Novanglus," 216
Nova Scotia, 37, 49, 120, 121, 123,
136, 238
Nowell, Samuel, 14, 15
Noyes, Oliver, 53, 64, 66, 68, 69, 72,
73, 74

Oakes, Thomas, 15, 18, 20–21, 25, 27,
45, 48
Ohio Valley, 6, 150, 159, 161, 235
Old Lights, 120, 168
Old tenor, 130, 132, 133. *See also*
Money
Oliver, Andrew, 95, 128, 131; and
Land Bank issue, 108; and
bimetallism, 133; and religious
unity, 168; as Stamp Master,
192–193, 196, 216; death of, 204;
writing as "Freeman," 217, 223;
as moderate, 227

# Index

Oliver, Peter, 69, 216–224 passim, 227
Oswego expedition, 137
Otis family, 3, 150, 229
Otis, James, Jr., 153, 161, 168, 172–173, 174, 175, 202; attack on Writs of Assistance, 1, 166, 220–221; and search warrant case, 165; and judicial system, 166–167; purges council of Tories, 192; revolutionary philosophy of, 194, 217, 219, 225, 238
Otis, James, Sr., 129, 153, 161, 162, 167, 173
Otis, John, 118
Otis, Samuel Alleyne, 164, 192

Paine, Thomas, 117, 202
Palfrey, William, 200
Palmer, Thomas, 79
Pamphleteering, 72, 192, 197
Parties. See Country faction; Court faction; Factionalism
Partridge, Oliver, 168
Partridge, Richard, 101, 106
Patronage practices, 45; in Massachusetts and England compared, 3–4; and Belcher, 93, 101; and Pownall, 152; and Bernard, 160–162
Paxton, Charles, 164, 167, 201
Payne, William, 64, 66, 68
Peace and peacetime: British policy during, 5; effect of, on politics, 5–7. See also War and wartime
Peace of Ryswick, 36
Peagrum, Jonathan, 98
Peddlers, 188–189
Pemaquid, fort at, 25, 36, 47, 49, 50, 99
Pennsylvania, 2, 4, 5, 159, 175, 235
Penobscot, 77
Penobscot Indians, 100
Pepperrell, Sir William, 120, 127, 153
Phelps, Charles, 152–153
Philadelphia, 62, 235, 237
Phips, Constantine, 44
Phips, David, 170
Phips, Gov. William, 15, 16–17, 18, 38, 45, 46, 166, 186; administration of, 19–28
Phips, Spencer, 129, 131, 132, 137, 151–152
Piracy, 41
Pitt, William, 151
Plan of Union, 135–136

Plymouth, 9, 26, 38, 135, 196
Poetry, as political weapon, 192–193
Political activity, attitudes of revolutionaries and loyalists toward, compared, 221–224
Political parties. See Country faction; Court faction; Factionalism
Poll tax, in Boston, 154
Pontiac's Conspiracy, 235
Poor relief, 190
Pope's Day violence, 170, 191–192, 196
Popular faction. See Country faction
Port Royal, 16–17, 45, 48, 49, 51, 52, 120
Povey, Thomas, 47, 52, 186
Pownall, Gov. Thomas, 133, 137; administration of, 149, 152–158; as "Defender of American Liberty," 151; alienates Hutchinson and court faction, 152; quarrel with Loudoun, 153–154; military policies, 157–158; in New Jersey, 158
Pownall, John, 151, 152
Prat, Benjamin, 161
Prerogative faction. See Court faction
Presbyterians, 5, 39
Prescott, Benjamin, 97
Preston, Capt. Thomas, 194
Prisons, 188
Privy Council, 20, 38–39, 40, 97, 99, 168; and appointment of governors, 4, 40; rejects old-charter restoration, 18
Puritans and Puritanism, 1, 20, 23, 24, 42; and social and political stability, 9–11; minority rule of, protest against, 12; as popular heroes during American Revolution, 196
Putnam, Col. James, 125
Pynchon, John, 14

Quakers, 4, 5, 11, 12, 100, 235
Quebec, 16–17, 48, 52, 149, 152
Queen Anne's War, 35, 36, 45, 48, 52, 53, 61, 124
Quincy, Edmund, 107
Quincy, Edmund, and Sons, 156
Quincy, Josiah, Sr., 124, 196
Quincy, Samuel, 222, 227

Ralle, Sebastian, 71
Randolph, Edmund, 12–16, 27
Recession, 169–170
Regulator movements, 2, 235

311

# Index

Religion: conflicts, 2, 168; and politics, 10–13; decline of, 10–11; zeal, and wars, 121; and revolutionary philosophy, 224–227. *See also names of specific denominations;* Clergy
Remington, Jonathan, 66, 92
Revere, Paul, 1, 193, 194, 214
Revolution and revolutionaries. *See* American Revolution; Whigs
Rhode Island, 99, 101, 107, 130
Richards, John, 14, 25, 26
Richardson, Ebenezer, 216
*Rights of the British Colonies, The,* 173
Riot Acts, 122, 190
Riots. *See* Crowds
Robertson, Sir Robert, 185–186
Royall, Isaac, 153, 238
Ruggles, Gen. Timothy, 153, 167, 168, 198, 224
Russell, Chambers, 201

Saffin, John, 45
Salem, 11, 71, 135, 196; witch trials in, 23
Saltonstall, Nathaniel, 14, 15, 170
Saltonstall, Richard, 97
Savage, Habijah, 66, 94
Savage, Samuel Phillips, 198, 200
Scituate, 196
Scotch-Irish settlers, 2, 93, 98–99, 100
Scott, Capt. James, 189
Sergeant, Peter, 45
Servants, 121, 191, 197
Seven Years' War. *See* French and Indian War
Sewall, Samuel, 25, 26, 42–43, 46, 68, 162; and charter issue, 15; and Dudley, 49–50, 51, 53; and Land Bank issue, 64
Sewall, Stephen, 37, 45
Sexual repression, revolution and, 203
Sharpe, Jonathan, 101
Shays's Rebellion, 155
Shepard, Thomas, 10
Shirley, Gov. William, 96, 100–101, 104, 106, 151, 152, 189, 205; military policies of, 6, 119–125, 136; civil administration of, 115–119, 125–129, 176, 236; accused of corruption by *The Advertiser,* 126, 130; and excise controversy, 133–135, 136; removed from office, 137; effect on American history, 137; personal nature of triumphs, 154

Short, Capt. Richard, 22, 186
Shove, Edward, 97
Shrimpton, Samuel, 15, 17, 25, 38
Shute family, 158
Shute, Gov. Samuel, 65, 91, 157, 187, 190; administration of, 66–68, 70–73, 76, 77, 78
Silver Bank, 103–105
Smallpox, 72, 131, 170, 187
Smuggling, 221
Society for the Encouragement of Manufacturing, 163
Society for the Propagation of the Gospel, 168
Socioeconomic divisions, in other colonies, 1–2
Sons of Liberty, 192, 196, 199, 200, 220, 223, 227
South Carolina, 2, 37, 175, 235
South End, Boston's, 170, 191–192
Southern colonies, political factionalism in, 1–2, 36
Spain, 101, 150
Sprague, John, 187
Springfield, 12
Stamp Act, 7, 149, 155, 159, 160, 163, 172, 173–174, 191, 196, 216, 227
Stamp Act Congress, 168
Stamp Act riots, 1, 160, 171, 174, 192–193, 196, 198
Stamp tax, provincial, 135
Stanley, Lt. John, 187
Stoddard, John, 92, 97
Stoughton, William, 13, 14, 15, 23, 24, 26, 27, 28, 36, 162; administration of, 36–39, 40, 43
Sudbury, 12
Suffield, 12
Suffolk County, 3, 45, 66, 93, 162
Sugar Act, 150, 160, 163, 172
*Swift,* H.M.S., 186

Tailer, William, 52, 64, 65–66, 186
Taxes, 17, 18, 25, 36, 62–63, 94–95, 123, 132, 136, 237; and excise controversy, 133–135, 136, 192; stamp, provincial, 135; and French and Indian War, 154–155; and Otis, on representatives' right of taxation, 167; revolutionary arguments against, 225–226; and Declaratory Act, 227. *See also* Stamp Act
Tax lists, 198–199
Tay, Isaiah, 70
Taylor, Christopher, 187

# Index

Temple, Earl, 165
Temple, John, 165–166, 170
Thacher, Oxenbridge, 161–162, 169, 237–238
Thatcher, Peter, 226
Thaxter, Samuel, 66, 67
Thomas, Isaiah, 193
Thomas, Lt. Dalby, 187
Thomas, Nathaniel, 26
Thomlinson, John, 130
Thornton, Henry, 187
Ticonderoga. *See* Fort Ticonderoga
Tidmarsh, Giles Dulac, 187
Tories, 65, 155, 168, 192, 198, 238; ages of, 201, 213–214; as tyrannical father-figures, 202–204; characteristics of, compared with revolutionaries, 213–229; meaning of "liberty" to, 216–218; economic philosophy of, 218–221; attitudes toward political activity, 221–224; personality traits of, 223–224; modes of reasoning of, 224–226; lack of sense of historical mission in, 227; self-perception of as virtuous, 228
Townsend, Penn, 66
Townshend Acts, 160
Treasury, supplying, 97–98
Trenchard, William, 125, 126
Trescott, Zechariah, 188
Truman, Nathan, 226
Tyler, Royall, 134, 167
Tyng, John, 95, 153, 160, 161, 162, 213

Unemployment: and military as alternative, 121–122; and violent crime, 170
Usher, John, 20, 22, 23, 38–39

Vans, Hugh, 103, 104, 107, 118, 156
Vassall, William, 170, 201
Vermont, 235
Vetch, Samuel, 50, 51, 52
Vice-Admiralty Court, 41, 42, 47, 153, 165, 216. *See also* Navigation Acts
Viet Nam War, 1
Violence. *See* Crowds
Virginia, 2, 9, 23, 120–121, 175, 235
Voting rights, 10

Wadsworth, Joseph, 66, 67, 70
*Wager*, H.M.S., 189

Wager, Sir Charles, 101
Waldo, Samuel, 98–101, 127, 128, 133, 170, 213
Walker, Benjamin, 82
Walker, Sir Hovenden, 52
Walpole, Sir Robert, 61, 96, 100, 101, 134, 161, 163
Walton, Shadrach, 71, 77
War and wartime: British policy toward Massachusetts during, 5; effect on politics, 5–7, 16, 24, 28, 36, 51–53, 71, 76, 125, 176, 237; economic effect of, 62–63, 118, 125, 154–156, 237; as outlet for religious zeal and socioeconomic frustration, 120–122
Warning Out Lists, 202
War of 1812, 1
War of Jenkins' Ear, 101
Warren, Joseph, 226
Warren, Adm. Peter, 124
Waters, John, Jr., 202
Watts, Samuel, 165
Welfare system, 190
Welles, Samuel, 82, 94, 97, 165
Welsteed, William, 121
West Indies, 9, 53, 74, 101, 150, 151, 164, 221
*Weymouth*, H.M.S., 187
Wharton, Richard, 15, 18
Wheeler, Sir Francis, 23
Wheelwright, Nathaniel, 155
Whigs, 125–126, 137, 213. *See also* American Revolution
Whitefield, George, 120
White Pine Laws, 119
Wigglesworth, Edward, 74, 104
Wilkes, Francis, 81, 82, 101
Wilkes, John, 220
Willard, Samuel, 46
William of Orange, 15, 16, 18–19, 40, 44
Williams, Israel, 131, 152, 161, 169, 222, 227
Williams, Roger, 10
Winslow, Isaac, 201
Winthrop, Adam, 66
Winthrop family, 3
Winthrop, Wait, 15, 25–26, 40, 43, 45, 49, 53
Witches and witchcraft, 24, 203
Witt, Samuel, 130
Wolfe, Gen. James, 149
Worcester, 196
Worcester County, 3
Worthington, John, 214, 22
Writs of Assistance, 1, 150, 163,

164–165, 166, 167, 172, 175, 199, 220–221

Yale College, 214
Yeomans, John, 187
York County, 3, 71, 170
Young, Dr. Thomas, 214, 215